DAVID AHL'S
SMALL BASIC COMPUTER ADVENTURES

Special 25th Anniversary Edition

© Kidware Software LLC, 2011

Kidware Software LLC

PO Box 701

Maple Valley, WA 98038

http://www.ComputerScienceForKids.com

http://www.KidwareSoftware.com

PUBLISHED BY:

Kidware Software LLC
PO Box 701
Maple Valley, WA 98038

Copyright 2011, Kidware Software LLC. ALL RIGHTS RESERVED
All rights reserved. No part of the contents of this book may be reproduced or transmitted in any form or by any means without the written permission of the publisher.

ISBN 13: 978-1-937161-17-0

Microsoft® is a registered trademark of Microsoft Corporation.

Adapted with permission from *David Ahl's BASIC Computer Adventures,* published by Microsoft Press, 1986. Copyright 1986 By David H. Ahl

1984 Cover and Interior Text Design by Becker Design Associates
1984 Cover illustration by Scott McDougall
1984 Principal Typographer: Christopher Banks
1984 Principal Production artist: Becky Johnson
2011 Cover Update - Small Basic Edition by Kevin Brockschmidt
2011 Copy Editor: Philip Conrod & Stephanie Conrod
2011 Small Basic Programming: Philip Conrod & Lou Tylee

The software included with David Ahl's Small Basic Adventures is licensed to a single user. Copies of the book and the associated software are not to be distributed or provided to any other user. Multiple User licenses are available for educational institutions. Please contact Kidware Software LLC for educational multi-user license information.

The authors, Kidware Software LLC, and its officers and shareholders assume no liability for damage to personal computers or loss of data residing on personal computers arising due to the use or misuse of this material. Always follow instructions provided by the manufacturer of 3rd party programs that may be included or referenced by this book.

This guide refers to several software and hardware products by their trade names. These references are for informational purposes only and all trademarks are the property of their respective companies and owners. Microsoft, Visual Studio, Small Basic, Visual Basic, Visual J#, and Visual C#, IntelliSense, Word, Excel, MSDN, and Windows are all trademark products of the Microsoft Corporation.

The example companies, organizations, products, domain names, e-mail addresses, logos, people, places, and events depicted are fictitious. No association with any real company, organization, product, domain name, e-mail address, logo, person, place, or event is intended or should be inferred.

This book expresses the author's views and opinions. The information in this book is distributed on an "as is" basis, without and express, statutory, or implied warranties.

DEDICATION BY DAVID AHL (1986)

To Amelia Earhart, Francis Parkman, Marco Polo and the many other bold and resolute adventurers who proved that no frontier is beyond the reach of man.

DEDICATION BY PHILIP CONROD (2011)

To David Ahl, who inspired me to become a computer programmer in 1977. To Stephanie, Jessica, and Chloe who inspire me to be the best dad in the world and to my best friend Jesus who gives me the strength and grace to try.

About the Authors

David Ahl is the well-known author of more than 20 books covering the educational and recreational applications of computers, including the best-selling *BASIC Computer Games* and *More BASIC Computer Games*. In 1974, he founded *Creative Computing* magazine, the first consumer magazine devoted to personal computers. David has also written for such publications as *National Geographic World, Travel Weekly, Omni, Science Digest, The New York Times*, and *The Christian Science Monitor*.

Philip Conrod has authored, co-authored and edited numerous computer programming books for kids, teens and adults, including the best-selling *Beginning Microsoft Small Basic* and *The Developer's Reference Guide to Microsoft Small Basic*. Philip holds a BS in Computer Information Systems and a Master's certificate in the Essentials of Business Development from Regis University. Philip has also held various Information Technology leadership roles in companies like Sundstrand Aerospace, Safeco Insurance Companies, FamilyLife, Kenworth Truck Company, PACCAR and Darigold. In his spare time, Philip serves as the President & Publisher of Kidware Software, LLC. He is the proud father of three "techie" daughters and he and his beautiful family live in Maple Valley, Washington.

DAVID AHL'S

SMALL BASIC Computer Adventures

TABLE OF CONTENTS

Table of Contents

PREFACE

Although one can trace the origins of digital computers to the Analytical Engine of Charles Babbage or the punched card tabulating machines of Herman Hollerith, the real beginning of the computer age was in the late 1930s and early 1940s, sparked in large part by various aspects of World War II. In Britian, Alan Turing's group at Bletchley Park was trying to build a computer for code-breaking purposes. In Germany, Konrad Zuse built a relay-type machine that could store 64 floating point numbers for rocketry calculations. In the U.S., several developments were proceeding in parallel, but by far the most influential was the work of John Mauchly and J. Presper Eckert at the University of Pennsylvania on a machine which was eventually christened ENIAC (Electronic Numerical Integrator and Computer).

The Purpose of ENIAC was to integrate ballistic equations for gunnery tables. Such tables show the required angle of elevation of a gun for various target distances, shell weights, and wind speeds. A significant accomplishment at the dedication of ENIAC in February 1946 was the computation of the trajectory of a 16" naval shell in less than real time. Since World War II had ended by the time ENIAC was operational, there was no longer the urgent need for the firing tables that motivated its design. Thus, after it was moved to Aberdeen Proving Ground, it was put to use in atomic energy calculations, cosmic ray studies, thermal ignition research, wind tunnel design, and weather prediction as well as for its original purpose of computing ballistic tables for the Army and Air Force.

Unfortunately, today we tend to get a somewhat distorted view of the history of digital computers. Books written by writers in the computer field tend to focus on the early technology (vacuum tubes, mercury delay lines, paper tape), capacity, speed, and occasionally, people. On the other hand, general history books tend to focus on data processing and financial applications, and ignore the incredibly important role of the military in perhaps the most momentous development of the 20th century.

Equally salient is the fact that virtually all of the early applications of digital computers were simulations—of an artillery weapon, a nuclear reaction, a wind tunnel, the weather. It was not until some years later that computers were put to work in data processing, financial applications, and communications.

MY EARLY INVOLVEMENT

In 1957, just 11 years after the first digital computer was demonstrated, in my sophomore year at Cornell University, I got my first taste of computing. By then, of course, computers were being widely used for data processing and related applications, but I was far more fascinated with their ability to simulate the real world. Summers during college, I worked at Grumman Aircraft refurbishing war-worn airplanes, testing antenna configurations, and writing programs with the computer group. I'll never forget the countless hours I spent in the computer room as our project team tried to simulate the actions of an airplane pilot in various situations.

The following summer, I was in a group charged with writing programs to simulate the movements of an early satellite, the orbiting astronomical observatory (OAO). The experience I gained working on these simulations put me in a good position to undertake my senior project at Cornell, a massive program (in ALGOL) that simulated the acoustics of a concert hall. Given the size, shape, seating configuration, wall covering, and ceiling material of the hall, the program calculated the acoustical properties of various seating locations. Today, such a program seems almost primitive, but in 1960 it was a major accomplishment.

A year later, in the MBA program at Carnegie-Mellon University, I had the opportunity to work with the team that wrote the first management game, a simulation of three companies competing in the detergent market. Since then, as my career has progressed through positions at Management Science Associates, Digital Equipment Corp., AT&T, and Creative Computing, I have had fewer and fewer opportunities to program. However, over the years, in the back of my mind I tucked away ideas for future programs.

Thus, when Ziff-Davis decided to fold Creative Computing magazine, it was with a sense of anticipation that I remembered some of these program ideas. Claudette Moore, formerly an editor at Creative Computing, now at Microsoft Press, and I were chatting one day and I mentioned the idea of doing a series of travel simulations. She, with some enthusiasm, asked me to put together a proposal for a book. I did, and this is it. Now, I can only hope that you, the reader, learn as much from the stories and have as much fun taking the simulated journeys as I had researching and writing them.

In closing let me thank Betsy Staples for her enormous help and fanatic attention to detail in editing the manuscript, Claudette Moore for encouraging me to write the book in the first place, and Jody Gilbert, David Rygmyr, and all the other folks at Microsoft Press for seeing the project through to completion.

2011 UPDATE BY DAVID AHL

As I looked back at the preface that I wrote some 25 years ago for Basic Computer Adventures, I was pleasantly surprised to not find any glaring blunders or lame predictions. However, my comments about ENIAC must be updated. As a result of Britain finally declassifying the details of the Colossus computer developed for cracking the so-called German Tunny code, we now know that the first electronic digital computer was designed by Thomas H. Flowers and not by Mauchly and Eckert at the University of Pennsylvania.

The first working Colossus computer was delivered to Bletchley Park in early December 1943. It had 1,600 valves (vacuum tubes) and operated at 5,000 characters per second. It first ran on December 8, 1943 and decoded its first Tunny message on February 5, 1944.

The second version of Colossus, of which nine more were built, had 2,400 valves and operated at a speed of 25,000 characters per second.

Interestingly, the people at Bletchley never saw an actual Tunny machine until after the war, but they had described it exactly and programmed it into Colossus. In fact, Tunny was a 12-wheel Lornez SZ40 cipher machine. Bear in mind, Colossus was not a general purpose, stored program computer. It had just one purpose—breaking the Tunny codes. Nevertheless, it was these 10 Colossus machines that led to the first general purpose programmable computer built at the University of Manchester after the war.

What happened to the Colossus machines? At the express orders of Winston Churchill, all ten of them were broken up and secretly discarded.

What happened to Tommy Flowers, the true and sole inventor of the electronic digital computer? Britain gave him £1,000 for his 6 years at Bletchley, barely enough to cover his debts and said, "don't tell anyone what you've done." He went to work for British Telcom who thought his idea for using computers for telephone switching was ridiculous and he died a bitter and frustrated man. He gets practically no mention or recognition in any book or history of computers.

I might mention that one of the first computers I learned to program (1961) was the Bendix G15, which was one of the direct commercial descendents of Colossus. It used a language called GATE that was a cross between machine code and a few Algol-like commands. It's so obscure, it's not even mentioned in the Encyclopedia of Computer Science.

Unlike many educators today, I believe there is a great deal that can be learned from history. I urge you to make a pilgrimage to Bletchley Park, pick up some books about Alan Turning, Tommy Flowers, and Colossus and start looking at computers and the Internet from a vastly broadened perspective.

Oh, and have fun with the adventures in this book!

David Ahl
Morristown, New Jersey
October 2010

INTRODUCTION

WRITING A SIMULATION

When writing a large and complex program, the first question always is where to start? The answer is, start with a pad of paper and DON'T turn on the computer.

Writing a computer simulation of some real or imaginary system is not especially difficult. The much bigger job is gathering the data and learning as much as possible about the system so you can define the relationships among its various facets. Once you understand the whole system, you must then break it down into the smallest possible pieces, analyze each piece in depth, determine how to model it, and combine the pieces back into the whole.

In developing the algorithms and writing the programs for each piece, you must determine the most accurate and efficient way to proceed. Is it an exact process that can be represented by a mathematical formula? Is the process continuous or discontinuous? Is it ever interrupted abruptly? Are there random elements involved?

An enormous amount of time must be spent testing each piece. Does the simulation behave in a sensible way? What happens at various extremes? These same questions must be asked again and again as all of the pieces are combined into the whole system.

Like most real-world systems, most of the simulations in this book are a combination of well-defined processes and random elements. For example, Amelia Earhart's airplane flies and consumes fuel according to well-defined physical principles. On the other hand, in Southeast Asia in July, she has a 30% chance of running into a torrential rainstorm. If it occurs, the problems she faces will be quite different from those on a sunny day.

There are five distinct parts to each of the simulations: an introduction to the game, historical background, program notes, program variables, and the progam listings. I encourage you to read The Story (historical background) before taking each computerized journey. By doing so, you will have a much better understanding of the original journey and you will make better decisions as you go along.

Later, if you want to see why the program works the way it does, examine how a routine operates, or even modify the program, the program notes and the list of variables will serve as your guide. You may also find in these programs many interesting and useful routines that you can use in programs of your own.

The ten simulations in this book are rather diverse. Some require many decisions on the part of the player, and some require relatively few decisions. In some, they are easy to make, but random hazards make it difficult to finish the journey. In others, the decisions are more difficult, but the journey itself is easier.

The programs are arranged in chronological order ranging from Marco Polo (1271) to Voyage to Neptune (2100). I suggest you play them in the order in which they appear. Following is a brief preview of what to expect in each simulation. Other aspects of the programs are summarized in the following table:

The Game	The Date	The Mode of Transportation	The Duration
Marco Polo	1271	Camel, foot	3 years
Westward Ho!	1847	Wagon, oxen	6 months
The Longest Automobile Race	1908	Automobile	6 months
The Orient Express	1923	Train	4 days
Amelia Earhart	1937	Airplane	1 month
Tour de France	present	Bicycle	3 weeks
Appalachian Trail	present	Foot	5 months
Subway Scavenger	present	Subway train	8 hours
Hong Kong Hustle	1997	Mixed (bus, tram, ferry, train, subway)	1 day
Voyage to Neptune	2100	Spaceship	6 years

SUMMARY OF THE ADVENTURE SIMULATIONS

- Marco Polo simulates a three-year journey over the Silk Road in 1271. It is easy to play once you get the hang of using jewels in place of money. However, it is a challenge to complete the journey in three years and have enough jewels remaining for trading.

- Westward Ho! simulates a six-month journey over the Oregon Trail in 1850. It uses the same framework as Marco Polo but, because you have fewer resources, it is slightly more difficult to finish the trip.

- The Longest Automobile Race simulates the 1908 auto race from New York to Paris (east to west). In those days, the cars were unreliable, the roads were nothing more than cart tracks, and, as always, the weather was unpredictable. It is not too difficult to reach Paris, but quite difficult to win the race.

- The Orient Express simulates a mystery case aboard the famous train in 1923. You will almost always complete the trip, but the mystery is extremely difficult to solve.

- Amelia Earhart simulates the around-the-world flight attempt of the famous aviatrix in 1937. If you load enough fuel and pay attention to maintenance and repairs, you will have no trouble reaching Southeast Asia. From there on, it is tough going.

- Tour de France simulates the famous three-week bicycle race. Along with intelligent decisions, this game requires manual dexterity on the keyboard. It is reasonably easy to finish, but quite difficult to win.

- Appalachian Trail simulates the trek of a hiker walking from Georgia to Maine. Preparation is half the key to completing the hike, but sensible decisions along the Trail about eating, walking speed, and walking hours are important also.

- Subway Scavenger simulates the rounds of a messenger using the New York subway system. During the first few plays of the game, you must develop a map of the subway system. Even with the help of a map, you will find this an extremely challenging game to finish.

- Hong Kong Hustle simulates the Tai Pan collecting bags of gold from various locations around Hong Kong. Using the same framework as Subway Scavenger, you must first develop a map, then go for the gold.

- Voyage to Neptune simulates an imaginary journey to Neptune in the year 2100. It is a game of trading and tradeoffs. It is not difficult to get to Neptune; it is very difficult to do so in six years or less and have enough fuel left for the return trip.

I hope you have fun trekking through this volume. Good luck on your computerized journeys!

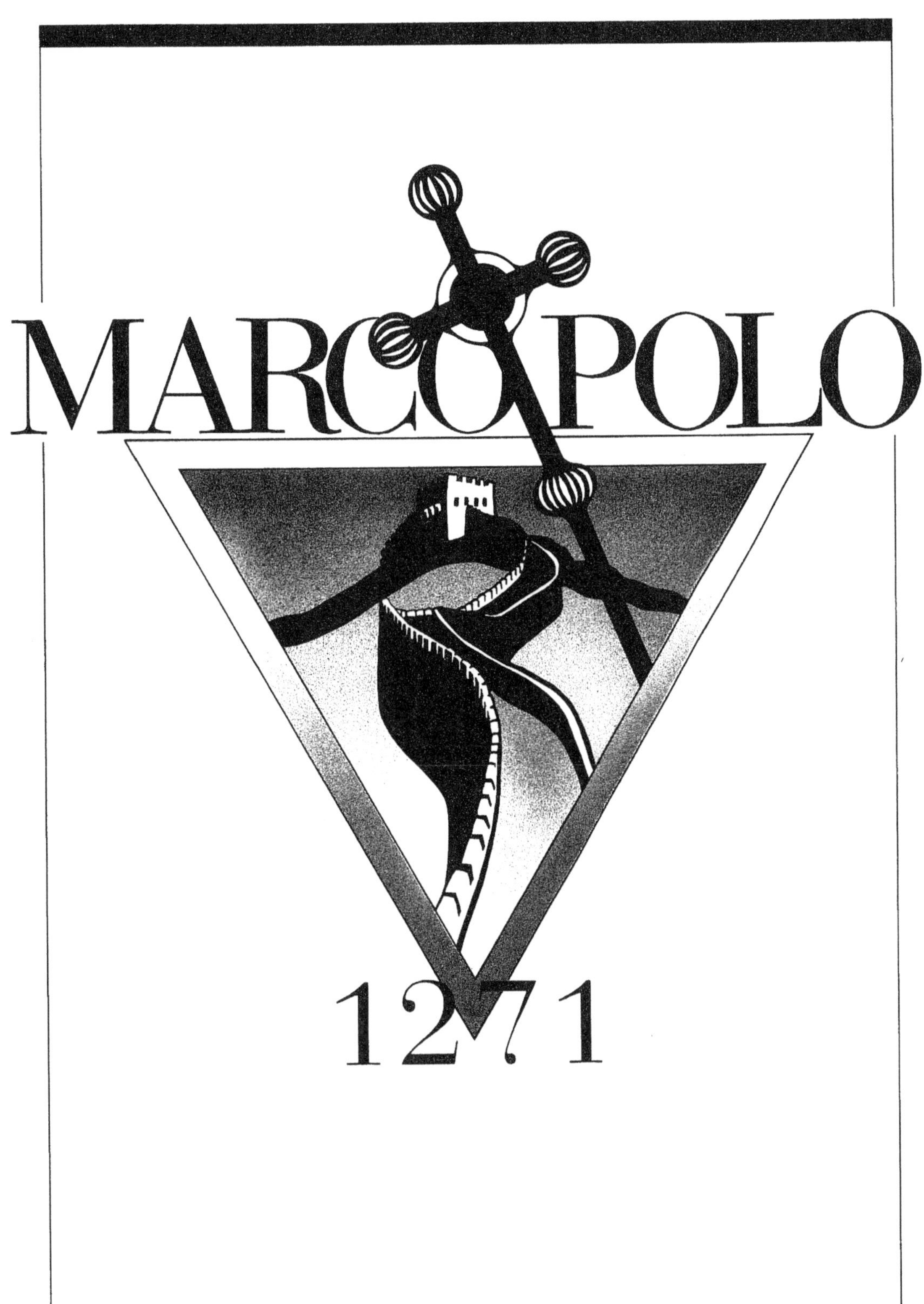
MARCO POLO
1271

Marco Polo

MARCO POLO
1271

In Marco Polo you are the leader of a group of merchants leaving on a business trip from Venice, Italy to Shang-tu, China. After sailing to Armenia at the east end of the Mediterranean Sea, you set out by camel on a 6000-mile trek across Asia to the court of the Great Kublai Khan in Shang-tu near the Pacific Ocean. To get your party safely to Shang-tu, you must know the rules of the Silk Road; the more important ones are noted here:

- At the beginning of the game, you are asked to rank your shooting ability. Since the program cannot really test your prowess with a crossbow, shooting ability is measured by how fast you can type a random shooting sound. A rating of I describes a reasonably good typist, while 4 should be reserved for those who use no more than two fingers. The game will be more fun if you rank yourself 1 or 2.
- Approximately every two months during your trip, you come upon a village that has a market where you may replenish your provisions. As prices vary widely from place to place, it is best to maintain a modest stock of goods so you are not forced to buy at high prices.
- Deciding how well to eat during each two-month period involves some tradeoffs. Eating better allows you to walk longer and cover more ground; you are also less susceptible to disease. However, food costs money (jewels), and your camels have a limited carrying capacity. If you run out of food on the trip, you can always eat a camel (assuming you have one left).
- Balm and unguents are used for treating wounds. If you run out, you face a much higher risk of getting a fatal infection.
- As a merchant, you are not a skilled hunter. However, occasionally you may be offered an opportunity to hunt. Count it a blessing if you get food in this way, but remember that your crossbow is the only weapon you have with which to drive off bandits. Hence, you should always keep a small supply of arrows in reserve.

Many hazards and surprises await you along the road to Shang-tu, so stay alert and keep your wits about you. The Polos completed the land journey in approximately 36 months. In the game, this means arriving at Shang-tu in March 1274. If you make only the best decisions and encounter no delays, it is possible to complete the computer journey in 24 months, but a more realistic goal is to complete the trip in the same 36 months it took the Polos. Can you do it?

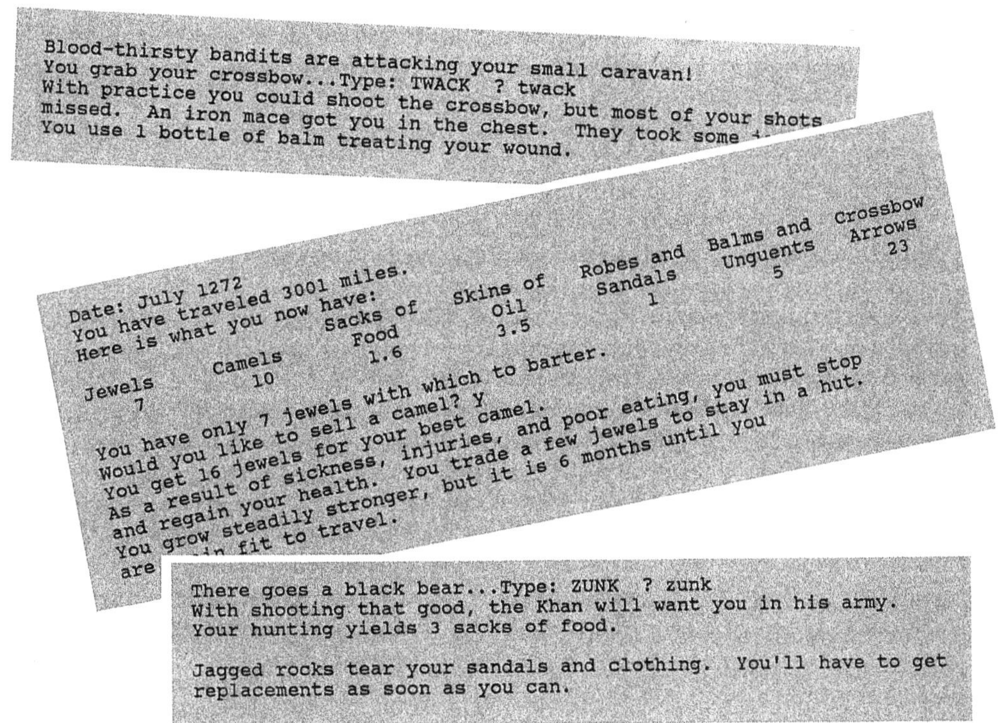

Blood-thirsty bandits are attacking your small caravan!
You grab your crossbow...Type: TWACK ? twack
With practice you could shoot the crossbow, but most of your shots
missed. An iron mace got you in the chest. They took some
You use 1 bottle of balm treating your wound.
Date: July 1272
You have traveled 3001 miles.
Here is what you now have:
Jewels 7
Camels 10
Sacks of Food 1.6
Skins of Oil 3.5
Robes and Sandals 1
Balms and Unguents 5
Crossbow Arrows 23
You have only 7 jewels with which to barter.
Would you like to sell a camel? y
You get 16 jewels for your best camel.
As a result of sickness, injuries, and poor eating, you must stop
and regain your health. You trade a few jewels to stay in a hut.
You grow steadily stronger, but it is 6 months until you
are fit to travel.
There goes a black bear...Type: ZUNK ? zunk
With shooting that good, the Khan will want you in his army.
Your hunting yields 3 sacks of food.
Jagged rocks tear your sandals and clothing. You'll have to get
replacements as soon as you can.

THE STORY

Today, a traveler flying into Venice, Italy lands at Marco Polo Airport. At the Doge's Palace in Piazza San Marco, one can view magnificent tapestries, porcelain, and jade carvings from China—the rewards of being at the western terminus of the "Silk Road" to the Far East, a route first traveled by Marco Polo in 1271.

Yet upon his return from his now famous journey to the Far East, Marco Polo's tales of strange people and far off places met with disbelief. For hundreds of years, to call something a "Marco Polo" was to label it a tall tale or even an outright falsehood. Even after they were published, his stories were thought to be largely fictional accounts. Indeed, there is little to indicate that a single one of Marco Polo's contemporaries believed much of his story. And, on his deathbed his friends pleaded with him, for the peace of his soul, to retract some of the incredible statements made in his book. Instead, he refused and is said to have replied, "I have not told half of what I saw."

As his accounts were set down many years before the development of printing, the volumes were copied by hand, and variations in wording and numerous embellishments crept into the work.

In all, more than 100 different manuscripts were produced—some in Italian, some in Latin, and some in French. The earliest printed edition is dated 1559, and an English translation did not appear until 1818.

Not until the late 1800's did scholars attempt to piece together a truly original edition, as reports from later travelers and explorers began to indicate that the majority of Marco Polo's accounts were accurate and unexaggerated. Unfortunately, not one edition treating the entire work as a travel narrative has ever appeared, nor has the story ever been translated into contemporary English. Thus, to this day, for most Americans, the myths and the realities remain intertwined.

Marco Polo was born in Venice in 1254, son of Niccolò, one of the great merchants and noblemen of the city. An uncle, Maffeo, worked directly with his father, and together the team of brothers traveled to many distant lands.

Niccolò Polo and his brother Maffeo made their first great journey east in 1260. They visited their third brother in Constantinople and from there set out on a trading trip along the Tigris River to the great city of Bokhara in the Persian Empire (today, the city of Bukhara is in south central Russia). There they met an ambassador of the Great Khan (Supreme Lord), Kublai, son of the conquering Gengis Khan, who lived at the eastern extremity of the continent in Shang-tu (today, the inconsequential town of Shangdu about 200 miles northwest of Beijing, China).

Kublai Khan had never seen a native of Italy and requested an audience with the two brothers. Convinced that they had no choice in the matter, the brothers made an incredible year-long journey across Tibet and Mongolia to the eastern-most part of the Empire of the Great Khan (Cathay, or China).

As the first Europeans to set foot in the court of the Great Khan, they were entertained with feasts and plied with extravagant gifts. Kublai Khan questioned the brothers at length and became convinced that his Empire could benefit greatly from European learning (although, it should be mentioned, the Khanates were in many respects better governed and more civilized than much of Europe at that time). Consequently, Kublai Khan asked the brothers to relay to the Pope a request for 100 men of learning who could be stationed throughout his extensive empire to disseminate the best of Western culture.

THE "SILK ROAD" RAN 6000 MILES ACROSS ASIA.

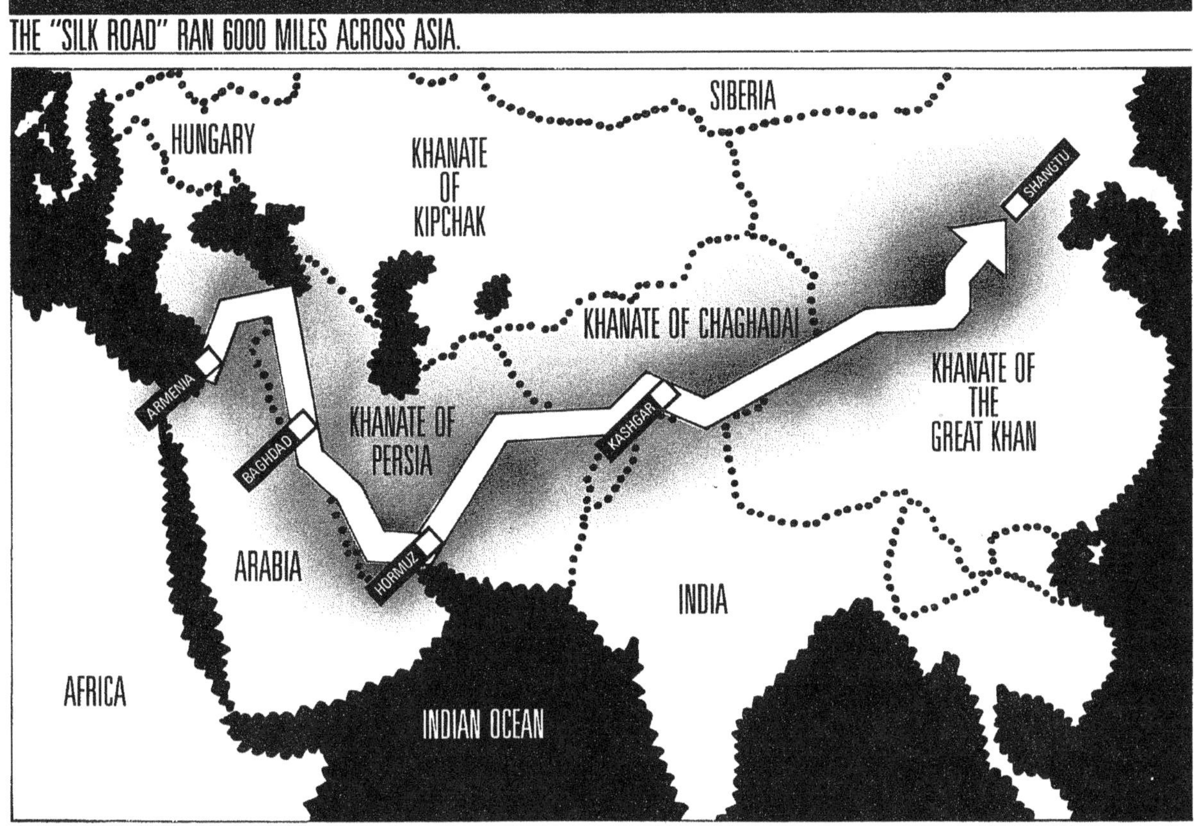

Although furnished with escorts, provisions, and everything necessary for their return journey, the Polos remained subject to the hazards of travel—extreme cold, snow, floods, deserts, and diseases—and it was three years before they reached the seaport of Laissus in Armenia and set sail for Venice.

Back in Italy, they found that Pope Clement IV had just died.

Two years passed before they could relay the Khan's request to the new Pope, Gregory X, who, instead of furnishing 100 men of learning, dispatched two friars of the Order of Preachers to accompany the Polos on their return trip. Having heard accounts of warring tribes along the route, the friars feared for their lives and, after just a few days' journey, turned back. This was not the only time this happened; as H.G. Wells in *The Outline of History* reports, "This abortive mission was only one of a number of attempts to communicate, and always they were feeble and feeble-spirited attempts, with nothing of the conquering fire of the earlier Christian missions."

Manuel Komroff in *The Travels of Marco Polo* goes further. "A hundred cultured men living in China at this time and returning home at various periods would have changed the course of human events. Europe was just awakening from a long, barbaric sleep, while China was already cultured in many fields. Marco Polo came to exchange merchandise, while 100 cultured men would have returned to exchange ideas. It is the traffic of ideas that is of greater profit to humanity."

On the second journey, the two Polo brothers decided to bring Niccolò's 16-year-old son, Marco, along. Marco was, first and foremost, a merchant, and much of his journals discuss trade, finance, risk, and profit. He also had an eye for nature and described many varieties of birds, trees, and other plants and animals. But beyond the realms of commerce and nature he was largely without vision and simply reported what he saw in a matter-of-fact style with little analysis of the underlying whys and wherefores.

The second journey of the Polos resembled the first—the main difference being the eyewitness account provided by young Marco's notes. As mentioned, these notes are not in the form of a travel narrative, but rather a description of things and places. Moreover, in setting down his account, Marco rearranged his notes to tell of a country (or city) and its immediate neighbors, thus making it difficult to define the actual route taken.

However, by comparing Marco's accounts with other historical information, excavations, and legends, historians have accurately reconstructed the route of this second legendary journey. Rather than starting in Constantinople, the second journey started in the port of Laissus in Lower Armenia (today, near Adana in south central Turkey). From there the travelers headed northeast along the Euphrates River and then turned southward along the Tigris River to Babylon (Baghdad) and continued on south to the Persian Gulf.

From there they continued south to Hormuz, where the caravan turned almost due north to cross the Dasht-e Lut and Dasht-e Kavir desert regions of Persia to Herat (then in the Khanate of Persia, today in Afghanistan). Next they followed a difficult trek across the mountains of Afghanistan, skirting north of Kashmir to Kashgir, the capital city of the Khanate of Chaghadai (today, Kashi, China).

Continuing in the mountains, the Polos then descended and crossed the narrowest part of the desert of Lop, which took a month. As Marco described, "During these days the journey is invariably over either sandy plains or barren mountains. In this tract, neither beasts or birds are met with, because there is no kind of food for them." He also described "excessive troubles and dangers that must unavoidably be encountered" such as mirages, malevolent spirits, eerie noises, and the danger of losing the path. This is one of the only places in which Marco Polo discussed the dangers of the route, so it must be supposed that they made a great impression on him. To this day this bone-strewn and barren waste has been crossed by very few travelers, and it remains one of the most desolate regions of the world.

The caravan then continued into the province of Tanguth in the Khanate of the Great Khan along what is today the border of Tibet (Xizang) and Sinkiang (Xinjiang). They continued generally eastward, veering off to the north before reaching Xian, the legendary eastern terminus of the Silk Road. The northern route followed the Yellow River for 550 miles, but unfortunately it also obliged the Polos to cross a portion of the Gobi Desert to reach Shang-tu.

Marco did not dwell as long on the Gobi Desert as he did on the Lop, although he did mention that one must "lay in provisions for at least 40 days because that space of time is employed in traversing the desert, where there is not any appearance of a dwelling, nor are there any inhabitants."

Finally, after traveling for three and a half years, the Polos arrived in the court of the Great Khan and bowed low before the emperor. In place of 100 learned men, they had with them a few letters from the new Pope, a little sacred oil from the Holy Land, and a few items to trade. By this time Marco was 21, the year, 1275.

Kublai Khan took a liking to Marco Polo, who at once applied himself to learning the written and spoken languages of the country. The Emperor, seeing that the young man was both clever and tactful, began to send him on public missions to other parts of the empire.

Marco Polo had observed that the Khan was often bored by the dry reports of his administrators but enjoyed hearing about the manners and oddities of people in other regions. Thus Marco started to keep small notebooks of strange facts that were likely to amuse and interest Kublai Khan. It was from these notebooks that Marco eventually transcribed the account of his travels back in Italy.

The Polos prospered in the court of Kublai Khan, and the Khan became very attached to them. Although they wanted to return to Italy, the Khan apparently felt that in a small way they were serving in place of the 100 men he had requested and declined to let them go.

However, 20 years later the Khan of Persia lost his favorite wife and asked Kublai Khan to send him another from the same Mongol tribe from which she had come. The Polos, who were expert navigators, proposed to the Khan that they be allowed to pilot the ships that would carry the party to Persia. Reluctantly, the Khan consented.

The Polos exchanged all their acquired possessions for jewels and set sail on a long and dangerous two-year voyage through the South China Sea and the Indian Ocean to Persia.

A year later, after having left the spectacular court of Kublai Khan, Niccolò, Maffeo, and Marco Polo arrived in their old home, Venice. Their clothes were tattered and foreign, their faces reflected the ravages of travel, and they had practically forgotten their native tongue. They had long been thought dead, and the distant relatives occupying their house refused to admit them after their absence of 26 years.

They finally succeeded in convincing their kindred that they were not imposters, and a great feast was arranged. All their old friends and relatives were invited. The Polos dressed in new velvet and damask garments for the meal, but when the table had been cleared and all the servants asked to leave, Marco Polo produced the coarse, shabby costumes they had worn on their arrival. Then, taking sharp knives, they ripped the seams and let fall to the table quantities of rubies, sapphires, diamonds, pearls, and other jewels. The guests were amazed and dumbfounded, the story spread, and the Polos became the most illustrious merchants of Venice.

Because the Polos were merchants, they immediately set themselves up in business and again began to trade. At the time, there were fierce rivalries among the great Italian merchant cities of Venice, Pisa, and Genoa. These rivalries had reached the point of open warfare, and most merchant families maintained one or more war galleys to protect their harbors and trading ships from both pirates and truculent rivals.

In a major battle, the Venetian and Genoese fleets met on September 7, 1298, just three years after the Polos' return from the Far East. In the battle, the Genoese captured the entire Venetian fleet and took 7000 Venetians, including Marco Polo, prisoner. Most were released in exchange for ransom, but the Genoese refused to release Marco Polo.

Thus, in a Genoese jail, Marco Polo dictated the notes of his travels to a fellow prisoner, Rusticien, a scribe from Pisa, and they were set down on parchment. Within a year, the merchant war between Venice and Genoa was over, Marco Polo was released, and the world got its first, disbelieving glimpse of the strange and fascinating land of Asia.

BIBLIOGRAPHY

Fairbank, J. K., Reischauer, E. O., and Craig, A. M. *East Asia: Tradition and Transformation.* Boston: Houghton Mifflin, 1973.

Komroff, Manuel. *The Travels of Marco Polo.* New York: The Modern Library, 1953.

Wells, H. G. *The Outline of History: A Plain History of Life and Mankind.* Boston: Doubleday, 1971.

THE PROGRAM

The Marco Polo program consists of a very short main program that simply calls a series of ten major subroutines. Ten shorter subroutines perform frequently used operations such as checking for a yes/no answer or centering a printed line. The program uses the same framework as the Westward Ho! program which includes extensive program notes; hence these notes describe only those sections that are unique. Both the subroutine to deal with the purchase of initial supplies (Sub720) and the one to deal with bartering for supplies along the way (Sub1190) require the player to specify quantities of six items. These quantities must be in a range, the lower limit of which is usually zero and the upper limit of which is defined by the number of jewels the player has. Hence, before each ReadNumber statement, the upper limit is set:

```
A2 = Math.Floor(JL / RN)
```

in which A2 is the upper limit, JL is the number of jewels, and RN is the cost of the item. The cost is a random function which varies over a small range. After setting the limit, a ReadNumber statement gets the answer, following which a subroutine (Sub3790), which checks to see if the answer is within the acceptable range, is called. If not, a message saying, "That is too few" or "That is too many," is printed and the input request is stated again.

Consider the expression in LN1580:

```
FR = Math.Floor(.5 + 10 * (F - FE)) / 10
```

The purpose of this expression is to calculate a fractional value (to 1/10) of the food reserve (FR), which is food (F) less food eaten (FE). This function is necessary because the computer may not calculate fractional values absolutely correctly (2/5 may come out 0.40000001, for example) and we do not want to print these extraneous digits or, worse yet, compound the error as the program proceeds. Because the integer (Math.Floor) function actually truncates the decimal places, it is necessary to add 0.5 to ten times the number to retain the correct decimal value. Try calculating the value of FR with and without the 0.5 for values of F–FE equal to 3.299999 and 3.300001.

Another expression frequently used in the program is found at Line 2160:

```
IF FC = 1 THEN
XD = ""
ELSE
XD = "S"
ENDIF
```

This is used when printing the reference to an item, in this case sacks of food that could have a value of zero, one, or more. When printing, we want the singular or plural form of the item to correspond to the numeric value, i.e., "I sack" and "2 sacks." Thus, the WriteLine statement uses the string XD as follows:

```
TextWindow.WriteLine("You'll have to sell " +FC+ " sack"+ XD +" of food or
skin"+ XD+ " of oil.")
```

Notice the spacing. A string (XD) has no automatic spaces and because we want a space following the word "sack" or "sacks," we leave a space inside the quotes following XD.

Look at the method of reading the probabilities of events occurring in this program (Sub3560). The cumulative value of the events is stored into the array EPArray. EPArray [1] = 6, EPArray [2] = 10, EPArray[3] = 14, and so on. The final value is EPT.

The function in Sub1940 determines which event occurs:

```
RN = Math.Floor(EPT * Math.GetRandomNumber(999)/1000)
```

This function selects a value between 1 and EPT. If RN is between 1 and 6, event 1 occurs; between 6 and 10, event 2; between 10 and 14, event 3; and so on.

The shooting subroutines in Marco Polo (Sub3620) and Westward Ho! are very similar. First, a random shooting word (SPLAT, TWACK, etc.) is selected which you are directed to type. Then, the current time (in seconds) is read from the real-time clock of the computer; this is the starting time S1. A Read statement in LN3650 accepts your typed word which is then compared with the requested word. If the two words match, the ending time is read from the real-time clock, the starting time subtracted from it, and the resulting elapsed time is used to calculate your ranking as a marksman.

If the word you entered did not match the requested word (the comparison is done in uppercase), the routine then checks to see whether you might have typed the word in lowercase letters. The code after the Read statement converts the letters of the requested word. If there is still no match, you are told, "That's not it. Try again."

At the beginning of the program when you were asked to rank your shooting ability (Sub600), the number that you input (HX) effectively becomes the number of seconds you have to type the requested shooting word in order to be ranked as an excellent marksman. Hence, if you claimed to be able to "hit a charging boar at 300 paces," in order to hit a bandit or animal dead center, you will have to type the correct word in one second or less. Actually, because of the way the real-time clock works, the allowable time may be as much as 1.99 seconds. Of course, you can "cheat" and rank yourself as a poor marksman (which will give you more time to type the correct word), but doing so makes the game less challenging and fun.

Many of the shorter subroutines are explained in the program notes in the next three chapters. Be sure to read them if you are having trouble understanding how anything works in this program.

PROGRAM VARIABLES

A	Answer to input query, numeric
AD	Answer to input query, string
A1, A2	Upper and lower limit to input answer
B	Beasts (camels)
BA	Beast quality
BL	Beast load capacity
BSK	Beast sickness indicator
C	Clothes (changes)
CZ	No clothes indicator
D	Distance (miles per trip segment)
DT	Distance, total
DZ	Desert indicator
EPArray[n]	Event probabilities (n = 1, 14)
F	Food (sacks)
FArray[n]	Food, names of animals for hunting
FC	Food carrying capacity of beast
FE	Food eaten on current trip segment
FP	Food eaten on previous trip segment
FQ	Food quality on current and previous trip segment
FR	Food reserve
HX	Hunting expertise level
I	Iteration variable
J	Trip segments (2-month periods)
K	Iteration variable
JL	Jewels
L	Oil (skins)
M	Medicines (bottles of balm)
MO	Month
MOD[n]	Month name (n = -1, 6)
PFD	Person food indicator
PSK	Person sickness indicator
PSKT	Person sickness total
PWD	Person wound indicator
PWDT	Person wounds total
R	Rate of speed
RN	Random number variable
SArray[n]	Shooting words (n = 1, 4)
S1, S2	Shooting timer start and stop
SR	Shooting response
W	Weapons (crossbow arrows)
XD	Temporary string variable
XAD	Temporary string variable
YR	Year

PROGRAM LISTINGS

```
TextWindow.CursorTop = 10
XD = "The Journey of Marco Polo, 1271"
Sub3760()
TextWindow.CursorTop = 13
XD = "(c) by David H. Ahl, 1986"
Sub3760()
TextWindow.CursorTop = 23
Sub3720()
TextWindow.Clear()
JL = 300
C = 2
W = 30
M = 5
FP = 5
BSK = 99
DT = 0
'Initial quantities of stuff
Sub360()
Sub3560()
'Display the scenario

TextWindow.WriteLine("")
Sub720()
'Purchase initial supplies
Sub600()
'Input hunting skill level
XD = "Press Enter to begin your trek!"
Sub3760()
JJJ = TextWindow.Read()
TextWindow.WriteLine("")
'
'Main program
LN220:
J = J + 1
Sub3510()
'Next two-month segment
DT = DT + D
If DT > 6000 Then
  Goto LN3360 'Reached end of trip?
EndIf
D = 40 + BA * 20 + Math.Floor(100 * Math.GetRandomNumber(999)/1000)
TextWindow.WriteLine("You have traveled "+ DT+ " miles.")
TextWindow.WriteLine("Here is what you now have: ")
Sub3200()
Sub910()
'Check for no jewels or clothes
Sub1020()
'Check for sickness
If BSK = J Then
BSK = 99
BL = B
BA = BA + 1 'Camel recover yet?
EndIf
```

```
If J > 1 AND JL > 1 Then
  Sub1190() 'Barter for supplies
EndIf
If C = 0 Then
  Sub1400() 'No clothes?
EndIf
Sub1500()
'Eating routine
If DZ = 0 AND Math.GetRandomNumber(999)/1000 < .18 Then
Sub3020() '18% chance to hunt for food
EndIf
TextWindow.WriteLine("")
Sub1780()
'Desert sections
If DZ = 0 Then
  Sub1940() 'Event happens
EndIf
Sub3110()
Goto LN220
'
Sub Sub360
'Subroutine to TextWindow.WriteLine( initial scenario
XD = "The Journey of Marco Polo-1271"
Sub3760()
TextWindow.WriteLine("")
TextWindow.WriteLine(" Starting from Venice in 1271 you travel by sailing
ship to the")
TextWindow.WriteLine("port of Armenia. Upon arrival, you prepare for a 6000-
mile trek to")
TextWindow.WriteLine("the court of the Great Kublai Khan in Shang-tu, Cathay.
Having set")
TextWindow.WriteLine("aside " +JL+ " precious jewels to finance your planned
3-year trip, you")
TextWindow.WriteLine("must barter for the following supplies in Armenia:")
TextWindow.WriteLine(" * Camels (Sturdier animals will cost more. You will
probably")
TextWindow.WriteLine(" want 8 to 10 camels to carry your many supplies.")
TextWindow.WriteLine(" * Food (You must barter for food as you travel along.
However,")
TextWindow.WriteLine(" prices tend to be lower in port cities, so you should
pack")
TextWindow.WriteLine(" in a good supply at the start.")
TextWindow.WriteLine(" * Oil for lamps and cooking (Over much of the trip,
you will be")
TextWindow.WriteLine(" able to use wood to build fires. However, in the
Persian,")
TextWindow.WriteLine(" Lop, and Gobi deserts you will need oil.)")
TextWindow.WriteLine("")
TextWindow.WriteLine(" From Venice you have also packed clothing, weapons
(crossbows),")
TextWindow.WriteLine("and medicines (balms and unguents); however, your
provisions will be")
TextWindow.WriteLine("depleted as you go along and you must replenish them.
The selection")
```

```
TextWindow.WriteLine("and price of supplies is quite different in various regions, so you")
TextWindow.WriteLine("must barter wisely. As a merchant, you are not skilled in fishing")
TextWindow.WriteLine("or hunting, although occasionally you might be able to try to get")
TextWindow.WriteLine("some food in this way.")
Sub3720()
TextWindow.Clear()
EndSub
'
Sub Sub600
'Subroutine to initialize hunting skill level
SArray[1] = "SPLAT"
SArray[2] = "SPRONG"
SArray[3] = "TWACK"
SArray[4] = "ZUNK"
FArray[1] = "wild boar"
FArray[2] = "big stag"
FArray[3] = "black bear"
TextWindow.WriteLine("")
TextWindow.WriteLine("Before you begin your journey, please rank your skill with")
TextWindow.WriteLine("the crossbow on the following scale:")
TextWindow.WriteLine(" (1) Can hit a charging boar at 300 paces")
TextWindow.WriteLine(" (2) Can hit a deer at 50 paces")
TextWindow.WriteLine(" (3) Can hit a sleeping woodchuck at 5 paces")
TextWindow.WriteLine(" (4) Occasionally hit own foot when loading")
LN680:
TextWindow.Write("How do you rank yourself? ")
HX = TextWindow.ReadNumber()
If HX > 0 AND HX < 5 Then
TextWindow.WriteLine("")
Goto LN719
EndIf
TextWindow.WriteLine("Please enter 1, 2, 3, or 4")
Goto LN680
LN719:
EndSub
'
Sub Sub720
'Subroutine to get initial supplies
TextWindow.WriteLine(" After three months at sea, you have arrived at the seaport of")
TextWindow.WriteLine("Laiassus, Armenia. There are many merchants in the port city and")
TextWindow.WriteLine("you can easily get the supplies you need. Several traders offer you")
A1 = 17
A2 = 24
TextWindow.WriteLine("camels at prices between " +A1 +" and " +A2+ " jewels each.")
TextWindow.Write("How much do you want to pay for a camel? ")
A = TextWindow.ReadNumber()
Sub3790()
```

```
BA = A
TextWindow.WriteLine("You will need at least 7 camels, but not more than
12.")
A1 = 7
A2 = 12
TextWindow.Write("How many camels do you want to buy? ")
A = TextWindow.ReadNumber()
Sub3790()
B = A
JL = JL - BA * B
A2 = 3 * B - 6
'Camels?number, cost, amount they can carry
TextWindow.WriteLine(" One large sack of food costs 2 jewels. You will need
at least")
TextWindow.WriteLine("8 sacks to get to Babylon (Baghdad); you can carry a
maximum of "+ A2)
A1 = 8
TextWindow.Write("sacks. How many do you want? ")
A = TextWindow.ReadNumber()
Sub3790()
F = A
JL = JL - A * 2
A2 = 3 * B - A
'Food & cost, amount of oil camels can carry
TextWindow.WriteLine(" A skin of oil costs 2 jewels each. You should have at
least 6")
TextWindow.WriteLine("full skins for cooking in the desert. Your camels can
carry " +A2)
A1 = 5
TextWindow.Write("skins. How many do you want? ")
A = TextWindow.ReadNumber()
Sub3790()
BL = B
L = A
JL = JL - 2 * L
'Oil-amount and cost
EndSub
'
Sub Sub910
'Subroutine to check for being out of jewels and clothes
If JL > 15 Then
  Goto LN980 'Still have a few jewels?
EndIf
TextWindow.WriteLine( "You have only "+ JL+ " jewels with which to barter." )
If B > 2 Then
  Goto LN950
EndIf
LN940:
TextWindow.WriteLine("You push on with your "+ B+ " camels.")
Goto ln1019
LN950:
TextWindow.Write("Would you like to sell a camel? ")
AD = TextWindow.Read()
Sub3840()
If AD = "N" Then
```

```
  Goto LN940
EndIf
RN = Math.Floor(8 + 9 * Math.GetRandomNumber(999)/1000)
TextWindow.WriteLine("You get " +RN+ " jewels for your best camel.")
JL = JL + RN
B = B - 1
BL = BL - 1
'Add jewels, subtract camel
LN980:
If C > 0 Then
  Goto ln1019 'Have some clothes?
EndIf
TextWindow.WriteLine("You should try to replace that tent you have been
wearing as a")
TextWindow.WriteLine("robe. It is badly torn and the Tartars find it
insulting.")
LN1019:
EndSub
'
Sub Sub1020
'Subroutine to deal with sickness
If PSK > 0 Then
PSKT = PSKT + PSK
PSK = 0 'Sickness total
EndIf
If PWD > 0 Then
PWDT = PWDT + PWD
PWD = 0 'Injuries total
EndIf
If FE = 3 Then
  PFD = PFD + .4
EndIf
If PSKT + PWDT + PFD < 3 Then
  Goto ln1189
EndIf
If Math.GetRandomNumber(999)/1000 > .7 Then
  Goto ln1189 '70% chance of delay due to recurring illness
EndIf
TextWindow.WriteLine("As a result of sickness, injuries, and poor eating, you
must stop")
TextWindow.WriteLine("and regain your health. You trade a few jewels to stay
in a hut.")
RN = Math.Floor(1 + 3.2 * Math.GetRandomNumber(999)/1000)
If RN > 3 Then
  Goto LN1160 '6% chance of dying
EndIf
TextWindow.WriteLine("You grow steadily stronger, but it is " +RN * 2 +"
months until you")
TextWindow.WriteLine("are again fit to travel.")
PSKT = 0
PWDT = 0
PFD = 0
J = J + RN
M = Math.Floor(M / 2)
F = F / 2
```

```
If F < 3 Then
  F = 3
EndIf
If JL > 20 Then
JL = JL - 10
ELSE
JL = Math.Floor(JL / 2) 'Costs money for lodging
EndIf
Sub3510()
Goto ln1189
LN1160:
For I = 1 To 2500
endfor
Goto ln1189
TextWindow.WriteLine("You stay for " +RN+ " months but grow")
TextWindow.WriteLine("steadily weaker and finally pass away.")
J = J + RN
Sub3280()
ln1189:
EndSub
'
Sub Sub1190
'Subroutine to barter for supplies
TextWindow.Write("You have " +JL)
TextWindow.Write(" jewels. Do you want to barter here? ")
AD = TextWindow.Read()
Sub3840()
If AD = "N" Then
  Goto LN1380
EndIf
RN = Math.Floor(17 + 8 * Math.GetRandomNumber(999)/1000)
TextWindow.Write("Camels cost "+ RN+ " jewels here. ")
A1 = 0
A2 = Math.Floor(JL / RN)
TextWindow.Write("How many do you want? ")
A = TextWindow.ReadNumber()
Sub3790()
B = B + A
BL = BL + A
BA = BA - A
'Lower quality animals along route
JL = JL - A * RN
RN = Math.Floor(2 + 4 * Math.GetRandomNumber(999)/1000)
TextWindow.Write("Sacks of food cost " +RN+ " jewels. ")
LN1260:
A2 = (Math.Floor(JL / RN))
TextWindow.Write("How many do you want? ")
A = TextWindow.ReadNumber()
Sub3790()
F = F + A
If F + L > 3 * BL Then
TextWindow.WriteLine( "Camels can't carry that much.")
F = F - A
GOTO LN1260
EndIf
```

```
JL = JL - A * RN
RN = Math.Floor(2 + 4 * Math.GetRandomNumber(999)/1000)
TextWindow.Write("Skins of oil cost "+ RN+ " jewels. ")
LN1290:
A2 = (Math.Floor(JL / RN))
TextWindow.Write("How many do you want? ")
A = TextWindow.ReadNumber()
Sub3790()
L = L + A
If F + L > 3 * BL Then
TextWindow.WriteLine( "Camels can't carry that much.")
L = L - A
GOTO LN1290
EndIf
JL = JL - A * RN
RN = Math.Floor(8 + 8 * Math.GetRandomNumber(999)/1000)
TextWindow.Write("A set of clothes costs "+ RN)
A2 = (Math.Floor(JL / RN))
TextWindow.Write(" jewels. How many do you want? ")
A = TextWindow.ReadNumber()
Sub3790()
C = C + A
JL = JL - A * RN
TextWindow.Write("You can get a bottle of balm for 2 jewels. ")
A2 = JL / 2
TextWindow.Write("How many do you want? ")
A = TextWindow.ReadNumber()
Sub3790()
JL = JL - 2 * A
M = M + A
A2 = JL
RN = Math.Floor(6 + 6 * Math.GetRandomNumber(999)/1000)
TextWindow.WriteLine("You can get " +RN+ " arrows for 1 jewel.")
TextWindow.Write("How many jewels do you want to spend on arrows? ")
A = TextWindow.ReadNumber()
Sub3790()
JL = JL - A
W = W + RN * A
If C > 1 Then
  CZ = 0
EndIf
LN1380:
TextWindow.WriteLine("")
TextWindow.WriteLine("Here is what you now have:")
Sub3200()
EndSub
'
Sub Sub1400
'Subroutine to deal with no clothes
TextWindow.WriteLine("")
TextWindow.WriteLine("You were warned about getting more modest clothes.")
TextWindow.WriteLine( "Furthermore, your sandals are in shreds.")
If CZ = 1 Then
  Goto LN1470
EndIf
```

```
TextWindow.Write("The Tartars chase you from town and ")
If Math.GetRandomNumber(999)/1000 > .2 Then
TextWindow.WriteLine( "warn you not to return.")
CZ = 1
Goto ln1499
EndIf
LN1450:
TextWindow.WriteLine("stone you.")
TextWindow.Write("You are badly wounded and vow to get")
TextWindow.WriteLine("new clothes as soon as possible.")
PWD = 1.5
CZ = 1
Goto ln1499
LN1470:
TextWindow.WriteLine("Word has been received about your disreputable
appearance.")
TextWindow.Write("The people are not willing to deal with you and they  ")
Goto LN1450
ln1499:
Endsub
'
Sub Sub1500
'Subroutine to eat
If F < 3 Then
  Goto LN1650 'Out of food?
EndIf
LN1520:
TextWindow.WriteLine("On the next stage of your journey, how do you want to
eat:")
TextWindow.WriteLine(" (1) Reasonably well (can walk further; Less chance of
sickness)")
LN1540:
TextWindow.Write( " (2) Adequately, or (3) Poorly? ")
A =TextWindow.ReadNumber()
If A > 0 AND A < 4 Then
  Goto LN1560
EndIf
TextWindow.Write("That's not a choice. Now then, (1) Well, ")
Goto LN1540
LN1560:
FE = 6 - A
If FE <= F Then
  Goto LN1580
EndIf
TextWindow.WriteLine("You don't have enough food to eat that well. Try
again.")
Goto LN1520
LN1580:
FR = Math.Floor(.5 + 10 * (F - FE)) / 10
If FR > 3 Then
  Goto LN1630
EndIf
If FR = 1 Then
XD = ""
ELSE
```

```
XD = "s"
EndIf
TextWindow.WriteLine( "Your food reserve will then be just " +FR+ " sack"+
XD)
If A = 3 Then
  Goto LN1630
EndIf
TextWindow.Write("Do you want to change your mind about how much you will
eat? ")
AD = TextWindow.Read()
Sub3840()
If AD = "Y" Then
  Goto LN1520
EndIf
LN1630:
F = F - FE
D = D - (A - 1) * 50
FQ = FP + FE
FP = FE
Goto LN1779
'
LN1650:
'Out of food section
TextWindow.WriteLine("You don't have enough food to go on.")
If JL < 15 Then
  Goto LN1730
EndIf
TextWindow.WriteLine("You should have bought food at the market. Now it will
cost you")
RN = Math.Floor(5 + 4 * Math.GetRandomNumber(999)/1000)
TextWindow.Write(RN +" jewels per sack. ")
A1 = 1
A2 = (Math.Floor(JL / RN))
TextWindow.Write(" How many sacks do you want? ")
A = TextWindow.ReadNumber()
Sub3790()
F = F + A
JL = JL - A * RN
If F >= 3 Then
  Goto ln1779
EndIf
TextWindow.WriteLine("You still don't have enough food and there is nothing
to hunt.")
LN1730:
If B < 1 Then
Goto LN1760
ELSE
textwindow.write("Do you want to eat a camel? ")
AD = TextWindow.Read()
EndIf
Sub3840()
If AD = "N" Then
Sub3280()
ELSE
B = B - 1
```

```
RN = Math.Floor(3 + 2 * Math.GetRandomNumber(999)/1000)
F = F + RN
EndIf
TextWindow.WriteLine("You manage to get about " +RN+ " sacks of food out of
it.")
Goto ln1520
LN1760:
TextWindow.WriteLine("You don't even have a camel left to eat.")
Sub3280() ' game over
ln1779:
Endsub
'
Sub Sub1780
'Subroutine for desert sections
DZ = 0
If DT < 2100 OR DT > 5900 Then
  Goto ln1919 'No desert at far ends
EndIf
If DT > 2600 AND DT < 4100 Then
  Goto ln1919 'Tigris River Valley
EndIf
If DT > 4600 AND DT < 5400 Then
  Goto ln1919 'No desert in middle
EndIf
If DT < 4100 Then
XD = "Dasht-e-Kavir (Persian)"
GOTO LN1840
EndIf
If DT > 5399 Then
XD = "Gobi (Cathay)"
ELSE
XD = "Taklimakan (Lop)"
EndIf
LN1840:
TextWindow.WriteLine("You are in the " +XD+ " desert.")
If L >= 3 Then
L = L - 3
TextWindow.WriteLine( "Use 3 skins of oil for cooking.")
GOTO ln1900
EndIf
TextWindow.WriteLine("You ran out of oil for cooking.")
If L > 1 Then
IF Math.GetRandomNumber(999)/1000 > .5 THEN
L = 0
GOTO ln1900
endif
EndIf
TextWindow.WriteLine("You get horribly sick from eating raw and undercooked
food.")
L = 0
PSK = 1
D = D - 80
M = M - 1
LN1900:
JJJ= Math.Floor(1 + 7 * Math.GetRandomNumber(999)/1000)
```

```
If (JJJ = 1) Then
  Sub2250()
ElseIf (JJJ = 2) Then
  Sub2310()
ElseIf (JJJ = 3) Then
  Sub2420()
ElseIf (JJJ = 4) Then
  Sub2450()
ElseIf (JJJ = 5) Then
  Sub2480()
ElseIf (JJJ = 6) Then
  Sub2510()
ElseIf (JJJ = 7) Then
  Sub1920()
EndIf
LN1910:
DZ = 1
Sub3110()
ln1919:
EndSub

Sub Sub1920
TextWindow.WriteLine("You get through this stretch of desert without
mishap!")
DZ = 1
Sub3110()
EndSub
'

Sub Sub1940
'Subroutine to deal with special events
RN = Math.Floor(EPT * Math.GetRandomNumber(999)/1000)
For I = 1 To 14
'Iterate thru possible events
If RN <= EPArray[i] then
  Goto LN1941
endif
endfor
i=14
ln1941:
If I > 10 Then
  Goto LN1990
EndIf
If (I = 1) Then
  Sub2000()
ElseIf (I = 2) Then
  Sub2250()
ElseIf (I = 3) Then
  Sub2310()
ElseIf (I = 4) Then
  Sub2340()
ElseIf (I = 5) Then
  Sub2360()
ElseIf (I = 6) Then
  Sub2380()
```

```
ElseIf (I = 7) Then
  Sub2400()
ElseIf (I = 8) Then
  Sub2420()
ElseIf (I = 9) Then
  Sub2450()
ElseIf (I = 10) Then
  Sub2480()
EndIf
LN1990:
If (I - 10 = 1) Then
  Sub2540()
ElseIf (I - 10 = 2) Then
  Sub2570()
ElseIf (I - 10 = 3) Then
  Sub2600()
ElseIf (I - 10 = 4) Then
  Sub2660()
EndIf
EndSub

Sub Sub2000
TextWindow.WriteLine("A camel injures its leg. Do you want to (1) Nurse it
along or")
LN2010:
TextWindow.Write("(2) Abandon it, or (3) Sell it? ")
A = TextWindow.ReadNumber()
If A = 1 Then
Goto LN2040
ElseIf A = 2 THEN
goto ln2050
ElseIf A = 3 THEN
goto ln2090
EndIf
TextWindow.WriteLine("That is not a choice. Answer (1) to Nurse it along, ")
Goto LN2010
LN2040:
BSK = J + 2
Sub2120()
Goto ln2121
LN2050:
B = B - 1
sub2120()
FC = 3 * BL - F - L
If FC <= 0 Then
  Goto ln2121
EndIf
TextWindow.WriteLine( "You kill the camel for food.")
If FC > 2 Then
  FC = 3
EndIf
F = F + FC
If FC = 1 Then
XD = ""
ELSE
```

```
XD = "s"
EndIf
TextWindow.WriteLine("You get the equivalent of " +FC+ " sack"+ XD+ " of
food.")
Goto ln2121
LN2090:
B = B - 1
TextWindow.WriteLine("It is a poor beast and you can get only 10 jewels for
it.")
JL = JL + 10
Sub2120()
LN2121:
EndSub
'

Sub Sub2120
'Exceed load carrying capacity of camels?
BL = B
If BSK <= J Then
BL = B - .6
BA = BA - 1 'If sick camel reduce load, speed
EndIf
If F + L <= 3 * BL Then
  Goto ln2249
EndIf
TextWindow.WriteLine("You have too large a load for your camels.")
FC = Math.Floor(F + L - 3 * BL + .9)
LN2160:
If FC = 1 Then
XD = ""
ELSE
XD = "s"
EndIf
TextWindow.WriteLine("You'll have to sell " +FC+ " sack"+ XD +" of food or
skin"+ XD+ " of oil.")
FS = Math.Floor(FC / 2)
LS = FC - FS
'How much to sell of food and oil
LN2190:
If LS > L Then
LS = LS - 1
FS = FS + 1
GOTO ln2190
EndIf
LN2200:
If FS > F Then
FS = FS - 1
LS = LS + 1
GOTO ln2200
EndIf
F = F - FS
L = L - LS
JL = JL + FS + LS
'Decrease food and oil, add jewels
```

```
TextWindow.Write("You sell " +FS+ " of food, " +LS+ " of oil for which you
get only")
TextWindow.WriteLine((FS + LS)+ " jewel" +XD+ ".")
LN2249:
EndSub

'
Sub Sub2250
TextWindow.WriteLine("One of your camels is very sick and can't carry a full
load.")
LN2260:
TextWindow.Write("Want to (1) Keep it with you, (2) Slaughter it, or (3) Sell
it? ")
A = TextWindow.ReadNumber()
If A = 1 Then
Goto LN2290
ELSEIF A = 2 THEN
'taken from ln2050 above - can't call line from subroutine
B = B - 1
sub2120()
FC = 3 * BL - F - L
If FC <= 0 Then
  Goto ln2309
EndIf
TextWindow.WriteLine( "You kill the camel for food.")
If FC > 2 Then
  FC = 3
EndIf
F = F + FC
If FC = 1 Then
XD = ""
ELSE
XD = "s"
EndIf
TextWindow.WriteLine("You get the equivalent of " +FC+ " sack"+ XD+ " of
food.")
Goto ln2309
B = B - 1
TextWindow.WriteLine("It is a poor beast and you can get only 10 jewels for
it.")
JL = JL + 10
Sub2120()
Goto ln2309
ELSEIF A = 3 THEN
B = B - 1
TextWindow.WriteLine("It is a poor beast and you can get only 10 jewels for
it.")
JL = JL + 10
Sub2120()
Goto ln2309
EndIf
TextWindow.WriteLine("That is not a choice. Again, please.")
Goto LN2260
LN2290:
BSK = J + 2
```

```
Sub2120()
LN2309:
EndSub
'
Sub Sub2310
TextWindow.WriteLine("Long stretch with bad water. Costs time to find clean
wells.")
D = D - 50
EndSub

Sub Sub2340
TextWindow.WriteLine("You get lost trying to find an easier route.")
D = D - 100
EndSub

'
Sub Sub2360
TextWindow.WriteLine("Heavy rains completely wash away the route.")
D = D - 90
EndSub
'
Sub Sub2380
TextWindow.WriteLine("Some of your food rots in the humid weather.")
F = F - 1
EndSub
'
Sub Sub2400
TextWindow.WriteLine("Marauding animals got into your food supply.")
F = F - 1
EndSub
'
Sub Sub2420
TextWindow.WriteLine("A fire flares up and destroys some of your food and
clothes.")
F = F - .4
C = C - 1
Sub3110()
If L < 1 Then
Goto ln2421
ELSE
L = L - .5
Goto LN2421
EndIf
LN2421:
EndSub

'
Sub Sub2450
TextWindow.WriteLine("Two camels wander off. You finally find them after
spending")
TextWindow.WriteLine("several days searching for them.")
D = D - 20
EndSub
'
Sub Sub2480
```

```
TextWindow.WriteLine("You get a nasty burn from an oil fire.")
PWD = .5
Sub2840()
EndSub
'
Sub Sub2510
TextWindow.WriteLine("High winds, sand storms, and ferocious heat slow you
down.")
D = D - 70
EndSub
'
Sub Sub2540
TextWindow.WriteLine("A gash in your leg looks infected. It hurts like the
blazes.")
Sub2840()
D = D - 50
PWD = .7
EndSub
'
Sub Sub2570
TextWindow.WriteLine("Jagged rocks tear your sandals and clothing. You'll
have to get")
TextWindow.WriteLine("replacements as soon as you can.")
C = C - 1
D = D - 30
EndSub
'
Sub Sub2600
RN = Math.GetRandomNumber(999)/1000 * FQ
If RN < 2 Then
  Goto LN2610
ELSE
  IF RN < 3.5 THEN
    Sub2630()
  ELSE
    Goto ln2629
  endif
endif
LN2610:
TextWindow.WriteLine("All of you have horrible stomach cramps and intestinal
disorders")
TextWindow.WriteLine("and are laid up for over a month.")
D = D - 275
LN2629:
EndSub

Sub Sub2630
TextWindow.WriteLine("You're running a high fever and your muscles feel like
jelly.")
TextWindow.WriteLine("Your party slows down for you.")
PSK = .7
D = D - 125
EndSub
'
Sub Sub2660
```

```
TextWindow.WriteLine("Blood-thirsty bandits are attacking your small
caravan!")
TextWindow.Write("You grab your crossbow... ")
Sub3620()
If W > 5 Then
Goto LN2700
ELSE
TextWindow.WriteLine( "You try to drive them off, but you run out")
EndIf
TextWindow.WriteLine("of arrows. They grab some jewels and food.")
F = F - 1
Goto LN2720
LN2700:
If SR <= 1 Then
Goto LN2810
ELSE
IF SR <= 3 THEN
goto LN2780
EndIf
EndIf
TextWindow.WriteLine("Better stick to trading; your aim is terrible.")
LN2720:
If Math.GetRandomNumber(999)/1000 > .8 Then
  Goto LN2750 '80% chance of surviving attack
EndIf
TextWindow.WriteLine("They are savage, evil barbarians ? they kill you and
take")
TextWindow.WriteLine("your remaining camels and jewels.")
JL = 0
B = 0
Goto LN3320
LN2750:
TextWindow.WriteLine("You caught a knife in the shoulder. That's going to
take quite")
TextWindow.WriteLine("a while to heal.")
Sub2840()
PWD = 1.5
JL = JL - 10
W = W - 4 - 2 * SR
Sub3110()
Goto LN2828
LN2780:
TextWindow.WriteLine("With practice you could shoot the crossbow, but most of
your shots")
TextWindow.WriteLine("missed. An iron mace got you in the chest. They took
some jewels.")
PWD = 1
JL = JL - 5
Sub2840()
W = W - 3 - 2 * SR
Sub3110()
Goto LN2828
LN2810:
TextWindow.WriteLine("Wow! Sensational shooting. You drove them off with no
losses.")
```

```
W = W - 4
LN2828:
EndSub

'
Sub Sub2840
'Subroutine to deal with using balm
RN = Math.Floor(1 + 2 * Math.GetRandomNumber(999)/1000)
If RN > 1 Then
XD = "s"
ELSE
XD = ""
EndIf
If Math.GetRandomNumber(999)/1000 > .5 Then
XAD = "balm"
ELSE
XAD = "unguent"
EndIf
M = M - RN
If M < 0 Then
M = 0
GOTO LN2890
EndIf
TextWindow.WriteLine("You use "+ RN+ " bottle"+ XD +" of "+ XAD +" treating
your wound.")
Goto LN3019
LN2890:
TextWindow.WriteLine( "You need more " +XAD+ " to treat your wound." )
If JL < 8 Then
  Goto LN2940
EndIf
TextWindow.WriteLine("Fortunately, you find some nomads who offer to sell you
2 bottles")
TextWindow.WriteLine("of "+ XAD +" for the outrageous price of 4 jewels
each.")
TextWindow.Write( "Do you want to buy it? ")
AD = TextWindow.Read()
Sub3840()
If AD = "N" Then
  Goto LN2950
EndIf
TextWindow.WriteLine("It works well and you're soon feeling better.")
M = 0
JL = JL - 8
Goto ln3019
LN2940:
TextWindow.WriteLine("But, alas, you don't have enough jewels to buy any.")
LN2950:
TextWindow.Write( "Your wound is badly infected,  ")
If Math.GetRandomNumber(999)/1000 < .8 Then
  Goto LN3000
EndIf
TextWindow.WriteLine("but you keep going anyway.")
TextWindow.WriteLine("")
```

```
TextWindow.WriteLine("Unfortunately, the strain is too much for you and,
after weeks of")
TextWindow.WriteLine("agony, you succumb to your wounds and die in the
wilderness.")
Goto LN3320
LN3000:
TextWindow.WriteLine("but you push on for the next village.")
PWD = 3
ln3019:
EndSub
'
Sub Sub3020
'Subroutine to hunt for food
If W < 15 Then
  TextWindow.WriteLine( "You don't have enough arrows to hunt for food." )
  Goto LN3009
EndIf
TextWindow.Write("There goes a " +FArray[Math.Floor(1 + 3 *
Math.GetRandomNumber(999)/1000)] + "_ ")
W = W - 15
Sub3620()
If SR <= 1 Then
  Goto LN3080
ELSE
  IF SR <= 3 THEN
    Goto LN3070
  EndIf
EndIf
TextWindow.WriteLine("Were you too excited? All your shots went wild.")
Goto LN3009
LN3070:
TextWindow.WriteLine("Not bad; you finally brought one down.")
FA = 2
Goto LN3090
LN3080:
TextWindow.WriteLine("With shooting that good, the Khan will want you in his
army.")
FA = 3
LN3090:
TextWindow.WriteLine("Your hunting yields "+FA +" sacks of food.")
F = F + FA
LN3009:
EndSub
'
Sub Sub3110
'Subroutine to check for zero quantities
If JL < 0 Then
  JL = 0 'Can't have negative jewels
EndIf
If F < 0 Then
  F = 0 'or food
EndIf
If L < 0 Then
  L = 0 'or oil
EndIf
```

```
If C < 0 Then
  C = 0 'or clothing
EndIf
If M < 0 Then
  M = 0 'or medicine
EndIf
If W < 0 Then
  W = 0 'or arrows
EndIf
EndSub
'
Sub Sub3200
'Subroutine to TextWindow.WriteLine( inventory
TextWindow.WriteLine("Jewel Camel                    Balms and")
TextWindow.WriteLine("Sacks Skins Food Oil  Clothes Unguents   Arrows")
Sub3110()
TextWindow.CursorLeft = 1
TextWindow.Write(JL)
TextWindow.CursorLeft = 7
TextWindow.Write(B)
TextWindow.CursorLeft = 12
TextWindow.Write(F)
TextWindow.CursorLeft = 17
TextWindow.Write(L)
TextWindow.CursorLeft = 25
TextWindow.Write(C)
TextWindow.CursorLeft = 33
TextWindow.Write(M)
TextWindow.CursorLeft = 42
TextWindow.Write(W)
TextWindow.WriteLine("")
TextWindow.WriteLine("")
EndSub
'
Sub Sub3280
'End game - out of food
TextWindow.WriteLine("You keep going as long as you can, trying to find
berries and")
TextWindow.WriteLine("edible plants. But this is barren country and you fall
ill and,")
TextWindow.WriteLine("after weeks of suffering, you collapse into eternal
sleep.")
LN3320:
TextWindow.WriteLine("")
J = J + 1
Sub3510()
TextWindow.WriteLine("You had the following left at the end:")
Sub3200()
TextWindow.WriteLine("You traveled for "+ J * 2+ " months!")
TextWindow.WriteLine("")
TextWindow.WriteLine("Sorry, you didn't make it to Shang-tu.")
Goto LN3490
'
LN3360:
'End of trip section
```

```
Sub3110()
'Can't have negative jewels at end
For I = 1 To 3000
EndFor
TextWindow.Clear()
For I = 1 To 10
XD = "CONGRATULATIONS !"
TextWindow.CursorTop = 12
Sub3760()
Program.Delay(100)
TextWindow.Clear()
Program.Delay(50)
EndFor
TextWindow.Clear()
TextWindow.WriteLine("You have been traveling for " +J * 2 +" months !")
TextWindow.WriteLine("")
TextWindow.WriteLine("You are ushered into the court of the Great Kublai
Khan.")
TextWindow.WriteLine("He surveys your meager remaining supplies:")
Sub3200()
TextWindow.WriteLine("... and marvels that you got here at all. He is
disappointed")
TextWindow.WriteLine("that the Pope did not see fit to send the 100 men of
learning")
TextWindow.WriteLine("that he requested and, as a result, keeps the three of
you as")
TextWindow.WriteLine("his personal envoys for the next 21 years. Well done!")
TextWindow.WriteLine("")
'
LN3490:
TextWindow.WriteLine("")
TextWindow.Write("Press Enter to End")
AD = TextWindow.Read()
Program.End()
endsub

'
Sub Sub3510
'Subroutine to print
MO = J
While MO>6
MO = MO - 6
EndWhile
YR = 1271 + Math.Floor(J / 6)
TextWindow.WriteLine("")
TextWindow.WriteLine("Date: " + MOD[mo] +" "+ YR )
EndSub
'
Sub Sub3560
'Subroutine to read event probabilities
EPArray[1] =6
EPArray[2] =10
EPArray[3] =14
EPArray[4] =20
EPArray[5] =26
```

```
EPArray[6] =32
EPArray[7] =38
EPArray[8] =42
EPArray[9] =46
EPArray[10] =47
EPArray[11] =53
EPArray[12] =61
EPArray[13] =79
EPArray[14] =89
EPT = EPArray[14]
MOD[1] = "March"
MOD[2] =  "May"
MOD[3] = "July"
MOD[4] = "September"
MOD[5] = "November"
MOD[6] = "January"
EndSub
'
Sub Sub3620
'Subroutine to shoot crossbow
RN = 1 + Math.Floor(4 * Math.GetRandomNumber(999)/1000)
'print random shooting word
's1 is seconds
S1 = 60 * Clock.Minute + Clock.Second
'Start timer
LN3650:
TextWindow.Write( "Type : " +SArray[RN] +"  ")
XD = TextWindow.Read()
If XD = SArray[RN] Then
  Goto LN3680
EndIf
For I = 1 To Text.GetLength(XD)
'Iterate through letters for possible lowercase
If Text.getsubtext(SArray[RN], I,
1)<>Text.GetCharacter(Text.GetCharacterCode(Text.GetSubText(XD, I, 1)) - 32)
Then
  Goto LN3700
  EndIf
endFor
LN3680:
S2 = 60 * Clock.Minute + Clock.Second
'End timer
SR = S2 - S1 - HX
Goto LN3719
'Shooting response
LN3700:
TextWindow.Write("That's not it. Try again. ")
Goto LN3650
ln3719:
EndSub
'
Sub Sub3720
'Subroutine to hit enter key
XD = "Press any Enter to continue."
Sub3760()
```

```
JJJ = TextWindow.Read()
RN = RN + 1
EndSub
'
Sub Sub3760
'Subroutine to TextWindow.WriteLine( a centered line
TextWindow.CursorLeft = (35 - Text.GetLength(XD)/2)
TextWindow.WriteLine(XD)
EndSub
'
Sub Sub3790
'Subroutine to check if answer entered is in range
LN3800:
If A >= A1 AND A <= A2 Then
  Goto LN3839
EndIf
If A < A1 Then
  XD = "few"
ELSE
  XD = "many"
EndIf
TextWindow.Write("That is too " +XD)
TextWindow.Write(". Your answer please? ")
A = TextWindow.ReadNumber()
Goto LN3800
LN3839:
EndSub
'
Sub Sub3840
'Subroutine to process a yes/no answer
LN3850:
Sub3880()
If AD = "Y" OR AD = "N" Then
  Goto LN3851
EndIf
TextWindow.Write("Don't understand answer. Enter 'Y' or 'N' please? ")
AD = TextWindow.Read()
Goto LN3850
LN3851:
EndSub
'
Sub Sub3880
'Subroutine to extract the first letter of an answer
If AD = "" Then
  AD = "Y"
 Goto LN3881
EndIf
AD = Text.GetSubText(AD,1, 1)
If AD >= "A" AND AD <= "Z" Then
  Goto LN3881
EndIf
AD = Text.GetCharacter(Text.GetCharacterCode(AD) - 32)
LN3881:
EndSub
```

Westward Ho!

In Westward Ho! you are the head of a family of five setting out from Independence, Missouri, in the spring of 1847 on the Oregon Trail. Your objective is to arrive safely in Oregon City, Oregon.

Having saved about $420 you must purchase a wagon for $70, and with the remaining money you must also buy enough equipment, supplies, and livestock to sustain you on your strenuous 2000-mile journey. As you travel, you encounter the same hazards and conditions that American pioneers faced during the Great Migration: wagon fires, polluted water, wild animals, bad weather, illness, and topographical obstacles. The following hints will help you on the Trail:

- In Independence you decide how much of your money to spend on the things you need for the trip. You can spend all of your money there, but if you do, you will not be able to buy supplies at forts along the way.
- The trip is divided into two-week segments. Between segments you have an opportunity to stop and hunt for game. Hunting may augment your food supply, but it always consumes valuable time.
- At the beginning of the game, you are asked to rank your shooting (typing) ability. When you are hunting or being attacked by hostile Indians, you are asked to type a word that sounds like a gunshot; the faster you type it, the more likely you are to hit your target. Of course, not all Indians that approach your wagon are hostile, and shooting at friendly Indians costs you time and ammunition.

If you make the correct decisions along the way, you and your family will join the hundreds of thousands of pioneers who settled and developed the land west of the Rockies. If you prepare poorly or if you make foolish decisions, your bones will serve as a warning to those who come after you on the Oregon Trail. Good luck!

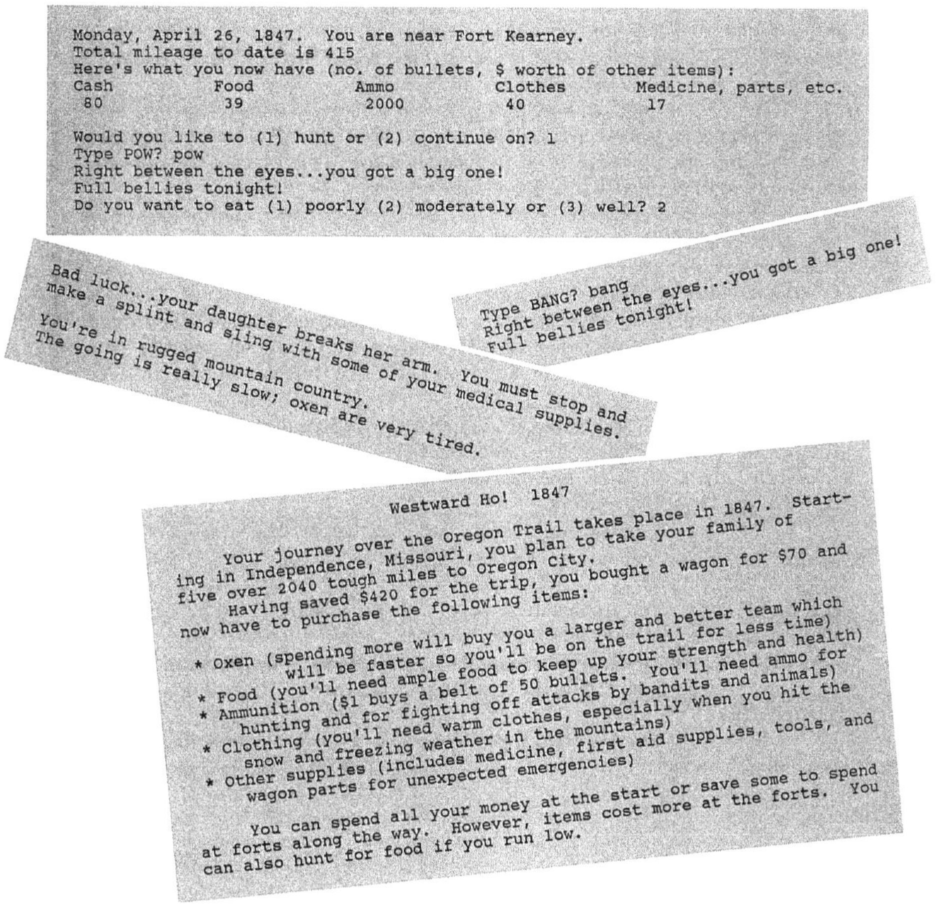

```
Monday, April 26, 1847.  You are near Fort Kearney.
Total mileage to date is 415
Here's what you now have (no. of bullets, $ worth of other items):
Cash        Food        Ammo        Clothes       Medicine, parts, etc.
 80          39         2000         40            17

Would you like to (1) hunt or (2) continue on? 1
Type POW? pow
Right between the eyes...you got a big one!
Full bellies tonight!
Do you want to eat (1) poorly (2) moderately or (3) well? 2
```

```
Bad luck...your daughter breaks her arm.  You must stop and
make a splint and sling with some of your medical supplies.
You're in rugged mountain country.
The going is really slow; oxen are very tired.
```

```
Type BANG? bang
Right between the eyes...you got a big one!
Full bellies tonight!
```

```
                        Westward Ho! 1847

   Your journey over the Oregon Trail takes place in 1847.  Start-
ing in Independence, Missouri, you plan to take your family of
five over 2040 tough miles to Oregon City.
   Having saved $420 for the trip, you bought a wagon for $70 and
now have to purchase the following items:

 * Oxen (spending more will buy you a larger and better team which
     will be faster so you'll be on the trail for less time)
 * Food (you'll need ample food to keep up your strength and health)
 * Ammunition ($1 buys a belt of 50 bullets.  You'll need ammo for
     hunting and for fighting off attacks by bandits and animals)
 * Clothing (you'll need warm clothes, especially when you hit the
     snow and freezing weather in the mountains)
 * Other supplies (includes medicine, first aid supplies, tools, and
     wagon parts for unexpected emergencies)

   You can spend all your money at the start or save some to spend
at forts along the way.  However, items cost more at the forts.  You
can also hunt for food if you run low.
```

THE STORY

No one can say when it began. A thousand little rivulets of water trickling downhill go unnoticed until they merge into a thundering river. So it was at the beginning of the greatest mass migration of people that this country, or any other, has ever known. There was only one way to go: west. West to farmlands in Ohio, west along the Erie Canal to the Great Lakes, west to the tributaries of the Mississippi and Ohio rivers, and west to the rolling hills of Kentucky.

By 1825, steamboats were plying the Mississippi and Ohio rivers, and the states of Michigan, Illinois, and Indiana were considered settled. Settlers pushed west into Iowa and Missouri until, by 1830, Independence, Missouri, then the westernmost post office in the United States, defined the boundary of the frontier.

Independence was on the very threshold of the frontier, and for more than a decade it remained the focal point for the western march of the pioneers. Independence was ideally situated for such a role. It was three miles south of the big bend in the Missouri River, where, after flowing southeast for 2000 miles from its headwaters in the Rocky Mountains, the great river changed direction and flowed due east to join the Mississippi a few miles north of St. Louis. A few miles to the west began the vast undulating prairies and high plains that stretched unbroken to the distant Rockies.

With the lands east of the Mississippi settled, adventurers, either by choice or compulsion, gravitated to an even newer frontier—the lands west of the Mississippi. Like their fathers, they were traders, trappers, hunters, and explorers—almost certainly not farmers or settlers.

An early lure of the west was the lower Rio Grande, where inexpensive Spanish and Mexican linens and fabrics could be bought from Spanish traders. New England textile merchants smacked their lips at the thought of profits from capturing that trade. Trade with various Indian tribes was also of interest, and by 1825 a regular route across the Kansas prairie, along the Arkansas and Purgatoire Rivers, and across the Sangre de Cristo Mountains, had been established from Independence to Santa Fe, New Mexico. This, the first of the major trails west, was known as the Santa Fe Trail.

By 1830, adventurers had started looking westward to destinations other than New Mexico. In 1831, Joseph Smith, Jr., set out from Independence and, upon reaching what is now Salt Lake City, declared, "This is the place." Tens of thousands of Mormons followed in his footsteps over the next three decades to escape religious persecution in Ohio and Missouri.

Meanwhile, Stephen Watts Kearney, a determined U.S. Army general, had pushed west over a southern route from Santa Fe through Arizona to San Diego, and other people had extended the northern trails west across the mountains to San Francisco (the Overland Trail) and to Willamette Valley (the Oregon Trail). In addition, steamboats of the American Fur Company had been able to navigate up the Missouri as far as Fort Pierre, South Dakota, while smaller vessels had gotten to Fort Benton, Montana. To cement its foothold, this privately owned company was busy establishing outposts and forts throughout the northern states.

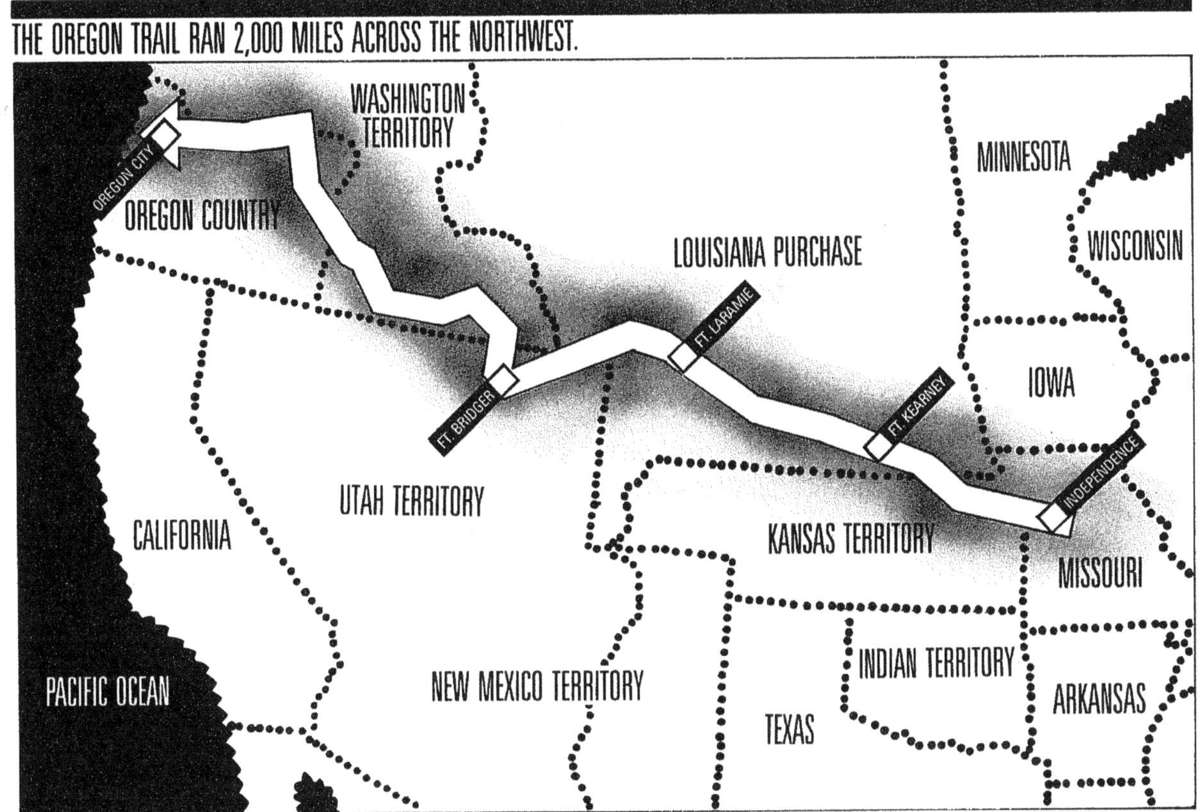

THE OREGON TRAIL RAN 2,000 MILES ACROSS THE NORTHWEST.

Independence, absorbed with the Santa Fe trade to the south and the fur trade to the north, had paid little attention to the trickle of emigrants who, for several years, had been setting out for California and Oregon. However, as glowing reports began to come back from the early pioneers, the trickle swelled to a flood—900 emigrants left Independence in 1843, 3000 in 1845, and more than 5000 in 1847. These new pioneers bore little resemblance to the traders plying the Santa Fe Trail or to the trappers in the North. They were men of the land, traveling with their wives and children. They were movers, but they had a destination, a promised land called Oregon—about which they knew as little as they knew about the road that would take them there.

Historically, the Conestoga wagon, which originated in eastern Pennsylvania, has always been associated with the great migration to Oregon and is depicted in scores of paintings. The truth, however, is much less colorful. The Conestoga wagon was in fact far too heavy for the long haul across the prairies and mountains, and a flatbed farm wagon, sometimes fitted with high wheels and a tent of waterproof sheeting, was generally the transport of choice. Such a wagon, sometimes called a Murphy wagon, required a team of six to ten mules or oxen to pull it when heavily laden. Most families also had a cow or two, a saddle horse, and a plow lashed to the rear of the wagon.

A bare-bones Murphy wagon cost about $50 to $70; high wheels, a waterproof covering, yokes, harnesses, and spare parts could bring the total cost up to $100. A team of two oxen cost about

$25; most travelers bought six to ten animals. Although horse teams could travel faster than oxen, ox teams were sturdy, dependable, and less likely to be stolen by Indians. And if worst came to worst and food ran out, the oxen could be eaten.

A guidebook of the time recommended the following food supplies for one adult for the five- to six-month journey: 150 lbs. of flour, 25 lbs. of bacon or pork, 15 lbs. of coffee, 25 lbs. of sugar, and smaller quantities of rice, beans, dried fruit, molasses, vinegar, salt, pepper, tea, spices, and baking soda. Also on the recommended list were tobacco, soap, whiskey, medicines, and matches.

It was essential that the wagon carry spare parts and tools such as oxen yokes, harnesses, lead bars, open chain links, horseshoes, nails, ropes, hammers, axes, mallets, saws, and spades. Tar buckets were also necessary, some filled with resin and grease to use on the axles, and others filled with tar to seal and waterproof the wagon before fording or floating it across a river.

When they arrived in Independence, most families already had some supplies and clothing. However, tales of harsh weather in the mountains inspired all but the most foolhardy travelers to procure additional warm clothing.

For protection as well as hunting, travelers carried breech loading rifles, Colt revolvers, and a plentiful supply of ammunition. Most also took along mirrors, ribbons, cloth, tobacco, and assorted trinkets for trading with the Indians.

Most families joined others in Independence and made up wagon trains of from four to as many as 100 wagons. Each season, the first of these trains set out as soon as the winter snows melted and was followed by a steady stream of departures throughout the spring and into early summer.

The wagon trains usually went only a short distance the first day, making a sort of trial run. While they were still close to Independence, the men could ride back if necessary to buy supplies that had been forgotten.

The first weeks of travel in the spring were generally very difficult. The men frequently were not experienced at handling teams, wagons, or weapons. The snows had just melted, so the trails were like mud bogs. Most families had no idea how to pack and wound up with dangerously top-heavy or unbalanced loads. Oxen became entangled in their ropes at night and sometimes, breaking free, wandered off.

The first stop for most travelers, usually reached in two or three days, was the Shawnee Methodist Mission only 15 miles from Independence. Once this was left behind, travelers would not see any signs of civilization for many long miles. After leaving the Mission, the wagon trains lumbered over the rolling prairie south of the Kansas River, following the deep ruts of the Santa Fe Trail as far as the present-day town of Gardner, Kansas. There a sign bore the simple legend "Road to Oregon."

From there on, the wagons kept to the high prairies as much as possible, although there were many streams and rivers to be crossed. The Wakarusa, Kansas, Red Vermillion, Black Vermillion, and Big Blue rivers were especially difficult for the travelers; smaller streams could be forded, but it was a daylong ordeal to cross a river. First, the wagons had to be unloaded and the joints and seams packed with tar. After that, they were let down the bank with ropes and floated across. Supplies were floated by makeshift raft or carried by horse. Frequently tools and heavier provisions slid into the river. After the oxen had crossed, they were taken to the top of the bank, harnessed by long ropes to the wagon, and, with them pulling and all the family members pushing, the wagon inched to the top of the bank.

Indians, particularly the Pawnee in the area of the Red Vermillion river, did not welcome the constant stream of white men crossing their hunting grounds. In 1849, for example, after a cholera epidemic for which the Indians blamed the whites, the Pawnee, Oglala, and Sioux began attacking wagon trains with great frequency. Wagons were particularly vulnerable when crossing rivers, so the Indians often chose fords for their attacks.

In a sense, the Indians were correct about the source of cholera. It had been carried from Asia to the U.S. by sailors and passengers on ships. It reached the frontier by way of New Orleans and the Mississippi and traveled west with the wagon trains. No amount of planning or preparation could save the settlers from this hazard. Afflicted with severe pain, vomiting, and cramps, a person might display the first symptoms in the morning and be dead by noon.

In 1852, Ezra Meeker kept a log and estimated that more than 5000 people had died of cholera on the trail that year.

Living in fear of disease, the emigrants were prone to dose themselves with large quantities of medicine at the first sign of any illness, on the theory that the larger the dose the quicker the recovery that might be expected. In fact, many patients were killed rather than cured by the injudicious use of medicine.

River crossings slowed the journey through Kansas and Nebraska, and most wagon trains took about three weeks to travel the 175 miles to the ford across the Big Blue River in southern Nebraska known as Independence Crossing. About six miles northwest of this crossing, trails from St. Joseph and Fort Leavenworth converged, thence following the Platte River to Fort Kearney. Having reached the Platte, the pioneers could follow its valley west, past Chimney Rock, Scott's Bluff, and to the last outposts of civilization, Fort Laramie and Fort Fetterman.

The Platte River marked the beginning of buffalo country, and few men missed the chance to enjoy some good hunting and to add to their food supply. Unfortunately, most of them had no idea how to preserve the meat. The animals were generally shot in midafternoon and left in the hot sun until sunset, when they were gutted. Perhaps one was roasted that night, but the rest were left unskinned and undivided to rot and provide a meal for the scavengers of the plain.

Along the North Platte River Valley, the wagons could generally make a speed of about two miles per hour, thus covering, in a good day, about 15 to 18 miles. If it had been possible to maintain this speed for the entire journey, the 2040 miles from Independence to Oregon City could have been covered in about 4 1/2 months. However, everything seemed to conspire to slow the trip: river crossings, Indian and bandit attacks, hunting, burying the dead, wagon breakdowns, muddy trails, oxen wandering off, and losing the trail.

Some wagon trains even rested on Sunday, observing it as a day of worship and, more often than not, repair.

Fort Laramie stood at the fork of the Laramie and North Platte rivers in eastern Wyoming. There the traveler had his first opportunity in many weeks to send letters home, buy provisions, and get information about the trail ahead. There, too, was a place to relax a bit from the constant caution so necessary on the march.

After Fort Laramie, the next objective was the Sweetwater River Valley in central Wyoming, the entrance to which was marked by Independence Rock, on which thousands of emigrants carved their names. "The Great Register of the Desert," Father Pierre Jean de Smet, a Jesuit missionary, called it. If things were going well, most travelers had reached the rock by July 4.

Looking west from Independence Rock, the emigrants could see, six miles in the distance, a V-shaped split in a rocky ridge known as Devil's Gate. The preferred route skirted Devil's Gate Canyon, but there was no question that it marked the beginning of a new and more difficult phase of the journey. Although there were many alternative routes to the Sweetwater Valley, all trails converged there for the long ascent to South Pass across the Continental Divide. Even in mid-July, the steep mountain walls often blocked the sun, and snow and ice frequently covered the ground. The ascent from the Sweetwater Valley was long and gradual, and the South Pass many miles in width. Hence the only real hindrances to good progress were the occasional snow and damage to wagon wheels from the rocky trail. The travelers, having left the boredom of the plains and knowing that they had reached the halfway point of the trip, were usually in good spirits as they entered South Pass.

Beyond the South Pass, the trail began a gradual but rocky descent of about 60 miles, across the Green River near the Wyoming-Idaho border. This crossing was an extremely dangerous one; the river was wide, deep, powerful, and ice cold. Those who successfully made this crossing were much relieved to follow the Bear River Valley for a way to Soda Springs, whence they headed northwest for 50 miles to Fort Hall, Idaho, on the Snake River. There they were forced to decide whether to continue on to Oregon or turn south to California.

Fort Hall was a welcome stop for the wagon trains. Originally built by Captain Nathaniel J. Wyeth of Boston in 1834, the fort offered needed supplies and protection from the hostile Blackfoot Indians. After leaving the fort, the trail crossed the Portneuf River and Bannock Creek and then passed the American Falls on the Snake River. This treacherous crossing led, a few miles on, to two enormous rocks known as Massacre Rocks because hostile Indians often used them as a place from which to ambush wagon trains.

The trail then followed the Snake River for some 300 miles as it traced its circuitous course across the barren, lava-covered Snake River Plains; it finally broke out of the canyon at the mouth of the Little Boise River near the Oregon border. As they crossed the Snake at Fort Boise, the travelers took their first steps in Oregon.

But one more barrier loomed between the settlers and the Promised Land: the terrible Blue Mountains. Several times during the crossing of these mountains, wagons had to be lowered with ropes from one part of the trail to another, and canyon walls too narrow for the wagons frequently had to be chipped away. Wagons were often abandoned, their occupants continuing the journey on foot. Others, searching for a better route, became hopelessly lost and eventually died of hunger and thirst.

John Kerns, in his diary, recorded this about the Blue Mountains: "...it was the roughest road we have encountered on the journey, being up and down sidling mountains, into the brush and across a creek every 200 or 300 yards, and over stony places enough to hide all despairing sinners."

Those pioneers who traversed the final obstacle, Deadman's Pass, saw the trail emerge from the mountains and wind down the bald face of Emigrant Hill from which they were treated to one of the most spectacular views in the world. Mt. Hood and Mt. Adams could be seen in the distance, while in the foreground lay the rolling hills and fertile valleys of the Columbia River Basin.

From Walla Walla, Washington, on, still 250 miles across Oregon to the coastal settlements, most travelers kept going, driven by sheer exhilaration and determination. By all accounts, it was one of the most difficult parts of the journey. As Medorem Crawford, an emigrant traveler, recorded, "From Walla Walla to Willamette Falls (Oregon City) occupied about 20 days, and, all things considered, was the hardest part of the entire journey—what with drifting sands, rocky cliffs, and rapid streams along the Columbia, and the gorges, torrents, and thickets of the Cascade Mountains, it seems incredible how, with our worn out and emaciated animals, we ever reached our destination." But many did, and they were well rewarded for their perseverance.

J.M. Shively, writer of one of the guidebooks about the trail, closed with the thought, "Be of good cheer—you will find a country in Oregon that will fill your desires, and repay you for all your toil."

BIBLIOGRAPHY

Coons, Frederica B. *The Trail to Oregon.* Portland, OR: Binfords & Mort, 1954.

Ghent, William J. *The Road to Oregon.* New York: Longmans, Green & Co., 1929.

Meeker, Ezra. *Ox Team Days on the Oregon Trail.* New York: E. Meeker, 1907.

Morgan, Dale L. *Overland in 1846.* Georgetown, CA: Talisman Press, 1963.

Parkman, Francis. *The Oregon Trail.* Boston, MA: Little, Brown & Co., 1925.

Rawitsch, Dan. *MECC Oregon User Manual.* Lauderdale, MN: Minnesota Educational Computer Consortium, 1977.

THE PROGRAM

Westward Ho! is a substantial revision of the Oregon Trail program written by Dan Rawitsch and Bill Heinemann in 1972–73 on the Hewlett Packard 2000 timesharing system of the Minnesota Educational Computer Consortium. The original Oregon Trail program was subsequently converted to Microsoft BASIC and appeared in *Creative Computing* magazine in 1977. Play of the game is similar in this new version, but the program has been structured (to some extent), simplified, and shortened by more than 300 lines.

The program consists of a main section, initialization and closing sections with five related subroutines, eight major subroutines, and six minor subroutines.

The initialization section dimensions variables, puts data in them, displays the initial scenario, and asks you for your initial purchases. At the outset, you have $420, the average amount of money that a family setting out on the Oregon Trail had in 1847. A wagon costs $70, and you can spend the rest of your money on oxen, food, ammunition, clothing, and miscellaneous supplies such as medicine, bandages, and repair parts. You can spend all of your money at the outset, or you can save some to spend at forts along the way to replenish supplies when they run low. This is a tradeoff: Supplies cost 50% more at the forts. However, if you lose supplies while fording a river or in a bandit attack, you may not have enough to continue.

Food is important to maintain the strength and health of your family. A guidebook of the time recommends for each adult 150 lbs. of flour, 25 lbs. of sugar, 25 lbs. of bacon, 15 lbs. of coffee, and smaller quantities of other staples. The average family of five (your family in the simulation) eats about as much as four adults. The above commodities in 1850 cost about 10 cents a pound in Missouri; thus an adequate food stock for your family would cost about $60 to $100. Of course, along the way you will hunt for fresh meat and, hopefully, find some edible plants and berries.

Although you are wearing some clothes, most travelers had to purchase additional clothing for the cold weather they would encounter in the mountains. In 1850, $15 would buy several warm outfits; thus an appropriate budget for clothes would be at least $50 or so for your family of five.

You will want to have plenty of ammunition for your rifle to hunt, ward off attacks by wild animals, and defend yourself against bandits and hostile Indians. A belt of bullets costs $1, and in general you can expect to use one or two belts per week on the trail.

A brief explanation of these purchases is displayed in the Sub490 subroutine, and the amounts are accepted as input in the Sub690 subroutine. Note the conditional (IF) statements in this subroutine that do not allow you to buy less than the minimum you need, or to spend more than you have.

The main program iterates through the journey in two-week segments. If you have been on the trail for more than 20 weeks, the program branches to an end-game routine. Under normal circumstances, at the beginning of a two-week trip segment, the date will be printed, injuries and illnesses treated (assuming you have enough money to pay a doctor), the mileage updated, and your inventory of supplies printed.

The expected mileage over the next two weeks is then calculated in LN390. In general, you will travel 200 miles plus some additional distance which depends upon the quality of your team of oxen. This mileage figure is an ideal, assuming nothing goes wrong. If you run into problems, mileage is subtracted from this ideal figure; the revised total is printed at the start of the next trip segment.

You are then asked whether you wish to hunt, continue on, or, if it is an even-numbered trip segment, stop at a fort. In 1847, forts and missions were spaced about 300 to 400 miles apart along the Oregon Trail. On average you will cover about 75 miles a week and thus you can expect to hit a fort about every four weeks (or every other trip segment). Note the function at the beginning of Sub1000 that determines whether or not you are on an even-numbered trip segment; if the integer value of J/2 equals J/2, J is even; if not, J is odd.

If you stop at a fort (Sub1100), you have an opportunity to purchase supplies, but they cost 50% more than at the start. The running total of most items in your inventory is kept in dollars. Your supply of ammunition, however, is expressed as a number of bullets. This makes it easier to calculate ammunition consumption when you use your gun to hunt, fight, or scare off animals.

If you decide to hunt, the subroutine at Sub1200 is called. If you have fewer than 40 bullets, you do not have enough to hunt and you are given the option of stopping at a fort (if there is one on this trip segment) or continuing on. Hunting costs several days of travel (45 miles) and, of course, some ammunition.

Since there is no good way to determine how skilled a marksman you are, the program asks you to rank yourself at the start of the trip (Sub920). From then on, each time you are confronted with a situation in which you must use your rifle, you will be asked to type in a word that sounds like a gunshot (pow, blam, or bang).

The faster you type the word and hit Return, the better luck you will have in hitting your target.

The shooting subroutine is found at Sub3870. When this subroutine is entered, a random shooting word is selected. Then a timer is started. The timer uses the real-time clock of the computer to get a starting time in seconds (S1) in milliseconds. You then type in the shooting word, which is compared to the requested word. If your typing was in error, you are asked to type the word again. This continues until the word is typed correctly, at which time the time in seconds is again calculated. The starting time is subtracted from the ending time, and the resulting elapsed time in seconds less your ranking as a marksman is put into variable BR. A good typist should be able to type a four-letter word in two seconds or less, while a less skilled, hunt-and-peck typist might take four or five seconds.

Control is then returned to the hunting subroutine, and ammunition consumption calculated as a function of the value of BR. The slower you shoot (the higher the value of BR), the greater the probability that you are unsuccessful in your hunting (see function after LN1230).

The eating subroutine is called next (Sub1310). In it you are asked how well you want to eat, and your food consumption is calculated. If you do not have enough food to eat as well as you would like, you must choose to eat at a diminished level.

Next, a subroutine is called to determine whether or not you are attacked by bandits or Indians (Sub1390). The probability of attack is determined by the function at the beginning of the subroutine. Toward the beginning of your journey, especially around 400 to 500 miles from Independence in what is now western Nebraska and Wyoming, you have the highest probability of encountering bandits and Indians. As you get into the mountains, these probabilities decrease drastically (see graph on page 36). The function within the IF ... THEN statement increases the probability from 20% at 0 miles (M) to a maximum of 50% at 500 miles and then gradually decreases the rest of the way.

If riders approach, you may choose one of four strategies: run, attack, ignore them, or circle wagons. Each strategy has a different cost in miles and supplies and also depends upon whether the riders were hostile or friendly. If you choose to attack, the program again goes to the shooting subroutine. If you are slow on the draw, you may pick up a flesh wound, which sets the injury flag and requires treatment by a doctor the next time you stop.

The longest subroutine (Sub1800) deals with hazards and special events. A random number selected at the beginning determines which event occurs; the program then branches to the appropriate routine to handle that event. The probability of each event is determined by the difference between successive numbers in the event array (EPArray, established in Sub3700). For example, if a random number between 0 and 6 is selected, event 1 occurs; between 6 and 11, event 2; between 11 and 13, event 3; and so on. Thus we see that there is the highest probability that event 19 (value between 69 and 95) will occur; this event has to do with illness from not eating well.

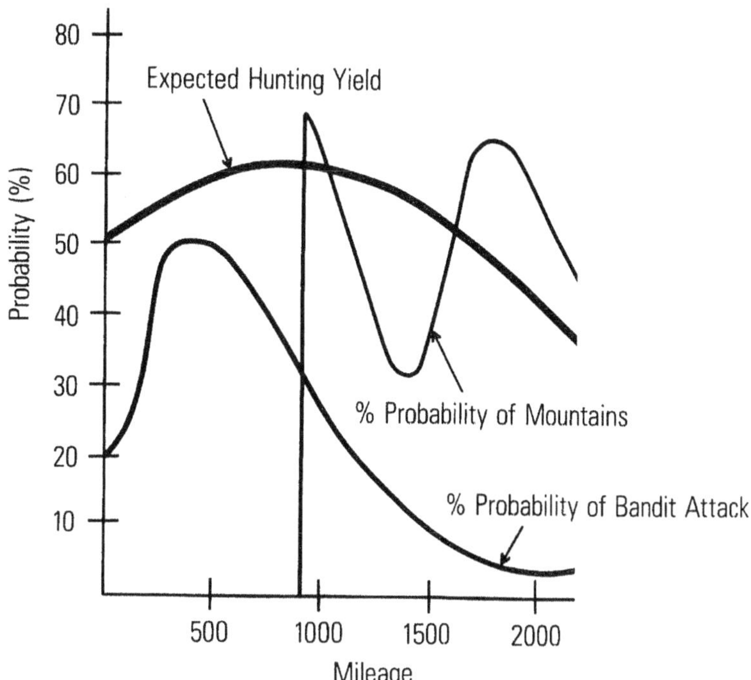

Most events are handled in a very straightforward manner: A message is printed, mileage subtracted, and supplies used. On the other hand, four of the events are more complicated: cold weather, bandit attack, wild-animal attack, and illness.

The cold-weather routine (starts at LN2130) checks to see if you have adequate clothing to keep warm. If not, the illness subroutine (Sub2880) is called. This routine is also called if you are not eating well enough (starts at LN2560).

In the illness routine, depending upon how well you have been eating, you may contract a mild, bad, or very serious illness. Mild and bad illness can be treated with your own medicine—if you have any left—whereas serious illness requires the services of a doctor (the illness flag, KS, is set) at the start of the next trip segment.

The bandits attack routine (starts at LN2180) is very similar to the attack by Indians routine in the previous section, except that bandits are always bad and you have no choice but to fight them.

The last major subroutine called by the main program deals with travel through the mountains (Sub2640). In the mountains, you are vulnerable to cave-ins along the trail, losing your way, and just plain slow going. In addition, you must traverse the South Pass and the Blue Mountains. The probability is set to 80% that you will get stuck in the South Pass when you first reach it, but a flag (KP) prevents you from being stuck there for the entire journey. Likewise, you have a 70% chance of getting stuck in the Blue Mountains, but you will eventually get through. Blizzards, on the other hand, can occur on every trip segment while you are in the mountains, and there is a good chance that this will happen.

If you do not have adequate food, clothing, ammunition, or medical supplies when you encounter the various hazards of the journey, chances are very high that you will die on the trail (starts at LN3000). If you die, a short message is displayed telling you what happened, how far you traveled, and your remaining inventory of supplies.

It is not known today what percentage of the travelers who set out on the Oregon Trail actually reached their destination. Certainly it was fewer than 50%, and perhaps fewer than 20%. If you are among the lucky few, the program tell you how long it took, and display your remaining supplies, if any.

It is not easy to reach Oregon. Your decisions must be well reasoned, and Lady Luck must be traveling with you. But if you don't make it, you, unlike actual families in 1847, at least, will get a chance to try again.

PROGRAM VARIABLES

A	Money spent on animals
AS	Money to question (Y or N), user input
B	Money spent on ammo, also number of bullets
BR	Response time for typing shooting word
C	Money spent for clothing
C1	Flag for insufficient clothes
D	Total days traveled
DD	Days of last month
DM	Total months traveled
DADArray[n]	Date, n = 1 - 20
DR	Shooting expertise level
E	Eating quality
EPArray[n]	Event probability, n = 1 - 20
EV	Event counter
F	Money spent on food
GH	Riders description (0 hostile, 1 friendly)
GT	Choice of tactics when riders approach
I	Temporary iteration variable
J	Trip segment counter
KB	Flag for blizzard
KF	Flag for stop at fort
KH	Flag for injury
KM	Flag for Blue Mountains
KP	Flag for South Pass
KQ	Flag for not enough ammo to hunt
KS	Flag for illness
M	Total trip mileage
MA	Mileage through previous turn
MP	Mileage flag for South Pass
P	Amount spent at fort
R	Money for medicine and repair parts
RN	Random number for choosing events
SD[n]	Shooting words, n = 1 - 4
S1, S2	Response time temporary variables
T	Cash
X	Choice of action, temporary
X$	Temporary string variable

PROGRAM LISTINGS

```
TextWindow.CursorTop = 10
TextWindow.CursorLeft = 31
TextWindow.WriteLine("Westward Ho! 1847")
TextWindow.WriteLine("")
TextWindow.WriteLine("")
TextWindow.CursorLeft = 28
TextWindow.WriteLine("(c) David H. Ahl, 1986")
TextWindow.CursorTop = 23
TextWindow.CursorLeft = 21
'
'Initialization
Sub3430()
Sub3530()
Sub3700()
'Put data in variables
TextWindow.WriteLine("Press Enter when you're ready to go")
JJJ = TextWindow.Read()
textwindow.Clear()
Sub490()
'Display the scenario
Sub690()
'Make initial purchases
Sub920()
'How good a shot are you?
TextWindow.WriteLine("")
TextWindow.WriteLine(" Your trip is about to begin ... ")
TextWindow.WriteLine("")
Sub3830()
'
'Main program
LN260:
If M > 2039 Then
finished = "true" 'Reached the final segment?
Sub3110()
EndIf
J = J + 1
'Iterate through 2-week trip segments
If J > 20 Then
  Goto LN3080 'On the trail too long?
EndIf
TextWindow.WriteLine("")
TextWindow.Write("Monday, " +DADArray[J] +", 1847. You are ")
FOR I = 1 TO 15
If M <= MPArray[I] Then
Goto GotMP
endIf
EndFor
GotMP:
TextWindow.WriteLine( PLArray[I])
If F < 6 Then
  TextWindow.WriteLine("You're low on food. Better buy some or go hunting
soon.")
EndIf
```

```
If KS<>1 AND KH<>1 Then
  Goto LN370 'Any sickness or injuries?
EndIf
T = T - 10
If T < 0 Then
Goto LN3010
ELSE
TextWindow.Write("Doctor charged $10 for his services ")
EndIf
TextWindow.Write("to treat your ")
If KS = 1 Then
TextWindow.WriteLine("illness." )
ELSE
TextWindow.WriteLine("injuries.")
EndIf
KS = 0
KH = 0
'Set illness and injury flags to normal
M = Math.Floor(M)
MA = M
'Update cumulative mileage
LN370:
If MP = 1 Then
TextWindow.WriteLine("Total mileage to date is 950." )
MP = 0
GOTO LN400
EndIf
TextWindow.WriteLine("Total mileage to date is "+ Math.Floor(M + .5))
LN390:
M = M + 200 + (A - 110) / 2.5 + 10 * Math.GetRandomNumber(999)/1000
'Calculate how far we travel in 2 weeks
LN400:
TextWindow.WriteLine("Here's what you now have (no. of bullets, $ worth of
other items):")
Sub3350()
'Print inventory
Sub1000()
'Stop at fort, hunt, or push on routine
Sub1310()
'Eating routine
Sub1390()
TextWindow.WriteLine("")
'Riders - attack routine
Sub1800()
TextWindow.WriteLine("")
'Hazards - and - events routine
Sub2640()
'Mountains routine
Goto LN260
'End of the 2-week trip segment
'
Sub Sub490
'Subroutine to print initial scenario
TextWindow.CursorLeft = 23
TextWindow.WriteLine("Westward Ho! 1847")
```

```
TextWindow.WriteLine("")
TextWindow.WriteLine(" Your journey over the Oregon Trail takes place in
1847. Starting")
TextWindow.WriteLine("in Independence, Missouri, you plan to take your family
of")
TextWindow.WriteLine("five over 2040 tough miles to Oregon City.")
TextWindow.WriteLine(" Having saved $420 for the trip, you bought a wagon for
$70 and")
TextWindow.WriteLine("now have to purchase the following items:")
TextWindow.WriteLine("")
TextWindow.WriteLine(" * Oxen (spending more will buy you a larger and better
team which")
TextWindow.WriteLine(" will be faster so you'll be on the trail for less
time)")
TextWindow.WriteLine(" * Food (you'll need ample food to keep up your
strength and health)")
TextWindow.WriteLine(" * Ammunition ($1 buys a belt of 50 bullets. You'll
need ammo for")
TextWindow.WriteLine(" hunting and for fighting off attacks by bandits and
animals)")
TextWindow.WriteLine(" * Clothing (you'll need warm clothes, especially when
you hit the")
TextWindow.WriteLine(" snow and freezing weather in the mountains)")
TextWindow.WriteLine(" * Other supplies (includes medicine, first-aid
supplies, tools, and")
TextWindow.WriteLine(" wagon parts for unexpected emergencies)")
TextWindow.WriteLine("")
TextWindow.WriteLine(" You can spend all your money at the start or save some
to spend")
TextWindow.WriteLine("at forts along the way. However, items cost more at the
forts. You")
TextWindow.WriteLine("can also hunt for food if you run low.")
TextWindow.WriteLine("")
EndSub
'
Sub Sub690
'Subroutine to get initial purchases of player
LN700:
TextWindow.WriteLine("")
TextWindow.Write("How much do you want to pay for a team of oxen? ")
A = TextWindow.ReadNumber()
A = Math.Floor(A)
If A < 100 Then
TextWindow.WriteLine("No one in town has a team that cheap.")
GOTO LN700
EndIf
If A < 151 Then
  Goto LN760
EndIf
TextWindow.WriteLine("You choose an honest dealer who tells you that $"+ A+ "
is too much for")
TextWindow.WriteLine("a team of oxen. He charges you $150 and gives you $"
+(A - 150)+" change.")
A = 150
LN760:
```

```
TextWindow.Write("How much do you want to spend on food? ")
F = TextWindow.ReadNumber()
F = Math.Floor(F)
If F > 13 Then
Goto LN790
ELSE
TextWindow.Write("That won't even get you to the Kansas River")
EndIf
TextWindow.WriteLine(" ...  better spend a bit more.")
Goto LN760
LN790:
If A + F > 300 Then
TextWindow.WriteLine("You won't have any for ammo and clothes.")
GOTO LN760
EndIf
LN800:
TextWindow.Write("How much do you want to spend on ammunition? ")
B = TextWindow.ReadNumber()
B = Math.Floor(B)
If B < 2 Then
TextWindow.WriteLine("Better take a bit just for protection.")
GOTO LN800
EndIf
If A + F + B > 320 Then
TextWindow.WriteLine("That won't leave any money for clothes.")
GOTO LN800
EndIf
LN830:
TextWindow.Write("How much do you want to spend on clothes? ")
C = TextWindow.ReadNumber()
C = Math.Floor(C)
If C > 24 Then
Goto LN860
ELSE
TextWindow.Write("Your family is going to be mighty cold in")
EndIf
TextWindow.WriteLine(" the mountains.")
TextWindow.WriteLine("Better spend a bit more.")
Goto LN830
LN860:
If A + F + B + C > 345 Then
TextWindow.WriteLine("That leaves nothing for medicine.")
GOTO LN830
EndIf
LN870:
TextWindow.Write("How much for medicine, bandages, repair parts, etc.? ")
R = TextWindow.ReadNumber()
R = Math.Floor(R)
If R < 5 Then
TextWindow.WriteLine("That's not at all wise." )
GOTO LN870
EndIf
If A + F + B + C + R > 350 Then
TextWindow.WriteLine("You don't have that much money.")
GOTO LN870
```

```
EndIf
T = 350 - A - F - B - C - R
TextWindow.WriteLine("")
TextWindow.WriteLine("You now have $"+ T+ " left.")
B = 50 * B
EndSub
'
Sub Sub920
'Subroutine to initialize shooting routine
TextWindow.WriteLine("")
TextWindow.WriteLine("Please rank your shooting (typing) ability as
follows:")
TextWindow.WriteLine(" (1) Ace marksman (2) Good shot (3) Fair to middlin'")
TextWindow.WriteLine(" (4) Need more practice (5) Shaky knees")
LN960:
TextWindow.Write("How do you rank yourself? ")
DR = TextWindow.ReadNumber()
If DR > 0 AND DR < 6 Then
  Goto LN999
EndIf
TextWindow.WriteLine("Please enter 1, 2, 3, 4, or 5.")
Goto LN960
LN999:
EndSub
'
Sub Sub1000
'Subroutine to stop at fort, hunt, or push on
If Math.Floor(J / 2)<>J / 2 Then
  Goto LN1060 'Are we on an even trip segment?
EndIf
LN1020:
TextWindow.Write("Want to (1) stop at next fort, (2) hunt, or (3) push on? ")
X = TextWindow.ReadNumber()
If X < 1 OR X > 3 Then
TextWindow.WriteLine("Enter a 1, 2, or 3 please." )
GOTO LN1020
EndIf
If X = 3 Then
goto LN1099
ELSE
If X = 1 Then
Sub1100()
ElseIf X = 2 then
Sub1200()
EndIf
EndIf
If KQ = 1 Then
Goto LN1020
ELSE
Goto LN1099 'Not enough ammo to hunt?
EndIf
LN1060:
TextWindow.Write("Would you like to (1) hunt or (2) continue on? ")
X = TextWindow.ReadNumber()
If X < 1 OR X > 2 Then
```

```
TextWindow.WriteLine("Enter a 1 or 2 please.")
GOTO LN1060
EndIf
If X = 2 Then
goto LN1099
ELSE
Sub1200()
EndIf
LN1099:
EndSub
'
Sub Sub1100
'Subroutine to stop at a fort
If T > 0 Then
Goto LN1130
ELSE
TextWindow.WriteLine("You sing with the folks there and get a good")
EndIf
TextWindow.WriteLine("night's sleep, but you have no money to buy anything.")
Goto LN1199
LN1130:
TextWindow.WriteLine("What would you like to spend on each of the
following;")
TextWindow.Write("Food? ")
P1 = TextWindow.ReadNumber()
TextWindow.Write("Ammunition? ")
P2 = TextWindow.ReadNumber()
TextWindow.Write("Clothing? ")
P3 = TextWindow.ReadNumber()
TextWindow.Write("Medicine and supplies? ")
P4 = TextWindow.ReadNumber()
P = P1 + P2 + P3 + P4
P1 = .67 * P1
P2 = 33 * P2
TextWindow.WriteLine("The storekeeper tallies up your bill. It comes to $"+
P)
If T >= P Then
T = T - P
F = F + P1
B = B + P2
C = C + .67 * P3
R = R + .67 * P4
Goto LN1199
EndIf
TextWindow.WriteLine("Uh, oh. That's more than you have. Better start over.")
GOTO LN1130
LN1199:
Endsub
'
Sub Sub1200
'Subroutine to hunt
KQ = 0
If B > 39 Then
  Goto LN1230 'Enough ammo to hunt?
EndIf
```

```
TextWindow.WriteLine("Tough luck. You don't have enough ammo to hunt.")
KQ = 1
Goto LN1299
LN1230:
M = M - 45
SUB3870()
If BR <= 1 Then
  Goto LN1270
EndIf
If 100 * Math.GetRandomNumber(999)/1000 < 13 * BR Then
  Goto LN1290
EndIf
TextWindow.WriteLine("Nice shot ... right on target ... good eatin'
tonight!")
F = F + 24 - 2 * BR
B = B - 10 - 3 * BR
Goto LN1299
LN1270:
TextWindow.WriteLine("Right between the eyes ... you got a big one!")
F = F + 26 + 3 * Math.GetRandomNumber(999)/1000
TextWindow.WriteLine("Full bellies tonight!")
B = B - 10 - 4 * Math.GetRandomNumber(999)/1000
Goto LN1299
LN1290:
TextWindow.WriteLine("You missed completely ... and your dinner got away.")
LN1299:
EndSub
'
Sub Sub1310
'Subroutine to eat
If F < 5 Then
  Goto LN3000 'Not enough food?
EndIf
LN1330:
TextWindow.Write("Do you want to eat (1) poorly (2) moderately or (3) well?
")
E = TextWindow.ReadNumber()
If E < 1 OR E > 3 Then
TextWindow.WriteLine("Enter a 1, 2, or 3, please.")
GOTO LN1330
EndIf
F = F - 4 - 2.5 * E
If F > 0 Then
  Goto LN1389 'Eating more food than you have?
EndIf
If E = 1 Then
  Goto LN1389
EndIf
F = F + 4 + 2.5 * E
TextWindow.WriteLine("You don't have enough to eat that well.")
Goto LN1330
LN1389:
EndSub
'
Sub Sub1390
```

```
'Subroutine for riders attack
If Math.GetRandomNumber(999)/1000 * 10 > (Math.Power(M / 100 - 4, 2) + 72) /
(Math.Power(M / 100 - 4, 2) + 12) - 1 Then
  Goto LN1799
EndIf
XD = ""
GH = 0
If Math.GetRandomNumber(999)/1000 > .2 Then
XD = "don't "
GH = 1
EndIf
TextWindow.WriteLine("")
TextWindow.WriteLine("Riders ahead! They " +XD+ "look hostile.")
TextWindow.WriteLine("You can (1) run, (2) attack, (3) ignore them, or (4)
circle wagons.")
LN1440:
TextWindow.Write("What do you want to do? ")
GT = TextWindow.ReadNumber()
If GT < 1 OR GT > 4 Then
TextWindow.WriteLine("Please enter 1, 2, 3, or 4.")
GOTO LN1440
EndIf
If Math.GetRandomNumber(999)/1000 < .2 Then
  GH = 1 - GH 'Maybe they're hostile after all
EndIf
If GH = 1 Then
  Goto LN1680 'Are they friendly?
EndIf
If (GT = 1) Then
  Goto LN1510
ElseIf (GT = 2) Then
  Goto LN1540
ElseIf (GT = 3) Then
  Goto LN1610
ElseIf (GT = 4) Then
  Goto LN1650
EndIf
'
'Try to run away
LN1510:
M = M + 20
R = R - 7
B = B - 150
A = A - 20
Goto LN1730
'Lose stuff when you run
'
'Attack the riders
LN1540:
Sub3870()
B = B - BR * 40 - 80
'Firefight uses ammo
LN1550:
If BR <= 1 Then
TextWindow.WriteLine("Nice shooting ... you drove them off.")
```

```
GOTO LN1730
EndIf
If BR <= 4 Then
TextWindow.WriteLine("Kind of slow with your Colt .45.")
GOTO LN1730
EndIf
TextWindow.WriteLine("Pretty slow on the draw, partner. You got a nasty flesh
wound.")
KH = 1
TextWindow.WriteLine("You'll have to see the doc soon as you can.")
Goto LN1730
'
'Ignore the riders
LN1610:
If Math.GetRandomNumber(999)/1000 > .8 Then
TextWindow.WriteLine("They did not attack. Whew!")
Goto LN1799
EndIf
B = B - 150
R = R - 7
Goto LN1730
'
'Circle wagons
LN1650:
Sub3870()
B = B - BR * 30 - 80
M = M - 25
Goto LN1550
'
'Cost of each tactic if riders were friendly
LN1680:
If GT = 1 Then
M = M + 15
A = A - 5
GOTO LN1730
EndIf
If GT = 2 Then
M = M - 5
B = B - 100
GOTO LN1730
EndIf
If GT = 3 Then
Goto LN1730
ELSE
M = M - 20
EndIf
'
'Final messages about riders
LN1730:
If GH = 0 Then
  Goto LN1750 'Were riders hostile?
EndIf
TextWindow.WriteLine("Riders were friendly, but check for possible losses.")
Goto LN1799
LN1750:
```

```
TextWindow.WriteLine("Riders were hostile. Better check for losses!")
If B >= 0 Then
goto LN1799
ELSE
TextWindow.WriteLine("")
SUB3740()
TextWindow.Write("Oh, my gosh! ")
EndIf
TextWindow.WriteLine("They're coming back and you're out of ammo! Your dreams
turn to")
TextWindow.WriteLine("dust as you and your family are massacred on the
prairie.")
finished="false"
sub3110()
LN1799:
EndSub
'

Sub Sub1800
'Subroutine to deal with hazards and special events
RN = 100 * Math.GetRandomNumber(999)/1000
'RN determines which event happens
For I = 1 To 15
'Iterate through possible events
If RN <= EPArray[I] Then
Goto GotEP 'If event happened, exit loop
EndIf
EndFor
I = 16
GotEP:
If I > 8 Then
  Goto LN1860
EndIf
If (I = 1) Then
  Goto LN1880
ElseIf (I = 2) Then
  Goto LN1910
ElseIf (I = 3) Then
  Goto LN1940
ElseIf (I = 4) Then
  Goto LN1980
ElseIf (I = 5) Then
  Goto LN2010
ElseIf (I = 6) Then
  Goto LN2040
ElseIf (I = 7) Then
  Goto LN2080
ElseIf (I = 8) Then
  Goto LN2180
EndIf
LN1860:
If (I - 8 = 1) Then
  Goto LN2290
ElseIf (I - 8 = 2) Then
  Goto LN2320
```

```
ElseIf (I - 8 = 3) Then
  Goto LN2350
ElseIf (I - 8 = 4) Then
  Goto LN2410
ElseIf (I - 8 = 5) Then
  Goto LN2440
ElseIf (I - 8 = 6) Then
  Goto LN2530
ElseIf (I - 8 = 7) Then
  Goto LN2560
ElseIf (I - 8 = 8) Then
  Goto LN2610
EndIf
'
LN1880:
TextWindow.WriteLine("Your wagon breaks down. It costs you time and supplies
to fix it.")
M = M - 15 - 5 * Math.GetRandomNumber(999)/1000
R = R - 4
Goto LN2639
'
LN1910:
TextWindow.WriteLine("An ox gores your leg. That slows you down for the rest
of the trip.")
M = M - 25
A = A - 10
Goto LN2639
'
LN1940:
TextWindow.WriteLine("Bad luck ... your daughter breaks her arm. You must
stop and")
TextWindow.WriteLine("make a splint and sling with some of your medical
supplies.")
M = M - 5 - 4 * Math.GetRandomNumber(999)/1000
R = R - 1 - 2 * Math.GetRandomNumber(999)/1000
Goto LN2639
'
LN1980:
TextWindow.WriteLine("An ox wanders off and you have to spend time looking
for it.")
M = M - 17
Goto LN2639
'
LN2010:
TextWindow.WriteLine("Your son gets lost and you spend half a day searching
for him.")
M = M - 10
Goto LN2639
'
LN2040:
TextWindow.WriteLine("Nothing but contaminated and stagnant water near the
trail.")
TextWindow.WriteLine("You lose time looking for a clean spring or creek.")
M = M - 2 - 10 * Math.GetRandomNumber(999)/1000
Goto LN2639
```

```
'
LN2080:
If M > 950 Then
  Goto LN2130 'If in mountains, go to snow; otherwise rain
EndIf
TextWindow.WriteLine("Heavy rains. Traveling is slow in the mud and you break your spare")
TextWindow.WriteLine("ox yoke using it to pry your wagon out of the mud. Worse yet, some")
TextWindow.WriteLine("of your ammo is damaged by the water.")
M = M - 5 - 10 * Math.GetRandomNumber(999)/1000
R = R - 7
B = B - 400
F = F - 5
Goto LN2639
LN2130:
TextWindow.Write("Cold weather ... Brrrrrrr! ... You ")
If C < 11 + 2 * Math.GetRandomNumber(999)/1000 Then
TextWindow.Write( "don't ")
C1 = 1
EndIf
TextWindow.WriteLine("have enough clothing to keep warm.")
If C1 = 0 Then
Goto LN2639
ELSE
SUB2880()
Goto LN2639
EndIf
'
LN2180:
TextWindow.WriteLine("Bandits attacking!")
Sub3870()
B = B - 20 * BR
If B > 0 Then
Goto LN2220
ELSE
T = T / 3
EndIf
TextWindow.WriteLine("You try to drive them off but you run out of bullets.")
TextWindow.WriteLine("They grab as much cash as they can find.")
Goto LN2230
LN2220:
If BR <= 1 Then
  Goto LN2260 'Good response time?
EndIf
LN2230:
TextWindow.Write("You get shot in the leg  ...   ")
Sub3740()
KH = 1
TextWindow.WriteLine("and they grab one of your oxen.")
A = A - 10
R = R - 2
TextWindow.WriteLine("Better have a doc look at your leg ... and soon!")
Goto LN2639
LN2260:
```

```
TextWindow.WriteLine("That was the quickest draw outside of Dodge City.")
TextWindow.WriteLine("You got at least one and drove 'em off.")
Goto LN2639
'
LN2290:
TextWindow.WriteLine("You have a fire in your wagon. Food and supplies are
damaged.")
M = M - 15
F = F - 20
B = B - 400
R = R - 2 * 6 * Math.GetRandomNumber(999)/1000
Goto LN2639
'
LN2320:
TextWindow.WriteLine("You lose your way in heavy fog. Time lost regaining the
trail.")
M = M - 10 - 5 * Math.GetRandomNumber(999)/1000
Goto LN2639
'
LN2350:
TextWindow.WriteLine("You come upon a rattlesnake and before you are able to
get your gun")
TextWindow.WriteLine("out, it bites you.")
B = B - 10
R = R - 2
If R < 0 Then
  Goto LN2390
EndIf
TextWindow.WriteLine("Fortunately, you acted quickly, sucked out the poison,
and")
TextWindow.WriteLine("treated the wound. It is painful, but you'll survive.")
Goto LN2639
LN2390:
TextWindow.WriteLine("You have no medical supplies left, and you die of
poison.")
Goto LN3060
'
LN2410:
TextWindow.WriteLine("Your wagon gets swamped fording a river; you lose food
and clothes.")
M = M - 20 - 20 * Math.GetRandomNumber(999)/1000
F = F - 15
C = C - 10
Goto LN2639
'
LN2440:
TextWindow.WriteLine("You're sound asleep and you hear a noise ... get up to
investigate.")
Sub3740()
TextWindow.WriteLine("It's wild animals! They attack you!")
Sub3870()
If B > 39 Then
Goto LN2480
ELSE
TextWindow.WriteLine("You're almost out of ammo; can't reach more.")
```

```
EndIf
TextWindow.WriteLine("The wolves come at you biting and clawing.")
KH = 1
Goto LN3030
LN2480:
If BR > 2 Then
  Goto LN2500
EndIf
TextWindow.WriteLine("Nice shooting, pardner ... They didn't get much.")
Goto LN2639
LN2500:
TextWindow.WriteLine("Kind of slow on the draw. The wolves got at your food
and clothes.")
B = B - 20 * BR
C = C - 2 * BR
F = F - 4 * BR
Goto LN2639
'
LN2530:
TextWindow.WriteLine("You're caught in a fierce hailstorm; ammo and supplies
are damaged.")
M = M - 5 - 10 * Math.GetRandomNumber(999)/1000
B = B - 150
R = R - 2 - 2 * Math.GetRandomNumber(999)/1000
Goto LN2639
'
LN2560:
'Problems from not eating well enough?
If E = 1 Then
SUB2880()
Goto LN2639 'If eating poorly, go to sickness routine
EndIf
If E = 2 AND Math.GetRandomNumber(999)/1000 > .25 Then
SUB2880()
Goto LN2639
EndIf
If E = 3 AND Math.GetRandomNumber(999)/1000 > .5 Then
SUB2880()
Goto LN2639
EndIf
'
LN2610:
TextWindow.WriteLine("Helpful Indians show you where to find more food.")
F = F + 7
LN2639:
EndSub
'
Sub Sub2640
'Subroutine to travel through mountains
If M <= 975 Then
  Goto LN2879 'Not in mountains yet?
EndIf
If 10 * Math.GetRandomNumber(999)/1000 > 9 - (Math.Power(M / 100 - 15, 2) +
72) / (Math.Power(M / 100 - 15, 2) + 12) Then
  Goto LN2750
```

```
EndIf
TextWindow.WriteLine("You're in rugged mountain country.")
If Math.GetRandomNumber(999)/1000 > .1 Then
  Goto LN2700
EndIf
TextWindow.WriteLine("You get lost and lose valuable time trying to find the
trail.")
M = M - 60
Goto LN2750
LN2700:
If Math.GetRandomNumber(999)/1000 > .11 Then
  Goto LN2730
EndIf
TextWindow.WriteLine("Trail cave in damages your wagon. You lose time and
supplies.")
M = M - 20 - 30 * Math.GetRandomNumber(999)/1000
B = B - 200
R = R - 3
Goto LN2750
LN2730:
TextWindow.WriteLine("The going is really slow; oxen are very tired.")
M = M - 45 - 50 * Math.GetRandomNumber(999)/1000
'
LN2750:
'South Pass routine
If KP = 1 Then
  Goto LN2790 'Is the South Pass clear?
EndIf
KP = 1
If Math.GetRandomNumber(999)/1000 < .8 Then
  Goto LN2840 '80% chance of blizzard
EndIf
TextWindow.WriteLine("You made it safely through the South Pass....no snow!")
LN2790:
If M < 1700 Then
  Goto LN2810
EndIf
If KM = 1 Then
  Goto LN2810 'Through Blue Mts yet?
EndIf
LN2810:
KM = 1
If Math.GetRandomNumber(999)/1000 < .7 Then
Goto LN2840
ELSE
Goto LN2879 'Get through without mishap?
EndIf
MP = 1
Goto LN2879
'Set South Pass flag
'
LN2840:
TextWindow.WriteLine("Blizzard in the mountain pass. Going is slow; supplies
are lost.")
KB = 1
```

```
M = M - 30 - 40 * Math.GetRandomNumber(999)/1000
F = F - 12
B = B - 200
R = R - 5
If C < 18 + 2 * Math.GetRandomNumber(999)/1000 Then
Sub2880()
ELSE
Goto LN2879 'Enough clothes?
EndIf
LN2879:
EndSub
'
Sub Sub2880
'Subroutine to deal with illness
If 100 * Math.GetRandomNumber(999)/1000 < 10 + 35 * (E - 1) Then
  Goto LN2930
EndIf
If 100 * Math.GetRandomNumber(999)/1000 < 100 - (40 / Math.power(4, E - 1))
Then
  Goto LN2950
EndIf
TextWindow.WriteLine("Serious illness in the family. You'll have to stop and
see a doctor")
TextWindow.WriteLine("soon. For now, your medicine will work.")
R = R - 5
KS = 1
Goto LN2970
LN2930:
TextWindow.WriteLine("Mild illness. Your own medicine will cure it.")
M = M - 5
R = R - 1
Goto LN2970
LN2950:
TextWindow.WriteLine("The whole family is sick. Your medicine will probably
work okay.")
M = M - 5
R = R - 2.5
LN2970:
If R > 0 Then
goto LN3099
ELSE
TextWindow.WriteLine("  ... if only you had enough." )
GOTO LN3020
EndIf
'
'Many ways to die on the trail
LN3000:
TextWindow.WriteLine("You run out of food and starve to death.")
finished="false"
sub3110()
LN3010:
T = 0
TextWindow.WriteLine("You need a doctor badly, but can't afford one.")
Goto LN3030
LN3020:
```

```
TextWindow.WriteLine("You have run out of all medical supplies.")
LN3030:
TextWindow.WriteLine("")
TextWindow.Write("The wilderness is unforgiving and you die of ")
If KH = 1 Then
TextWindow.WriteLine("your injuries.")
GOTO LN3060
EndIf
TextWindow.WriteLine("pneumonia.")
LN3060:
TextWindow.Write("Your family tries to push on, but finds the going too
rough")
TextWindow.WriteLine(" without you.")
finished="false"
sub3110()
LN3080:
TextWindow.WriteLine("Your oxen are worn out and can't go another step. You
try pushing")
TextWindow.WriteLine("ahead on foot, but it is snowing heavily and everyone
is exhausted.")
TextWindow.WriteLine("")
Sub3740()
TextWindow.WriteLine("You stumble and can't get up....")
finished="false"
sub3110()
LN3099:
EndSub

Sub Sub3110
If finished then
Goto LN3190
EndIf
TextWindow.WriteLine("")
Sub3740()
TextWindow.WriteLine("Some travelers find the bodies of you and your")
TextWindow.WriteLine("family the following spring. They give you a decent")
TextWindow.WriteLine("burial and notify your next of kin.")
TextWindow.WriteLine("")
D = Math.Floor(14 * (J + ML))
DM = Math.Floor(D / 30.5)
DD = Math.Floor(D - 30.5 * DM)
TextWindow.WriteLine("At the time of your unfortunate demise, you had been on
the trail")
TextWindow.WriteLine("for " +DM +" months and " +DD+ " days and had covered "
+Math.Floor(M + 70)+ " miles.")
TextWindow.WriteLine(" You had a few supplies left:")
Sub3350()
TextWindow.WriteLine("")
Goto LN3310
'
LN3190:
'Made it!
ML = (2040 - MA) / (M - MA)
F = F + (1 - ML) * (8 + 5 * E)
Sub3830()
```

```
TextWindow.WriteLine("You finally arrived at Oregon City after 2040 long
miles.")
TextWindow.WriteLine("You're exhausted and haggard, but you made it! A real
pioneer!")
D = Math.Floor(14 * (J + ML))
DM = Math.Floor(D / 30.5)
DD = Math.Floor(D - 30.5 * DM)
TextWindow.WriteLine("You've been on the trail for " +DM+ " months and " +DD+
" days.")
TextWindow.WriteLine("You have few supplies remaining:")
Sub3350()
TextWindow.WriteLine("")
TextWindow.WriteLine("President James A. Polk sends you his heartiest")
TextWindow.WriteLine("congratulations and wishes you a prosperous life in
your new home.")
Goto LN3310
'
'Play - again query
LN3310:
TextWindow.WriteLine("")
TextWindow.Write("Press Enter to End")
AD = TextWindow.Read()
Program.End()
EndSub
'
Sub Sub3350
'Subroutine to print inventory
TextWindow.WriteLine("Cash   Food   Ammo   Clothes   Medicine, parts, etc.")
If F < 0 Then
F = 0
ELSE
F = Math.Floor(F)
EndIf
If B < 0 Then
B = 0
ELSE
B = Math.Floor(B)
EndIf
If C < 0 Then
C = 0
ELSE
C = Math.Floor(C)
EndIf
If R < 0 Then
R = 0
ELSE
R = Math.Floor(R)
EndIf
TextWindow.Write(T)
TextWindow.CursorLeft = 7
TextWindow.Write(F)
TextWindow.CursorLeft = 14
TextWindow.Write(B)
TextWindow.CursorLeft = 21
TextWindow.Write(C)
```

```
TextWindow.CursorLeft = 31
TextWindow.WriteLine(R)
TextWindow.WriteLine("")
EndSub
'
Sub Sub3430
'Subroutine to read shooting words and dates
SD[1] = "POW"
SD[2] = "BANG"
SD[3] = "BLAM"
SD[4] = "WHOP"
SD[5] = "pow"
SD[6] = "bang"
SD[7] = "blam"
SD[8] = "whop"
DADArray[1] = "March 29"
DADArray[2] = "April 12"
DADArray[3] = "April 26"
DADArray[4] = "May 10"
DADArray[5] = "May 24"
DADArray[6] = "June 7"
DADArray[7] = "June 21"
DADArray[8] = "July 5"
DADArray[9] = "July 19"
DADArray[10] = "August 2"
DADArray[11] = "August 16"
DADArray[12] = "August 31"
DADArray[13] = "September 13"
DADArray[14] = "September 27"
DADArray[15] = "October 11"
DADArray[16] = "October 25"
DADArray[17] = "November 8"
DADArray[18] = "November 22"
DADArray[19] = "December 6"
DADArray[20] = "December 20"
EndSub
'

Sub Sub3530
'Subroutine to read distances and place names
MPArray[1] =  5
PLArray[1] = "on the high prairie."
MPArray[2] = 200
PLArray[2] = "near Independence Crossing on the Big Blue River."
MPArray[3] = 350
PLArray[3] = "following the Platte River."
MPArray[4] = 450
PLArray[4] = "near Fort Kearney."
MPArray[5] = 600
PLArray[5] = "following the North Platte River."
MPArray[6] = 750
PLArray[6] = "within sight of Chimney Rock."
MPArray[7] = 850
PLArray[7] = "near Fort Laramie."
MPArray[8] = 1000
```

```
PLArray[8] = "close upon Independence Rock."
MPArray[9] = 1050
PLArray[9] = "in the Big Horn Mountains."
MPArray[10] = 1150
PLArray[10] = "following the Green River."
MPArray[11] = 1250
PLArray[11] = "not too far from Fort Hall."
MPArray[12] = 1400
PLArray[12] = "following the Snake River."
MPArray[13] = 1550
PLArray[13] = "not far from Fort Boise."
MPArray[14] = 1850
PLArray[14] = "in the Blue Mountains."
MPArray[15] = 2040
PLArray[15] = "following the Columbia River."
EndSub

Sub Sub3700
'Read probabilities of events
EPArray[1] = 6
EPArray[2] = 11
EPArray[3] = 13
EPArray[4] = 15
EPArray[5] = 17
EPArray[6] = 22
EPArray[7] = 32
EPArray[8] = 35
EPArray[9] = 37
EPArray[10] = 42
EPArray[11] = 44
EPArray[12] = 54
EPArray[13] = 64
EPArray[14] = 69
EPArray[15] = 95
EndSub
'
Sub Sub3740
'Subroutine to create a short pause
Program.Delay(1000)
EndSub
'
Sub Sub3770
'Subroutine to read a yes/no answer
LN3780:
XD = Text.GetSubText(AD,1, 1)
If XD = "Y" OR XD = "y" Then
A = 0
Goto LN3789
EndIf
If XD = "N" OR XD = "n" Then
A = 1
Goto LN3789
EndIf
TextWindow.WriteLine("Don't understand your answer of " +AD+ ".")
TextWindow.Write("Please enter Y for 'yes' or N for 'no.' Which is it? ")
```

```
AD = TextWindow.Read()
Goto LN3780
LN3789:
EndSub
'
Sub Sub3830
'Subroutine to play a fanfare
Sound.PlayAndWait(Program.Directory +"\tada.wav")
EndSub
'
Sub Sub3870
'Subroutine to shoot gun
RN = 1 + Math.Floor(4 * Math.GetRandomNumber(999)/1000)
'Pick a random shooting word
S1 = Clock.ElapsedMilliseconds
'Start timer
LN3900:
TextWindow.Write("Type " +SD[RN]+" ")
XD = TextWindow.Read()
If SD[RN]<>XD AND SD[RN + 4]<>XD Then
  TextWindow.Write("Nope. Try again. ")
  GOTO LN3900
EndIf
S2 = Clock.ElapsedMilliseconds
'End timer
BR = (S2 - S1)/1000 - DR - 1
EndSub
```

The Longest Automobile Race

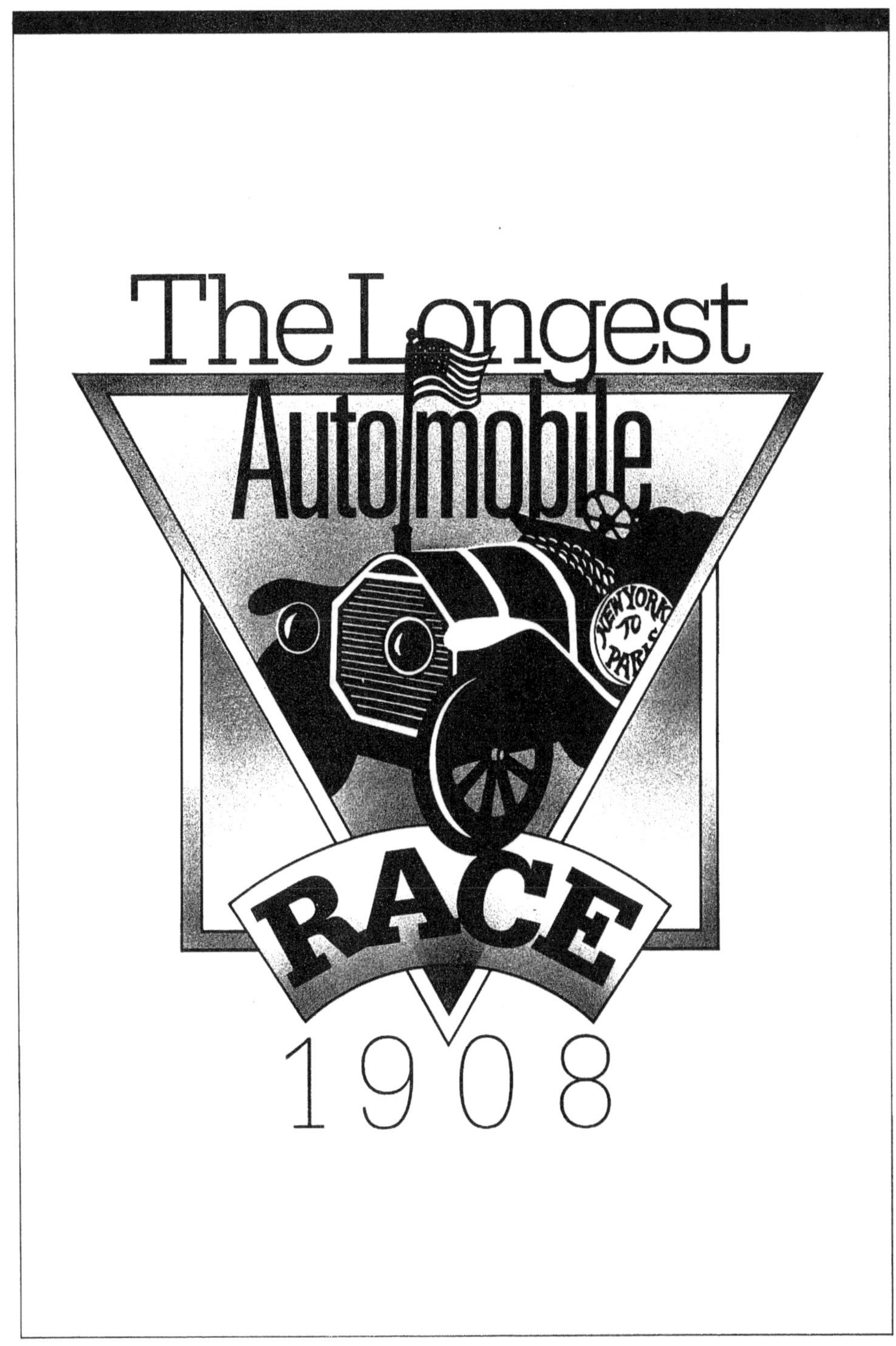

The Longest Automobile Race 1908

The Longest Automobile Race puts you in the driver's seat. In this simulation of a 1908 race from New York to Paris—across the U.S., Japan, Russia, and Europe—you are the captain of the American team. It is your job to get the Thomas Flyer to Paris as quickly as possible—and before your money runs out.

Soon after your departure on February 12, 1908, you encounter some of the worst snows of the decade. From Chicago on, you face a different array of problems: accidents, fatigue, mechanical breakdowns, and more bad weather. Japan and Russia have their own problems (narrow cart tracks in Japan, no gas or lubricants in Russia).

Your chances of beating the other contestants to Paris will be increased if you note the following:

- Buy as much gas as you need, but no more. Prices are high between stops, and any gas remaining at the end of a segment goes to waste. Your car gets approximately 14 miles per gallon, but with changing terrain your mileage could vary by 20%.
- At speeds in excess of 35 mph, the probability of mechanical breakdown increases dramatically. Likewise, driving more than six and a half hours per day increases your chances of having an accident.
- If you get stuck in a snowdrift, a ditch, or mud, you can either pay someone to pull you out or try to extricate yourself. The former costs you money; the latter, time.
- You can choose whether to repair a mechanical problem on the spot or nurse the car along to the next city. On-the-spot repairs are generally more costly, but a second malfunction on top of the first forces you to retire from the race.

On July 30, 1908, nearly six months after starting the race, the weary Thomas Flyer crew limped down the Champs-Elysees and was declared the winner of the race. Can you improve on the performance of the American team—or will your opponents pass as you are permanently bogged down in Siberian mud?

```
Date: August 4 , 1908
You dozed off and your car has run into a farmer's wagon.
You can try to fix it or get a tow to the next village for $15.
Want to try to bang out the damage on the spot? n
The tow costs $15 and the repairs cost $ 25
```

```
You are at New York, New York.
You currently have $1000.00
Roads to the west of here are hard packed gravel.
The weather forecast is snow and sleet.
You set a goal of making 897 miles in the next 6 days.
Gas costs 21 cents per gallon here.
How many gallons do you want for the segment ahead? 80
That will cost $16.80
How fast (mph) do you want to drive? 30
How many hours do you want to drive each day? 6
```

```
Date: August 22 , 1908
You are at Paris, France.
You currently have $402.36

You have driven 12698 miles in 193 days.

                    CONGRATULATIONS !

You made it to Paris! The German Protos beat you by
25 days but just to finish is a great honor!

You reached Paris in 193 days. In 1908, the Thomas Flyer
won the race reaching Paris on July 30 after 169 days.

Would you like to try again (Y or N)?
```

```
Date: March 31 , 1908
You are at Seattle, Washington.
You currently have $200.38
It took 3 days on the steamer. The next steamer for Valdez
leaves in 2 days. Nothing to do but wait.

Press any key when you're ready to go aboard.
```

THE STORY

In 1908, barely 15 years after the automobile was invented, the seemingly preposterous suggestion that an automobile race be run from New York to Paris was made. This race, proposed by newspapermen of the *New York Times* and *Le Matin* of Paris, was to be made over untried roads; the sponsors believed it would be possible to drive in Alaska by widening dog trails and, in the far North, driving on the crust of the snow that, according to one *Times* document, "froze so solidly overnight that it would bear the weight of a car." They also believed that contestants would be able to drive a car on frozen rivers and to cross the Bering Strait between Alaska and Siberia on an ice bridge.

THE MOST DIFFICULT STRETCH OF THE RACE WAS ACROSS MANCHURIA AND RUSSIA.

This sort of misinformation, coupled with the daring, adventuresome spirit of early automobile makers and the promise of honor and glory, lured thirteen contestants to sign up for the race.

However, on February 12, 1908, the day the race was to begin, only six teams actually showed up. The entrants included three cars made in France and one each made in Italy, Germany, and the United States.

The French entries included a 30 hp Motobloc, a big De Dion, and a tiny one-cylinder, 15 hp Sizaire-Naudin. Italy was represented by a Zust, Germany by a big Protos, and the U.S. by a year-old, 60 hp Thomas Flyer. All of the cars had four cylinders (except the Sizaire-Naudin), open bodies with no windshields, narrow spoked wheels, no heaters, and only the most basic seating for driver and passengers.

Each team consisted of a driver and one or more mechanics. In addition, each car was required to carry a writer/observer from one of the sponsoring newspapers.

The race got underway in front of the Times Building on 43rd Street at 11:15 A.M. on Abraham Lincoln's birthday, 1908.

The Sizaire-Naudin driven by Auguste Pons led the procession up Broadway and onto the Albany Post Road. It was the only time Pons had the lead; while climbing a hill only 40 miles from the city, his car broke an axle. There were no spare parts available for his car, and Pons spoke no English. Thus the race ended for him on the very first day.

Language was also a problem for the crew of the French Motobloc. They stopped for lunch at a hotel in Dobbs Ferry, New York, and after waiting two hours to be served, became furious and accused the proprietor of overcharging and delaying them. To add injury to insult, just a few miles north at Peekskill, the Motobloc skidded in the snow and landed in a ditch, delaying it further. Snow and language difficulties continued to plague the Motobloc team, and they finally dropped out of the race three weeks later in western Iowa.

The remaining four cars fought on—although their battles were as much or more with Mother Nature as with one another.

From the newspaper stories, one can piece together a fascinating description of the race. However, a somewhat more coherent account is found in the book, *The Longest Auto Race*, by George Schuster, the mechanic on the American Thomas Flyer. Moreover, Schuster and the Flyer team stayed in the race long after even the hardiest newspapermen had dropped out.

Schuster records constant problems with snow as the cars progressed along the route from New York to Albany, Buffalo, Erie, Cleveland, South Bend, and Chicago. In fact, Ohio and Indiana had one of the worst blizzards of the decade just after the cars left Buffalo.

What should have been a two- or three-day trip from Buffalo to Chicago became a week-long ordeal for the Flyer team: in and out of snow drifts, driving on railroad tracks, hiring teams of horses to pull the car a few miles, and dealing with every sort of mechanical problem.

Beyond South Bend, the team was forced to hire teams of six or eight horses to drag the car along. On February 22 Schuster spent $80 on horse teams and covered only 15 miles. The next day, the Flyer team struggled for 22 hours and covered a grand total of eight miles.

The chores of draining the water from the cooling system every night (antifreeze had not yet been invented) and making constant small repairs added to the frustration of slow progress.

Finally, at 4:25 P.M. on February 25, the Flyer team reached the South Shore Country Club, the official arrival point in Chicago. Schuster notes that it took 13 1/2 days to travel the 1403 miles from New York, eight days of which were required to cover the last 256 miles. All of the teams spent a few days in Chicago recuperating and making needed repairs before starting westward on "tracks of half-frozen ruts" on the morning of February 28.

Now the battle was with thick, gooey mud, which the wheels and tires threw in big gobs onto the fenders, running boards, and interior of the car. Schuster records that when the Flyer team pulled into Clarence, Iowa, to stop for the night, someone suggested that they take the car to the fire station to get the mud washed off. The high-pressure three-inch stream was so effective that the Flyer crew visited fire stations whenever they could from then on. The thrill of the trip had worn thin for the *Times* correspondent, and a day later in Cedar Rapids he bade the American crew good bye and returned to New York.

The Plains States brought more rain and mud, which, as the cars reached the mountains, turned into sleet, hail, and snow.

Conditions were so bad in Utah and eastern Nevada that it became clear that crossing the Sierra Nevada Mountains (the direct route to San Francisco) would be impossible. So the Flyer team took a 700-mile detour south through the Nevada desert and Death Valley to Bakersfield, California and back up along the San Joaquin Valley to San Francisco.

The Flyer team made it to San Francisco on March 24, a total of 3836 miles and 41 days after leaving New York. At the time, the Italian Zust was in Utah and the French De Dion and the German Protos were in Wyoming, all pushing west. With the help of the Thomas Flyer dealer in San Francisco, that car was prepared, as much as possible, for the unknown rigors of Alaska and Siberia that lay ahead. Springs, transmission, wheels, drive chains, and many other parts were replaced in the three days before the car was loaded on the steamer City of Pueblo for the three-day voyage to Seattle. There, five tires—all that could be found—were purchased and Schuster wired owner Mr. Thomas at the factory for additional funds.

The crew and car sailed north on a leisurely seven-day voyage to Valdez, Alaska. There they learned the truth about the proposed route: Dog trails didn't exist, snow would not support a car, and there was no ice bridge across the Bering Strait. They telegraphed this information to New York and soon received a response: "Return to Seattle. Route changed. Go by steamer to Vladivostock." Meanwhile, the Zust and the De Dion had arrived in San Francisco, while the Protos, much in need of repairs, had been shipped by its crew aboard a railroad flatcar from Idaho across the Sierra Nevadas to Seattle, avoiding the 700-mile "detour" taken by the other cars.

The Protos sailed immediately for Vladivostock; the other teams, unable to get a steamer for Russia, sailed instead for Japan. The Flyer crew, afraid that those teams would get credit for driving across Japan, decided to take a steamer for Kobe, Japan. On the voyage, the leather aprons with which the Flyer crew had replaced their metal fenders were removed by the Chinese crew to make sandals. The captain ordered the ship's carpenter to replace the aprons with canvas and, Schuster reported, "except for that our voyage was uneventful." As it turned out, the Flyer crew need not have worried about the newly added Japan segment.. The race committee ruled that the Protos would be penalized 15 days for not driving all the way across the U.S. and that the Flyer crew would be given a 15-day advantage for going to Alaska.

The trip across Japan from Kobe to Tsuruga was only 350 miles, but torturous miles they were. Japanese roads were designed for narrow carts, and the big cars could barely negotiate the sharp turns and steep hills. What should have been an easy two-day drive turned into a four-day ordeal punctuated by delays for religious processions, detours, wrong turns, and skids into ditches. Although it was commonly thought that the Japanese worked for coolie wages, one group of workmen insisted on 50 yen ($25) for manning a towrope to let the Flyer down a steep hillside.

Sailing from Tsuruga on May 16, the Flyer and its crew finally arrived in Vladivostock in a gloomy rain on May 18. The other cars were all there, but the eccentric Count De Dion, his team having already driven and won the Peking to Paris race the year before, decided he had much to lose and little to gain by continuing on, and pulled his team out of the race.

Gasoline was extremely scarce in Russia, and the Protos and Zust teams had lined up most of the existing supplies. Schuster was thus forced to cash his last letter of credit to buy 400 gallons of gasoline at exorbitant prices ($1.00 to $1.25 per gallon). Most of this was then shipped ahead by rail to be stored along the route where the team could retrieve it in the days ahead. This was necessary because there were no filling stations, and gasoline would not be commercially available until the cars reached Europe. The teams stocked up on food and supplies and were ready to go on May 22. "You are mad," a Russian officer told them. "You will never get through." It rained during 17 of the next 20 days and, recounted one driver, "we drove out into a dismal, flat, rain-drenched country, over or rather through a road that was a streak of mud as far as the eye could reach." The Flyer drove in low or second gear with chains on the rear wheels.

In one of the most memorable events of the race, the Flyer came upon the Protos so deep in the mud that only the tops of the rear wheels showed above the mire. The three Germans and a Russian officer/guide were trying to pry it out, but with the churning of the wheels it was only sinking deeper. After a brief debate among themselves, the Flyer crew passed a towrope to the Germans and managed to pull the Protos to solid ground. Lt. Koeppen, the German team captain, uncorked a bottle of champagne and poured drinks as thanks for what he called "a gallant, comradely act."

Finally, unable to make any progress in the muddy cart tracks, the Flyer crew took to driving along railroad tracks, a strategy they had successfully used—at great cost to the wheels, tires, and springs—on several stretches in the U.S. Two tires quickly blew out, and four more were worn to the cords in the next 150 miles. The organizers had ruled that the cars would not be permitted to fit special wheel flanges that would allow them to drive on the rails but that driving on the ties was permitted.

Soon, however, the pounding on the ties began to take an even greater toll than the tires and springs. A sharp noise signaled a six-inch crack in the Flyer transmission housing and the stripping of six gear teeth from the drive pinion. Schuster then made a five-day trip to Harbin where he cabled the factory to send a new transmission by way of Europe. Meanwhile, the crew made makeshift repairs—new teeth were welded to the drive pinion at a blacksmith shop—and slowly pushed on.

Mechanical devices, much less automobiles, were virtually unknown in Manchuria and Siberia, and lubricants were unavailable. Thus the crew was forced to buy 40 lbs. of Vasoline in Chita to quiet the gears and allow them to keep moving. At Irkutsk, completely out of money, Schuster again wired the factory for more. He received it, but Thomas warned him that he was disinclined to pour any more money into this adventure. Also at Irkutsk when the mud was washed from the car, he discovered a broken motor support. Schuster replaced it with a piece of boiler plate from the railroad shops, but the break had thrown the motor out of line, making it difficult to shift gears.

It rained so constantly through Siberia that the road was a continuous bog. The car frequently got stuck, and laborers or horse teams had to be hired to pull it out. Near Kansk was a swollen river with a quicksand bottom and no bridge; there the Flyer crew hired four teams of Cossacks' horses to rush the car across a fording spot. The next day they came upon a river so deep it could not be forded, so the crew hired villagers to make a log raft to float the car across.

Deep ditches across the roads were frequent hazards in Siberia. On one occasion, completely worn brake drums failed to stop the Flyer in time at one of these ditches; there was a sudden snap, and the left side of the car sagged. The frame was broken, creating an awkward problem in the middle of nowhere. Finally, angle iron was secured from a railroad shop and bolted to the broken frame.

The Protos had been in the lead across most of Russia, but finally, near the village of Kolnokowa, the Flyer caught up with and passed the German competitor. However, a few days later, on July 1 in Omsk, 3408 miles from Vladivostock, the makeshift transmission repairs on the Flyer gave out. The new transmission had been shipped two weeks earlier aboard the SS President and should have been waiting. It wasn't, so again the crew laboriously forged new teeth at a blacksmith shop and welded them on. This cost three days, but on July 4, the Flyer was back on the road. The Protos, too, had run into trouble and was obliged to wait in Kansk for five days until a new rear axle could be shipped from the factory in Germany.

Schuster, fearing that the transmission would soon fail permanently, sent two crew members (two mechanics from teams that had dropped out had joined the Flyer crew) to check all the railroad depots in the area for the missing transmission while the car pushed slowly on toward Perm. There he received word that the missing transmission had been located at Kasan, 350 miles ahead and more or less on the route west. However, the mud was so bad that the car could never be shifted out of low, and three days out of Perm—still 215 miles from Kasan—the transmission failed for good.

Schuster then used the last of his money to arrange relays of farm wagons to fetch the 600-lb. transmission. It took five days, by which time Schuster, walking with the wagons day and night, was sick with chills and a high fever. Installing the transmission took another day, and on July 18 the team finally reached Kasan where they took a steam ferry across the Volga River. A wrong turn, a leaky radiator, and another break in the frame slowed the Flyer, but finally at Gorky they reached the relatively smooth pavement of some of the oldest roads in Europe.

But there were problems with these roads, too. When driven at speed on a good surface, the Flyer wobbled all over the road; the repaired motor support broke again and was out of alignment with the clutch and transmission. The tires were worn through, and the radiator was still leaking. Thus, the team had to stop for several days in Moscow to make more repairs.

The Flyer team reached St. Petersburg on the afternoon of July 22, four days behind the Protos; three days later, the Flyer crossed the border into Germany. The radiator sprang yet another leak and was removed for more repairs at the ancient fortress city of Konigsberg. The crew reached Berlin on July 27, and there heard the disheartening news that the Protos had arrived in Paris the night before. Rolling along perfectly smooth road outside of Hanover, the car slowed down and finally coasted to a stop. The makeshift clutch shaft installed in Moscow had worn away completely, again necessitating complete disassembly and repair. The 30-lb. assembly was hauled to a machine shop many miles away where it took another half day to make and install a new part.

At noon the next day, having had little food or rest, the Flyer crew drove into Cologne, looking forward to a washup and a good meal. "Not here, not here," said the head waiter of the Dom Hotel, shaking his head and waving the motley crew out of the restaurant. After an unsatisfying meal at a small cafe, they left the city and crossed the Rhine into Liege, Belgium, to spend the night.

Leaving early on July 30, they followed the Meuse River and crossed into France at Fumay. Accelerator to the floor, they attained a speed of 50 mph, the highest since they had left the United States. Approaching Paris late in the afternoon, they were stopped by gendarmes who refused to let them pass without headlamps (they had broken weeks before in Siberia). A passing Frenchman gallantly offered one from his bicycle. When the lamp could not be detached, the bicycle was lifted onto the car, and the journey was resumed amid cheering crowds.

At 6:00 P.M. on July 30, the Thomas Flyer pulled up in front of the offices of *Le Matin* and, with the credit for going to Alaska and the penalty against the Protos, was declared the winner of the longest automobile race in history by 26 days. The only other car still in the race, the Italian Zust, finally reached Paris on September 17, missing second place by only three days.

Winning the race briefly spurred sales of the Thomas Flyer, but the euphoria was short-lived. In 1909, Henry Ford introduced the Model T, thus ending the age of expensive hand-crafted automobiles. A year later, only 913 Thomas Flyers were produced, and the following year the company left the business.

Note: The restored chassis of the competing Protos is on display in the Deutches Museum in Munich, Germany, and the restored Thomas Flyer is at the Harrah Automotive Museum in Reno, Nevada. The Zust was not preserved.

BIBLIOGRAPHY

Schuster, George with Tom Mahoney. *The Longest Auto Race.* New York: The John Day Co., 1966.

The New York Times. Various accounts between February and August, 1908.

THE PROGRAM

The Longest Automobile Race program consists of a main program, initialization section, summary section, 12 major subroutines, and five lesser subroutines.

In the initialization section at the beginning, text and numeric data are read into variables in three subroutines. The main program consists of two main sections. The first section (starts at LN260) obtains data for the next section of the race, specifically weather (W), distance (D), and the number of days that it took the winning car to complete the segment in 1908 (TE). The current date, location, and summary information of the race to that point are then printed. If the racer has managed to limp along with an unfixed problem that developed on the road, repairs are made at this location (starting at LN310).

If the next segment of the race is an ocean voyage, the ocean voyage subroutine (Sub2290) is called. If the next race segment is a normal land segment, the main program prints a description of the expected weather and road conditions, and establishes a time and distance.

Next, three subroutines that accept input from the user are called: the amount of fuel to be put in the car and spotted at villages ahead (in many locations, the racing teams had to send cans of gasoline ahead by train), the desired driving speed, and the desired number of driving hours per day.

The second major section of the main program (starting at LN520) loops through each day of the race. For each day, subroutines that deal with weather conditions, mechanical breakdowns, and accidents and special situations, are called. After this, the program calculates daily and cumulative distance traveled and gasoline consumption. If a race segment is completed, the program branches back to the beginning of the main program to start the next segment.

In the gas-and-oil subroutine (Sub640), you are asked how many gallons of fuel you want to purchase. The price of gasoline varies between 17 and 39 cents per gallon; the average is 25 cents. However, if you run out of gasoline on the road, the base price is 33 cents per gallon, although it can be as low as 23 cents or as high as 52 cents. In general, the best strategy is to buy enough gas for a segment at the outset. However, extra gas goes to waste, as it cannot be shipped ahead to the next race segment. In general, the car will get approximately 14 miles per gallon, but mileage varies by plus or minus 20%. After calculating the total cost of the gas you want to buy, the program goes to the payment subroutine at Sub2660 (discussed later). If you don't have enough money to buy the amount of gasoline you want, you get as much as you can afford.

The subroutine to accept the desired speed (Sub730) will accept any speed between 8 mph and 54 mph, the top speed of the Thomas Flyer. In snowy weather, the program limits the maximum speed to 30 mph. Of course, your average speed on the road will be lower than the speed you input, because you must slow down to go through villages, make detours, make rest stops, and deal with unexpected problems. The probability of a mechanical breakdown is related to speed by the formula at LN790 and increases rather quickly as speed exceeds 35 mph. You must, of course, balance the risk of mechanical problems with that of driving too slowly to be competitive.

The driving-hours subroutine (Sub820) accepts the desired driving hours per day (HP), establishing an upper limit of eight and a lower limit of two. If you have consistently been driving for an average of more than seven and a half hours, you are advised not to push yourself and your crew quite so hard. The probability of a problem resulting from driver fatigue (PF) is related to driving hours and starts to rise sharply when six and a half hours per day is exceeded (LN910). The formula for this probability is:

```
PF = HP * HP * HP / 1000 - .15
```

Cubing the hours causes the very sharp rise from nil at five hours per day to 6.6% at six hours, 19.3% at seven hours, and 36.2 at eight hours.

The date subroutine (Sub940) simply takes the day counter (TD) and converts it into the proper month and day. If the date goes beyond August 31—one full month after the first car crossed the finish line in 1908—you are obliged to withdraw from the contest.

The weather subroutine (Sub1120) is the longest in the program. It is divided into five sections, representing major types of weather conditions, and a subroutine having to do with getting stuck in a ditch.

Each of the five major weather-subroutine sections is structured similarly. First, a random number is generated to determine if something nasty happens. For example, in the heavy snow section (starts at LN1150), there is a 33% chance of hitting a blizzard of major proportions. In this case the speed factor (PW) ranges from .03 to .10; i.e., your actual speed will be only 3% to 10% of what you input. You also have a 17% chance of getting stuck in a snowdrift, in which case you are sent to the stuck-in-the-ditch subroutine. Under "normal" heavy-snow conditions, the speed factor is about .22 or 22% of what you input.

In regular snowy conditions there is a 10% chance of skidding off the road, but in all cases your speed is much reduced (starts at LN1230).

Rainy weather was a much greater problem in 1908 than it is today, because the dirt roads turned into virtual quagmires into which a car could sink 10 or 15 inches. There is a 20% chance of this occurring (LN1290). Furthermore, if you do get stuck, getting out is usually rather time-consuming.

In the cloudy-and-mixed-weather section (starts at LN1350), there is a 1% chance of a sudden downpour, an 8% chance of coming to a river with no bridge, and a 92% chance of smooth sailing. Although a river without a bridge doesn't seem to be related to cloudy weather, in the actual 1908 race most of the rivers across which the contestants had to be ferried were reached during stretches of cloudy or mixed weather. The program gives you a choice of being ferried across (for a fee) or driving north to a bridge (an unknown distance away).

If you get stuck in a snowdrift, a ditch, or mud, you can usually find a farmer to pull you out for $5 to $20 (Line 1540). If you want to pay him to pull you out, the program calls the payment routine. If not, you and your mechanic have at it with prybars, shovels, and a winch. To get out by yourself takes at least one day and sometimes two (at LN1610).

The mechanical-breakdowns subroutine (Sub1640) is perhaps the most complex in the program. First, a random number is compared to the breakdown probability to determine if there actually is a breakdown. Then, the specific problem is determined by the subsequent random number functions; the first 13 malfunctions are twice as likely to occur as the last five.

```
F = Math.Floor(1 + 15 * Math.GetRandomNumber(999)/1000)
If F > 13 Then
  F = Math.Floor(14 + 5 * Math.GetRandomNumber(999)/1000) 'What malfunction
EndIf
```

The problem is then presented to you, and you are asked whether or not you want to fix it and which type of repair you want to use in the event that more than one is available. One is usually a new part and the other a homebrew approach. Each repair has a time and cost associated with it. If you have enough money, the repairs are made; otherwise the car must be nursed along to the next city at half speed, a procedure with a 60% chance of success. Also, if there is a second unrepaired malfunction, the combination of the two forces the car to be retired. In general, the only time you might not want to do a repair right away is when you are nearing the next city, because you won't lose much time at the reduced speed and also a sympathetic automobile dealer will usually fix your car for free (at LN310).

The accidents-and-special-situations subroutine (Sub1930) is divided into three sections. The first determines whether or not there is an accident. As mentioned earlier, the probability of an accident is related to the average driving hours per day. If there is an accident—you dozed off and ran into something: a tree, hole, or farmer's wagon—you can try to fix it on the spot (costs time) or get a tow to the next village and get it repaired there (costs money). At the time of the accident, the farmer will tell you the cost of a tow to the next village, but, of course, you will not know how much the repairs will cost.

In the four race segments in which the roads are particularly bad or blocked with snow, you may be able to get permission to drive on the railroad tracks (starts at LN2100). While this will save you time—the speed factor is multiplied by 1.7—the constant pounding of tires on the uneven railroad ties is extremely hard on the car.

Although the wheels, tires, suspension, transmission, and chassis take the biggest beating, in the program the current overall probability of all problems is simply multiplied by 1.25, i.e., an increase of 25%.

In the two race segments in central Russia between Chita and Omsk, very few mechanical supplies of any sort were available in 1908. Gasoline, oil, grease, and all spare parts had to be carried on the cars or shipped ahead, or substitutions made on the spot. During this segment, the Thomas Flyer developed a serious crack in its transmission. The team requested that a replacement be shipped from the factory, but they had to push on to meet the transmission in Perm.

A portion of this adventure is simulated in the no-grease routine (starts at LN2190). Also, the time for a transmission repair is set to forty hours, which is five eight-hour workdays. The forty hours is converted to days in LN1790 so it can be added to the cumulative travel time.

The ocean-voyage subroutine (Sub2290) simulates the five steamer voyages: San Francisco to Seattle, Seattle to Valdez, Valdez to Seattle, the long 21-day trip to Kobe, Japan, and the short voyage from Tsuruga to Vladivostock, Russia. There is not much decision-making on these segments. Your waiting time in port varies from one to four days and is produced by the formula at the beginning of the subroutine.

A short subroutine takes care of time delays and hotel stays (Sub2590). It simply increments the day counters by TZ, a variable set in various other subroutines representing days needed for repairs, tows, river crossings, and port stays. For each day of the trip, except those on ships, you pay an average of $10 for food and accommodations for you and your mechanic.

All bills—repairs, tows, hotels, gasoline, and ferries—are paid in a four-line subroutine (Sub2660). The cost of an item (ZN) is simply subtracted from your cash reserve (Z). If you don't have enough money to pay your bills and can't get it from home, an indicator (A) is set to 1 and program execution is returned to the place the bill was incurred. The consequences of not paying your bills can range from mild (if you can't pay for as much gasoline as you want, you are given as much as you can afford) to severe (unpaid repair and hotel bills take you out of the race).

If you run out of money, you can wire Mr. Thomas at the factory in Buffalo for more (Sub2710). In 1908, Mr. Thomas was wildly enthusiastic about the race before it started and while the cars were in the U.S. However, as the months wore on his enthusiasm turned to disenchantment, and he became much less willing to supply additional funds to the crew. The growing disillusionment of Mr. Thomas as well as his somewhat temperamental nature is simulated in the program.

You can go back and ask for money three times before Mr. Thomas gets totally fed up. You can get up to $1000 on each of the first two requests and up to $500 on the third. But if you don't say the right things you may get less or you may have to wait for the money. Code starting at LN2790 picks apart the contents of your telegram to Mr. Thomas in three-letter groups. I won't spoil the fun of playing the game by telling you what the telegram must say, although close analysis of the program will give you the answer.

Three subroutines (Sub2970, Sub3060, Sub3310) read numeric and alphabetic data into the proper variables. These routines use two data files weather.txt and breakdown.txt. The subroutine at Sub3530 checks for a yes or no answer to an Read statement. The telegraph and warning beeper subroutines make simple sounds, the "Ready to go?" subroutine halts the program until a key is pressed, while the pause subroutine creates a short pause in program execution.

The simulated race can end in one of two ways: You make it to Paris or you don't. If you make it, the program tells you how long it took and where you placed in the race. If you don't make it, a consoling message is printed.

PROGRAM VARIABLES

```
A Answer of user (0 = Yes, 1 = No)
AD Answer to string input query, user input
AP Telegram-politeness indicator
ATD 3-letter group from telegram
AS Telegram-urgency indicator
C[n] Road conditions by location, index of C$(n), n = 1 - 20
CD[n] Road-conditions descriptor, n = 1 - 20
D Distance of segment
DA Distance, cumulative within segment
DC Distance, cumulative
DD Distance, daily
DX[n] Distance of segment, n = 1 - 20
F Mechanical failure, index for FAD, FBD, FCD, FL, FT
FAD[n] Mechanical-failure descriptor, n = 1 - 18
FBD[n] Mechanical-failure fix descriptor, n = 1 - 18
FCD[n] Mechanical-failure 2nd fix descriptor, n = 1 - 18
FDD Mechanical failure, hours or days descriptor
FL[1][n] Mechanical-failure cost of 1st fix, n = 1 - 18
FL[2][n] Mechanical-failure cost of 2nd fix, n = 1 - 18
FQ Mechanical-failure, how to fix, user input
FT[1][n] Mechanical-failure time for 1st fix, n = 1 - 18
FT[2][n] Mechanical-failure time for 2nd fix, n = 1 - 18
FU Mechanical failure, fix time
FX Mechanical-failure indicator
GF Gasoline base price per gallon
GG Gasoline reserve
GM Gasoline used by day
GP Gasoline price
HC Hours per day, cumulative
HP Hours per day to drive, user input
I Temporary index
J Journey-segment number
JV Ocean-voyage indicator
K Temporary indicator and index
LAD[n] City, n = 1 - 20
LBD[n] State or country, n = 1 - 20
MD Day of month
MOD Month
PB Probability of mechanical breakdown
PF Probability of fatigue problem
PW Probable speed factor due to weather and road conditions
RN Random variable for random number
RQ Random variable for hours
SP Speed, user input
T Time-into-race segment

TD Time, cumulative
TE Time of 1908 winning car to complete segment
TL Time, cumulative of 1908 race leader
TT Temporary date indicator
TX[n] Time of 1908 winning car to complete segment, n = 1 - 20
TZ Time delay
W Weather on the trip, index of w$(n)
```

```
WD[n] Weather descriptor, n = 1 - 6
WX[n] Weather, probable at each location, n = 1 - 20
X Temporary variable
XD Temporary string variable
Z Cash balance of racing team
ZN Cash expenditure during race
```

Note: all variables use the following measurement units:

```
D       Distance        Miles
G       Gasoline        Gallons
H       Time            Hours
P       Probabilities   0 to 1
T       Time            Days
Z       Money           Dollars and cents
```

PROGRAM LISTINGS

```
TextWindow.CursorTop = 10
TextWindow.CursorLeft = 23
TextWindow.WriteLine("The Longest Automobile Race, 1908")
TextWindow.WriteLine("")
TextWindow.WriteLine("")
TextWindow.CursorLeft = 29
TextWindow.WriteLine("(c) David H. Ahl, 1986")
TextWindow.CursorTop = 23
TextWindow.CursorLeft = 21

'Initialization
'Z = 1000
GF = .25
'Starting cash and gas price
Sub2970()
'Initialize text variables
Sub3060()
'Initialize location data
Sub3310()
'Initialize mechanical breakdown data
TextWindow.WriteLine("Press Enter when you're ready to go")
JJJ = TextWindow.Read()
Sub4010()
'
'Main program
LN260:
J = J + 1
T = 0
Sub3710()
Sub3630()
'New location, road data, etc.
DA = 0
W = WX[J]
D = DX[J]
TE = TX[J]
'Set variables for new location
Sub940()
'Print the date
TextWindow.WriteLine("You are at "+ LAD[J]+ ", " +LBD[J] +".")
ZValue = Z
FormatZ()
TextWindow.WriteLine("You currently have $" + ZDisplay)
If J = 1 Then
  Goto LN420
EndIf
LN310:
If FX = 0 Then
  Goto LN340 'Any unfixed mechanical parts?
EndIf
TextWindow.WriteLine("A sympathetic garage owner will fix the " +FAD[FX]+ "
here.")
FX = 0
TZ = Math.Floor(1 + 3 * Math.GetRandomNumber(999)/1000)
```

```
TextWindow.WriteLine("It will take "+ TZ+ " day(s).")
Sub2590()
LN340:
If J > 7 AND J < 11 Then
  Sub2290() 'Ocean voyage?
EndIf
If JV = 1 Then
JV = 0
TL = TL + TE
GOTO LN260 'End of ocean voyage?
EndIf
TextWindow.WriteLine("")
TextWindow.WriteLine("You have driven "+ Math.Floor(DC)+ " miles in "+TD+ "
days.")
If J = 20 Then
  finished = "true"
  Sub3740() 'Finished the race?
EndIf
If TD < TL Then
Goto LN400
ELSEIF TD = TL THEN
goto LN410
EndIf
TextWindow.WriteLine("The race leader passed this point " +(TD - TL)+ "
day(s) ago.")
Goto LN420
LN400:
TextWindow.WriteLine("You are the race leader and are " +(TL - TD)+ " day(s)
ahead.")
Goto LN420
LN410:
TextWindow.WriteLine("You and the Italian Zust are running even with each
other.")
LN420:
TL = TL + TE
'Elapsed time of race leader
If J = 7 OR J = 12 Then
  Sub2290() 'Ocean voyage after land segment?
EndIf
If JV = 1 Then
JV = 0
GOTO LN260 'End of ocean voyage?
EndIf
TextWindow.WriteLine("Roads to the west of here are " +CD[C[J]]+ ".")
TextWindow.WriteLine("The weather forecast is "+ WD[W]+ ".")
TextWindow.WriteLine("You set a goal of making "+ D+ " miles in the next "+(
TE - 2)+ " days.")
Sub640()
'Buy gas and oil
Sub730()
'Get desired speed
Sub820()
'Get desired driving hours per day
'
LN520:
```

```
'Go through this race segment day by day
TZ = 1
Sub2590()
'Increment through each day of travel
Sub1120()
'Weather subroutine
Sub1640()
'Mechanical breakdown subroutine
Sub1930()
'Accident subroutine
DD = SP * HP * PW
DA = DA + DD
DC = DC + DD
'Daily and cumulative distances
GM = .07 * DD * (.8 + .4 * Math.GetRandomNumber(999)/1000)
'Gas used today
If GM < GG Then
GG = GG - GM
GOTO LN620 'Subtract gas used from supply
EndIf
Sound.PlayAndWait(Program.Directory + "\ding.wav")
Sound.PlayAndWait(Program.Directory + "\ding.wav")
Sub940()
TextWindow.WriteLine("You ran out of gas on the road.")
GF = .33
Sub640()
GG = GG - GM
'Buy gas
LN620:
If DA >= D Then
Goto LN260
ELSE
goto LN520 'Complete a travel segment?
EndIf
'
Sub Sub640
'Fuel and oil subroutine
GP = GF * (.7 + .6 * Math.GetRandomNumber(999)/1000)
TextWindow.WriteLine("Gas costs " +math.Floor(100 * GP)+ " cents per gallon
here.")
TextWindow.Write("How many gallons do you want for the segment ahead? ")
GG = TextWindow.ReadNumber()
GF = .25
ZN = GG * GP
TextWindow.Write("That will cost $")
ZValue = ZN
FormatZ()
TextWindow.WriteLine(ZDisplay)
Sub2660()
'Do you have enough money?
If A = 0 Then
  Goto LN639 'Enough money now?
EndIf
If Z < 2 Then
TextWindow.WriteLine("Your car won't run on fumes. It's all over.")
```

```
finished="false"
Sub3740()
EndIf
GG = Math.Floor(Z / GP)
TextWindow.WriteLine("Sorry, you could only get "+ GG +" gallons.")
LN639:
EndSub
'
Sub Sub730
'Input desired speed subroutine
LN740:
TextWindow.Write("How fast (mph) do you want to drive? ")
SP = TextWindow.ReadNumber()
If SP > 54 Then
TextWindow.Write("Top speed of your car is only 54 mph." )
GOTO LN740
EndIf
If SP < 8 Then
TextWindow.Write("At that rate, you'll never get there.")
GOTO LN740
EndIf
If W < 3 AND SP > 30 Then
Goto LN780
ELSE
goto LN790
EndIf
LN780:
TextWindow.WriteLine("That's too fast for these weather and road
conditions.")
Goto LN740
LN790:
PB = SP * SP / 7000
'Probability of mechanical breakdown is related to speed
EndSub
'
Sub Sub820
'Input desired driving hours subroutine
K = 0
'Counter for pushing too hard
LN840:
TextWindow.Write("How many hours do you want to drive each day? ")
HP = TextWindow.ReadNumber()
If K = 1 Then
  Goto LN910 'Did we ask about pushing too hard already?
EndIf
If HP > 8 Then
TextWindow.WriteLine("That's too much for both you and your car.")
GOTO LN840
EndIf
If HP < 2 Then
TextWindow.WriteLine("No one is that lazy!")
GOTO LN840
EndIf
HC = HC + HP
If J > 2 AND HC / J > 7.55 Then
```

```
Goto LN890
ELSE
goto LN910
EndIf
LN890:
TextWindow.WriteLine("You've been pushing yourself and your crew pretty hard.")
TextWindow.WriteLine("You should probably back off a bit.")
K = 1
Goto LN840
LN910:
PF = HP *HP*HP/ 1000 - .15
If PF < .01 Then
  PF = .01 'Probability of fatigue problem
EndIf
EndSub
'
Sub Sub940
'Date subroutine
If TT = TD Then
  Goto LN939 'Printed this date already?
EndIf
Sub960()
LN939:
EndSub

Sub Sub960
If TD < 19 Then
Goto LN990
ELSEIF TD < 50 THEN
goto LN1000
ELSEIF TD < 80 THEN
goto LN1010
EndIf
If TD < 111 Then
Goto LN1020
ELSEIF TD < 141 THEN
goto LN1030
ELSEIF TD < 172 THEN
goto LN1040
EndIf
If TD < 203 Then
Goto LN1050
ELSE
sub3630()
GOTO LN1070
EndIf
LN990:
MOD = "February"
MD = TD + 11
Goto LN1060
LN1000:
MOD = "March"
MD = TD - 18
Goto LN1060
```

```
LN1010:
MOD = "April"
MD = TD - 49
Goto LN1060
LN1020:
MOD = "May"
MD = TD - 79
Goto LN1060
LN1030:
MOD = "June"
MD = TD - 110
Goto LN1060
LN1040:
MOD = "July"
MD = TD - 140
Goto LN1060
LN1050:
MOD = "August"
MD = TD - 171
LN1060:
TextWindow.WriteLine("")
TextWindow.WriteLine("Date: " +MOD+" "+ MD +", 1908" )
TT = TD
Goto LN1119
LN1070:
TextWindow.WriteLine("")
TextWindow.WriteLine("It's September 1 and the winning car crossed the
finish")
TextWindow.WriteLine("line in Paris over a month ago. Your factory refuses to
give")
TextWindow.WriteLine("you any more money to continue. Better luck next
time.")
finished="false"
Sub3740()
ln1119:
EndSub
'
Sub Sub1120
'Weather subroutine
If (W = 1) Then
  Goto LN1150
ElseIf (W = 2) Then
  Goto LN1230
ElseIf (W = 3) Then
  Goto LN1290
ElseIf (W = 4) Then
  Goto LN1350
ElseIf (W = 5) Then
  Goto LN1350
ElseIf (W = 6) Then
  Goto LN1490
EndIf
'
LN1150:
'Heavy snow and blizzard conditions
```

```
RN = Math.GetRandomNumber(999)/1000
If RN < .33 Then
Goto LN1170
ELSEIF RN > .83 THEN
goto LN1190
ELSE
goto LN1210
EndIf
LN1170:
Sub960()
PW = .03 + .08 * Math.GetRandomNumber(999)/1000
'Speed factor in blizzard
TextWindow.WriteLine("Blizzard conditions. Tough going today.")
Sub3710()
Goto LN1499
LN1190:
Sub960()
PW = .05 + .1 * Math.GetRandomNumber(999)/1000
'Speed factor in very heavy snow
TextWindow.WriteLine("You're stuck in a huge snow drift.")
Sub1530()
Goto LN1499
LN1210:
PW = .14 + .17 * Math.GetRandomNumber(999)/1000
Goto LN1499
'Speed factor on heavy snow day
'
LN1230:
'Snow conditions
If Math.GetRandomNumber(999)/1000 < .1 Then
  Goto LN1260 '10% chance of getting stuck in snow
EndIf
PW = .3 + .4 * Math.GetRandomNumber(999)/1000
Goto LN1499
'Speed factor on normal snowy day
LN1260:
PW = .15 + .1 * Math.GetRandomNumber(999)/1000
Sub960()
TextWindow.WriteLine("You have skidded into a ditch.")
Sub1530()
Goto LN1499
'Hire farmer to pull you out of ditch?
'
LN1290:
'Rainy weather
If Math.GetRandomNumber(999)/1000 < .2 Then
Sub960()
GOTO LN1320 'Bogged down in mud?
EndIf
PW = .35 + .4 * Math.GetRandomNumber(999)/1000
Goto LN1499
'Speed factor on normal rainy day
LN1320:
PW = .02 + .04 * Math.GetRandomNumber(999)/1000
TextWindow.WriteLine("You are totally bogged down in the mud.")
```

```
Sub1530()
Goto LN1499
'Hire farmer to pull you out of mud?
'
LN1350:
'Cloudy and mixed weather
RN = Math.GetRandomNumber(999)/1000
If RN > .08 Then
Goto LN1470
ELSE
Sub960() 'Normal cloudy day?
EndIf
If RN < .01 Then
TextWindow.WriteLine("An unexpected downpour!")
GOTO LN1320
EndIf
LN1380:
TextWindow.WriteLine("River ahead with no bridge. Some locals tell you there
is a bridge")
TextWindow.WriteLine("'some distance' north. They also offer to take you
across by boat")
ZN = 3 + 2 * Math.Floor(3 * Math.GetRandomNumber(999)/1000)
ZValue = ZN
FormatZ()
TextWindow.Write("for $" +ZDisplay)
TextWindow.Write(". Want to go by boat? ")
AD = TextWindow.Read()
Sub3530()
If A = 1 Then
  Goto LN1450 'Not willing to pay?
EndIf
Sub2660()
'Go to pay the bill routine
If A = 1 Then
  Goto LN1450 'Still not enough money?
EndIf
TextWindow.WriteLine("They got you across in "+( 2 + Math.Floor(3 *
Math.GetRandomNumber(999)/1000))+ " hours.")
PW = .3
Goto LN1499
LN1450:
TZ = Math.Floor(1 + 2 * Math.GetRandomNumber(999)/1000)
TextWindow.Write("It took " +TZ+ " day(s) for you to drive north ")
TextWindow.WriteLine("and find the bridge.")
Sub2590()
Goto LN1499
LN1470:
PW = .4 + .4 * Math.GetRandomNumber(999)/1000
Goto LN1499
'Normal cloudy day
'
LN1490:
'Clear and sunny
If Math.GetRandomNumber(999)/1000 < .025 Then
Sub960()
```

```
GOTO LN1380 'River with no bridge
EndIf
'Normal sunny day
PW = .45 + .5 * Math.GetRandomNumber(999)/1000
LN1499:
EndSub
'
Sub Sub1530
'Pull you out of ditch subroutine
ZN = 5 * Math.Floor(1 + 4 * Math.GetRandomNumber(999)/1000)
ZValue = ZN
FormatZ()
TextWindow.WriteLine("A farmer offers to pull you out for $" +ZDisplay)
TextWindow.Write("Do you want to pay him to pull you out? ")
AD = TextWindow.Read()
Sub3530()
If A = 1 Then
  Goto LN1610 'Not willing to pay?
EndIf
Sub2660()
'If not enough money try to get some
If A = 1 Then
  Goto LN1610 'Still not enough money?
EndIf
RQ = Math.Floor(1.5 + 5 * Math.GetRandomNumber(999)/1000)
TextWindow.WriteLine("It took " +RQ+ " hours for him to pull you out.")
If RQ < 5 Then
Goto LN1639
ELSE
TZ = 1
Sub2590()
PW = PW * 1.5
Goto LN1639
EndIf
LN1610:
TZ = Math.Floor(1 + 1.3 * Math.GetRandomNumber(999)/1000)
TextWindow.WriteLine("It took "+ TZ +" day(s) for you and your mechanic")
TextWindow.WriteLine("to pull the car out by yourselves.")
Sub2590()
PW = PW * 1.5
LN1639:
EndSub
'
Sub Sub1640
'Mechanical breakdowns subroutine
If Math.GetRandomNumber(999)/1000 > PB Then
  Goto LN1929 'If no mechanical breakdown then return
EndIf
F = Math.Floor(1 + 15 * Math.GetRandomNumber(999)/1000)
If F > 13 Then
  F = Math.Floor(14 + 5 * Math.GetRandomNumber(999)/1000) 'What malfunction
EndIf
Sound.PlayAndWait(Program.Directory + "\ding.wav")
Sound.PlayAndWait(Program.Directory + "\ding.wav")
Sub940()
```

```
'Sound warning beeper and print date
TextWindow.WriteLine("Uh oh. You have a problem. It's a " +FAD[F] +".")
TextWindow.WriteLine("Here's what you can do about the problem:")
TextWindow.CursorLeft = 7
TextWindow.WriteLine("(1) Try to keep going with it")
TextWindow.CursorLeft = 7
ZValue = FL[1][F]
FormatZ()
TextWindow.WriteLine("(2) "+ FBD[F]+ ", cost $" +ZDisplay)
If FCD[F] = "" Then
  Goto LN1740 'Only one way to fix it?
EndIf
TextWindow.CursorLeft = 7
ZValue = FL[2][F]
FormatZ()
TextWindow.WriteLine("(3) " +FCD[F] +", cost $"+ ZDisplay)
LN1740:
TextWindow.Write("Which would you like to do? ")
FQ = TextWindow.ReadNumber()
If FQ = 1 Then
  Goto LN1840 'Decided to do nothing?
EndIf
If FQ = 2 OR FQ = 3 Then
Goto LN1770
ELSE
TextWindow.WriteLine("Please enter a number." )
GOTO LN1740
EndIf
LN1770:
FQ = FQ - 1
FU = FT[FQ][F]
If FU < 8 Then
FDD = "hours"
ELSE
goto LN1790
EndIf
If FU < 5 Then
Goto LN1810
ELSE
TZ = 1
GOTO LN1800 'Lose a day for repairs?
EndIf
LN1790:
FU = FT[FQ][F] / 8
TZ = FU
If FU = 1 Then
FDD = "day"
ELSE
FDD = "days"
EndIf
LN1800:
PW = PW * 1.5
Sub2590()
'Allow for 1/2 day driven & increase day counters
LN1810:
```

```
ZN = FL[FQ][F]
ZValue = ZN
FormatZ()
TextWindow.WriteLine("Repairs will take " +FU+" "+FDD+ " and will cost $"
+ZDisplay)
Sub2660()
'Pay the repair bill
If A = 0 Then
  Goto LN1929 'Enough money?
EndIf
LN1840:
TextWindow.WriteLine("You try to nurse the car along to the next major
city.")
If FX = 0 Then
  Goto LN1870 'Any unfixed malfunction?
EndIf
TextWindow.WriteLine("But with the other problem you just can't make it and")
Goto LN1890
LN1870:
If Math.GetRandomNumber(999)/1000 > .4 Then
  Goto LN1900 '60% chance that you can nurse it along
EndIf
Sub3710()
TextWindow.WriteLine("")
TextWindow.WriteLine("Unfortunately, it just won't make it and")
LN1890:
TextWindow.WriteLine("reluctantly you admit defeat.")
finished="false"
Sub3740()
LN1900:
TextWindow.WriteLine("It looks like you'll make but at a drastically reduced
speed.")
PW = PW * .5 'Cut speed factor in half, note unfixed item
FX = F
LN1929:
EndSub

'
Sub Sub1930
'Accidents and special situations subroutine
If Math.GetRandomNumber(999)/1000 > PF Then
  Goto LN2100 'If driving long hours is not a problem, go on
EndIf
Sound.PlayAndWait(Program.Directory + "\ding.wav")
Sound.PlayAndWait(Program.Directory + "\ding.wav")
Sub940()
TextWindow.Write("You dozed off and your car has run ")
JJJ = Math.Floor(1 + 4 * Math.GetRandomNumber(999)/1000)
If (JJJ = 1) Then
  Goto LN1970
ElseIf (JJJ = 2) Then
  Goto LN1980
ElseIf (JJJ = 3) Then
  Goto LN1990
ElseIf (JJJ = 4) Then
```

```
  Goto LN2000
ElseIf (JJJ = 5) Then
  Goto LN2000
EndIf
LN1970:
TextWindow.WriteLine("into a tree.")
TZ = 2
ZN = 24
Goto LN2010
LN1980:
TextWindow.WriteLine("off the road.")
TZ = 1
ZN = 12
Goto LN2010
LN1990:
TextWindow.WriteLine("into a gaping hole.")
TZ = 1
ZN = 18
Goto LN2010
LN2000:
TextWindow.WriteLine("into a farmer's wagon.")
TZ = 2
ZN = 25
LN2010:
TextWindow.WriteLine("You can try to fix it or get a tow to the next village
for $15.00")
TextWindow.Write("Want to try to bang out the damage on the spot? ")
Ad = TextWindow.Read()
Sub3530()
If A = 0 Then
Goto LN2070
ELSE
ZValue = ZN
FormatZ()
TextWindow.WriteLine("The tow costs $15 and the repairs cost $" +ZDisplay)
EndIf
ZN = ZN + 15
Sub2660()
'Pay the bills
If A = 0 Then
  Goto LN2100 'Enough money now?
EndIf
TextWindow.WriteLine("The locals impound your car for your unpaid debt.")
finished="false"
Sub3740()
LN2070:
TextWindow.WriteLine("You finally manage to do it but it takes " +TZ+ "
day(s).")
PW = PW * 1.5
Sub2590()
'Allow for 1/2 day driven & increase day counters
'
LN2100:
'Drive on railraod ties routine
If J<>2 AND J<>5 AND J<>13 AND J<>14 Then
```

```
  Goto LN2190 'In area with railroads?
EndIf
If Math.GetRandomNumber(999)/1000 > .4 Then
Goto LN2190
ELSE
Sub940() '40% chance to drive on rwy tracks
EndIf
TextWindow.WriteLine("In this area of terrible roads, you can save some time
by driving")
TextWindow.WriteLine("on the railraod tracks. However, it is murder on your
wheels,")
TextWindow.Write("tires, and whole car. ")
TextWindow.Write("Want to drive on the tracks? ")
Ad = TextWindow.Read()
Sub3530()
If A = 1 Then
  Goto LN2289
EndIf
PW = PW * 1.7
PB = PB * 1.25
Goto LN2289
'Increase speed and chance of trouble
'
LN2190:
'No grease routine
If J<>15 AND J<>16 Then
  Goto LN2289 'In central Russia?
EndIf
If Math.GetRandomNumber(999)/1000 > .2 Then
  Goto LN2289 '20% chance of no grease
EndIf
Sound.PlayAndWait(Program.Directory + "\ding.wav")
Sound.PlayAndWait(Program.Directory + "\ding.wav")
Sub940()
TextWindow.WriteLine("Your differential is dry and there is")
TextWindow.WriteLine("no grease available here. However, you can get
Vaseline.")
TextWindow.Write("Want to use it in place of grease? ")
Ad = TextWindow.Read()
Sub3530()
If A = 0 Then
TextWindow.WriteLine("Okay, you buy 20 jars for $4.00")
Z = Z - 4
Goto LN2289
EndIf
TextWindow.WriteLine("The gears sound horrible. You'll have to cut your speed
in half.")
PW = PW * .5
LN2289:
EndSub
'
Sub Sub2290
'Ocean voyage subroutine
JV = 1
TZ = Math.Floor(1 + 3.5 * Math.GetRandomNumber(999)/1000)
```

```
'Length of time in port
If J = 12 Then
Goto LN2510
ELSEIF J = 10 THEN
goto LN2480
EndIf
If J = 9 Then
Goto LN2420
ELSEIF J = 8 THEN
goto LN2390
EndIf
TextWindow.WriteLine("You're stuck in port for " +(TZ + 1) +" days before you
can get a steamer")
TextWindow.WriteLine("for Seattle. You use the time to get new countershaft")
TextWindow.WriteLine("housings, springs, wheels, drive chains, and tires.")
If Z > 300 Then
TextWindow.WriteLine("The cost of these items is $164.00")
Z = Z - 164
GOTO LN2380
EndIf
TextWindow.WriteLine("These were all furnished by the local Thomas Flyer
dealer.")
LN2380:
TZ = TZ + 1
TD = TD + 3
Sub2590()
Sub3660()
Goto LN2589
LN2390:
TextWindow.WriteLine("It took 3 days on the steamer. The next steamer for
Valdez")
TextWindow.WriteLine("Leaves in " +TZ+ " days. Nothing to do but wait.")
Sub2590()
Sub3660()
TD = TD + 7
Goto LN2589
LN2420:
TextWindow.WriteLine("The steamer made many stops up the coast and it took 7
days.")
TextWindow.WriteLine("It is apparent that the race organizers have never been
in Alaska")
TextWindow.WriteLine("and have no idea that it is impossible to drive on the
snow and")
TextWindow.WriteLine("ice at all, much less across the Bering Strait to
Russia. You'll")
TextWindow.WriteLine("have to return to Seattle. Next steamer goes in "+ TZ+
" days.")
Sub2590()
Sub3660()
TD = TD + 7
Goto LN2589
LN2480:
TextWindow.WriteLine("It took 7 days to get back to Seattle. Now you have a
"+ TZ+ " day")
TextWindow.WriteLine("wait before you can get a freighter for Japan.")
```

```
Sub2590()
Sub3660()
TD = TD + 21
Goto LN2589
LN2510:
TextWindow.WriteLine("The freighter across the Pacific takes a leisurely 21
days making")
TextWindow.WriteLine("stops at Hawaii, Guam, and the Philippines. Also the
Chinese")
TextWindow.WriteLine("crewmen made sandals out of your leather fenders and
mud flaps.")
TextWindow.WriteLine("You can't replace them in Japan, but you can at
Vladivostock,")
TextWindow.WriteLine("Russia. There you'll have to spend several days
arranging for")
TextWindow.WriteLine("fuel also. But hurry now. A steamer to Russia leaves
tonight.")
Sub3660()
TD = TD + 7
LN2589:
EndSub
'
Sub Sub2590
'Time delay and hotel bills routine
T = T + TZ
TD = TD + TZ
'Increment time counters
ZN = 10 * TZ
Sub2660()
'Pay for hotel and meals
If A = 0 Then
  Goto LN2659 'Did we have enough money?
EndIf
TextWindow.WriteLine("")
TextWindow.WriteLine("You don't even have enough money to pay for meals.")
TextWindow.WriteLine("That's the end of the road for you.")
TextWindow.WriteLine("")
finished="false"
Sub3740()
LN2659:
EndSub

Sub Sub2660
'Pay the bills routine
If Z < ZN Then
Sub2710()
ELSE
goto LN2690 'Enough money to pay bills?
EndIf
If Z < ZN Then
A = 1
Goto LN2709 'Couldn't get money from home
EndIf
LN2690:
Z = Z - ZN 'Subtract money from kitty
```

```
A = 0
LN2709:
EndSub

'
Sub Sub2710
'Need more money subroutine
ZB = ZB + 1
If ZB < 3 Then
ZW = 1000
ELSE
ZW = 500 'Money request and amount
EndIf
TextWindow.WriteLine("")
TextWindow.WriteLine("You don't have enough money to continue. Your only hope
is")
TextWindow.WriteLine("to send a telegram back to Mr. Thomas at the factory
and ask")
TextWindow.WriteLine("for more money. Remember, telegrams in 1908 used all
capital")
TextWindow.WriteLine("letters, had no commas, and were short.")
TextWindow.Write("What is your message? ")
Ad = TextWindow.Read()
TextWindow.WriteLine("Sending telegram now ... ")
sub3590()
If ZB > 3 Then
  Goto LN2940
EndIf
AS = 0
AP = 0
L = Text.GetLength(Ad)
If L < 12 Then
  Goto LN2920
EndIf
LN2790:
For I = 1 To L - 2
ATD = Text.GetSubText(ATD, I, 3)
'Look at 3-letter groups in telegram
If ATD = "PLE" OR ATD = "BEG" OR ATD = "SOR" OR ATD = "IMP" Then
  AP = 1
EndIf
If ATD = "SOO" OR ATD = "QUI" OR ATD = "EAR" OR ATD = "FAS" OR ATD = "HUR"
Then
  AS = 1
EndIf
If ATD = "IMM" OR ATD = "ONC" OR ATD = "URG" Then
  AS = 1
EndIf
ENDFOR
If AP = 0 Then
Goto LN2880
ELSEIF AS = 0 THEN
GOTO LN2860
EndIf
ZValue = ZW
```

```
formatz()
TextWindow.WriteLine("Mr. Thomas wired back $"+ZDisplay+" and said 'GOOD
LUCK!")
Z = Z + ZW
Goto LN2969
LN2860:
ZValue = ZW
formatz()
TextWindow.WriteLine("Mr. Thomas didn't know you needed the money right away
and waited")
TextWindow.WriteLine("3 days before wiring back $"+ ZDisplay)
Z = Z + ZW
TZ = 3
Sub2590()
Goto LN2969
LN2880:
If AS = 0 Then
  Goto LN2910
EndIf
TextWindow.WriteLine("Mr. Thomas wired back, 'YOU COULD AT LEAST BE POLITE,'
but did")
ZW = ZW / 2
ZValue = ZW
FormatZ()
TextWindow.WriteLine("include a draft for $" +ZDisplay)
Z = Z + ZW
Goto LN2969
LN2910:
TextWindow.WriteLine("Mr. Thomas was offended by your telegram and refused
to")
Goto LN2930
LN2920:
TextWindow.WriteLine("Your message was short all right. Too short. Mr. Thomas
didn't")
LN2930:
TextWindow.WriteLine("send any money. Sorry.")
Goto LN2969
LN2940:
TextWindow.WriteLine("Mr. Thomas wires back: I AM FED UP WITH THIS ADVENTURE
STOP")
TextWindow.WriteLine("YOU WILL GET NO MORE MONEY FROM ME STOP")
LN2969:
EndSub
'
Sub Sub2970
'Subroutine to put verbal data into constants
CD[1] = "hard packed gravel"
CD[2] = "muddy ruts"
CD[3] = "slightly improved wagon tracks"
CD[4] = "built for narrow carts"
CD[5] = "practically non-existent"
CD[6] = "horrible"
WD[1] = "blizzard conditions"
WD[2] = "snow and sleet"
WD[3] = "rain"
```

```
WD[4] = "cloudy with a chance of rain"
WD[5] = "mixed"
WD[6] = "sunny and dry"
EndSub
'
Sub Sub3060
'Location, expected weather, road conditions, need to use rail,
' expected days to next location, distance to next location
CLINE = 1
DataFile = Program.Directory +"\weather.txt"
FileLine = File.ReadLine(DataFile, CLINE)
For I = 1 To 20
  GetNextItem()
  X = NextItem
  GetNextItem()
  LAD[I] = NextItem
  GetNextItem()
  LBD[I] = NextItem
  GetNextItem()
  WX[I] = NextItem
  GetNextItem()
  C[I] = NextItem
  GetNextItem()
  TX[I] = NextItem
  GetNextItem()
  DX[I] = NextItem
EndFor
EndSub

Sub GetNextItem
  'find comma in FileLine
  KK = Text.GetIndexOf(FileLine, ",")
  If KK <> 0 Then
    NextItem = Text.GetSubText(FileLine, 1, KK - 1)
    FileLine = Text.GetSubTextToEnd(FileLine, KK + 1)
  Else
    NextItem = FileLine
    CLINE = CLINE + 1
    FileLine = File.ReadLine(DataFile, CLINE)
  EndIf
EndSub

'
Sub Sub3310
'Mechanical breakdown descriptions, time to fix, cost
CLINE = 1
DataFile = Program.Directory +"\breakdown.txt"
FileLine = File.ReadLine(DataFile, CLINE)
For I = 1 To 18
  GetNextItem()
  X = NextItem
  GetNextItem()
  FAD[I] = NextItem
  GetNextItem()
  FBD[I] = NextItem
```

```
  GetNextItem()
  FCD[I] = NextItem
  GetNextItem()
  FT[1][I] = NextItem
  GetNextItem()
  FL[1][I] = NextItem
  GetNextItem()
  FT[2][I] = NextItem
  GetNextItem()
  FL[2][I] = NextItem
EndFor
EndSub
'
Sub Sub3530
LN3530:
'Check for yes or no answer
If AD = "" OR AD = "Y" OR AD = "y" Then
A = 0
Goto ln3589
EndIf
If AD = "N" OR AD = "n" Then
A = 1
Goto ln3589
EndIf
TextWindow.WriteLine("Don't understand your answer of "+AD+ ".")
TextWindow.Write("Please enter Y for 'yes' or N for 'no.'? ")
AD = TextWindow.Read()
Goto LN3530
LN3589:
EndSub
'
Sub Sub3590
'Telegraph routine
For I = 1 To 4
X = 1 + 3 * Math.GetRandomNumber(999)/1000
For K = 1 To X
Sound.PlayAndWait(Program.Directory + "\ding.wav")
EndFor
For K = 1 To 500
EndFor
EndFor
EndSub
'
Sub Sub3630
'Warning beeper routine
TextWindow.WriteLine("")
For I = 1 To 3
Sound.PlayAndWait(Program.Directory + "\ding.wav")
For K = 1 To 500
EndFor
EndFor
EndSub
'
Sub Sub3660
'Ready to go? routine
```

```
TextWindow.WriteLine("")
TextWindow.WriteLine("Press Enter when you're ready to go aboard.")
JJJ = TextWindow.Read()
EndSub
'
Sub Sub3710
'Pause routine
Program.Delay(500)
EndSub
'
Sub Sub3740
If finished = "false" Then
Goto LN3890
EndIf
LN3740:
'Finished the race in Paris!
For K = 1 To 3
Sub3710()
Sound.PlayAndWait(Program.Directory + "\Carsnd.wav")
EndFor
TextWindow.Clear()
TextWindow.WriteLine("")
TextWindow.WriteLine("")
If TD < TL Then
Goto LN3830
ELSEIF TD = TL THEN
goto LN3850
EndIf
TextWindow.WriteLine("You made it to Paris! The German Protos beat you by")
TextWindow.WriteLine((TD - TL)+" days but just to finish is a great honor!")
Goto LN3860
LN3830:
TextWindow.WriteLine("You reached Paris first! The next car is " +(TL - TD)+"
days behind.")
Goto LN3860
LN3850:
TextWindow.WriteLine("You reached Paris in a dead tie with the French
Motobloc!")
LN3860:
TextWindow.WriteLine("")
TextWindow.WriteLine("You reached Paris in " +TD+ " days. In 1908, the Thomas
Flyer")
TextWindow.WriteLine("won the race reaching Paris on July 30 after 169
days.")
Goto LN3970
'
LN3890:
'End of race and summary statistics
TextWindow.WriteLine("")
Sub3630()
TextWindow.WriteLine("")
LN3910:
TextWindow.WriteLine("Sorry you were unsuccessful. Only three of the")
TextWindow.WriteLine("cars in the 1908 race ever finished.")
TextWindow.WriteLine("")
```

```
TextWindow.WriteLine("In the " +TD+ " days since the start of the race on
February 12, 1908,")
TextWindow.Write("you covered "+Math.Floor(DC)+ " miles. You almost made it
to "+LAD[J + 1]+ ", ")
TextWindow.WriteLine(LBD[J + 1] +". ")
TextWindow.WriteLine("Not bad, but you can do better.")
TextWindow.WriteLine("")
'
LN3970:
TextWindow.WriteLine("")
TextWindow.Write("Press Enter to End")
AD = TextWindow.Read()
Program.End()
EndSub

Sub Sub4010
'Subroutine to print the instructions
TextWindow.Clear()
TextWindow.CursorLeft = 18
TextWindow.WriteLine("The Longest Automobile Race, 1908")
TextWindow.WriteLine("")
TextWindow.WriteLine(" In this program, you are the captain of the Thomas
Flyer team.")
TextWindow.WriteLine("It is your job to get the car from New York to Paris
... east to west ...")
TextWindow.WriteLine("as quickly as possible. The race starts on Febraury 12,
1908.")
TextWindow.WriteLine(" You must overcome many problems: bad weather,
accidents,")
TextWindow.WriteLine("mechanical breakdowns, fatigue, and a lack of gas
stations.")
TextWindow.WriteLine(" For each leg of the trip, buy as much gas as you need,
but no")
TextWindow.WriteLine("more. You car gets approximately 14 mph, although this
will vary.")
TextWindow.WriteLine("You will carry what fuel you can and ship the rest
ahead by rail to")
TextWindow.WriteLine("locations along your route to be held for you (called
'spotting').")
TextWindow.WriteLine(" Your car has a top speed of 54 mph. However, the
probability")
TextWindow.WriteLine("of a breakdown increases substantially at speeds over
35 mph. Like-")
TextWindow.WriteLine("wise, driving more than six hours per day increases
your chance of")
TextWindow.WriteLine("having an accident. But don't forget, this IS a race.")
TextWindow.WriteLine(" If you get stuck, you can pay someone to pull you out
(costs")
TextWindow.WriteLine("money) or try to get out on your own (costs time).")
TextWindow.WriteLine(" You can choose to repair a mechanical problem on the
spot or")
TextWindow.WriteLine("wait until the next large town to get it fixed. Either
choice has")
TextWindow.WriteLine("associated risks.")
```

```
TextWindow.WriteLine(" If and when you run out of money, you can wire Mr. 
Thomas for")
TextWindow.WriteLine("more, but your request must be carefully and politely 
worded Also,")
TextWindow.WriteLine("your telegram must be in all UPPER CASE letters.")
TextWindow.CursorLeft = 21
TextWindow.WriteLine("")
TextWindow.CursorLeft = 21
TextWindow.WriteLine("Press Enter to Continue")
JJJ = TextWindow.Read()
TextWindow.Clear()
EndSub

Sub FormatZ
  Dollars = Math.Floor(ZValue)
  Cents = Math.Floor((ZValue - Dollars) * 100)
  ZDisplay = Text.Append(Dollars , ".")
  If Cents < 10 Then
    ZDisplay = Text.Append(ZDisplay, "0")
  EndIf
  ZDisplay = Text.Append(ZDisplay, Cents)
EndSub
```

The Orient Express

The Orient Express places you aboard that famous train bound from London, England to Constantinople in February 1923. As a secret agent your assignment is to make contact with an arms dealer who has tired of his life of crime, and arrest the killer of one of his former associates.

Some of the passengers on the train (all of whom are historical characters who actually rode the Express in their day) have information that can help you complete your assignment. As you work your way through the mystery, you participate in many of the things—delicious meals, stops at stations along the way, and occasional delays due to snow, derailment, and bandits—that made the Orient Express an unforgettable experience for those who rode it.

Solving the puzzle is not easy. You will probably want to make notes about meaningful clues and take some time to think—hours perhaps—before talking to the Turkish police (who will help you) at Uzunkopru. Bear the following in mind as you play the game:

- You must identify and protect the sender of the note and identify and arrest the killer of Baron Wunster.
- Five notorious arms dealers, all of different nationalities, are currently operating in Europe under an uneasy truce. Each of them deals in a different type of weapon, and all are known to have different tastes and habits.
- Not all of the passengers with whom you speak have useful information. You cannot talk to passengers during sleeping segments of the trip.
- Unless you have extraordinary deductive powers, it will probably take you at least an hour of play to solve the mystery. (Of course, you can cheat and do some sleuthing in the program listing, but that will probably take you almost as long and be a lot less fun.)

So grab your notebook and your ticket, and start asking questions. Remember, a man's life is at stake!

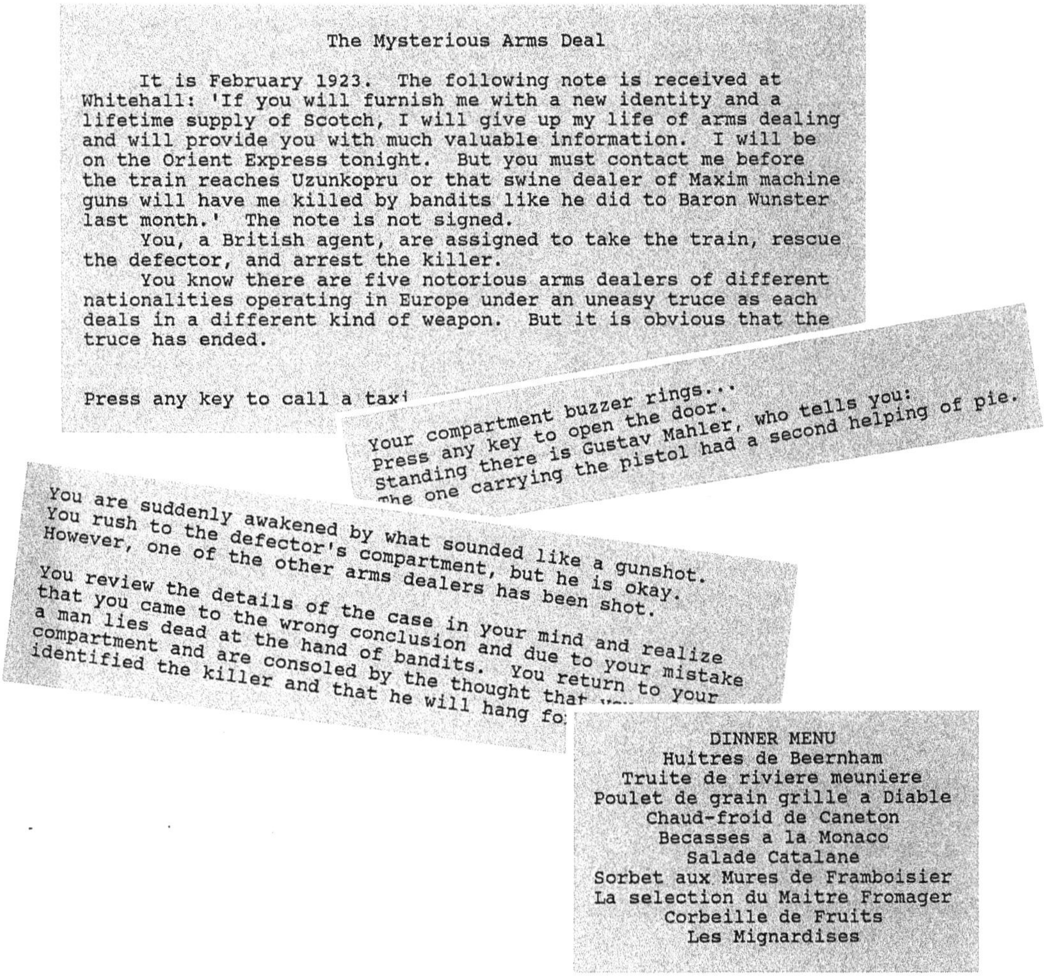

```
                 The Mysterious Arms Deal

     It is February 1923.  The following note is received at
Whitehall: 'If you will furnish me with a new identity and a
lifetime supply of Scotch, I will give up my life of arms dealing
and will provide you with much valuable information.  I will be
on the Orient Express tonight.  But you must contact me before
the train reaches Uzunkopru or that swine dealer of Maxim machine
guns will have me killed by bandits like he did to Baron Wunster
last month.'  The note is not signed.
     You, a British agent, are assigned to take the train, rescue
the defector, and arrest the killer.
     You know there are five notorious arms dealers of different
nationalities operating in Europe under an uneasy truce as each
deals in a different kind of weapon.  But it is obvious that the
truce has ended.

Press any key to call a taxi
```

```
Your compartment buzzer rings...
Press any key to open the door.
Standing there is Gustav Mahler, who tells you:
The one carrying the pistol had a second helping of pie.
```

```
You are suddenly awakened by what sounded like a gunshot.
You rush to the defector's compartment, but he is okay.
However, one of the other arms dealers has been shot.
You review the details of the case in your mind and realize
that you came to the wrong conclusion and due to your mistake
a man lies dead at the hand of bandits.  You return to your
compartment and are consoled by the thought that yo
identified the killer and that he will hang fo
```

```
           DINNER MENU
        Huitres de Beernham
      Truite de riviere meuniere
   Poulet de grain grille a Diable
       Chaud-froid de Caneton
        Becasses a la Monaco
          Salade Catalane
   Sorbet aux Mures de Framboisier
   La selection du Maitre Fromager
        Corbeille de Fruits
          Les Mignardises
```

THE STORY

What image comes to mind at the mention of the Orient Express? Adventure? Luxury? Intrigue? Reliability? Awe? The famous train was all of these things and much more. Very few people ever traveled on the Orient Express, even at its peak, because the cost was prohibitive for all but the super rich. However, no form of public transportation has fascinated more authors, journalists, and filmmakers than the Orient Express. Thus, it has assumed a dimension almost larger than life. D.H. Lawrence had Lady Chatterley and her lover travel on the Orient Express. Agatha Christie, who was, in fact, a regular traveler on the Orient Express, used it as the setting for one of her most compelling Hercule Poirot stories, *Murder on the Orient Express*. Graham Greene's *Stambol Train* is about the Orient Express. Eric Ambler also used it as the setting for *The Mask of Dimitrios*, and one of the most accurate descriptions of the postwar train is found in the final chapters of Ian Fleming's *From Russia with Love*. And there are scores of others. How did this magnificent train come into existence and how did it achieve such fame and notoriety?

In the 30 or so years following 1825, when the first steam railroad was put into operation in England, every country in Europe began building its own railroad system. Political conditions were unsettled, and the threat of war hung heavy in the air. Hence railway builders would deliberately use track widths and rolling stock incompatible with those of their neighbors to thwart the movement of invaders by rail. Transcontinental travelers thus had to change trains at every border, and frequently used a ship or stagecoach to make connections.

Moreover, railroad coaches had evolved from horse-drawn carriages and were quite uncomfortable. Trains had no lavatories, no restaurant cars, no connections between coaches, no corridors, no lighting, hard seats, and little heat. Although progress was being made in Europe, it was in America that the real advances in rail travel were taking place. There, consistent with the democratic principles on which the country had been founded, railroad cars had open seating in contrast with the tiny boxed-in compartments found on European trains. Distances in the U.S. were longer, so provision had to be made for eating and other necessities. The three most important advances in American railroading sprang from necessity. First, much track in America had been poorly laid, so derailments were common. To overcome this problem, the fixed wheel-and-axle design was discarded, and railroad cars were equipped with bogies, swiveling four-wheel trucks with independent springs. Second, American trains were much longer and heavier than European trains, and the locomotive brakes required a very long distance to stop a train. So, for greater efficiency, George Westinghouse developed a system of compressed air brakes. The third advance was George Pullman's development of a combined parlor/sleeping car. Georges Nagelmackers, son of a wealthy Belgian banker, journeyed to the U.S. in 1869 and was very impressed by American railroads and particularly by Pullman's luxurious cars. By the time he returned to Europe in 1870, Nagelmackers was obsessed with the idea of establishing luxury, long-distance, through rail service throughout Europe.

His indulgent father was impressed with his son's enthusiasm and proposed to King Leopold II of Belgium that he would forgive the King's substantial overdue bank loans if the King would agree to head the list of subscribers to the venture. The King, seeing a way out of a difficult financial situation, agreed, and the new company of Nagelmackers et Cie. gained an endorsement. Soon their stock sales promotion had every social climber in Belgium clamoring to get aboard.

The new company's first train was to run from Paris to Berlin by way of Belgium. Five cars, ordered from a coach-building company in Vienna, arrived in early July to begin service later in the month. Then, on July 19, 1870, France declared war on Prussia. Discouraged, but still determined, Nagelmackers negotiated a route from Ostend, Belgium, through France, and down to Brindisi. The route was very successful—for one year. Then, on September 17, 1871, the French opened a tunnel through the Alps under Mount Cenis. Rights were reserved for French-owned rail-roads, so Nagelmackers was forced to continue using the much longer (18 hours) route through the Brenner Pass. As losses mounted, the service was reduced. With only ten cars as assets and debts far exceeding his capital, Nagelmackers disbanded the company and formed a new one under a name that was to become world famous: La Compagnie Internationale des Wagons-Lits. The company was struggling along, only slightly better off than the old one, when Nagelmackers received a letter inviting him to come to London to "discuss matters of mutual commercial interest." The invitation was from Colonel William Mann of Perkins, Ohio. Although charming and urbane, Mann was fundamentally dishonest. He once ran a tavern—profitable only because he didn't pay his bills. Later he sold stock in a non-existent oil field, collected taxes for the federal government (he turned in $4.7 million and pocketed $5 million), and ran several railroad-related swindles. His last misadventure in America was an attempt to compete with George Pullman using Mann-designed boudoir cars. Rather than having seats that converted into beds, each Mann car was divided into two separate sections, one for sitting and one—with real beds—for sleeping. The cars accommodated only 16 passengers, half the number who could share a Pullman, and cost more to build; thus they were quite unprofitable. Mann soon admitted defeat and took two of his cars to England where he held lavish receptions to drum up interest in them. The European railroad executives were unenthusiastic, except for young Nagelmackers who swallowed hook, line, and sinker everything Mann told him about his grandiose plans. Moreover, he even agreed to make his company a subsidiary of the Mann Boudoir Sleeping Car Company.

Nagelmackers, with boundless energy, traveled around Europe trying to sell cars to kings, nobles, and anyone else he thought could afford one. He quickly sold more than 50 cars and, in the process, became more convinced that there was a need for luxury train service across Europe. By now completely disenchanted with Mann, who was in London enjoying himself on the money that was rolling in, Nagelmackers and his financial backers bought him out for $5 million and reinstituted the company under its old name in 1876.

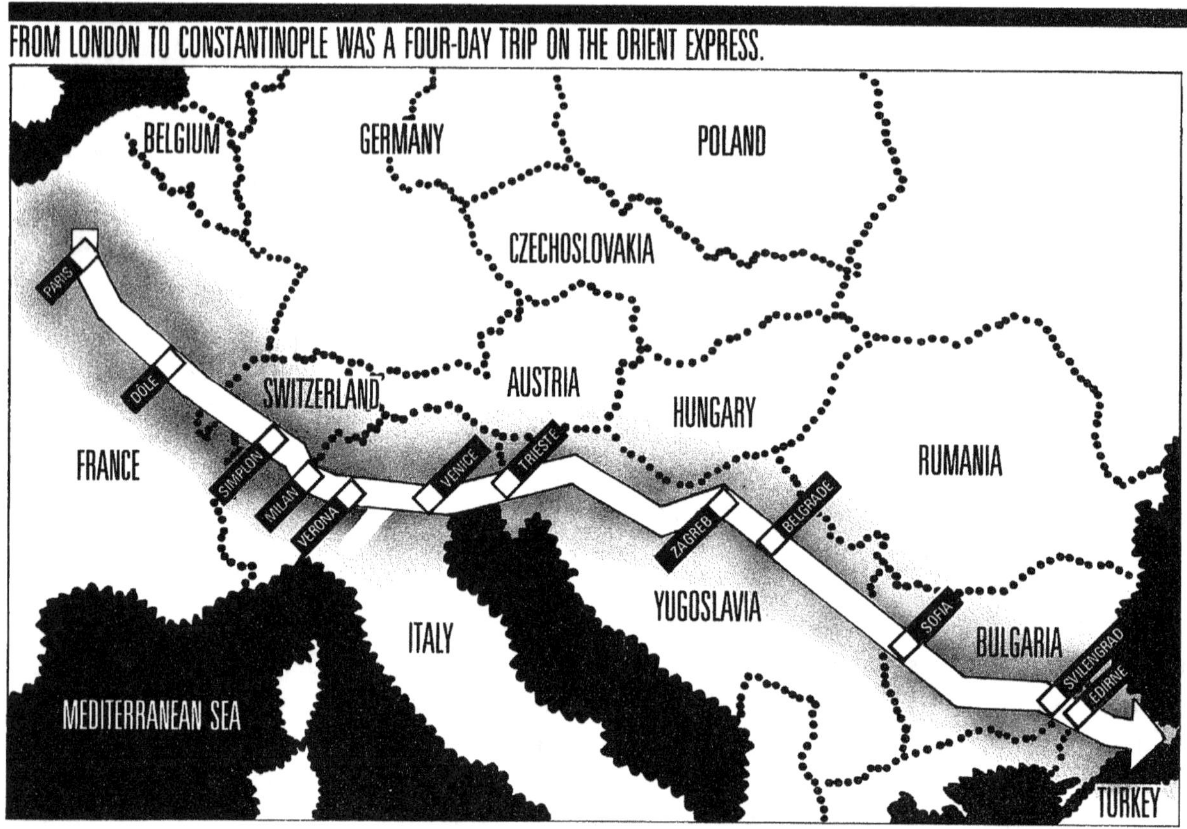

FROM LONDON TO CONSTANTINOPLE WAS A FOUR-DAY TRIP ON THE ORIENT EXPRESS.

Railroad executives were not convinced that the luxury service Nagelmackers described would be profitable, so they granted him only a few short-term contracts to attach some of his cars to various trains between Paris and Vienna, Paris and Cologne, Ostend and Berlin, and some other routes of less consequence. To the amazement of everyone but Nagelmackers, the cars were well patronized and frequently sold out. With some assistance from the influential King Leopold II, Nagelmackers started negotiating with many European countries, states, and kingdoms for a route from Paris to Constantinople. It took him almost a year to reach agreements with the eight national railway companies involved: the Eastern Railroad Company of France, the Imperial Railways of Alsace-Lorraine, the Kingdom of Württemburg State Railways, the Grand Duchy of Baden State Railways, the Royal Bavarian Lines of Communication, the Imperial and Royal Austrian State Railways, the Royal Rumanian Railways, and the Austrian Lloyd Shipping Company (for the last section by sea to Constantinople).

The route selected by Nagelmackers ran from Paris through Strasbourg, Munich, Salzburg, Vienna, Budapest, and Bucharest to Giurgiu on the Danube in Rumania. From there, the passengers were obliged to take a ferry across the river to Rustchuk, Bulgaria, where Nagelmackers had made a somewhat shaky arrangement for a special train to take them on to Varna (a port on the Black Sea coast). From there, a steamer took the passengers on an 18-hour sea voyage to Constantinople. Scheduled time was 81 hours and 40 minutes eastbound and 77 hours and 49 minutes westbound.

The service had no formal name, but newspapers quickly dubbed it the Orient Express, and Nagelmackers decided to make the inaugural run on October 4, 1883 under this name. The train was made up of two sleeping cars, a restaurant car, a luggage van, and a mail van. Each sleeping car had five compartments, each of which accommodated four people in comfortable bench seats by day and four berths at night. Washbasins and toilet compartments were at one end of each car. The large number of journalists invited on the inaugural run furnished many memorable accounts of the occasion. Nagelmackers spared no effort to ensure the success of the trip; elaborate food, excellent wine, beautiful crystal and linen, and impeccable service combined to create an ambience of unmistakable elegance and grandeur. In addition, many official receptions and welcomes were held along the way. Hungarian minstrels boarded the train at Szegedin and played vigorously for more than two hours without a stop. Passengers were even invited to the castle of the rather morose King of Bulgaria. Thus the most famous train of all time was put into service. After the euphoria of the inaugural trip wore off, the Orient Express settled into a regular routine. By 1884, it had become a daily service as far as Budapest and, a year later, to Bucharest with several alternative routings onward. By 1889, a link of track near Nish, Bulgaria, was finished, which meant that finally the same coaches could travel all the way from Paris to Constantinople. The route then became important for mail as well as passengers. Nagelmackers died of a heart attack on July 10, 1905, two weeks after his sixtieth birthday. He did not live to see the opening of the Simplon Tunnel, an incredibly important link through the Alps between Switzerland and Italy. Almost immediately, Wagons-Lits began to offer service between Paris and Venice. This became known as the Venice Simplon Orient Express (V-S-O-E) and is the only service still in operation today, thanks to its meticulous restoration by James Sherwood in 1982.

People often think of the Orient Express as one train running one route. In fact, the company operated more than 1000 coaches on routes throughout Europe and the Near East with such destinations as Lisbon, Madrid, Naples, Ankara, Beirut, Baghdad, Saint Petersburg, Berlin, Amsterdam, and London. From 1908 until the new communist regime appropriated the company's cars and property in 1919, Wagons-Lits operated all the Trains de Luxe on the Trans-Siberian Railway.

During the Great War (now called World War I), many Wagons-Lits services were halted, and because of the German occupation of Belgium, the company was forced to move to Paris. Prior to the war, the Simplon service terminated in Trieste, then a part of the Austrian Empire, because Austrian authorities would not permit international trains to traverse the Empire without stopping in Vienna. However, the Treaty of Versailles, which ended the War, specified that new international through routes be opened in Italy, Trieste, and the newly created country of Yugoslavia, formerly the southern part of the Austrian Empire.

Thus, a new and much faster southern route via the Simplon Tunnel and across Italy and Yugoslavia to Constantinople was inaugurated on April 11, 1919. A few years later, the route was extended on the western end to London, creating probably the single most popular route of the Orient Express. This route was in service until the Germans occupied France during World War II, and then reinstated from the end of the war until the last run on May 19, 1977. The train ran from London to Paris, through the Mont d'Or tunnel to Lausanne and Brig, through the Simplon Tunnel to Milan, Venice, and Trieste, and into Yugoslavia. A second train, originating in Munich, met the first train in Ljubljana, and continuing cars were joined for the run to Belgrade. At Crveni Krst the train was divided, some cars being routed to Athens and the main train going to Constantinople via Sofia, Bulgaria. The trip from London to Constantinople took exactly 96 hours and the train was rarely late. While the train was occasionally slowed by snow, it generally made up the lost time on the straight runs in France and Italy. One exception was in February 1929, when the train was marooned for six days in huge snowdrifts near Cherkes Keui, just 70 miles from Constantinople. Indeed, in its long history, the Orient Express suffered very few mishaps. Minor accidents occurred in January 1901, when a locomotive jumped the rails and ran into the restaurant hall of the Frankfurt-am-Main Central Station, and in November 1911, when the Orient Express ran into a stationary freight train near Vitry-le-Francois because of incorrectly set signals. No one was seriously injured in either of these accidents. On the other hand, holdups in the Balkan areas near the end of the run occurred with disturbing frequency in the early days of the Express. As political stability increased in the '30s, however, the number of railway robberies declined. On any given run of the Orient Express one could be certain that deals were being made, plots were being hatched, and fortunes were changing hands. The booking lists in the archives of the train company read like pages from the *International Who's Who*. Royalty from Europe and the East were frequent passengers on the Orient Express as were military officers, entertainers, musicians, bankers, industrialists, bishops, and, of course, spies. The train was known to be a hotbed of intrigue and mystery.

Basil Zaharoff, the notorious arms dealer, always reserved all the seats in compartment seven for himself when he rode the train. The dancer Margaretha Gertrud Zelle, otherwise known as Mata Hari, was a frequent passenger, and Lord Kitchener traveled on the train as a young military intelligence officer gathering information about Austrian and Turkish fortifications. But we'll never know the identities of most of the spies, secret agents, saboteurs, and couriers who repeatedly crossed the continent on mysterious missions. All of which leads us to speculate and wonder: What was it really like to travel the Orient Express?

BIBLIOGRAPHY

Barsley, Michael. *The Orient Express*. London: Macdonald & Co., 1966.

Cookridge, E. H. *Orient Express*. New York: Random House, 1978.

Sherwood, Shirley. *Venice Simplon Orient-Express*. London: Weidenfeld & Nicolson, 1983.

THE PROGRAM

The Orient Express program consists of a main program, initialization section, end-game section, nine major subroutines, and nine short subroutines.

In the initialization section, text and numeric data are read into variables in four separate subroutines. These subroutines use as data files: mealsetc.txt, statements.txt, passengers.txt, menus.txt.

The last function performed in the initialization section is the shuffling of 24 integers. These are used later to determine the order in which the conversations with various passengers occur. Shuffling is an important function in many games, particularly those involving cards. In mathematical terms, shuffling is defined as a random permutation, that is, generating the numbers from 1 to N in a random order without repetition. Consider this routine, commonly found in beginning programming texts, for shuffling 10 integers into M[1] to M[10]:

```
For I = 1 To 10
LN20:
  K = Math.Floor(1 + 10 * Math.GetRandomNumber(999)/1000)
  For J = 1 To I
    If M[J] = K Then
      GoTo LN20
    EndIf
  EndFor
  M[I] = K
EndFor
```

A random number between 1 and 10 is generated in LN20. This is then checked against all of the elements of M to see if it has already been used; if not, the current element of M, that is, M[I], is set equal to K. If it has been used, a new value of K is generated in LN20. The routine is short, easy to understand, and horribly inefficient (the execution speed is proportional to the square of the numbers to be shuffled).

Consider this approach:

```
For I = 1 To 10
  M[I] = I
EndFor
For I = 1 To 9
  K = I + Math.Floor((11 - I) * Math.GetRandomNumber(999)/1000)
  T = M[I]
  M[K] = M[I]
  M[I] = T
EndFor
```

The execution speed for this code is much faster than the previous algorithm, as it is proportional to two times the numbers to be shuffled. The heart of the algorithm is found at first line of the second For loop. The first time through the loop, this function selects a random integer between 1 and 10; the second time through, between 2 and 10; the third time, between 3 and 10; and so on. The elements chosen are then exchanged with the values currently in those elements. If we think of the elements as cards, we could think of picking up one random card at a time from the deck, placing it on a pile, and then picking the next card. The final pile will thus be thoroughly shuffled. In the program, this subroutine is found at Sub2760.

The main program prints the scenario and then iterates through the 24 segments of the train journey. For each segment, the date is printed followed by the location and the arrival time. The scheduled arrival time is found in the data variable TA[n] The actual arrival time is determined by a random function at LN310 and can be from 8 minutes early to 18 minutes late.

In some cases this function will produce a time like 271 or 1460. This problem is cured in the subroutine that prints out the time (Sub3060). The last two digits of the time are examined at the beginning of the subroutine, and if they are found to exceed 59, one hour is added and 60 minutes are subtracted; this is accomplished by simply adding the integer 40 to the numeric value of the time. This subroutine then divides the time into strings representing hours and minutes and prints it in the correct format such as 3:11 or 15:00. The integer 10000 is added to the numeric value of the time so that the leading zeroes will be printed.

If an intermediate station is reached at night during sleeping hours, arrival and departure times are simply noted, and the program proceeds. If the stop is during waking hours, you are given a chance to get off the train and stretch your legs.

On the first segment of the trip out of London, you ask passengers to keep alert for information of value. Each segment of the trip has a series of data values which indicate the number of conversations with passengers that can take place (CN[n]), the meal to be served (ME[n]), and the potential hazards (HZ[n]). After the subroutines for each of these items are called, the program goes on to the next trip segment.

The breakfast and dinner subroutines (Sub640 and Sub770) are similar. Each one asks if you are ready to go to the restaurant car for the meal and waits until you press Enter. The menu is then presented. Menu items are selected at random and printed on the screen. Items are centered by CursorLeft and CursorTop statements, which takes the length of the item, 80 (the width of the screen), divides by two, and moves the cursor to that location to start printing. At the conclusion of the meal, you press Enter to clear the screen, in the Sub2950.

The subroutine (Sub860) to present the conversations you have with the passengers iterates through the conversations, if any, on the current trip segment. If a conversation is to be held, the number of that conversation, CS[CM], is selected from the previously shuffled list.The length of the string containing the conversation is checked. If it is fewer than 80 characters long, it is displayed on one screen line. If it is longer than 80 characters, the For loop using KA starts iterating from the 79th character backward looking for a space. When one is found, the left side of the string up to that point (the first part of the conversation) is printed and, on the next line, the right side of the string from the space on is printed (the last part of the conversation).

Two subroutines for hazards—snowdrifts, bandits, and derailments—are nearly identical except for the dialog. There is a 65% chance of snow on three of the trip segments (top of Sub970). If it is snowing heavily, there is a 1% chance of getting stuck in a snowdrift.

If this happens, the trip is delayed for two days until the snow is cleared from the tracks. This routine could be made much more elaborate to simulate the time the train was stuck in a snowdrift for six days in 1929. However, that was an isolated incident, and every other time the train was stuck it resulted only in a delay and very little discomfort to the passengers.

On two trip segments in Bulgaria and Turkey, there is a 4% chance that bandits will board the train and rob the passengers. On the actual Orient Express robberies were an infrequent occurrence and, except for two instances in May and October 1891 when people on the train were kidnapped and held for ransom, bandits rarely hurt anyone, being content to steal money and jewelry.

On all trip segments there is a 2% chance of a derailment. In the event that this occurs, the locomotive, tender, and first mail coach will leave the track, and you will be stranded somewhere for a day until the track is repaired and a replacement locomotive obtained.

The probability of any of the above three hazards occurring in the program is much higher than it was in actuality. However, if the probabilities were reduced to the few thousandths of one percent that existed in reality, you might have to play the game tens of thousands of times to experience even a single misadventure.

The final major subroutine (Sub1490) checks the identities of the killer and defector that you input in the previous subroutine (Sub1340) with the actual identity. There are seven possible situations which can lead to any of five different eventual outcomes (see chart).

IF YOU DO THIS			THEN THIS HAPPENS	
Killer identified as	Defector identified as	Defector killed by bandits	You killed by killer	Defector wrongly arrested
Killer	Defector	No	No	No
Killer	Nobody	Yes	No	No
Nobody	Defector	No	Yes	No
Nobody	Nobody	Yes	Yes	No
Nobody	Killer	No	Yes	Yes
Defector	Nobody	Yes	Yes	No
Defector	Killer	No	Yes	Yes

The correct dialog for the three possible nasty events (defector killed, you killed, and defector wrongly arrested) can be selected with just three IF...THEN statements. If you get both identities correct, the indicator A5 is set equal to 1 so that you receive a congratulatory message when you arrive in Constantinople.

The short subroutines (Sub2760) are all self-explanatory; they simply produce pauses in program execution, make train noises, check for yes/no answers, and the like. The end-game segment (Sub3190) presents an end-game message, displays a message of congratulations if you got both identities correct, and stops the program.

PROGRAM VARIABLES

```
A Answer of user (0 = yes, 1 = no)
AD Answer to string-input query, user input
A1, A2 Answer to identity of defector and killer, user input
A3, A4 Actual identity of defector and killer
A5 Indicates if user identifications were correct
CD[n] Conversations of passengers, n = 1 - 24
CM Conversation number, index of CS
CN[n] Number of conversations per trip segment, n = 1 - 24
CP[n] Conversation indicator (0 = passenger, 1 = waiter, 2 = cook), n = 1 -
24
CS[n] Conversation number, n = 1 - 24
DA[n] Day of trip by trip segment, n = 1 - 24
HW Hazard, derailment indicator
HX Hazard, bandit-attack indicator
HY Hazard delay in days
HZ[n] Hazards on each trip segment, n = 1 - 24
I Index indicator
J Trip-segment indicator
K, KA Index indicators
LAD[n] City, n = 1 - 24
LBD[n] Country, n = 1 - 24
MBD[n] Meal, breakfast, name of menu item, n = 1 - 13
MDD[n] Meal, dinner, name of menu item, n = 1 - 25
ME[n] Meal indicator by trip segment, n = 1 - 24
ND[n] Names of passengers, n = 1 - 25
RN Random seed for random-number generator
T Time, temporary for printing
TD Time, string variable, temporary for printing
TA[n] Time of arrival, scheduled, by trip segment, n = 1 - 24
TB Time of arrival, actual
TD[n] Time of departure by trip segment, n = 1 - 24
TN Time, minutes early or late
X Temporary variable
XD Temporary string variable
```

PROGRAM LISTINGS

```
TextWindow.CursorTop = 10
TextWindow.CursorLeft = 27
TextWindow.WriteLine("The Orient Express, 1923")
TextWindow.CursorTop = 13
TextWindow.CursorLeft = 28
TextWindow.WriteLine("(c) David H. Ahl, 1986")
TextWindow.CursorTop = 23
TextWindow.CursorLeft = 27
TextWindow.WriteLine("Press Enter to continue.")
JJJ=TextWindow.Read()
TextWindow.Clear()
TextWindow.CursorLeft = 22
TextWindow.WriteLine("The Mysterious Arms Deal")
TextWindow.WriteLine("")
Sub1710()
'
'Initialization
Sub1880()
'Read data about journey segments
Sub2160()
'Read statements of travelers
Sub2430()
'Read names of those on the train
Sub2530()
'Read menu selections
Sub2760()
'Shuffle 24 integers for later use
TextWindow.WriteLine("Press Enter to call a taxi ... ")
JJJ=TextWindow.Read()
'
'Main program
For J = 1 To 24
'Iterate through locations
TextWindow.WriteLine("")
TextWindow.WriteLine("February " + (DA[J] + 13 + HY) +", 1923")
'Print date
LN310:
TN = 18 - Math.Floor(27 * Math.GetRandomNumber(999)/1000)
TB = TA[J] + TN
T = TB
If J = 1 Then
  Goto LN450
EndIf
Sub3110()
TextWindow.Write("You have arrived at "+ LAD[J] +", "+ LBD[J] +" at ")
Sub3060()
If TN > 1 Then
  TextWindow.WriteLine("just " +TN+ " minutes late.")
  GOTO LN360
EndIf
```

```
If TN < -1 Then
  TextWindow.WriteLine("almost "+ MATH.Abs(TN) +" minutes early.")
  GOTO LN360
EndIf
TextWindow.WriteLine(" ...  right on time!")
LN360:
If TB > TD[J] -2 Then
  T = TB + 4
ELSE
  T = TD[J] 'Make sure departure is after arrival
EndIf
If J = 24 Then
  Sub3190()
ELSE
  IF ME[J] < 4 THEN
    goto LN400 'Is it daytime?
  EndIf
EndIf
TextWindow.WriteLine("Asleep in your compartment, you barely notice that
the")
TextWindow.Write("departure was right on time at ")
Sub3060()
Sub2860()
Goto LN490
LN400:
If J = 23 Then
  Sub1340() 'Time to identify the killer and defector?
EndIf
TextWindow.Write("Departure is at ")
Sub3060()
TextWindow.WriteLine("")
TextWindow.Write("Would you like to get off and stretch your legs? ")
AD = TextWindow.Read()
Sub2810()
If A = 1 Then
  TextWindow.WriteLine("Okay, you stay in your compartment.")
  GOTO LN470
EndIf
TextWindow.WriteLine("Okay, but be sure not to miss the train.")
Goto LN470
LN450:
TextWindow.WriteLine("The taxi has dropped you at Victoria Station in
London.")
TextWindow.WriteLine("The Orient Express is standing majestically on Track
14.")
LN470:
TextWindow.WriteLine("")
Sound.PlayBellRingAndWait()
Sub2860()
TextWindow.Write("All aboard ... ")
Sub2860()
TextWindow.WriteLine("train is leaving.")
Sub2860()
LN490:
Sub2990()
```

```
'Train noises
Sub2860()
If J > 1 Then
  Goto LN570 'First leg of trip?
EndIf
X = 3 + Math.Floor(20 * Math.GetRandomNumber(999)/1000)
TextWindow.WriteLine("")
TextWindow.WriteLine("You speak to some of the passengers ... " +ND[X]+ ",")
TextWindow.WriteLine(ND[X + 1]+ ", " +ND[X + 2]+ " and others ... and ask
them to keep")
TextWindow.WriteLine("their eyes and ears open and to pass any information
... no")
TextWindow.WriteLine("matter how trivial ... to you in compartment 13. The
Channel")
TextWindow.WriteLine("crossing is pleasant and the first part of the trip
uneventful.")
LN570:
If J = 23 Then
  Sub1490() 'Time to identify the killer and defector?
EndIf
If ME[J] > 0 AND ME[J] < 4 Then
'Meals
  If ME[J] = 1 Then
    Sub770()
  ElseIf ME[J] = 2 Then
    Sub720()
  ElseIf ME[J] = 3 Then
    Sub640()
  EndIf
EndIf
Sub860()
'Talk to passengers
If HZ[J] > 0 Then
  'Snow or bandits on this leg?
  If HZ[J] = 1 Then
    Sub970()
  ElseIf HZ[J] = 2 Then
    Sub1110()
  EndIf
EndIf
Sub1220()
'Other hazards
EndFor
'
Sub Sub640
'Subroutine to serve breakfast
TextWindow.WriteLine("")
TextWindow.WriteLine("Breakfast is now being served in the restaurant car.")
TextWindow.WriteLine("Press Enter when you're ready to have breakfast.")
JJJ = TextWindow.Read()
TextWindow.Clear()
TextWindow.CursorTop = 3
TextWindow.CursorLeft = 33
TextWindow.WriteLine("BREAKFAST MENU")
For I = 1 To 4
```

```
X = 3 * (I - 1) + 1 + Math.Floor(3 * Math.GetRandomNumber(999)/1000)
TextWindow.CursorTop = 4 + 3 * I
TextWindow.CursorLeft = (80 - Text.GetLength(MBD[X])) / 2
TextWindow.WriteLine(MBD[X])
EndFor
TextWindow.CursorTop = 19
TextWindow.CursorLeft = 20
TextWindow.WriteLine(MBD[13])
Sub2950()
EndSub
'
Sub Sub720
'Subroutine to serve lunch
TextWindow.WriteLine("")
TextWindow.Write("An enormous buffet luncheon has been laid out in the ")
TextWindow.WriteLine("restaurant car.")
TextWindow.Write("Press Enter when you have finished.")
JJJ=TextWindow.Read()
TextWindow.WriteLine(" B-U-R-P !")
EndSub
'
Sub Sub770
'Subroutine to serve dinner
TextWindow.WriteLine("")
TextWindow.WriteLine("Dinner is now being served in the restaurant car.")
TextWindow.WriteLine("Press Enter when you're ready to have dinner.")
JJJ=TextWindow.Read()
TextWindow.Clear()
TextWindow.CursorTop = 1
TextWindow.CursorLeft = 34
TextWindow.WriteLine("DINNER MENU")
For I = 1 To 7
X = 3 * (I - 1) + 1 + Math.Floor(3 * Math.GetRandomNumber(999)/1000)
TextWindow.CursorTop = 2 + 2 * I
TextWindow.CursorLeft = (80 - Text.GetLength(MDD[X])) / 2
TextWindow.WriteLine(MDD[X])
EndFor
TextWindow.CursorTop = 18
TextWindow.CursorLeft = 24
TextWindow.WriteLine(MDD[22])
TextWindow.CursorTop = 20
TextWindow.CursorLeft = 30
TextWindow.WriteLine(MDD[23])
TextWindow.CursorTop = 22
TextWindow.CursorLeft = 33
TextWindow.WriteLine(MDD[24])
Sub2950()
EndSub
'
Sub Sub860
'Subroutine to have conversations
For K = 1 To CN[J]
'Iterate through conversations in this trip segment
Sub2890()
CM = CM + 1
```

```
'Ring compartment buzzer and open door
If CP[CS[CM]] > 0 Then
X = CP[CS[CM]]
ELSE
X = 3 + Math.Floor(23 * Math.GetRandomNumber(999)/1000)
EndIf
TextWindow.WriteLine("Standing there is "+ND[X]+ ", who tells you: ")
X = CS[CM]
If Text.GetLength(CD[X]) < 81 Then
TextWindow.WriteLine(CD[X])
GOTO LN950 'If short message, print it
EndIf
CS[CN] = CS[CM]
For KA = 79 To 1 Step -1
If Text.GetSubText(CD[X], KA, 1)=" " Then
  Goto LN999 'Find a space near end of line
EndIf
EndFor
LN999:
TextWindow.WriteLine(Text.getsubtext(CD[X], 1, KA))
TextWindow.WriteLine(Text.GetSubTextToEnd(CD[X], KA + 1))
LN950:
EndFor
EndSub
'
Sub Sub970
'Subroutine for snow
X = Math.GetRandomNumber(999)/1000
If X > .65 Then
  Goto LN1099 '65% chance of snow
EndIf
TextWindow.WriteLine("")
TextWindow.Write("It is snowing heavily ")
If X < .01 Then
  Goto LN1030 '1% chance of getting stuck in the snow
EndIf
TextWindow.WriteLine("but the tracks have been cleared and the train")
TextWindow.WriteLine("will not be delayed.")
Goto LN1099
LN1030:
TextWindow.WriteLine("and the train is forced to slow down.")
TextWindow.WriteLine("")
TextWindow.WriteLine("Oh no! The train is coming to a stop. Let's hope this
is")
TextWindow.WriteLine("not a repeat of the trip of January 29, 1929 when the
Orient")
TextWindow.WriteLine("Express was stuck in snowdrifts for five days.")
TextWindow.WriteLine("")
Sub2860()
TextWindow.WriteLine("But it looks like it is!")
Sub2860()
TextWindow.WriteLine("You are stranded for two days until a snowplow clears
the track.")
TextWindow.WriteLine("The train is now exactly two days behind schedule.")
HY = HY + 2
```

```
LN1099:
EndSub
'
Sub Sub1110
'Subroutine for bandits
If Math.GetRandomNumber(999)/1000 > .04 Then
  Goto ln1209 '4% chance of bandits
EndIf
If HX = 1 Then
Goto ln1209
ELSE
HX = 1 'Only one bandit attack
EndIf
TextWindow.WriteLine("")
TextWindow.WriteLine("You are rudely awakened from a deep sleep by a loud
noise")
TextWindow.WriteLine("as the train jerks to a halt.")
Sub2890()
TextWindow.WriteLine("You are shocked to see a bandit waving a gun in your
face.")
TextWindow.WriteLine("He demands that you give him your wallet, jewelry, and
watch.")
TextWindow.WriteLine("")
Sub2860()
TextWindow.WriteLine("The bandits are off the train in a few moments with")
TextWindow.WriteLine("their loot. They disappear into the forest. No one")
TextWindow.WriteLine("was injured, and the train resumes its journey.")
LN1209:
EndSub
'
Sub Sub1220
'Subroutine to deal with miscellaneous hazards
If Math.GetRandomNumber(999)/1000 > .02 Then
  Goto Ln1329 '2% chance of derailment
EndIf
If HW = 1 Then
Goto Ln1329
ELSE
HW = 1 'Only one derailment
EndIf
TextWindow.WriteLine("")
TextWindow.WriteLine("You hear a loud screeching noise as the train comes to
a")
TextWindow.WriteLine("crashing stop. The engine, tender, and first coach
are")
TextWindow.WriteLine("leaning at a crazy angle. People are screaming.")
Sub2860()
TextWindow.WriteLine("")
TextWindow.WriteLine("While not as bad as the derailment at Vitry-le-Francois
in")
TextWindow.WriteLine("November 1911, there is no question that the front of
the")
TextWindow.WriteLine("train has left the track.")
Sub2860()
TextWindow.WriteLine("")
```

```
TextWindow.WriteLine("You are stranded for exactly one day while the track
is")
TextWindow.WriteLine("repaired and a new locomotive obtained.")
HY = HY + 1
LN1329:
EndSub
'
Sub Sub1340
'Subroutine to identify defector and killer
TextWindow.WriteLine("")
TextWindow.WriteLine("The Turkish police have boarded the train. They have
been")
TextWindow.WriteLine("asked to assist you, but for them to do so you will
have to")
TextWindow.WriteLine("identify the killer (the dealer in machine guns) and
the defector")
TextWindow.WriteLine("(the Scotch drinker) to them. The arms dealers are
lined")
TextWindow.WriteLine("up as follows:")
TextWindow.WriteLine("")
TextWindow.Write(" (1) Austrian, (2) Turk, ")
TextWindow.WriteLine("(3) Pole, (4) Greek, (5) Rumanian.")
TextWindow.WriteLine("")
TextWindow.Write("Who is the defector (a number please)? ")
A1 = TextWindow.ReadNumber()
TextWindow.Write("and who is the killer? ")
A2 = TextWindow.ReadNumber()
Sub2860()
TextWindow.WriteLine("")
TextWindow.WriteLine("The police take into custody the man you identified as
the")
TextWindow.WriteLine("killer and provide a guard to ride on the train with
the")
TextWindow.WriteLine("defector. You return to your compartment, praying
that")
TextWindow.WriteLine("you made the correct deductions and identified the
right men.")
TextWindow.WriteLine("")
Sub2860()
EndSub
'
Sub Sub1490
'Subroutine to check the identities
If A1 = A3 OR A1 = A4 Then
  Goto LN1600 'Defector saved?
EndIf
TextWindow.WriteLine("")
TextWindow.WriteLine("You are suddenly awakened by what sounded like a
gunshot.")
TextWindow.WriteLine("You rush to the defector's compartment, but he is
okay.")
TextWindow.WriteLine("However, one of the other arms dealers has been shot.")
Sub2860()
TextWindow.WriteLine("")
```

```
TextWindow.WriteLine("You review the details of the case in your mind and
realize")
TextWindow.WriteLine("that you came to the wrong conclusion and due to your
mistake")
TextWindow.WriteLine("a man lies dead at the hands of bandits. You return to
your")
TextWindow.WriteLine("compartment and are consoled by the thought that you
correctly")
TextWindow.WriteLine("identified the killer and that he will hang for his
crimes.")
'
LN1600:
If A2 = A4 Then
A5 = 1
Goto LN1699 'Killer is still on the train
EndIf
Sub2890()
TextWindow.WriteLine("A man is standing outside. He says, 'You made a")
TextWindow.WriteLine("mistake. A bad one. You see, I am the machine-gun
dealer.")
If A1<>A4 Then
  Goto LN1660 'Wrongly identified defector as killer?
EndIf
TextWindow.WriteLine("Moreover, you incorrectly identified the man who was
cooperating")
TextWindow.WriteLine("with you as the killer. So the state will take care of
him. Ha.")
LN1660:
TextWindow.WriteLine("")
Sub2860()
TextWindow.WriteLine("He draws a gun. BANG. You are dead.")
TextWindow.WriteLine("")
TextWindow.WriteLine("You never know that the train arrived at 12:30, right
on")
TextWindow.WriteLine("time at Constantinople, Turkey.")
Sub2860()
Sub2860()
TextWindow.WriteLine("")
TextWindow.WriteLine("")
Sub3190()
ln1699:
EndSub
'
Sub Sub1710
'Subroutine to set the scenario
TextWindow.WriteLine(" It is February 1923. The following note is received
at")
TextWindow.WriteLine("Whitehall: 'If you will furnish me with a new identity
and a")
TextWindow.WriteLine("lifetime supply of Scotch, I will give up my life of
arms dealing")
TextWindow.WriteLine("and will provide you with much valuable information. I
will be")
TextWindow.WriteLine("on the Orient Express tonight. But you must contact me
before")
```

```
TextWindow.WriteLine("the train reaches Uzunkopru or that swine dealer of
Maxim machine")
TextWindow.WriteLine("guns will have me killed by bandits like he did to
Baron Wunster")
TextWindow.WriteLine("last month.' The note is not signed.")
TextWindow.WriteLine(" You, a British agent, are assigned to take the train,
rescue")
TextWindow.WriteLine("the defector, and arrest the killer.")
TextWindow.WriteLine(" You know there are five notorious arms dealers of
different")
TextWindow.WriteLine("nationalities operating in Europe under an uneasy truce
as each")
TextWindow.WriteLine("deals in a different kind of weapon. But it is obvious
that the")
TextWindow.WriteLine("truce has ended.")
A4 = A5
TextWindow.WriteLine("")
TextWindow.WriteLine("")
Goto ln2159
TextWindow.WriteLine("Press Enter to call a taxi ... ")
JJJ = TextWindow.Read()
LN2159:
EndSub
'
Sub Sub1880
'subroutine to read meals, ...
CLINE = 1
DataFile = Program.Directory +"\mealsetc.txt"
FileLine = File.ReadLine(DataFile, CLINE)
For I = 1 To 24
  GetNextItem()
  X = NextItem
  GetNextItem()
  ME[I] = NextItem
  GetNextItem()
  HZ[I] = NextItem
  GetNextItem()
  CN[I] = NextItem
  GetNextItem()
  DA[I] = NextItem
  GetNextItem()
  TA[I] = NextItem
  GetNextItem()
  TD[I] = NextItem
  GetNextItem()
  LAD[I] = NextItem
  GetNextItem()
  LBD[I] = NextItem
EndFor
EndSub

Sub GetNextItem
  'find comma in FileLine
  KK = Text.GetIndexOf(FileLine, ",")
  If KK <> 0 Then
```

```
    NextItem = Text.GetSubText(FileLine, 1, KK - 1)
    FileLine = Text.GetSubTextToEnd(FileLine, KK + 1)
  Else
    NextItem = FileLine
    CLINE = CLINE + 1
    FileLine = File.ReadLine(DataFile, CLINE)
  EndIf
EndSub


Sub Sub2160
'Subroutine to read statements of travelers
CLINE = 1
DataFile = Program.Directory +"\statements.txt"
FileLine = File.ReadLine(DataFile, CLINE)
For I = 1 To 24
  GetNextItem()
  CS[I] = NextItem
  GetNextItem()
  CP[I] = NextItem
  GetNextItem()
  CD[I] = NextItem
EndFor
EndSub

Sub Sub2430
'Subroutine to read the names of those on the train
CLINE = 1
DataFile = Program.Directory +"\passengers.txt"
FileLine = File.ReadLine(DataFile, CLINE)
For I = 1 To 25
  GetNextItem()
  ND[I] = NextItem
EndFor
EndSub

Sub Sub2530
'Subroutine to read menus
CLINE = 1
DataFile = Program.Directory +"\menus.txt"
FileLine = File.ReadLine(DataFile, CLINE)
For I = 1 To 13
  GetNextItem()
  MBD[I] = NextItem
EndFor
For I = 1 To 25
  GetNextItem()
  MDD[I] = NextItem
EndFor
EndSub

Sub Sub2760
'Subroutine to shuffle 24 integers
For I = 1 To 23
K = I + Math.Floor((25 - I) * Math.GetRandomNumber(999)/1000)
```

```
X = CS[I]
CS[I] = CS[K]
CS[K] = X
EndFor
EndSub
'
Sub Sub2810
  'Subroutine to check for yes or no answer
  LN2810:
If Text.GetSubText(AD,1, 1) = "Y" OR Text.GetSubText(AD,1, 1) = "y" Then
A = 0
Goto ln2819
EndIf
If Text.GetSubText(AD,1, 1) = "N" OR Text.GetSubText(AD,1, 1) = "n" Then
A = 1
Goto ln2819
EndIf
TextWindow.Write("Please enter Y for 'yes' or N for 'no.' Which is it? ")
AD = TextWindow.Read()
Goto LN2810
LN2819:
EndSub
'
Sub Sub2860
'Subroutine creates a short pause
Program.Delay(1000)
EndSub
'
Sub Sub2890
'Subroutine to ring buzzer and open door
TextWindow.WriteLine("")
TextWindow.WriteLine("Your compartment buzzer rings ... ")
'Ring the buzzer
Sound.PlayAndWait(Program.Directory + "\buzzer1.wav")
TextWindow.WriteLine("Press Enter to open the door.")
JJJ=TextWindow.Read()
EndSub
'
Sub Sub2950
'Subroutine to finish eating
TextWindow.CursorTop = 24
TextWindow.CursorLeft = 18
TextWindow.Write("Press Enter when you have finished eating")
A3 = A3 + 5 * (J + 1) '- POS(X)
jjj=TextWindow.Read()
TextWindow.clear()
EndSub
'
Sub Sub2990
'Subroutine to produce train noises
TextWindow.WriteLine("")
TextWindow.WriteLine("Clackety clack ... clackety clack ... clackety clack")
If Math.GetRandomNumber(999)/1000 > .5 Then
  Goto ln3059
ELSE
```

```
  Sub3110()
EndIf
LN3059:
EndSub
'
Sub Sub3060
'Subroutine to print time
T = T + 10000
If Text.GetSubTextToEnd(T,4) > 59 Then
  T = T + 40
EndIf
TextWindow.WriteLine(Text.GetSubText(T, 2, 2) +":"+Text.GetSubTextToEnd(T,4))
EndSub
'
Sub Sub3110
'Subroutine to blow train whistle
Sound.PlayAndWait(Program.Directory +"\trainsnd.wav")
EndSub
'
Sub Sub3190
'End of journey
TextWindow.WriteLine("")
TextWindow.WriteLine("Your journey has ended. Georges Nagelmackers and the")
TextWindow.WriteLine("management of Cie. Internationale des Wagons-Lits ")
TextWindow.WriteLine("hope you enjoyed your trip on the Orient Express, the")
TextWindow.WriteLine("most famous train in the world.")
TextWindow.WriteLine("")
TextWindow.WriteLine("")
If A5<>1 Then
  Goto LN3310
ELSE
  X = 0
EndIf
TextWindow.WriteLine("Whitehall telegraphs congratulations for identifying
both")
TextWindow.WriteLine("the killer and defector correctly.")
Sub2860()
Sub2860()
LN3310:
TextWindow.Write("Press Enter to End")
AD = TextWindow.Read()
Program.End()
EndSub
```

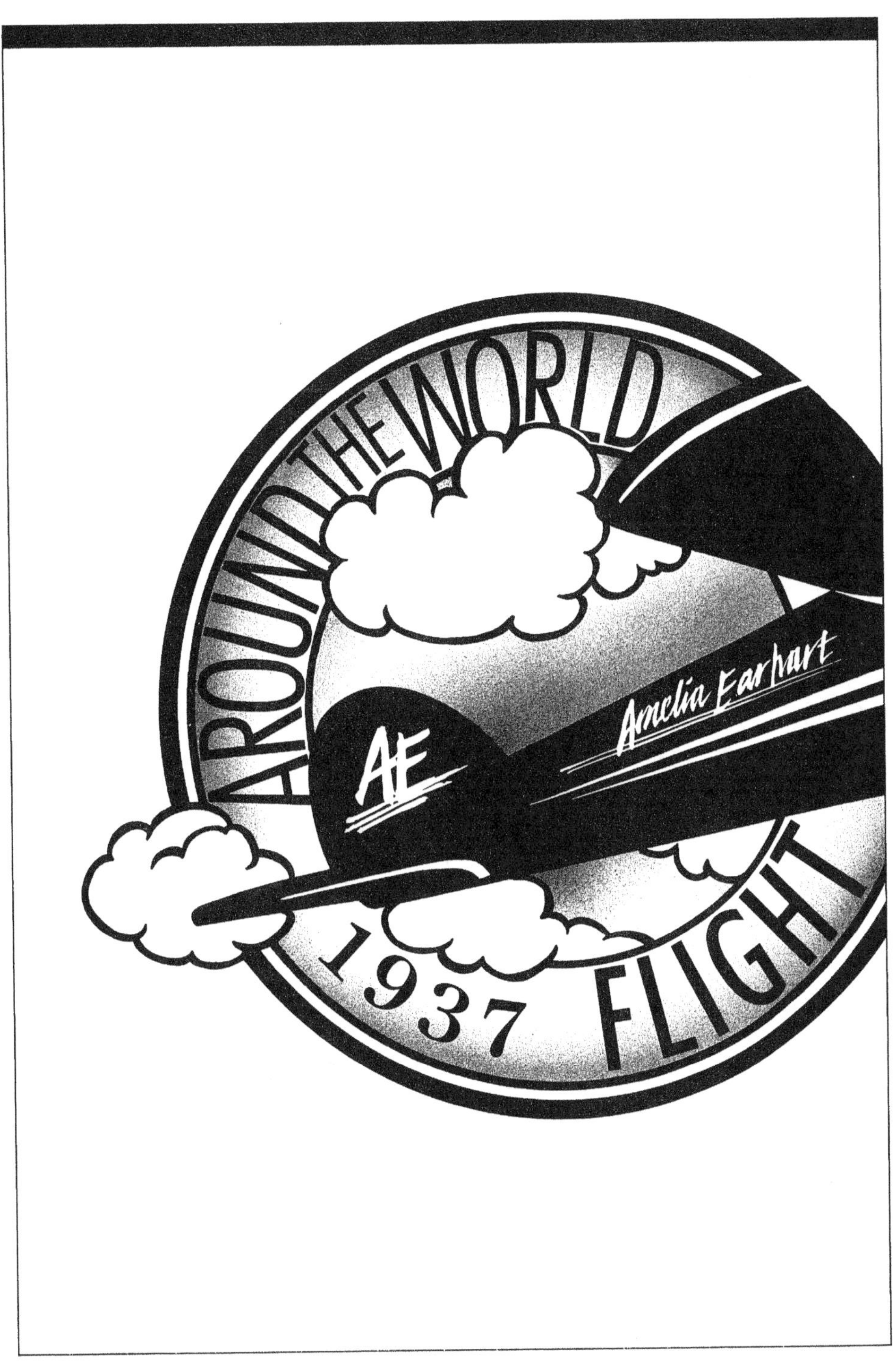
AROUND THE WORLD
Amelia Earhart
AE
1937
FLIGHT

Amelia Earhart: Around the World Flight

In this simulation of Amelia Earhart's around-the-world flight attempt, you take the place of the most famous aviatrix of all time. Flying in the cockpit of a twin-engine Lockheed Electra, you face the same decisions and hazards Amelia Earhart faced in 1937.

Prior to each flight, you are given information about your physical condition, the distance to the next destination, and the current weather. Once aloft, you may encounter a variety of problems: headwinds, heavy rain, engine malfunctions, excessive fuel consumption, and navigation difficulties.

Of course, your skill as an aviator is unquestioned, but to increase your chances of survival, remember the following:

- To find out the condition of the field before each landing, you attempt to contact someone on the ground—sometimes successfully, sometimes not. Should the runway be excessively muddy, you have the option to turn back.
- In case of a malfunction, you are asked if you want to make repairs, which, of course, take time. Not making repairs, however, substantially increases the probability of a major problem in the future.
- Similarly, your engines and other mechanical components will last longer if they are maintained judiciously. Flying for more than 40 hours between engine overhauls dramatically increases the probability of malfunction.
- You must balance the relationship between fuel consumption and weight. At 150 mph, the Electra gets approximately two miles per gallon. Bad weather increases fuel consumption.

As she left New Guinea for Howland Island, Amelia Earhart flew under some of the worst conditions of the trip—as you will discover—and she had to turn back for the Gilbert Islands, a decision that ultimately led to her death. Can you learn from her mistakes and make it to Howland, Hawaii, and finally back to Oakland?

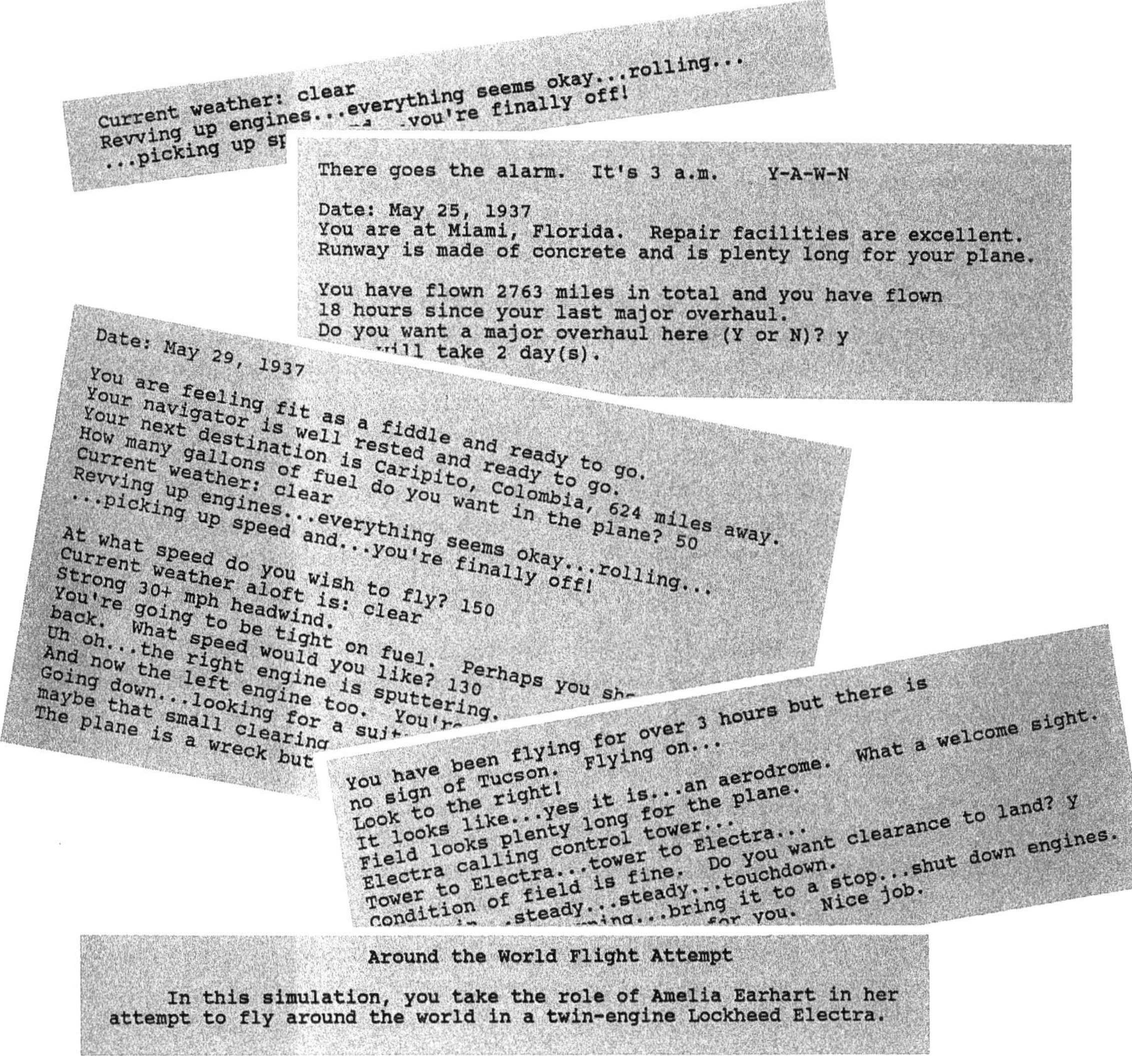

Current weather: clear
Revving up engines...everything seems okay...rolling...
There goes the alarm. It's 3 a.m. Y-A-W-N
Date: May 25, 1937
You are at Miami, Florida. Repair facilities are excellent.
Runway is made of concrete and is plenty long for your plane.
You have flown 2763 miles in total and you have flown
18 hours since your last major overhaul.
Do you want a major overhaul here (Y or N)? y
Date: May 29, 1937
You are feeling fit as a fiddle and ready to go.
Your navigator is well rested and ready to go.
Your next destination is Caripito, Colombia, 624 miles away.
How many gallons of fuel do you want in the plane? 50
Current weather: clear
Revving up engines...everything seems okay...rolling...
...picking up speed and...you're finally off!
At what speed do you wish to fly? 150
Current weather aloft is: clear
Strong 30+ mph headwind.
You're going to be tight on fuel.
back. What speed would you like? 130
Uh oh...the right engine is sputtering.
You have been flying for over 3 hours but there is
no sign of Tucson. Flying on...
Look to the right! What a welcome sight.
It looks like...yes it is...an aerodrome.
Field looks plenty long for the plane.
Electra calling control tower...
Tower to Electra...tower to Electra...
Condition of field is fine. Do you want clearance to land? y
Around the World Flight Attempt
In this simulation, you take the role of Amelia Earhart in her attempt to fly around the world in a twin-engine Lockheed Electra.

THE STORY

In the summer of 1920, on vacation from her pre-med studies at Columbia University, Amelia Earhart took a trip to California. She found the West exhilarating, but what she enjoyed most of all were the air meets, carnival-like affairs with stunt flying and barnstorming. She attended every air meet she could find and was finally rewarded with a chance to ride with the not-yet-famous barnstormer, Frank Hawks. She later recalled the flight: "By the time I had got two or three hundred feet off the ground I knew I had to fly." With some financial help from her understanding mother and against the wishes of her father, she bought her first plane, a secondhand, bright yellow Kinner Canary on her 25th birthday, July 24, 1922. She recalled: "The motor was so rough that my feet went to sleep after more than a few minutes on the rudder bar."

She did what flying she could afford for the next few years. She had dropped out of the pre-med program and taken jobs teaching English to foreign students in Boston and then doing social work at Denison House, one of America's oldest social settlements. Her salary of $60 a month didn't permit much flying, and, in fact, she was so short of cash that she arranged to lend her plane out for demonstrations so as not to be charged hangar storage, which she said, "would have annihilated my salary."

At Denison House in May 1928, she received a phone call from publishing heir and public-relations promoter George Putnam asking if she was interested in doing something dangerous in the air. She recalled, "At first I thought the conversation was a joke and said so. Several times before I had been approached by bootleggers who promised rich reward and no danger. But the frank admission of risk stirred my curiosity. References were demanded and supplied—good references." And then Putnam dropped the bombshell that would change her life forever: "Would you like to be the first woman to fly the Atlantic?"

Amelia's reply was a prompt yes—provided the equipment was adequate and the crew capable. She went to New York that same night and met Putnam. It turned out that he was looking for a female passenger—someone with social grace, education, charm, a pleasant appearance, and not necessarily a pilot. Still, Amelia showed Putnam her pilot's license, the first granted to a woman in the U.S. However, she came away from the meeting feeling that Putnam was not impressed with her credentials.

As it turned out, her impression was dead wrong, and three days later she was formally asked to make the flight. Indeed, Putnam was far more impressed with Amelia than he initally let on, and over the next two years he repeatedly proposed marriage, which she, just as consistently, turned down. Late in the fall of 1930, at the Lockheed factory in Burbank, California, Putnam asked Amelia to marry him. Her resistance worn down, she casually accepted, and they were married on February 7, 1931. In a departure for the 1930s, Amelia continued to use her maiden name, preferring to be called "AE." Similarly, she always called Putnam "GP."

AMELIA EARHART'S ROUTE CLOSELY TRACED THE EQUATOR.

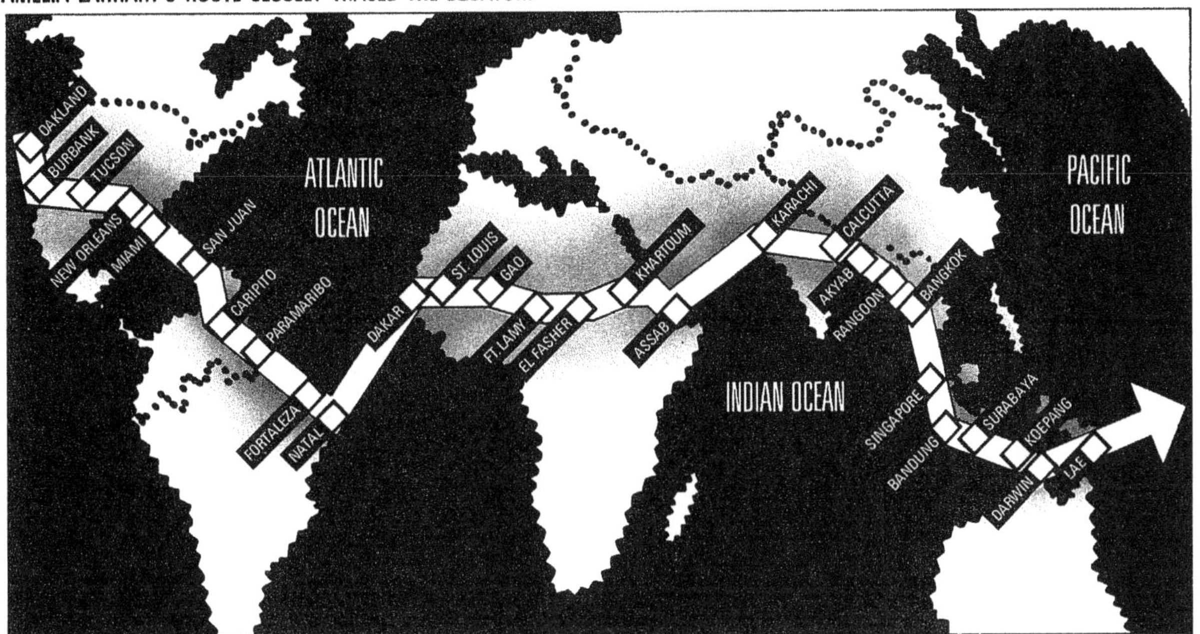

Although AE did not pilot the Atlantic flight, she was appointed honorary captain. As it turned out, this demanded far more courage than anyone anticipated. The plane—called "Friendship"—was a Fokker trimotor seaplane that had been purchased from Commander Richard E. Byrd by Mrs. Frederick (Amy) Guest. Byrd agreed to act as technical consultant for the flight, while pilot Wilmer L. "Bill" Stultz and mechanic Louis "Slim" Gordon prepared the plane itself.

All went according to plan, and on June 3, 1928, the Friendship, carrying Stultz, Gordon, and Earhart, left Boston Harbor on the initial flight leg to Halifax, Nova Scotia. On June 5, the trimotor reached Trepassey, Newfoundland, and was readied for the transoceanic flight leg.

Unfortunately, a long spell of bad weather set in, and the trio was stranded in Trepassey for 13 frustrating days. Faced with absolutely nothing to do, Stultz gave in to his one weakness, alcohol. For the next 12 days Amelia spent as much time with him as possible playing cards, talking, taking him for long walks on the beach, and otherwise trying to distract him from the bottle.

This was not the first time she had had to deal with alcoholism. Years earlier she had helped her mother hold their family together when her father became an alcoholic. When her parents were finally divorced, it was Amelia who paid all his bills and continued to think of him as an upright and virtuous man.

When, over the North Atlantic, a weather "window" finally opened on June 17, Stultz was totally inebriated and unable to rise from his bed under his own power. Putnam later recalled that "AE did what I suppose either was the bravest or silliest act of her whole career .... She simply got hold of her pilot and all but dragged him to the plane. It was a fine-drawn choice. He wasn't in good shape, but perhaps—once he took off—his flying instinct, which was so sure, so complete, would come uppermost."

Stultz tried to take off three times and aborted each time when the plane failed to reach the required 50 mph for liftoff. Finally, on the fourth try, Stultz managed to reach 50 mph, in spite of the two outboard engines "coughing salt water." However, from the moment of takeoff, Stultz drew from a deep reserve of skill and resolve, keeping the Friendship on course for 20 hours and 40 minutes and making an excellent landing at Burry Port, Wales, on the morning of June 18.

As she was not the pilot, Amelia expected the trip to be nothing more than an interesting adventure, after which she would slip back into a life of social work and anonymity. However, it was she who received most of the attention at receptions in Southampton and London. There was to be no return to her old way of life.

From then on, her life became a whirlwind of publicity tours, article writing, and, occasionally, flying. Putnam frequently arranged lecture tours consisting of as many as 27 or 28 engagements in a single month, with barely enough time to get from one to another.

Although she consoled herself that she was doing the causes of both aviation and women some good, she was sorely disappointed that because of her "success," she actually had less time to fly than before. Indeed, in 1932 she confided to some of her friends in the Ninety-Nines, a women's flying group, that she felt a fraud at times because of her lack of experience. As author Vincent Loomis observed in his book, *Amelia Earhart: The Final Story*, "There was little doubt that she was sincere in wanting to promote the cause of women in aviation, but there was not much regard for her ability as a pilot and she knew it. It was time to make a true record flight."

And make it, she did. Not just one, but many. On May 20, 1932, Earhart piloted a Lockheed Vega across the Atlantic, becoming the first woman to do so. Although her goal had been to land in Paris, she flew through five wicked hours of stormy North Atlantic weather and was forced to land in a meadow near Londonderry, Ireland. Nevertheless, five years to the day after Lindberg made the first solo flight across the Atlantic, she duplicated his feat. A few months later, on August 24, 1932, she set the women's transcontinental speed record, flying nonstop from Los Angeles to Newark in 19 hours and 5 minutes.

A year later, in July 1933, she entered the Bendix east-to-west transcontinental race. She was the third competitor to finish and the first woman. Six days later, flying back to Newark, she broke her own record, making the cross-country flight in 17 hours and 7 minutes.

In January 1934, six Navy aircraft made the first Pacific crossing from the mainland to Hawaii. Amelia resolved to do the same flight—solo—as soon as possible, but a heavy lecture schedule prevented her from attempting it until a year later. On Christmas Day 1934, Amelia's faithful

Vega was lashed to the aft tennis deck of a Matson cruise ship bound for Hawaii. Shortly after the first of the year, she and the plane were ready for the flight to the mainland. Unfortunately, the weather was not ready; torrential rains doused everyone's spirits for nearly a week. Finally, on the afternoon of January 11, 1935, the weather cleared enough for Amelia to slip out on what she announced was a test flight. Of course, it was no test flight and, after flying through the night and landing at Oakland, California, 2400 miles later, Amelia Earhart became the first person, male or female, to fly solo across any part of the Pacific Ocean. Now she was a legend in truth as well as in Putnam's public-relations campaigns.

Earhart made one more record flight, a 2185-mile trip from Mexico City to Newark nonstop in 14 hours and 19 minutes on May 8, 1935, before turning her attention to preparing for and financing a round-the-world flight attempt.

Amelia was increasingly uncomfortable flying single-engine planes over large bodies of water, so she decided she must have a twin-engine plane for the round-the-world attempt. Moreover, special fuel tanks and a fuel-management system would have to be fitted for the long Pacific Ocean flight legs. Also, a Sperry autopilot was to be installed to give Amelia some relief on the longer flight legs.

While Putnam was busy trying to raise money and obtain political support, Paul Mantz, AE's technical advisor, began to prepare the plane, and Amelia began as tight a flight-training regimen as she could squeeze between her lecture tours. (She gave 150 lectures in 1936.) She also had to learn to fly the Lockheed Electra, a relatively large twin-engine, 10-passenger transport plane.

In August and September 1936, Amelia, along with Mantz and mechanic Bo McKneely, made several long-distance shakedown flights. It was a good thing that they did. On one flight the fuel system didn't work properly, and the recently-installed navigation hatch blew open.

As the planning progressed, it became quite apparent that Amelia would not be able to fly the Electra and navigate at the same time. Thus it was decided that she would take along a navigator, at least for the Pacific Ocean flight legs. Harry Manning, a ship's captain who had explained the rudiments of celestial navigation to AE on the way back from England in 1928, was selected as the navigator.

Amelia decided to give Manning a small practical test of his abilities, and in early January 1937 she took him far out over the Pacific and asked him to plot a course back to Los Angeles. On the return, they hit the California coast about 200 miles north of Los Angeles. AE claimed the navigation was in error, while Manning said Amelia flew off course and tended to drift consistently to the left when trying to follow a heading. In any event, both of them agreed that an assistant navigator would be a wise precaution on the Pacific flights.

The best choice for an assistant navigator seemed to be Fred Noonan, one of Pan Am's finest navigators—at least until just two months earlier when the airline had fired him for drinking on the job. Pan Am manager Harry Drake recalled of Noonan, "Many were the nights I carried him home and rolled him into bed dead drunk." When Noonan was sober he was one of the ablest navigators in the world, and he promised Amelia that he would stay sober for the trip.

Originally, the round-the-world flight was intended to proceed from Oakland, California in a westward direction, beginning with the three long Pacific flight legs. Preparation was finally completed in early 1937, and the takeoff planned for March 15. The crew was assembled in Oakland in early March, but as it had been so many times in the past, the weather was uncooperative.

Finally, at 4:00 P.M. on March 17, the Electra was pulled from the hangar, and at 4:37 it lifted off for Hawaii. Poor weather returned as night fell, but Amelia handled the plane well while Manning and Noonan took star sightings, manned the radio, and continually plotted and replotted the course.

As the Electra neared Hawaii, the radio operators at Makapuu asked for a radio transmission one minute long from the aircraft to provide a fix on its position. Noonan held down the telegraph key, but the generator could not deliver the power required for such a long transmission and burned out. Fortunately, a second generator powered most of the other electrical gear on the aircraft, so the loss was not too serious.

The Electra touched down at Wheeler Field 15 hours and 52 minutes and 2410 miles after leaving Oakland. Early the next morning, the Electra was flown to Luke Field, which had a longer runway. There 590 gallons of high-octane military fuel were added to her tanks, bringing to 900 gallons the total fuel on board for the 1800-mile flight to Howland Island.

At 7:35 A.M. on March 20, with Manning and Noonan aboard, AE started the long taxi down the runway. As the plane gained speed, suddenly it pulled to the right, and ten seconds later it lay in a crumpled heap on the side of the runway. Witnesses differ in their accounts of the accident. Some claim a tire blew out. Amelia believed the right shock absorber gave way. But Paul Mantz thought that AE was jockeying the throttles—something he had warned her not to do many times in practice flights.

The plane was taken by ship back to California where—$25,000 and five weeks later—it was repaired and readied for another flight attempt. Manning decided to quit the adventure, giving as his reason that his leave time from his company was up. Much later he admitted that he had felt that "Amelia was responsible for the crash in Hawaii. She overcorrected to the left, then to the right."

The repairs delayed departure until May. That meant that AE would be making the Atlantic crossing in late June and the Caribbean flights in early July. Normal weather conditions for that period were considered unfavorable, so the direction of the flight was reversed. It would be made from west to east—from Oakland across the U.S., down to South America, across the

Atlantic, across Africa and the Arabian Gulf to India, across Southeast Asia down to Australia, then to New Guinea, Howland Island, Hawaii, and back to the U.S.

Early on May 21, Amelia, Putnam, Noonan, and McKneely climbed into the Electra for another shakedown flight. Without a word to the press or anyone else, the round-the-world flight attempt was underway. The flights from Oakland to Burbank to Tucson went off without a hitch. An engine fire on the ground at Tucson caused some minor damage to the rubber fittings but was cleaned up in a few hours.

The next morning a ferocious sandstorm temporarily blocked the way out of Tucson, but the Electra finally reached New Orleans on the night of May 22. On Sunday morning, May 23, AE took off for the 688-mile flight to Miami, where she settled in for a final week of preparation. The plane was fully serviced, checked, and rechecked; long-range weather forecasts were collected; and thousands of details were attended to.

On June 1, 1937, at 5:56 A.M., Earhart and Noonan lifted off from Miami bound for San Juan, Puerto Rico. Gorgeous weather was their welcome companion, and they set down in San Juan at 1:10 p.m., right on schedule. Getting up at 3:45 A.M. on June 2, Amelia hoped for a dawn departure, but she was not able to take off until nearly 7:00 A.M. on the flight to Caripito, Venezuela. The flight was short, 624 miles, but AE had to buck 30 mph headwinds the entire way.

Heavy black rain clouds hung thick about Caripito as the Electra lifted off early on the morning of June 3. Again, strong headwinds cut the average speed, and it took nearly 4 1/2 hours to cover the 610 miles to Paramaribo, Dutch Guiana.

A very early departure from Paramaribo the next day left AE and Noonan without a current weather report; nevertheless, after some ten hours of flying, the town of Fortaleza, Brazil, 1332 miles away, came into view. A fuel-gauge leak had to be fixed, and because Pan Am had excellent facilities there, AE decided to have an engine overhaul in Fortaleza in preparation for the Atlantic crossing, rather than at the jumping-off airport in Natal, Brazil.

The next day they took to the air at 4:50 A.M. and arrived, 270 miles later, in Natal at 6:55 A.M. The weather was unsettled all the way, and a tropical deluge caught the plane just as it landed. Amelia had hoped to leave that evening for Africa, but the rain squalls and muddy field prevented their departure. She finally got off at 3:15 A.M., using a secondary grass runway because a perverse wind was blowing directly across the longer, lighted runway. Noonan had been drinking heavily with his old Pan Am buddies, and observers at Natal sensed a growing tension between pilot and navigator that belied their outward cordiality.

Headwinds prevailed for most of the way. Then came a stretch of doldrums, some clear skies, and finally, in the words of AE, "the heaviest rain I ever saw. Tons of water descended, a buffeting weight bearing so heavily on the ship I could almost feel it." Although Dakar, French West Africa, was their objective, when they reached the coast a thick haze blanketed the landscape and there was no sign of civilization. Noonan thought that they should turn south, a correct judgment, because, as they later learned, they were 80 miles north of Dakar. However, AE decided to turn north, and half an hour later they found themselves at St. Louis, Senegal.

The following day, June 8, they flew the 163 miles to Dakar, where they were forced to lay over to repair a broken fuel gauge. AE also decided to have an overall engine check there. From June 9 to 14, they hopped across the African continent in six flights, varying in length from 340 to 1150 miles. A variety of problems were faced and overcome: weather, navigation, language, minor malfunctions, and fuel.

On June 15, the pair flew from Assab, Eritrea, to Karachi, India. A few hours out, the mixture control lever jammed, preventing AE from regulating the quantity of fuel consumed by the right engine. To economize, she reduced her speed dramatically. Nevertheless, they covered the 1920 miles in 13 hours and 10 minutes and became the first flyers ever to make a non-stop flight from the Red Sea to India.

In 1937, Karachi aerodrome, the main intermediate point for all air traffic from Europe to India, Australia, and the Far East, was one of the biggest in the world. AE and Noonan spent two days in Karachi having a major engine overhaul and replacing many small but important items for the first time on the trip.

On June 17, AE piloted the Electra 1390 miles to Calcutta, India. Despite a series of severe rain squalls, the Electra averaged 163 mph, making the trip to Calcutta in 8 1/2 hours.

Now, in the middle of the monsoon season, AE faced a number of risky situations. On June 18, the field at Calcutta was thoroughly soaked, making a takeoff very dangerous. However, there was a momentary break in the weather, and she knew that she might not get another chance to get out for several days or even weeks. She described the takeoff: "The plane clung for what seemed like ages to the heavy sticky soil before the wheels finally lifted, and we cleared with nothing at all to spare the fringe of trees at the airdrome's edge." A bit over two hours later she put down at Akyab, Burma, refueled, and took off for Rangoon. However, the weather grew increasingly hostile, until the pair found themselves in monsoon rains so savage that they beat patches of paint off the wings. After trying to get through for two hours, AE gave up and retreated to Akyab.

On June 19, the pair set out from Akyab bound for Bangkok, Siam, but again moonsoon rains forced a landing at Rangoon. Horrible weather continued to plague them as they barely managed to get through the following day to Bangkok for refueling, and then on to Singapore.

Early on June 21, they flew to Bandoeng, Java, where AE decided to lay over two days to let the local KLM mechanics give the Electra a good going over. At 3:45 A.M. on June 24, as AE was warming up the plane, she found that an instrument refused to function. Repairs took a good part of the day, and they did not get off until 2:00 P.M. AE reached Saurabaya, Java, late in the day but, because of continued problems with the instruments, she was forced to return to the much better facilities at Bandoeng for more repairs the next day.

The instrument problems seemed finally cured, and on June 27, Earhart and Noonan left Bandoeng for Australia. Bucking strong headwinds most of the way, AE was forced to put down at a tiny airstrip at Koepang on the island of Timor. Early the next morning they set out across the Timor Sea, again bucking strong headwinds, and landed at Port Darwin, Australia, four hours later. There they were pounced upon by a medical inspector and quarantined on the plane for ten hours.

At 6:29 A.M. on June 29, the pair took off for Lae, New Guinea. They covered the 1200 miles over a portion of the Indian ocean dotted with small islands in 7 hours and 43 minutes. Adverse wind conditions and threatening clouds held the flyers at Lae for two days. In addition, Noonan was unable because of radio difficulties to set the chronometers, which were vital to accurate navigation.

Discouraged by these problems and steadily losing faith in Noonan because of his drinking, AE worked out a revised flight plan with the assistance of Harry Balfour, the Guinea Airways radio operator at Lae. Amelia tried unsuccessfully to persuade Balfour to go with her in addition to or instead of Noonan. The new routing was slightly north of the original course but passed over Nauru Island, which, because of its giant phosphate mining lights, was one of the few islands visible at night.

AE took off from Lae at 10:00 A.M. on July 2 and reached Nauru 11 hours later, right on schedule. From there she turned slightly south to Howland. However, her old bugaboo, consistently drifting left when following a bearing, raised its ugly head again. Thus, eight hours later when she thought she was about 100 miles out of Howland, she was indeed 100 miles short but also 170 miles north. After briefly searching and finding no sign of Howland, she made a desperate about-face in an attempt to reach the Gilbert Islands four hours to the west.

However, she was again north of her intended course, so instead of hitting the Gilberts she reached Mili Atoll, one of the southernmost atolls of the Marshall Islands chain. As she tried to put down on a long stretch of coral at Barre Island, the landing gear caught on the coral, the plane was wrenched to a stop, a wing was torn off, and Noonan was thrown forward, injuring his forehead and knee.

Earhart and Noonan were aided by the Marshallese, but word of their landing spread, and several days later they were picked up by the Japanese military, who occupied the Marshalls. On July 14, the flyers and the wrecked Electra were put aboard the Koshu, a small Japanese survey ship. On July 19 the Koshu reached Truk Island, where Earhart and Noonan were transferred to a Japanese Navy seaplane and flown to Saipan, Japanese headquarters in the Pacific.

There they were accused by the Japanese of spying, and were mercilessly questioned. Between interrogations, they were held in small damp cells in Garapan prison where, on a diet of weak soup, both became ill with dysentery. Resenting the treatment, Noonan eventually lost his temper and threw his bowl of soup at a guard. He was immediately taken out and beheaded. Amelia's strong willpower kept her going for 14 months until finally, in August 1938, she died of dysentery.

In 1935, Charles Lindberg had given up flying and moved to England after the kidnapping and death of his son. That same year Wiley Post was killed in a crash on a flight with Will Rogers in Alaska. A few years earlier Eddie Rickenbacker had given up flying to become an airline executive, and Blanche Stuart Scott had given up her role as "Tomboy of the Air" for a career in radio and the movies. Thus, with the death of Amelia Earhart in 1938, the golden age of aviation came to a close.

BIBLIOGRAPHY

Earhart, Amelia. *Last Flight.* New York: Harcourt, Brace and Company, 1937.

Loomis, Vincent V. *Amelia Earhart: The Final Story:* New York: Random House, 1985.

THE PROGRAM

The Around-the-World Flight main program is quite short; most of the calculations and dialogue are contained in eight major subroutines, 19 sub-subroutines, an initialization section, and an end-of-game summary section.

In the initialization section, variables are dimensioned and initial values are entered by means of two subroutines (using two data files: verbaldata.txt and airports.txt). I have, of course, used city and country names as they were in 1937; most of the African names are different today.

For the most part, the main program simply calls one subroutine after another. Very short operations are done in the main program. These include printing the current location, airplane condition, and weather; determining if there is a delay in takeoff; resetting the day and date; and fueling the plane.

The date subroutine (Sub530) determines and prints the month and date based on the number of days into the flight (DY) from the starting date of May 20, 1937.

The aircraft-repairs subroutine (Sub640) looks to see if there has been a malfunction in a previous flight leg (M > 0). If so, you are asked if you want to make repairs. (Hint: You are well-advised to do so. Amelia Earhart always made necessary repairs, even to the smallest items, as soon as possible. Not making repairs substantially increases the probability of major problems on future flight legs.) If a repair is to be made, the time (in hours) to fix it is a direct function of the facilities of the airport; a minor repair will take three hours at a well-equipped airport and nine hours at a poorly-equipped one. If the repair time is five hours or more and the next destination is more than 600 miles away (more than four flying hours) or if the repair time is nine hours or more, you will not be able to take off the same day.

The major-overhaul subroutine (Sub730) is similar to the repairs subroutine. The program advises you to have a major overhaul "sometime soon" if flying time is between 39 and 60 hours and "as soon as possible" if flying time is more than 60 hours. You are also permitted to have a major overhaul at any of four very well-equipped airports: Miami, Fortaleza, Karachi, and Bandoeng. A major overhaul is not possible at airports with fair or poor facilities.

What is the probability of mechanical trouble? This is a function that took some thought and finally turned out to be quite simple. The mechanical condition of the plane is determined by the total number of flying hours and the speed flown. Although it is possible to push the plane to its limit, the engines and other mechanical components will last longer if they are used with, as Amelia put it, TLC. On the other hand, you can't fly too slowly, or fatigue becomes an overwhelming factor. Hence, the mechanical condition can be represented by cumulative distance times average speed. This is a better measure of wear and tear on the plane than just hours flown. Condition (PC) is normalized to 1.0 for 6000 miles at 150 mph (LN1500), or 40 flying hours. On her round-the-world flight attempt, Amela tried to have a preventative overhaul approximately every 40 flight hours.

However, you may be tempted to fly longer intervals between overhauls or may find yourself at an airport that does not have the facilities for a major overhaul. What then? Until the recommended overhaul interval is reached, the plane can be considered very reliable. (See major engine-problem code near LN1500). At one-half the overhaul interval there is a slim 3% chance of malfunction, and even at 80% of the interval, the chance of a problem has risen to only a little over 5%. However, beyond the overhaul interval, the probability of a malfunction rises dramatically; fly 1.3 times the recommended interval and the chance of a problem is nearly 78%, while flying 1.5 times the interval increases the chance of failure to 92%. Obviously, the probability can never exceed 100%.

If we plot these probabilities (see graph on next page), we see a very familiar curve. Although it can be expressed several ways, the tangent function is one of the simplest. The upper and lower limits of the tangent function are π/2 and -π/2, but we want the probability to range between 0 and 1. Okay, that's easy to fix by dividing the answer by pi and adding 0.5. However, we want the input variable to range between 0 (no flight hours) and 2 (a risk-taker flying twice the recommended interval before servicing). There are several pairs of constants that make the probability of a problem equal to 10% at the scheduled maintenance point (my estimated figure for Amelia's Lockheed Electra). I finally settled on the following equation in which PC represents the plane condition (ranges between 0 to 2 or more, depending upon speed and hours flown) and MP represents the probability of a mechanical problem (varies between 0 and 1):

```
MP = Math.ArcTan(14 * PC - 17) / 3.14159 + .5
```

This probability is compared to a random number between 0 and 1 to determine if there is an actual failure. If there is a failure in one engine, you have a 33.3% probability of being able to nurse the plane along to the next airport on one engine, a 33.3% chance of having to go back to the airport from which you just took off, and a 33.3% chance of a forced landing.

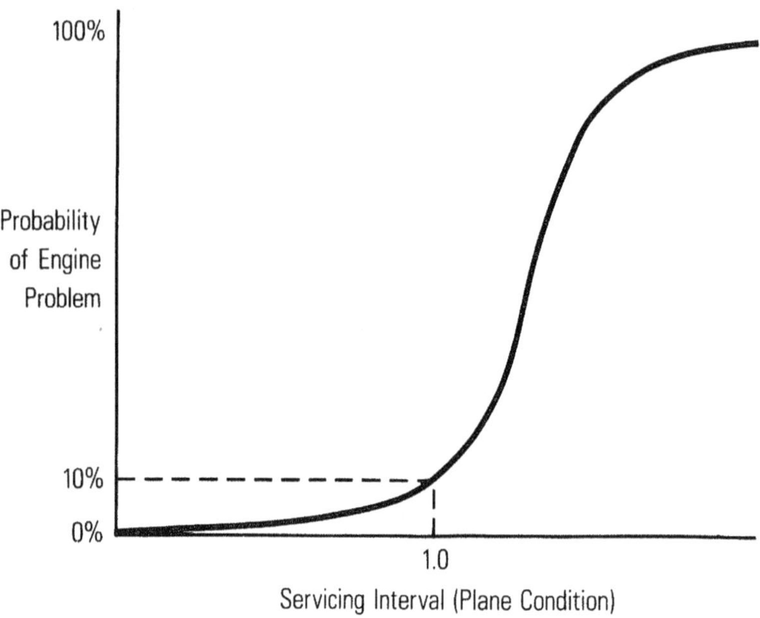

The forced landing routine (starts at LN1630) first checks to see if you are over water; if so, you don't have a prayer. If you are over land, you have an 80% chance of surviving a crash, although the crash ends the round-the-world flight.

Minor malfunctions, of which Amelia Earhart saw many, are annoying but seldom fatal (starts at LN1740). On the other hand, if a previous malfunction was never fixed, the combination of two or more minor malfunctions is equivalent to losing one engine. If you have just one minor malfunction, you are given an opportunity to push on or to return to the airport from which you took off. The longer you fly with a minor malfunction, the greater the probability that it will cause major problems—up to 5% if you cover the entire flight distance. Hence, if you are less than one-third of the way to the next location, you probably should turn back. Amelia usually lived with her minor malfunctions and turned back only once on her round-the-world flight attempt, when she had serious instrument problems between Bandoeng and Saurabaya, Java. This situation is re-created in the program (at LN2270).

Another serious problem facing the flyer is that of fuel consumption and weight (at LN1900), which, of course, are interrelated. More fuel means longer flying time, but it also means more weight and higher fuel-consumption. The Electra had dramatically different fuel consumption rates depending upon its speed; this is a key calculation. The Electra could cruise at between 120 and 170 mph. Amelia preferred a speed of just over 150 mph whenever possible to balance fuel consumption with flight time (and pilot fatigue). It would reduce the fun of playing the game to print the exact relationships here; but at 150 mph, the Electra gets approximately two miles per gallon. Amelia also reported several serious problems with the fuel/air mixture control system. A problem in this system requires you to throttle way back because fuel consumption increases enormously.

At Lae, New Guinea, Amelia stripped nearly everything nonessential out of the Electra in order to save precious weight and increase fuel range. This is simulated in LN1970.

Another problem related to the fuel load is that the takeoff distance is lengthened when the plane is heavier (Sub1080). This is a major factor at airports with short runways made of grass and dirt. When these fields are wet, which is frequently the case in Brazil and Southeast Asia, the plane may not be able to get off with a heavy fuel load. Indeed, in monsoon conditions or after days of heavy rain, the plane may be unable to break out of the mud at all—regardless of fuel load.

Another problem on takeoff is that of synchronizing the two engines. Amelia had serious problems with this and smashed the Electra on the takeoff from Honolulu on her first east-to-west round-the-world attempt (start at LN1200).

Weather conditions affect the round-the-world flight attempt in many ways. Bad weather may prevent you from taking off at all. In the case of bad weather, you can elect to delay your takeoff for a day or more—often a wise option if a monsoon is raging outside. The weather aloft (start at LN1330) can also be a headache. In the event of a monsoon, you have a 60% chance of getting through (or around) it and a 40% chance of having to turn back. In the Caribbean you will always face strong headwinds which lengthen flying times and increase fuel consumption; across the South Atlantic you face mixed weather conditions.

Weather also affects landings (start at LN2990). If it has been raining and the field is soggy, you run a risk of getting a wheel stuck in the mud on a grass and dirt field. You should try to contact the tower by radio to learn the condition of the field before you land. If it is soggy, you are given the option of going back. On short flight legs this is feasible, but on longer flights you probably won't have enough fuel.

One unusual problem that Amelia faced on her round-the-world flight attempt was a navigator with a serious alcohol problem. Although Fred Noonan had supposedly gone on the wagon before the flight, he soon reverted to his old ways, particularly as the flight went on; tensions increased, and delays grew longer (Sub920 and LN2040). In the program, if your navigator is drunk when you are ready to take off, you have the option of waiting a day on the chance that he will be sober tomorrow. If you take off with him not fully functional, you have to rely upon dead reckoning and landmarks—feasible over land, much more difficult over water.

Seven special situations, some of which Amelia Earhart faced, are simulated in the program. The navigation was incorrect on the Atlantic crossing (LN2130); this you must face, even if your navigator is stone sober. But it is not a serious problem; you simply hit the coast of Africa at the wrong place 95% of the time.

Out of Akyab, Burma, you will fly through a monsoon (LN2220). Because you are following the coast, this again is not a terribly serious problem, except that you may have to land at an intermediate destination.

Already mentioned are the instrument problems on the Bandoeng to Saurabaya flight leg. Also in this part of the world, the Australian authorities refused to recognize the signature of a doctor on Amelia's vaccination records and quarantined her, Noonan, and the Electra for ten hours at Port Darwin (LN3220).

Your most serious problem is on the flight leg from Lae, New Guinea, to Howland Island (start at LN2340). Your only visible guidance comes from the arc lights at the mines at Nauru. If your navigator is functional (Noonan wasn't), you have a 30% chance of finding Howland; if not, your chance is only 2%. If you turn back for the British Gilbert Islands, you have a 1.5% chance of finding them and a 98.5% chance of winding up—as Amelia did—at the Marshall Islands.

Two situations which, unfortunately, Amelia did not face are the flight legs of Howland Island to Honolulu (LN2700) and Honolulu to Oakland (LN2790).

Five frequently used subroutines are at the end. They check for yes/no answers to questions, provide a pause, and make beeping noises to represent a radio signal, warning indicator, and alarm clock..

The end-of-flight summary (Sub4030) provides you with some overall statistics of your flight and that of Amelia Earhart, and stops the game.

PROGRAM VARIABLES

```
A Answer of user (0 = Yes, 1 = No)
AD Answer of user (Y or N)
AB Abort flight for one day indicator
C[n] Runway construction (n = 1 - 32, index of C$)
CD[n] Runway construction description (n = 1 - 3)
D Distance over a flight leg
DA Day of month
DC Distance (cumulative) total
DF Distance, maximum based on speed and fuel
DJ Distance over a flight leg, temporary
DM Distance (cumulative) since last maintenance
DX[n] Distance over a flight leg (n = 1 - 32)
DY Day into flight
F Facilities (index of F$)
FD[n] Facilities description (n = 1 - 4)
FU Fuel for a flight leg, gallons (user input)
FX[n] Facilities by location (n = 1 - 32)
I Index variable, temporary
```

J Location (current) index
JA Location (destination) index
K Index variable, temporary
LAD[n] Location, city name (n = 1 - 32)
LBD[]n Location, state or country name (n = 1 - 32)
MD[n] Malfunction description (n = 1 - 11)
MOD Month
M Malfunction indicator (index for M$)
MD Miles flown prior to a malfunction on flight leg
ME Miles yet to fly after a malfunction
MJ Malfunction of instruments over Java indicator
MP Malfunction of engine probability
MQ Malfunction not fixed indicator
NC Navigator condition (scale of 1 to 100)
ND Navigator condition (0 = functional, 1 = not)
PC Plane condition (needs servicing when PC = 1.0)
PD Plane condition based on distance and time (DM * DM / TM)
R[n] Runway length (n = 1 - 32, index of R$)
RD[n] Runway length description (n = 1 - 3)
RF Radio frequency change indicator
RN Random probability of finding Howland Island also Randomize seed at start of program
S Speed over a flight leg (user input)
SA Speed over a flight leg, actual
SQ Speed, reduced because of fuel (user input)
SW Speed of wind over a flight leg
TC Flight time (cumulative) total
TE Flight time over a flight leg, expected actual
TF Flight time, maximum based on fuel and speed
TG Ground time, total at one location
TM Flight time (cumulative) since last maintenance also time in minutes at end of program
TP Ground time for overhaul
TQ Ground time for repairs
TR Flight time, temporary
W Weather, probable, at airport
WA Weather, actual, at airport (index of W$)
WD[n] Weather conditions description (n = 1 - 6)
WX[n] Weather, probable, at each airport (n = 1 - 32)
XD Temporary string variable
X Temporary variable for random number
Y Temporary variable
ZD[n] Type of crowd (n = 1 - 6)

Note: all variables use the following measurement units:

D	Distance	Miles
S	Speed	Miles/hour (mph)
T	Time (air)	Hours
T	Time (ground)	Days

PROGRAM LISTINGS

```
TextWindow.CursorTop = 10
TextWindow.CursorLeft = 17
TextWindow.WriteLine("Around the World Flight of Amelia Earhart, 1937")
TextWindow.WriteLine("")
TextWindow.WriteLine("")
TextWindow.CursorLeft = 29
TextWindow.WriteLine("(c) David H. Ahl, 1986")
TextWindow.CursorTop = 23
TextWindow.CursorLeft = 27
TextWindow.WriteLine("Press Enter to continue.")
JJJ= TextWindow.Read()

Sub4150()
'Print scenario
'
'Initialization
Sub3260()
Sub3450()
'Initialize text variables and airport data
TextWindow.Clear()
DC = 0
M=0
'
'Main program
LN230:
J = J + 1
DY = DY + 1
TG = 0
Sub3950()
Sub3980()
'New day & destination
F = FX[J]
W = WX[J]
D = DX[J]
'Set variables for new location
Sub530()
'Date subroutine
TextWindow.WriteLine("You are at "+LAD[J]+", "+LBD[J]+". Repair facilities
are "+FD[F]+".")
TextWindow.WriteLine("Runway is made of "+CD[C[J]]+" and is "+RD[R[J]]+" for
your plane.")
If DC = 0 Then
  Goto LN350 'Don't print mileage before you start
EndIf
TextWindow.WriteLine("")
TextWindow.WriteLine("You have flown " +DC+ " miles in total and you have
flown")
TextWindow.WriteLine(Math.Floor(TM + .5)+ " hours since your last major
overhaul.")
Sub640()
'Aircraft-repairs subroutine
Sub730()
'Major-overhaul subroutine
```

```
If TP + TQ = 0 Then
  Goto LN350 'Any delay for repairs or overhaul?
EndIf
TG = TG + TP + TQ
DY = DY + TP + TQ
TP = 0
TQ = 0
Sub530()
LN350:
Sub850()
'Pilot-condition subroutine
Sub920()
'Navigator-condition subroutine
If ND = 1 Then
  Goto LN460 'Delay a day because navigator is drunk?
EndIf
Sub1030()
'Next-destination subroutine
LN390:
TextWindow.Write("How many gallons of fuel do you want in the plane? ")
FU = TextWindow.ReadNumber()
If FU > 1150 Then
TextWindow.WriteLine("Maximum capacity is 1150 gallons.")
GOTO LN390
EndIf
'Actual weather may be slightly better or worse than expected
WA = Math.Floor(W + 1.6 * Math.GetRandomNumber(999)/1000 - .3)
If WA > 6 Then
WA = 6
ELSEIF WA < 1 THEN
WA = 1
EndIf
TextWindow.WriteLine("Current weather :  "+ WD[WA] )
If WA < 3 Then
  Goto LN480
EndIf
TextWindow.Write("Do you want to wait a day for better weather (Y or N)? ")
AD = TextWindow.Read()
Sub3820()
If A = 1 Then
  Goto LN480 'Abort flight because of weather?
EndIf
LN460:
AB = 0
TG = TG + 1
DY = DY + 1
Sub530()
'Increase day counters
Goto LN350
LN480:
Sub1080()
'Take-off subroutine
If AB = 1 Then
  Goto LN460 'Was flight aborted on takeoff?
EndIf
```

```
Sub1270()
'In-flight subroutine
Sub3950()
Goto LN230
'
Sub Sub530
'Date subroutine
If DY < 12 Then
Goto LN560
ELSEIF DY > 56 THEN
Goto LN590
ELSEIF DY > 41 THEN
goto LN570
EndIf
MOD = "June"
DA = DY - 11
Goto LN580
LN560:
MOD = "May"
DA = DY + 20
Goto LN580
LN570:
MOD = "July"
DA = DY - 41
LN580:
TextWindow.WriteLine("")
TextWindow.WriteLine("Date: " +MOD+" "+DA+", 1937" )
Goto LN639
ln590:
TextWindow.WriteLine("")
TextWindow.WriteLine("It's July 16 and your money has completely run out.")
TextWindow.WriteLine("Sorry, you were unsuccessful. Perhaps you and George
Putnam")
TextWindow.WriteLine("can raise enough money for a try again next year.")
success = "false"
Sub4030()
LN639:
EndSub
'
Sub Sub640
'Aircraft-repairs routine
TQ = 0
If M = 0 Then
  Goto LN729 'If no malfunctions, return to main program
EndIf
TextWindow.WriteLine("Your "+MDA[M]+" has been giving you problems.")
TextWindow.Write("Do you want to have it repaired here (Y or N)? ")
AD = TextWindow.Read()
Sub3820()
If A = 1 Then
  Goto LN729
EndIf
M = 0
TextWindow.Write("That will take " +(2 * F + 1)+ " hours")
If (DX[J + 1] > 600 AND F > 1) OR F > 3 Then
```

```
Goto LN710
ELSE
TextWindow.WriteLine(".")
Goto LN729
EndIf
LN710:
TextWindow.WriteLine(" and will prevent you from leaving today.")
TQ = 1
LN729:
EndSub
'
Sub Sub730
'Major-overhaul routine
TP = 0
If TM < 28 Then
Goto LN780
ELSEIF TM < 39 THEN
goto LN790 'Check flying hours
EndIf
TextWindow.Write("You should probably have a major overhaul ")
If TM > 60 Then
  Goto LN770
EndIf
TextWindow.WriteLine("sometime soon.")
Goto LN790
LN770:
TextWindow.WriteLine("as soon as possible.")
Goto LN790
LN780:
If (J = 5 OR J = 9 OR J = 19 OR J = 25) AND TM > 12 Then
Goto LN800
ELSE
Goto ln849
EndIf
LN790:
If F > 2 Then
  Goto LN849 'Major overhaul not possible at this airport
EndIf
LN800:
TextWindow.Write("Do you want a major overhaul here (Y or N)? ")
AD = TextWindow.Read()
Sub3820()
TP = 0
If A = 1 Then
  Goto LN849
EndIf
If Math.GetRandomNumber(999)/1000 > .7 Then
TP = F + 1
ELSE
TP = F '30% chance that overhaul takes
EndIf
DM = 0
TM = 0
TextWindow.WriteLine("That will take "+ TP +" day(s).")
'extra day
```

```
LN849:
EndSub
'
'
Sub Sub850
'Pilot-condition routine
X = 10 * Math.GetRandomNumber(999)/1000
TextWindow.WriteLine("")
TextWindow.Write("You are feeling ")
If X < 5 Then
Goto LN890
ELSEIF X < 8 THEN
goto LN900
EndIf
TextWindow.WriteLine("as if you could use some more sleep.")
Goto LN919
LN890:
TextWindow.WriteLine("pretty good, all things considered.")
Goto LN919
LN900:
TextWindow.WriteLine("fit as a fiddle and ready to go.")
LN919:
EndSub
'
Sub Sub920
'Navigator-condition routine
ND = 0
NC = .002 * DC + 15 * TG
TextWindow.Write("Your navigator is ")
If NC > 80 Then
Goto LN980
ELSEIF NC > 50 THEN
goto LN970
ELSEIF NC > 25 THEN
goto ln960
EndIf
TextWindow.WriteLine("well rested and ready to go.")
Goto LN1029
LN960:
TextWindow.WriteLine("a bit under the weather from drinking last night.")
Goto LN1029
LN970:
TextWindow.WriteLine("droopy and has a bad hangover.")
Goto LN990
LN980:
TextWindow.WriteLine("drunk and barely able to walk.")
LN990:
TextWindow.WriteLine("Do you want to wait until tomorrow and hope he will be
in")
TextWindow.Write("better shape (Y or N)? ")
AD =TextWindow.Read()
Sub3820()
If A = 1 Then
  Goto LN1029
EndIf
```

```
ND = 1
LN1029:
EndSub
'
Sub Sub1030
'Next-destination routine
If J = 10 OR J = 21 Then
JA = J + 2
ELSE
JA = J + 1
EndIf
TextWindow.WriteLine("Your next destination is "+LAD[JA]+", "+LBD[JA]+", "+
DX[JA]+ " miles away.")
EndSub
'
Sub Sub1080
'Take-off routine
TextWindow.WriteLine("Revving up engines ... everything seems okay ...
rolling ...")
TextWindow.Write("... picking up speed and ... ")
Sub3950()
X = Math.GetRandomNumber(999)/1000
If X > .99 Then
Goto LN1190
ELSEIF X > .98 THEN
goto LN1200 'Problem 2% of time
EndIf
Y = C[J] + R[J] + WA
'Runway condition and weather
If Y > 9 AND X > .85 Then
  Goto LN1160 'Monsoons and muddy runway?
EndIf
If Y > 8 AND FU > 900 AND X > .6 Then
  Goto LN1160 'Bad weather and big fuel load?
EndIf
TextWindow.WriteLine("you're finally off!")
TextWindow.WriteLine("")
Goto LN1269
LN1160:
TextWindow.WriteLine("the wheels just won't lift out of the mud!")
TextWindow.WriteLine("Reluctantly you concede there is no chance of a takeoff
today.")
AB = 1
Goto LN1269
LN1190:
TextWindow.WriteLine("the landing gear strut broke!")
Goto LN1220
LN1200:
TextWindow.WriteLine("engines aren't synchronized ... plane is turning!")
Sub3950()
Sound.PlayAndWait(Program.Directory+"\ding.wav")
TextWindow.WriteLine("")
LN1220:
TextWindow.WriteLine("Disaster! The Electra is lying helpless on the runway
with")
```

```
TextWindow.WriteLine("a broken wing, smashed engine, and structural damage
just")
TextWindow.WriteLine("as in the ill-fated March 20 takeoff from Honolulu. So
sorry.")
success = "false"
Sub4030()
'Flight failed, exit program
LN1269:
EndSub
'
Sub Sub1270
'In-flight routines (weather, equipment, fuel consumption, navigation)
LN1280:
TextWindow.Write("At what speed do you wish to fly? ")
S = TextWindow.ReadNumber()
If S > 119 AND S < 171 Then
  Goto LN1330
EndIf
TextWindow.WriteLine("Minimum cruising speed is 120 mph; maximum is 170
mph.")
Goto LN1280
'
'Weather-aloft routine
LN1330:
WA = Math.Floor(WA + 1.6 * Math.GetRandomNumber(999)/1000 - .3)
If WA > 6 Then
WA = 6
ELSEIF WA < 1 THEN
WA = 1
EndIf
TextWindow.WriteLine("Current weather aloft is: "+ WD[WA])
If J = 6 OR J = 7 Then
SW = 30
TextWindow.WriteLine("Strong 30+ mph headwind.")
EndIf
If J = 10 Then
SW = 15
TextWindow.WriteLine("Mixed weather ... doldrums ... headwinds.")
EndIf
If J < 20 OR J > 22 Then
  Goto LN1440
EndIf
SW = 20
TextWindow.Write("The plane is being buffetted about, ")
If Math.GetRandomNumber(999)/1000 > .4 Then
  Goto LN1420 '60% chance of getting thru a monsoon
EndIf
TextWindow.WriteLine("and you'll have to turn back.")
Goto LN1880
'Turning back
LN1420:
TextWindow.WriteLine("but you decide to push on.")
'
LN1440:
'Compute flight data and update cumulative figures
```

```
SA = S - SW
DJ = DX[JA]
TE = DJ / SA
'Actual speed, expected time
DC = DC + DJ
TC = TC + TE
'Cumulative distance and time
DM = DM + DJ
TM = TM + TE
'Cumulative maintenance distance and time
'
'Major-engine-problem routine
LN1500:
PC = DM * DM / (900000 * TM)
'Plane condition; needs maint when pc = 1.0
MP = Math.ArcTan(14 * PC - 17) / 3.14159 + .5
'Probability of major engine problem
If Math.GetRandomNumber(999)/1000 > MP Then
  Goto LN1740 'Actual failure?
EndIf
M = 11
Sub3920()
TextWindow.WriteLine("Right engine gauges are going crazy ... major engine
failure!")
TextWindow.Write("Want to try to limp along on one engine (Y or N)? ")
AD = TextWindow.Read()
Sub3820()
If A = 0 Then
  Goto LN1630 'Trying to limp along on one engine
EndIf
LN1570:
X = Math.GetRandomNumber(999)/1000
If X < .333 Then
Goto LN1600
ELSEIF X > .667 THEN
goto LN1650
EndIf
TextWindow.WriteLine("No chance of making "+LAD[JA]+". You'll have to turn
back.")
Goto LN1880
'Turning back
LN1600:
Sub3950()
TextWindow.WriteLine("Whew! It looks as if you can nurse it along.")
Goto LN2040
'Skip minor problems and fuel-consumption routines
'
LN1630:
'Forced-landing routine
LN1640:
If J = 4 OR J = 10 OR J = 27 OR J > 28 Then
  Goto LN1710 'Over water?
EndIf
LN1650:
```

```
TextWindow.WriteLine("Going down ... looking for a suitable place to land ...
nothing ... ")
If Math.GetRandomNumber(999)/1000 > .2 Then
  Goto LN1680 '80% chance of surviving a forced landing
EndIf
LN1670:
Sub3950()
TextWindow.WriteLine(" C R A S H ! No survivors.")
success = "false"
Sub4030()
LN1680:
TextWindow.Write("maybe that small clearing ... ")
Sub3950()
TextWindow.WriteLine("you made it!")
TextWindow.WriteLine("The plane is a wreck but at least you're alive.")
success = "false"
Sub4030()
'It's all over
LN1710:
TextWindow.WriteLine("Going down ... nothing but water..looking for a reef or
anything ... ")
Goto LN1670
'
LN1740:
'Minor malfunction
If Math.GetRandomNumber(999)/1000 > .3 Then
  Goto LN1900 '30% chance of a minor malfunction
EndIf
If M > 0 Then
MQ = M
ELSE
MQ = 0 'Previous malfunction not fixed?
EndIf
M = Math.Floor(1 + 10 * Math.GetRandomNumber(999)/1000)
Sub3920()
TextWindow.WriteLine("")
TextWindow.WriteLine("Malfunction in the " +MDA[M])
If MQ = 0 Then
  Goto LN1810
EndIf
TextWindow.WriteLine("This combined with the previous malfunction of the "
+MDA[MQ]+ " will")
TextWindow.WriteLine("create very serious problems for you.")
Goto LN1570
LN1810:
MD = Math.Floor(DJ * Math.GetRandomNumber(999)/1000)
'Miles flown in this flight leg
TextWindow.WriteLine("You have flown " +MD+ " miles of this flight leg. Do
you want to")
TextWindow.Write("push on (Y or N)? ")
AD =TextWindow.Read()
sub3820()
If A = 0 Then
ME = DJ - MD
ELSE
```

```
ME = MD
EndIf
If Math.GetRandomNumber(999)/1000 < .05 * ME / DJ Then
Goto LN1850
ELSE
goto LN1870 'Up to 5% chance of going down
EndIf
LN1850:
Sub3920()
TextWindow.WriteLine("Uh oh. Fuel-feed system has malfunctioned also.")
TextWindow.WriteLine("Things look pretty bad.")
TextWindow.WriteLine("")
Sub3950()
Goto LN1640
LN1870:
If A = 0 Then
  Goto LN1900 'Going on
EndIf
LN1880:
AB = 1
J = J - 1
JA = J
FU = .7 * FU
'Turning back
'
LN1900:
'Fuel consumption
TF = FU * (5.6 / S - .02)
'Flying time for amount of fuel
If TF * .8 > TE Then
  Goto LN2040 'Enough fuel for flight leg
EndIf
If S < 121 Then
TextWindow.WriteLine("Fuel consumption seems very high ... " )
GOTO LN1990
EndIf
TextWindow.WriteLine("You're going to be tight on fuel. Perhaps you should
throttle")
TextWindow.Write("back. What speed would you like? ")
SQ = TextWindow.ReadNumber()
LN1960:
If SQ < 120 Then
TextWindow.Write("Too slow. Now then, what speed? ")
SQ = TextWindow.ReadNumber()
GOTO LN1960
EndIf
LN1970:
If J > 28 AND FU > 1100 Then
  Goto LN2040 'Longer range on stripped plane
EndIf
If S - SQ < 9 Then
  Goto LN2000 'Cut back speed enough to make a difference?
EndIf
LN1990:
If TF * .96 > TE Then
```

```
  Goto LN2040 'Run out of fuel?
EndIf
LN2000:
TextWindow.WriteLine("Uh oh ... the right engine is sputtering?")
Sub3950()
TextWindow.WriteLine("And now the left engine too. You're out of fuel.")
Goto LN1630
'Go to forced-Landing routine
'
LN2040:
'Navigation
If NC < 51 Then
  Goto LN2090 'Is navigator functional?
EndIf
TextWindow.WriteLine("Your navigator isn't going to be of much use to you
today.")
TextWindow.WriteLine("You'll have to rely upon dead reckoning and
landmarks.")
If M = 5 OR M = 7 Then
  TextWindow.WriteLine("Moreover, your "+ MDA[M]+ " is on the fritz.")
EndIf
LN2090:
TR = Math.Floor(TE)
If TR < 2 Then
  TR = 1.2
EndIf
TextWindow.WriteLine("")
TextWindow.WriteLine("You have been flying for over " +TR+ " hours but there
is")
TextWindow.Write("no sign of ")
If AB = 0 Then
Goto LN2130
ELSE
AB = 0
GOTO LN2990
EndIf
'
LN2130:
'Special situations
If J<>10 Then
  Goto LN2220 'Atlantic crossing
EndIf
TextWindow.Write("land. Pushing onwards. ")
Sub3950()
TextWindow.WriteLine("Wow! Land! Look!")
TextWindow.Write("Approaching coast of Africa; ahead of you is ")
If Math.GetRandomNumber(999)/1000 > .95 Then
TextWindow.WriteLine("Dakar! Nice flying!")
J = 11
GOTO LN3010
EndIf
TextWindow.WriteLine("nothing but jungle. Turning north.")
Sub3950()
TextWindow.WriteLine("A half hour later you sight St. Louis, Senegal, and
decide to land.")
```

```
JA = 11
DX[12] = 163
Goto LN3010
'Distance between Dakar and St. Louis
'
LN2220:
If J<>21 Then
  Goto LN2270 'Moonsoons out of Akyab
EndIf
TextWindow.WriteLine("anything except the deluge of water. You'll have to put
down at")
TextWindow.WriteLine("Rangoon?if you can find it.")
Sub3950()
TextWindow.WriteLine("Look! There!")
JA = 22
Goto LN3000
'Reset destination to Rangoon
'
LN2270:
If J<>25 Then
  Goto LN2340 'Serious instrument problems in Java
EndIf
If MJ = 1 Then
  Goto LN2990 'Have we been through this already?
EndIf
TextWindow.WriteLine("civilization. Moreover, several of your instruments")
TextWindow.WriteLine("are behaving quite badly. Reluctantly, you turn back
to")
TextWindow.WriteLine("Bandoeng because you know that facilities at Saurabaya
are minimal.")
DC = DC - 300
DM = DM - 300
TC = TC - 2
TM = TM - 2
J = 24
JA = 24
MJ = 1
Goto LN3040
'
LN2340:
If J<>29 Then
  Goto LN2700 'Lae to Howland Island
EndIf
TextWindow.WriteLine("land. You spotted the arc lights at Nauru 8 hours
ago.")
LN2360:
TextWindow.Write("Calling Coast Guard cutter Itasca ... ")
Sub3880()
Sub3950()
If RF = 1 Then
Goto LN2390
ELSE
TextWindow.WriteLine("Nothing.")
EndIf
TextWindow.WriteLine("Switch radio frequency ... try again ... ")
```

```
RF = 1
Goto LN2360
LN2390:
TextWindow.WriteLine("Still nothing.")
Sub3950()
TextWindow.WriteLine("You're very low on fuel!")
TextWindow.WriteLine("You can search for Howland or turn back to the Gilbert
Islands.")
TextWindow.Write("Want to search (Y or N)? ")
AD = TextWindow.Read()
Sub3820()
If A = 1 Then
  Goto LN2470
EndIf
For K = 1 To 4
TextWindow.WriteLine("Searching ... ")
Sub3950()
EndFor
Sub3950()
If NC < 30 Then
RN = .3
ELSE
RN = .02 'If navigator okay, 30% chance of
EndIf
' finding Howland Island, otherwise only 2%
If Math.GetRandomNumber(999)/1000 > RN Then
  Goto LN1630 'Go to forced-landing routine
EndIf
TextWindow.WriteLine("My gosh! There it is! A tiny speck of land. WOW!")
Goto LN3010
LN2470:
TextWindow.WriteLine("Tuvalu, the only island in the Gilberts with a landing
strip,")
TextWindow.WriteLine("is almost 4 hours distant on a course almost due
west.")
For K = 1 To 4
TextWindow.WriteLine("Flying?")
Sub3950()
EndFor
Sub3950()
TextWindow.WriteLine("")
TextWindow.WriteLine("Look! Coral reefs. A small island.")
Sub3950()
TextWindow.WriteLine("Virtually no fuel left?both engines sputtering?try to
put")
TextWindow.WriteLine("it down in that flat area along the beach.")
Sub3950()
TextWindow.WriteLine("You made it down?a wing tore off the plane?navigator
injured.")
Sub3950()
TextWindow.WriteLine("Men in uniform are coming over the sand dunes.")
sub3950()
sub3950()
TextWindow.WriteLine("")
If Math.GetRandomNumber(999)/1000 > .985 Then
```

```
  Goto LN2650
EndIf
TextWindow.WriteLine("They're Japanese. An English-speaking native tells you that")
TextWindow.WriteLine("this is Mili Atoll in the Marshall Islands. You are put on a")
TextWindow.WriteLine("warship bound for Majuro. Days later you are put on another")
TextWindow.WriteLine("Japanese warship bound for Saipan. The Japanese accuse you")
TextWindow.WriteLine("of being a spy, torture you, and put you in a tiny prison cell.")
Sub3950()
TextWindow.WriteLine("")
Sub3950()
TextWindow.WriteLine("After months in a tiny, damp prison cell you contract dysentery.")
TextWindow.WriteLine("Your navigator is executed and in August 1938 you die of disease")
TextWindow.WriteLine("and thus become the first U.S. casualities of World War II.")
LN2650:
success = "false"
Sub4030()
TextWindow.WriteLine("They're British. You're safe. In three days the USS Itasca")
TextWindow.WriteLine("Fyespicks you up and deposits you in Honolulu a week later.")
success = "false"
Sub4030()
'
LN2700:
If J<>30 Then
  Goto LN2790 'Howland to Honolulu
EndIf
TextWindow.WriteLine("the Hawaiian Islands. But you're buoyed by the thought")
TextWindow.WriteLine("that you found Howland Island in the middle of the Pacific.")
For K = 1 To 4
TextWindow.Write("Flying ... ")
Sub3950()
EndFor
Sub3950()
TextWindow.WriteLine("")
TextWindow.WriteLine("Calling Honolulu ... come in please")
Sub3880()
Sub3950()
TextWindow.WriteLine("Honolulu to Electra: You're right on course. Weather is")
TextWindow.WriteLine("excellent. You should sight Diamond Head very soon.")
Sub3950()
TextWindow.WriteLine("")
TextWindow.WriteLine("Yes ... there it is. What a welcome sight!")
Goto LN3040
```

```
'
LN2790:
If J<>31 Then
  Goto LN2990 'Honolulu to Oakland
EndIf
TextWindow.WriteLine("the mainland. But you're confident you'll make it.")
Sub3950()
TextWindow.WriteLine("")
TextWindow.WriteLine("You've been flying nearly 20 hours and you're")
TextWindow.WriteLine("bone tired. You wish your navigator could relieve
you.")
Sub3950()
Sub3880()
TextWindow.WriteLine("Oakland calling Electra ... Oakland calling Electra ...
")
TextWindow.Write("Are you okay ... please respond ... are you okay? ")
AD = TextWindow.Read()
Sub3820()
If A = 0 Then
TextWindow.Write("Oakland : Glad to hear it. ")
GOTO LN2870
EndIf
TextWindow.WriteLine("Oakland: Sorry to hear that. Keep going. Just a short
way now.")
LN2870:
Sub3950()
TextWindow.WriteLine(" Oh yes, G.P. sends greetings.")
Sub3950()
TextWindow.WriteLine("")
TextWindow.WriteLine("And there it is; the Pacific coast and the Golden Gate
Bridge.")
TextWindow.WriteLine("What a beautiful sight! Coming into Oakland ... steady
... steady.")
TextWindow.WriteLine("Touchdown?slowing down ... HUGE crowds all around ...
stopping.")
For K = 1 To 4
Sub3950()
EndFor
TextWindow.Clear()
X = 0
For I = 1 To 30
For K = 1 To 100
EndFor
TextWindow.CursorTop = 10
TextWindow.Cursorleft = 30
TextWindow.WriteLine(Xd)
If X = 0 Then
XD = "CONGRATULATIONS !"
X = 1
Goto LN2950
EndIf
XD = " "
X = 0
LN2950:
EndFor
```

```
TextWindow.WriteLine("")
TextWindow.WriteLine("")
TextWindow.WriteLine("")
TextWindow.WriteLine("")
success="true"
Sub4030()
'
'Landing routine
LN2990:
TextWindow.WriteLine(LAD[JA] +". Flying on ... ")
Sub3950()
TextWindow.WriteLine("Look to the right!")
LN3000:
TextWindow.WriteLine("It looks like ... yes it is ... an aerodrome. What a
welcome sight.")
LN3010:
TextWindow.WriteLine("Field looks "+ RD[R[JA]]+ " for the plane.")
If M<>7 Then
Goto LN3040
ELSE
TextWindow.WriteLine( "Radio broken. You'll have to try to land")
EndIf
TextWindow.WriteLine("without establishing contact.")
TextWindow.WriteLine("")
Goto LN3090
LN3040:
TextWindow.WriteLine("Electra calling control tower ... ")
sub3880()
If Math.GetRandomNumber(999)/1000 < .1 Then
  Goto LN3110
EndIf
LN3050:
TextWindow.WriteLine("Tower to Electra ... tower to Electra ... ")
If WX[JA] > 3 Then
  Goto LN3080
EndIf
TextWindow.Write("Condition of field is fine. Do you want clearance to land?
")
AD = TextWindow.Read()
Sub3820()
If A = 0 Then
Goto LN3130
ELSE
TextWindow.Write("Repeat: ")
GOTO LN3050
EndIf
LN3080:
TextWindow.Write("Field is a bit soggy. Do you want clearance to land? ")
AD = TextWindow.Read()
LN3090:
sub3820()
If A = 0 Then
Goto LN3130
ELSE
TextWindow.Write("Do you want to turn back? ")
```

```
AD=TextWindow.Read()
EndIf
sub3820()
If A = 0 Then
Goto LN1880
ELSE
TextWindow.Write("Repeat: ")
GOTO LN3050
EndIf
LN3110:
TextWindow.Write("Can't establish contact. Do you want to land? ")
AD = TextWindow.Read()
Sub3820()
If A = 1 Then
TextWindow.WriteLine( "Circling ... circling ... trying radio again.")
GOTO LN3040
EndIf
LN3130:
TextWindow.Write("Coming in ... steady ... steady ... ")
Sub3950()
TextWindow.WriteLine("touchdown.")
If C[JA] + R[JA] + WX[JA] > 9 AND Math.GetRandomNumber(999)/1000 < .15 Then
Goto LN3150
ELSE
goto LN3170
EndIf
LN3150:
TextWindow.WriteLine("Field is soggy ... one wheel caught in mud ... plane is
tipping.")
Goto LN1220
LN3170:
TextWindow.WriteLine("Slowing down ... turning ... bring it to a stop ...
shut down engines.")
If JA = 11 OR JA = 2 Then
K = 6
ELSE
K = Math.Floor(1 + 4.9 * Math.GetRandomNumber(999)/1000) 'Type of crowd
EndIf
TextWindow.WriteLine("A " +ZD[K]+ " crowd is waiting for you. Nice job.")
LN3220:
If J<>28 Then
  Goto LN3333 'Are you in Darwin?
EndIf
'
TextWindow.WriteLine("Australian authorities claim that your medical papers
are")
TextWindow.WriteLine("not in order and hold you on the plane for 10 hours.
That")
TextWindow.WriteLine("costs you an extra day.")
DY = DY + 1
TG = TG + 1
LN3333:
EndSub
'
Sub Sub3260
```

```
'subroutine to put verbal data into constants
CLINE = 1
DataFile = Program.Directory +"\verbaldata.txt"
FileLine = File.ReadLine(Program.Directory +"\verbaldata.txt", CLINE)
For I = 1 To 4
  GetNextItem()
  FD[I] = NextItem
EndFor
For I = 1 To 3
  GetNextItem()
  CD[I] = NextItem
EndFor
For I = 1 To 3
  GetNextItem()
  RD[I] = NextItem
EndFor
For I = 1 To 6
  GetNextItem()
  WD[I] = NextItem
EndFor
For I = 1 To 11
  GetNextItem()
  MDA[I] = NextItem
EndFor
For I = 1 To 6
  GetNextItem()
  ZD[I] = NextItem
EndFor
EndSub

Sub GetNextItem
  'find comma in FileLine
  KK = Text.GetIndexOf(FileLine, ",")
  If KK <> 0 Then
    NextItem = Text.GetSubText(FileLine, 1, KK - 1)
    FileLine = Text.GetSubTextToEnd(FileLine, KK + 1)
  Else
    NextItem = FileLine
    CLINE = CLINE + 1
    FileLine = File.ReadLine(DataFile, CLINE)
  EndIf
EndSub
'
Sub Sub3450
'Airport location, repair facilities, runway construction,
' runway length, likely weather, miles from last airport
CLINE = 1
DataFile = Program.Directory +"\airports.txt"
FileLine = File.ReadLine(DataFile, CLINE)
For I = 1 To 32
  GetNextItem()
  X = NextItem
  GetNextItem()
  LAD[I] = NextItem
  GetNextItem()
```

```
  LBD[I] = NextItem
  GetNextItem()
  FX[I] = NextItem
  GetNextItem()
  C[I] = NextItem
  GetNextItem()
  R[I] = NextItem
  GetNextItem()
  WX[I] = NextItem
  GetNextItem()
  DX[I] = NextItem
EndFor
EndSub
'
Sub Sub3820
  LN3820:
'Check for yes or no answer
If AD = "Y" OR AD = "y" Then
A = 0
Goto LN3879
EndIf
If AD = "N" OR AD = "n" Then
A = 1
Goto ln3879
EndIf
TextWindow.WriteLine("Don't understand your answer of "+AD+ ".")
TextWindow.Write("Please enter Y for 'yes' or N for 'no.'? ")
AD = TextWindow.Read()
Goto LN3820
LN3879:
EndSub
'
Sub Sub3880
'Radio-signal routine
For I = 1 To 4
Sound.PlayAndWait(Program.Directory+"\ding.wav")
EndFor
EndSub
'
Sub Sub3920
'Warning-beeper routine
TextWindow.WriteLine("")
For I = 1 To 3
Sound.PlayAndWait(Program.Directory+"\ding.wav")
For K = 1 To 500
EndFor
EndFor
EndSub
'
Sub Sub3950
'Pause routine
Program.Delay(1000)
EndSub
'
Sub Sub3980
```

```
'Alarm-clock routine
TextWindow.WriteLine("")
TextWindow.WriteLine("There goes the alarm. It's " +Math.floor(3 + 3.7 *
Math.GetRandomNumber(999)/1000)+ " a.m. Y - A - W - N")
Sound.PlayChimesAndWait()
Sound.PlayChimesAndWait()
EndSub
'
Sub Sub4030
'End-of-flight summary routine
If success Then
  Goto LN4050
EndIf
Sub3950()
TextWindow.WriteLine("")
TextWindow.WriteLine("")
TextWindow.WriteLine("Sorry your flight was unsuccessful.")
LN4050:
TextWindow.WriteLine("")
TextWindow.Write("You flew " +DC+ " miles and were aloft for ")
T = Math.Floor(TC)
TM = Math.Floor(60 * (TC - T))
TextWindow.WriteLine(T +" hours and "+ TM +" minutes.")
TextWindow.WriteLine("Your flight started on May 20 and ended on "+ MOD+" "+
DA +", 1937.")
TextWindow.WriteLine("")
TextWindow.WriteLine("Amelia Earhart flew approximately 27,000 miles
between")
TextWindow.WriteLine("May 20 and July 2, 1937 before going down at Mili
Atoll")
TextWindow.WriteLine("in the Japanese-held Marshall Islands.")
Sub3950()
TextWindow.WriteLine("")
TextWindow.WriteLine("")
TextWindow.Write("Press Enter to End")
AD = TextWindow.Read()
Program.End()
EndSub

'
Sub Sub4150
'Subroutine to print the scenario
TextWindow.Clear()
TextWindow.CursorLeft = 20
TextWindow.WriteLine("Around the World Flight Attempt")
TextWindow.WriteLine("")
TextWindow.WriteLine(" In this simulation, you take the role of Amelia
Earhart in her")
TextWindow.WriteLine("attempt to fly around the world in a twin-engine
Lockheed Electra.")
TextWindow.WriteLine(" Prior to each flight leg, you are given information
about your")
TextWindow.WriteLine(" physical condition and that of your navigator, the
distance to your")
```

```
TextWindow.WriteLine("next destination, and the current weather. As pilot, you must make")
TextWindow.WriteLine("many decisions before taking off, while aloft, and prior to landing.")
TextWindow.WriteLine(" Under ideal conditions, at 150 mph, your plane can fly 2.3")
TextWindow.WriteLine("miles on one gallon of fuel, but conditions are seldom ideal.")
TextWindow.WriteLine("The Electra can hold up to 1150 gallons of fuel.")
TextWindow.WriteLine(" Your engine and mechanical components will last longer if they")
TextWindow.WriteLine("are maintained regularly; on the Electra, the recommended interval")
TextWindow.WriteLine("for a major overhaul is 40 hours. But remember, not all airports")
TextWindow.WriteLine("are equipped to service your aircraft.")
TextWindow.WriteLine(" If you have malfunctions along the way, you may want to have")
TextWindow.WriteLine("them fixed at a secondary aerodrome. Of course, this costs time.")
TextWindow.WriteLine(" You navigator has a serious alcohol problem. As long as your")
TextWindow.WriteLine("ground time is minimal, he won't have much chance to get lost in")
TextWindow.WriteLine("the bottle, but if you get trapped on the ground by a series of")
TextWindow.WriteLine("tropical storms and he gets drunk, you may find you have to rely")
TextWindow.WriteLine("on dead reckoning and landmarks when you get back in the air.")
TextWindow.WriteLine("")
TextWindow.CursorLeft= 20
TextWindow.WriteLine("Press Enter To Continue")
JJJ = TextWindow.Read()
EndSub
```

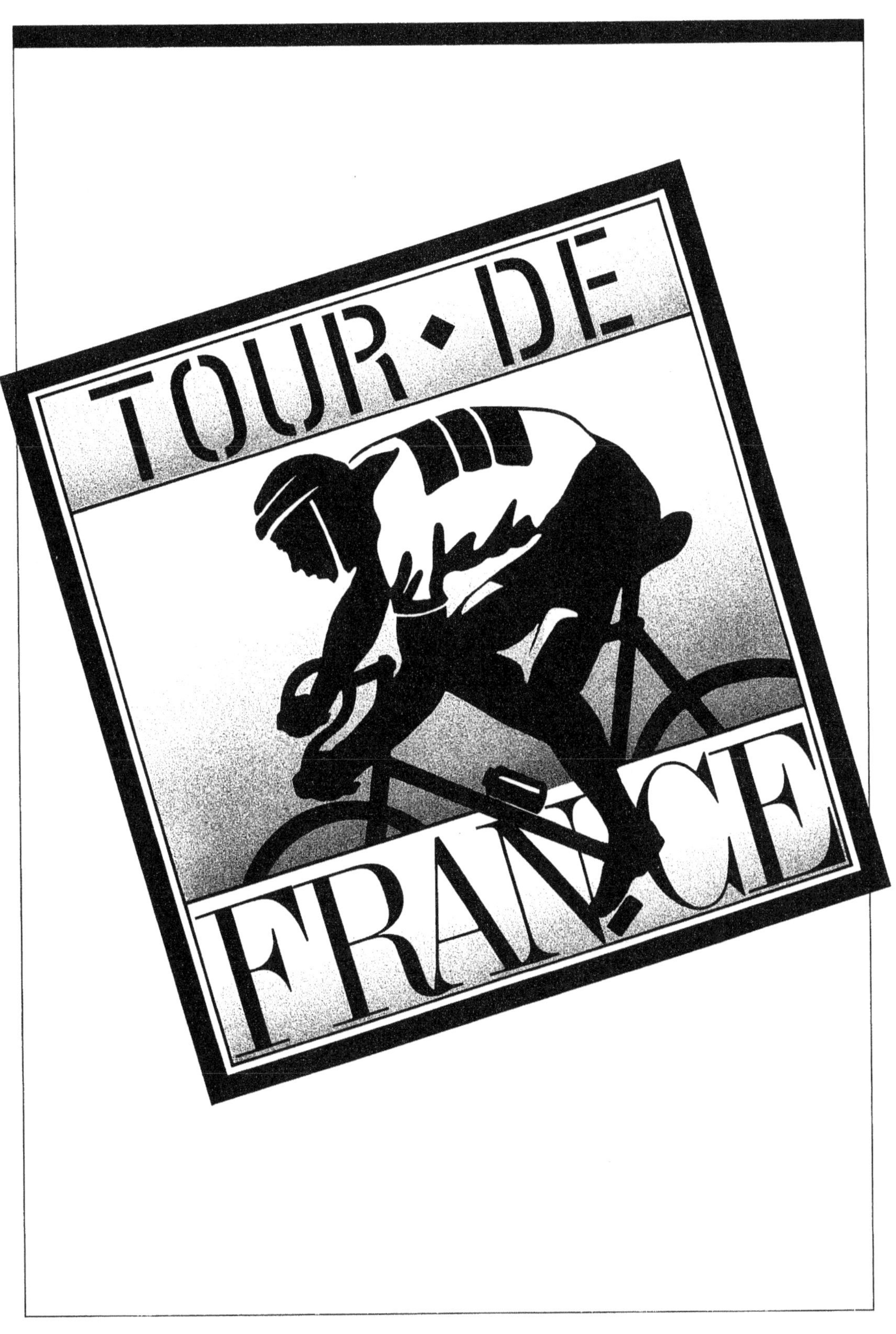
TOUR DE
FRANCE

Tour de France

In Tour de France, you are a bicycle racer whose objective is to win the famous three-week bicycle road race around France. The competition is fierce in this most grueling of all races: You must overcome physical pain, mechanical difficulties, rough terrain, and other problems.

Prior to the race, you are asked some questions about your physical condition and training. You are also given a chance to pedal your bicycle on a short practice run. To "pedal" your bicycle, strike two keys alternately on your keyboard. You can use the index finger of each hand or the index and middle finger of one hand. A well-practiced rider in excellent condition can pedal a bicycle at about 80 rpm.

Your bicycle is a 12-speed with ring gears (pedal) of 52 and 40 teeth, and cog gears (back wheel) of 13, 15, 17, 19, 21, 23, and 25 teeth. (See Table 1.) In your highest gear, 52/13, you will travel 8.61 meters for each pedal revolution, while in your lowest gear, 40/25, you will travel 3.45 meters. Your high gears are best for the flat, open road, while your low gears are necessary for climbing the steep mountains.

Cog Gear	**13**	**15**	**17**	**19**	**21**	**23**	**25**
Ring Gear							
52	8.61	7.45	6.59	5.88	5.32	4.87	
40		5.75	5.06	4.55	4.09	3.75	3.45

TABLE 1. Meters progressed for ring/cog combinations

Here are a few tips to help you place among the top finishers:

- Always use the highest gear possible for the terrain you encounter.
- You can have the computer do some of your pedaling, but it is an inconsistent performer, so you may be better off doing your own pedaling.
- There is a sprint at the end of each stage. The computer counts down the kilometers starting 10 km from the end of the stage. You must decide when to start your sprint. Start too soon and you may tire before you reach the finish line; start too late and you will not gain much time.

The Tour de France is probably the toughest athletic contest in the world One quarter of the starters never finish the race. But the others—despite collisions, concussions, gashes, and even broken bones—continue to compete, for simply to finish the Tour is a feat any cyclist can be proud of.

```
How many weeks do you intend to take off from work or school to
practice and prepare for the race? 12
To pedal your computer bike, you will strike two keys alternately
with two fingers (one hand or two, it's up to you).
Which key do you want for your left pedal? s
and which key for the right? l
Thank you.  Let's go out for a practice run.
Start pedaling NOW!
```

```
You're pushing yourself to the absolute limit and after 2 hours
you totally collapse.  The medics give you oxygen and bring you
around, but warn you against resuming the race.
But nothing can defeat your competitive spirit and you
vow to press on regardless.
```

```
Date: July 1     You are at Reims.
Your destination is Lille, 213 km from here.
Type of racing this stage: Mostly flat with small hills.
Naturally you will shift gears, but what will be your basic gear
range (ring and cog) for the day.  First the ring (40 or 52)? 52
Which cog (13, 15, 17, 19, 21, 23, or 25)? 15
That ratio sounds very high.  Do you want to change it? n
Your departure time is scheduled at 9:43
Start pedaling NOW!
```

THE STORY

What is the most popular sporting event in the world? The World Series? Wimbledon? The Olympic Games? Hardly. The World Soccer Cup? Getting warmer. The Indianapolis 500? Almost (it *is* the most popular one-day event). The Tour de France? Bingo! Every year, more than 20 million fans line the roads to catch just a quick glimpse of the bicycles flashing by in this most competitive race.

The Tour, which lasts three weeks, is a race of at least 4000 kilometers (2500 miles) winding through France, the Pyrenees, and the Alps, to the traditional finish line on the Champs-Elysèes in Paris. The riders who compete in the Tour de France are among the toughest and most courageous athletes in the world; they have to be to survive the formidable daily pace, full-speed sprints, 60 mph spills, treacherous weather, and fickle equipment.

The Tour de France was created in 1903 by Henri Desgranges as a promotional device to sell newspapers, and today it is still owned by *l'Equipe,* a sports paper. But over the years, the Tour has become practically a sovereign state with its own motorcycle police force, its own traveling bank, and more than 2000 full-time participants (officials, mechanics, trainers, doctors, chauffeurs, technicians, salesmen, reporters, and photographers) in addition to the 170 or so riders.

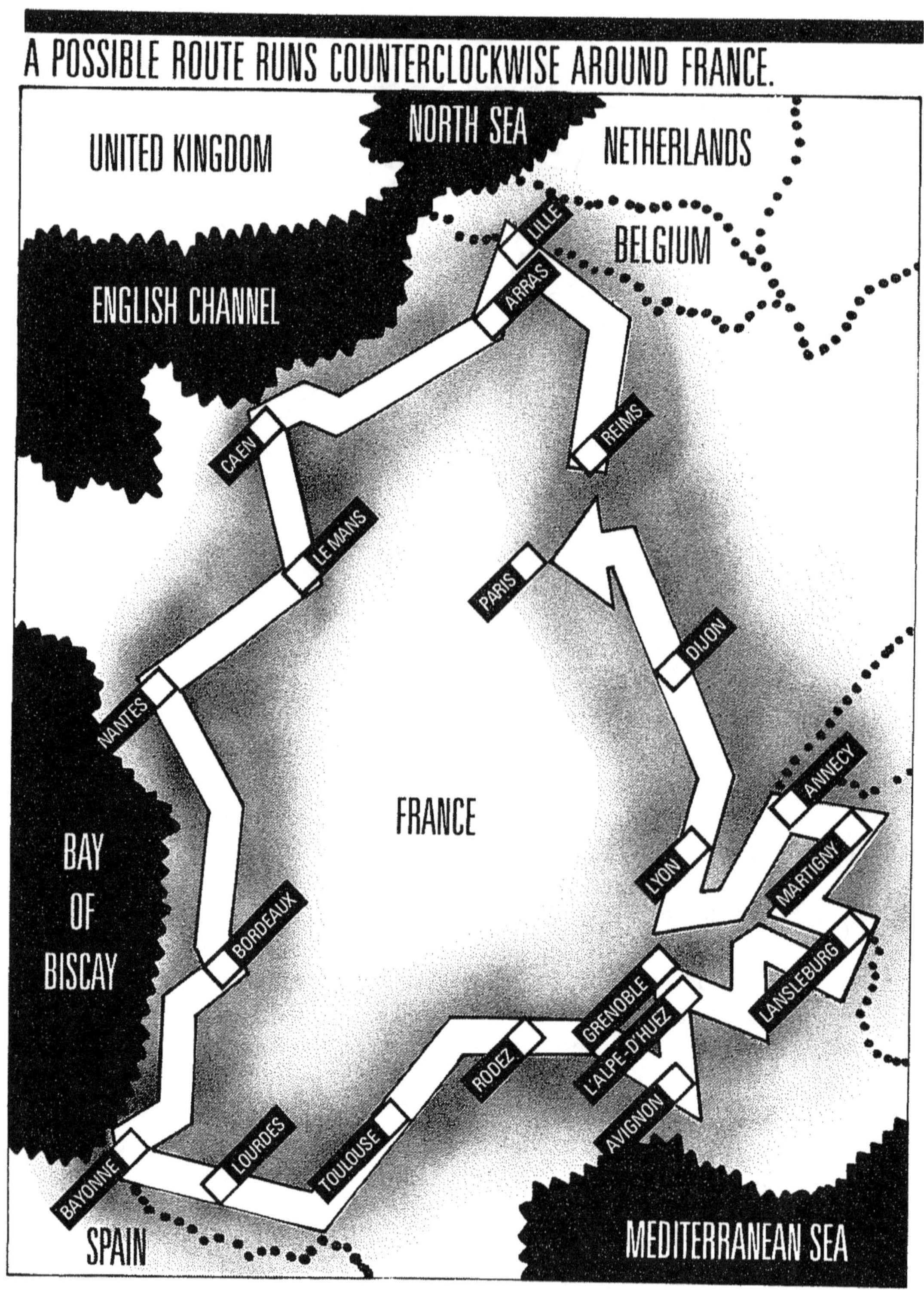
A POSSIBLE ROUTE RUNS COUNTERCLOCKWISE AROUND FRANCE.
UNITED KINGDOM
NORTH SEA
NETHERLANDS
BELGIUM
ENGLISH CHANNEL
LILLE
ARRAS
REIMS
CAEN
LE MANS
PARIS
DIJON
NANTES
FRANCE
ANNECY
MARTIGNY
LYON
BAY
OF
BISCAY
BORDEAUX
GRENOBLE
LANSLEBURG
L'ALPE-D'HUEZ
RODEZ
AVIGNON
TOULOUSE
LOURDES
BAYONNE
SPAIN
MEDITERRANEAN SEA

Although it is theoretically possible to enter the Tour de France as an individual, it is rarely done, not only because of the high cost, but because of the support personnel and equipment required. Thus, in recent years, all of the entries have been teams—each one consisting of ten competitors and a veritable army of support troops.

Many other countries have bicycle tours, but the majority of them are relatively unimportant to the professional teams because of length (too short), time of year (before or after the main European season), or location (Africa, Asia, and East Europe pose unmanageable logistical problems). Thus, only three tours remain significant—those of Spain, Italy, and France—and, of these three, the Tour de France reigns supreme.

The route of the Tour changes each year and, for a price, a small town or village can buy a few moments of recognition on European television by becoming an evening stopover point—the end of one stage and the beginning of the next. In these small towns, shops and banks close, and all of the townspeople turn out to welcome the riders as they struggle in at the end of the daily stage. Even more exciting is the half hour in the morning before the departure on the next stage: Young and old turn out in full racing regalia to glide on their bicycles among the riders, children seek autographs, and riders chat with their fans.

The price a town must pay to start the Tour is substantial—about a half million dollars. Therefore the race usually starts in a major city, not necessarily in France. Frankfurt was the starting city in 1980, Nice in 1981, and Basel in 1982. More recently, the organizers have been promoting the idea of a region—rather than a city—hosting the race start. Thus in 1983 the race began in the southeast of Paris, Val-de-Marne Department, and in 1984 the race began north of the capital in the Seine-Saint-Denis Department.

As the route of the Tour changes from year to year, so does the length. It is generally about 4000 kilometers long, although in 1968 it was stretched to a staggering 4664 kilometers. Sometimes the route is continuous, with each new stage starting at the end of the preceding stage, although in recent years there have been some notable breaks, including a 300-kilometer train trip between Stages 22 and 23 in the 1984 race.

Generally, one stage is run each day, although this is not a hard-and-fast rule. Occasionally, a time-trial stage may be run after one of the shorter flat stages. During time trials, racers compete against the clock, starting at one-minute intervals and race completely on their own to the finish line. The time trials are regarded as particularly painful events because a rider cannot use the slipstream or draft effect of his competitors, and because tactics are secondary to pure concentration and sheer physical effort.

Sometimes there may be one or two rest days—usually just one which comes two-thirds of the way through on July 14, Bastille Day. Distances to be covered in each stage are quite different, ranging from 350 kilometers in a flat stage to as little as 20 kilometers in a time trial or one of the high mountain stages.

Although most time trials are held over fairly short distances, there are some that range longer in length. One of the most prestigious long distance events is the Hour Record time trial. In this event a racer is challenged to cover the maximum amount of distance possible in one hour. Points are awarded for winning and placing in all the time trials and race stages. Thus, for determining the overall Tour winner (calculated by a complex formula including total elapsed time and points for stage wins), time trials loom as important events.

To get a feel for an actual race, let's accompany the riders in the 1984 Tour. Seventeen teams entered the 1984 race, each with ten riders. A short prologue stage was held on Friday, June 29, two days before the official start. This was a time trial held near Paris that took the winner, Bernard Hinault, only 6 minutes, 39 seconds to complete. The tenth place rider was only 14 seconds behind the leader, and most riders agreed that this was just a small warm-up and not indicative of the race to follow. Nevertheless, Hinault got to wear the coveted yellow jersey (awarded to the winner of each stage) for the start of the actual race.

The first "real" stage of the 1984 Tour started from Seine-Saint-Denis on Sunday, July 1. The route wound 249 kilometers over secondary roads towards Louvroil in the Nord Department. The day was hot, and would have been oppressively so except for a headwind that was strong enough to cool down the passion for breakaways. Moreover, the road was narrow, rarely allowing more than three men abreast; thus, escape from the pack was effectively blocked. During this stage, the riders seemed most concerned with staying out of each other's way and avoiding the grazing contacts that can cause mass spills. Nevertheless, on a tight corner at the 78th kilometer, Jean-Rene Bernaudeau fell, scraping a knee. Before the day was over, six other riders crashed, injuring shoulders, legs, arms, and heads.

Jaime Vilamajo was fined 75 francs and penalized 10 seconds for receiving a bag of food at kilometer 158, 16 kilometers beyond the feeding zone, a designated stretch where riders can grab a light sack of food. Another rider was fined 50 francs for stopping on the left side of the road, instead of the regulation right, when he had a flat tire. In the old days, each rider carried a spare tire strapped to his back. However, as it took about three minutes for a rider to change his own tire and it takes a team mechanic only 30 seconds, today a rider with a flat simply waits at the side of the road for his team mechanic to come along and change the tire. These days, riders don't even dismount but simply stand, straddling the frame of their bicycle, while a tire is changed or a minor mechanical problem is fixed by a mechanic.

The second day of the 1984 race consisted of two stages, a 51-kilometer team time trial and an 83-kilometer stage through predominantly flat country near the Belgian border. During the afternoon stage, there was a strong sidewind, and Belgian rider Adri van den Haute, running 96th in the standings, perhaps sparked by the proximity to his native land, made a strong breakaway and built an astounding 6 minute and 23 second lead. Crowds love a breakaway, and a great cheer greeted him as he entered Douai, about midway through the stage. However, as the kilometers wore on and the sidewind turned into a rainy headwind, his lead slowly diminished, and he finally finished at Bethune with a 1 minute, 3 second lead.

The next day in Stage 5, Paulo Ferreira, an unknown Portuguese rider, unexpectedly broke away at kilometer 3, just after the start of the race. Two other riders followed him and the three of them swapped the positions of setting the pace and riding the slipstream for the entire 207 kilometers of the stage from Bethune to Cergy-Pontoise. As their lead from the pack built up through 11 minutes, 19 minutes, and ultimately 27 minutes, they experienced the exhilaration of looking back over the small hills and seeing nobody following. Until this stage, there had never been more than 13 seconds difference between the total elapsed time of the first- and fourth-place riders. Now, three completely new riders were in the top three places—Vincent Barteau, Maurice Le Guilloux, and Ferreira—and there was more than a 17-minute gap to the former first place rider who had slipped to fourth place.

Stage 6 was a 202-kilometer run over flat country to Alençon. The stage was largely uneventful until, just ten kilometers from the end, two riders in the middle of the pack locked wheels, causing a mass crash of at least 30 other riders. "What's awful about bicycling," said Greg LeMond, the great American cyclist, "is that you're supposed to get up, get back on your bike, and finish. In any other sport they'd let you lie there for a while. What if you'd done something to your neck and they get you up and put you on your bike and break your neck and you're paralyzed the rest of your life?"

Except in the Benelux countries, helmets are not required for cycling in Europe. Nobody wears them, because they are too hot and, according to most riders, their protective value has not been proven. Race organizers like to point out that competitive cycling is quite safe: "After all," they say, "only six riders have died from injuries in the last 30 years." Of course, this argument ignores the scores of non-fatal injuries sustained in nearly every race: broken legs and arms, dislocated shoulders, amputated fingers, concussions, gashes, and sprains.

Thursday, July 5, saw the first serious individual time trial—67 hilly kilometers from Alençon to Le Mans. Riders were started at two-minute intervals in the inverse order of their overall ranking. On a long time trial, a rider must not think about the distance traveled or the distance to go; rather, he must just focus on the next 20 meters; his attention cannot wander and he cannot relax. His back may be aching, his lungs bursting, and his legs wobbly, but he must pedal on.

Laurent Fignon of the Renault team finished with a time of 1 hour, 27 minutes, 33 seconds, with an average speed of nearly 46 kph. Sean Kelly, an Irish rider, was 16 seconds behind, and Bernard Hinault, an unpopular Breton who had won the Tour four times since his debut in 1978, finished 49 seconds off Fignon's time. Barteau was still in the lead, but Fignon had made up more than five minutes on his total time and was in fourth place overall.

The eighth stage on Friday, July 6 was a largely flat 192-kilometer ride from Le Mans to Nantes at the mouth of the Loire River on the West Coast. Pascal Jules of the Renault team won the stage, although overall he was well down in the rankings. The ninth, another flat stage, saw the cyclists "riding forever," as LeMond put it, "forever" being the 338 kilometers between Nantes and Bordeaux.

At the end of one of the bonus sprints on this long and boring stage, Hinault, accompanied by 20 other riders, made a breakaway and gained 30 seconds on the pack. It didn't take long for the Renault, Panasonic, and Kwantum teams to react. Their riders fell into team time-trial formations and pushed the pace up to 60 kph in an effort to catch the Hinault group. When a team is chasing over a flat road and can see the gap narrowing, the chasers have the psychological advantage. On this particular July day, some additional aid to the chasers came from an unexpected ally, the wind, which shifted from the left side to a headwind. In 20 kilometers the pack had caught the renegades, and things settled down for the remaining 200 odd kilometers. Jan Raas of the Kwantum team was the winner with a time of 9 hours, 40 minutes. The order of the first six riders had not changed since Alençon, and Barteau, surprisingly, was still in first place overall, with the favored Fignon in fourth place, trailing the leader by more than 12 minutes.

The tenth stage—the prelude to the mountains—was held Sunday, July 8. It covered 198 kilometers from Bordeaux to Pau in the foothills of the Pyrenees. Eric Vanderaerden was the stage victor. Fignon displaced Ferreira from third place but was still more than 12 minutes behind race leader Barteau.

Compared to previous years, the climb in the Pyrenees from Pau to the ski resort at the summit of Guzet-Neige (1480 meters high) was relatively benign. Asked why the new route was chosen, the organizers claimed it was to avoid the steeper peaks close to the Spanish border where Spanish Basques, eager for publicity, might possibly disrupt the race. Robert Millar of Scotland was the easy winner with Luis Herrera of Colombia 41 seconds behind him. Overall, the first three places remained unchanged, but Ferreira, who had been holding on to fourth place, proved conclusively that he was not a climber by finishing dead last, 59 minutes and 43 seconds behind Millar.

Next came a series of four stages through the Massif Central, France's mountainous heartland and the transition between the Pyrenees and the Alps. This is a region of hills, gorges, short climbs, and sharp descents. The roads are bumpy and narrow. Stressful climbs, sharp turns, and bold descents took their toll on the riders—both physically and mentally. Grenoble, the start of the tough Alpine stages, was reached on July 14, Bastille Day and the only rest day of the Tour. At this point, after 15 stages, Barteau was still leading with a total elapsed time of 73 hours, 52 minutes, 19 seconds. Fignon had worked up to second place, 10 minutes, 13 seconds behind; Hinault was third, less than two minutes behind Fignon; LeMond was sixth and Kelly seventh, both a bit over 14 minutes behind the leader; and Millar had pulled up to ninth place. Barteau had held up far better than his two companions on the Cergy-Pontoise breakaway; Le Guilloux had dropped to thirty-third while Ferreira, totally defeated by the mountains, was running dead last in the field of 140 men remaining in the race.

The next five days in the Alps would answer many questions:

Could the young Barteau hold onto his lead? Could Hinault win a fifth victory? Could Fignon duplicate his win of the year before? How would the American LeMond make out? Would the

Scot, Millar, or the Irishman, Kelly, be any real challenge to the leaders? Would any of the Colombians, known for their mountain racing, be a factor in this race?

First in the Alps was a 22-kilometer individual time trial, followed by daily climbs to L'Alpe-d'Huez, La Plagne, Morzine, and Crans-Montana Mountain in Switzerland. Fignon won the time trial easily; Herrera was second, Delgado third, and Hinault fourth.

The first climb was 151 kilometers; the second, 185 kilometers; the third, 186 kilometers; and the fourth, 140 kilometers. In the first mountain stage, Barteau was unseated from his first-place position. (He continued to slip and finally finished the Tour in 28th place, exactly one hour behind the leader.) By the end of the second of these mountain stages, it was clear that Fignon would win the race unless he was injured or did something very stupid. Hinault was running second, almost nine minutes behind Fignon, but it was clear that he could not close the gap. LeMond was third, just a little more than one minute behind Hinault, and Millar was just 20 seconds behind him.

As it turned out, these places did not change from the second Alps stage, the eighteenth stage of the race, to the end of the Tour. On the other hand, the mountains exacted a terrible toll from the rest of the pack. Delgado, a fast Spanish rider, got a puncture just before the Morzine finish line, crashed, broke his shoulder, and left the race. Tonon, an experienced Italian rider, hit a spectator who had wandered onto the road with his bike; both were rushed to a hospital by helicopter, Tonon with a fractured skull, the spectator with "grave injuries." In all, 16 riders were forced to retire from the race with injuries during these four stages.

The twenty-first stage was another long one—320 kilometers, from Crans-Montana to Villefranche-sur-Saône, across the Beaujolais wine country. The riders, exhausted from their days in the mountains, appealed to the race organizers to shorten the stage; they won a reduction, and the first 30 kilometers were covered in team cars.

Little was at stake during this stage and during the ten hot and dreary hours, the riders decided to clown a bit. Barteau pretended to read a newspaper, Castaing did a giant crossword puzzle, Brun turned his handlebars up like a casual Sunday rider, and the pack goaded Cabrera, a timid little Colombian, to win two of the bonus sprints. Kelly was not having any of it; while Cabrera was playfully being allowed to win his first sprint, Kelly was right behind him, gaining an eight-second reduction in his overall time. By the end of the day, Kelly had worked his way up from seventh place to fifth. Kelly, desperate for a stage victory, kept pressing on and eventually won a mock victory at the midpoint of the stage.

The next day was a 51-kilometer time trial, and Kelly, determined to earn the coveted stage victory, went all out to win. His time was a sensational 1 hour, 7 minutes, 9 seconds; Hinault was second, 36 seconds behind; and LeMond third, 41 seconds behind. Only Fignon, last to start, was still out on the road. He finished the race with a long sprint in the same time as Kelly; when the timers calculated the time to thousandths of a second, they gave the race to Fignon by

48/1000 seconds. Disappointed and frustrated, Kelly had no use for the condolences of other riders.

Later that day, July 21, the riders boarded a train for Paris. For all intents and purposes, the race was over, although there was one last 196-kilometer stage run around the suburbs of Paris that would pass the Arc de Triomphe six times before it swept down the Champs-Elysées to the finish line at the Place de la Concorde. This was a sprinter's stage, and it was won by Vanderaerden, with Jules, Hoste, Hinault, and Kelly following.

Finishers: 124 out of 170. First: Laurent Fignon. Second: Bernard Hinault. Third: Greg LeMond. Fourth: Robert Millar. Fifth: Sean Kelly. First Colombian finisher: Luis Herrera, twenty-seventh place. Leading climber (polka-dot jersey): Millar. Points leader (green jersey): Franck Hoste. Leading neophyte (white jersey): LeMond. Top team by time: Renault. Top team by points: Panasonic/Raleigh.

Months later, as the season came to a close, Hinault came back to win two prestigious one-day classics; Barteau, being in great demand, rode several six-day races; and Sean Kelly was awarded the Super Prestige Pernod trophy as the season's top-ranked professional bicyclist. LeMond left the Renault team and signed a $1 million contract with the La Vie Claire team. Three other teams disbanded. And riders mounted their exercise machines to wait for the start of the next season.

BIBLIOGRAPHY

Abt, Samuel. *Breakaway: On the Road with the Tour de France.* New York: Random House, 1985.

Leete, Harley M., ed. *The Best of Bicycling!* New York: Trident Press, 1970.

Walton, Bill and Rostaing, Bjarne. *Bill Walton's Total Book of Bicycling.* New York: Bantam Books, 1985.

THE PROGRAM

The Tour de France program consists of a main program (with five sections and five associated subroutines), two introductory sections (with five associated subroutines), a closing section, and five utility subroutines.

In the introductory section, the title screen is displayed followed by a screen of instructions. While this screen is being displayed, data are read in subroutines at Sub1430, Sub3050 (uses routes.txt data file), and Sub3300. After all the data have been read, you are instructed to "Press Enter to continue," and program execution proceeds.

In the pre-race data section (starts at LN300), you are asked to enter information about your physical fitness and your practice time.

The routine to select the gear range (starts at LN650) is straightforward. If you select a gear range that is too high for the terrain, you will have to shift much more than you should, and appropriate penalties are accessed in LN830. In addition, using a gear range that is too high in the mountains increases physical exertion and the risk of collapse. Code after the 'Physical problems comment line tests for these conditions and, if they exist, increases the probability of physical collapse by ten percentage points (from 11% to 21%). If nothing happens, probabilities are returned to normal.

In the sprint routine (after 'Sprint at end of stage comment), a counter, which counts down in 0.1-kilometer increments starting 10 km from the end of the race, will start. You enter how far into the countdown you want to start you sprint.

After the sprint finish, daily elapsed times for five other riders are calculated. The program assumes they are all in excellent physical condition and that they use the correct gear for the terrain. They have their share of delay-causing problems (1.4 * Math.GetRandomNumber(999)/1000) which tend to be in the same range as your delay time.

Event probabilities (Sub1430) are handled in the same generalized way as in the Marco Polo program, the difference being that Tour de France has three different sets of events: road hazards, mechanical breakdowns, and physical problems. Each of these sets of events has its own subroutine. Various events cause delays of between 0.1 hours (6 minutes) and 1 hour (physical collapse, assuming you recover). A few "events" are simply informative and cause no delay: a nice day in the French countryside, bicycle running like a charm, and feeling fit as a fiddle.

All the other subroutines either are straightforward and self-explanatory or are explained in the program notes for other programs.

PROGRAM VARIABLES

```
A Answer to input query, numeric
AD Answer to input query, string
BD Temporary string variable
CG Teeth on cog
CL Physical-collapse indicator
CR Crash indicator
DAY Day of race
DIST[d] Distance to cover (d = day)
DSP Distance of sprint
FIT Physical-fitness factor (.1 = poor, .5 = excellent)
GDGR Good gear indicator (0 = poor, 1 = good)
GQ Gear ratio x distance (for calculating performance of other riders)
GR Gear ratio
I Temporary iteration variable
K Temporary iteration variable
KPH Speed over route
KSR Speed of sprint
PAUSE Temporary iteration variable
PFRQ Pedaling frequency (1 = low, 10 = high)
PLACED[d] Destination for day (d = day)
PM[n] Probability of mechanical problem (n = problem no.)
PMT Total probabilities of all mechanical problems
PP[n] Probability of physical problem (n = problem no.)
PPT Total probabilities of all physical problems
PR[n] Probability of road hazard (n = hazard no.)
PRT Total probabilities of all road hazards
PT Pedaling time
RN Random number
RNG Teeth on ring gear
RPM Pedal speed
RPS RPM-speed multiplier
TDEP Time of departure
TDL Time for delays
TMSD Time to ride sprint distance
TMRD Time to ride route distance
TTM[r] Total time for stage (r = rider)
TTR[r] Total time for race to date (r = rider)
TTS Total stage time, leader
TTT Total race time, leader
TYPE[d] Type of terrain (d = day)
TYPED[t] Type of terrain, description
WK Weeks of practice
WS Winner of stage
WSG[r] Stages won by each rider (r = rider)
WT Winner of race to date
XD Temporary string variable
```

Note: Distances are in kilometers
Times in hours and fractions
Speeds in kilometers per hour

PROGRAM LISTINGS

```
TextWindow.CursorTop = 10
XD = "Tour de France Bicycle Race"
Sub3470()
TextWindow.CursorTop = 13
XD = "(c) David H. Ahl, 1986"
Sub3470()
TextWindow.CursorTop = 23
XD = "Press Enter to continue."
Sub3470()
JJJ = TextWindow.Read()
TextWindow.Clear()
Sub3500()
'Display initial scenario
'DIM PLACED[23), TYPE[23), DIST[23), PP[14)
GDGR = 1
PLACED[0] = "Reims"
Sub1430()
'Read event probabilities
Sub3050()
Sub3300()
'Read data about places
TextWindow.CursorTop = 23
XD = "Press Enter to continue."
Sub3470()
JJJ = TextWindow.Read()
TextWindow.Clear()
'
'Calculate pedaling time (takes 20 seconds)
LN300:
TextWindow.WriteLine("")
TextWindow.WriteLine("About your physical fitness: are you (1) in fantastic
health,")
TextWindow.WriteLine(" (2) excellent shape, (3) quite good, (4) okay, (5)
poor")
LN320:
TextWindow.Write(" Please enter a number between 1 and 5? ")
A = TextWindow.ReadNumber()
If A < 1 OR A > 5 Then
TextWindow.WriteLine("Huh? I don't understand.")
GOTO LN320
EndIf
FIT = .57 - .04 * A 'Physical fitness factor
TextWindow.WriteLine("")
LN350:
TextWindow.WriteLine("How many weeks do you intend to take off from work or
school to")
TextWindow.Write("practice and prepare for the race? ")
WK =TextWindow.Read()
If WK > 12 Then
  WK = 12
EndIf
If WK > 5 Then
Goto LN390
```

```
ELSE
TextWindow.WriteLine("You must be joking. You'll need at least six")
TextWindow.WriteLine("weeks if you want to be a real contender. Now ... ")
Goto LN350
EndIf
LN390:
FIT = FIT - (12 - WK) * .05 'Modify fitness factor for amount of practice
TextWindow.WriteLine("")
'Beginning of main riding section
LN540:
DAY = DAY + 1
TextWindow.WriteLine("")
TextWindow.WriteLine("Date: July "+ DAY+ " You are at " +PLACED[DAY - 1]+
".")
If TYPE[DAY] < 5 Then
  Goto LN580
EndIf
TextWindow.WriteLine("Today, thank goodness, is a rest and recuperation
day.")
Goto LN540
LN580:
TextWindow.WriteLine("Your destination is "+ PLACED[DAY]+ ", "+ DIST[DAY]+ "
km from here.")
TextWindow.WriteLine("Type of racing this stage: "+ TYPED[TYPE[DAY]])
If TYPE[DAY]<>TYPE[DAY - 1] Then
  Goto LN650
EndIf
'
'Select gear range
TextWindow.Write("Do you want a different basic gear range than yesterday? ")
AD = TextWindow.Read()
sub3350()
If AD = "N" Then
Goto LN850
ELSE
GDGR = 1
EndIf
LN650:
TextWindow.WriteLine("Naturally you will shift gears, but what will be your
basic gear")
TextWindow.Write("range (ring and cog) for the day. First the ring (40 or
52)? ")
RNG = TextWindow.ReadNumber()
LN670:
If RNG = 40 OR RNG = 52 Then
Goto LN690
ELSE
TextWindow.WriteLine("You don't have that ring.")
EndIf
LN680:
TextWindow.Write("Enter 40 or 52 please? ")
RNG = TextWindow.ReadNumber()
Goto LN670
LN690:
TextWindow.Write("Which cog (13, 15, 17, 19, 21, 23, or 25)? ")
```

```
CG = TextWindow.ReadNumber()
If CG = 13 OR CG = 15 OR CG = 17 OR CG = 19 OR CG = 21 OR CG = 23 OR CG = 25
Then
  Goto LN720
EndIf
TextWindow.WriteLine("Sorry, you don't have that cog. Please try again.")
Goto LN690
LN720:
If (CG = 13 AND RNG = 40) OR (CG = 25 AND RNG = 52) Then
Goto LN730
ELSE
GR = RNG / CG
GOTO LN750
EndIf
LN730:
TextWindow.WriteLine("The chain line will be badly skewed with that
combination.")
LN740:
TextWindow.Write("Let's do it again. First the ring.  ")
Goto LN680
LN750:
If TYPE[DAY] = 4 Then
  Goto LN850
EndIf
If GR > 3.2 Then
XD = "high"
ELSEIF GR < 1.8 THEN
XD = "low"
ELSE
GOTO LN790
EndIf
TextWindow.Write("That ratio sounds very "+ XD)
TextWindow.Write(". Do you want to change it? ")
AD = TextWindow.Read()
sub3350()
If AD = "Y" Then
  Goto LN740
EndIf
LN790:
If TYPE[DAY] = 3 AND GR > 2.3 Then
Goto LN800
ELSE
goto LN830
EndIf
LN800:
TextWindow.WriteLine("For mountainous terrain, that's a rather high basic
gear ratio.")
TextWindow.Write("Do you want to stick with it? ")
AD=TextWindow.Read()
sub3350()
If AD = "N" Then
  Goto LN740
EndIf
GDGR = 1.3 - .19 * GR
Goto LN840
```

```
LN830:
'Penalty for too high gear ratio in mts
If GR > 3 Then
  GDGR = 1.35 - .14 * GR  'Penalty for too high gear on flat route
EndIf
LN840:
'
LN850:
'Start of stage
TDEP = 100 + Math.Floor(59 * Math.GetRandomNumber(999)/1000)
TextWindow.WriteLine("")
TextWindow.Write("Your departure time is scheduled at 9:")
TextWindow.WriteLine(Text.GetSubTextToEnd(TDEP, text.getlength(tdep) - 2 +
1))
Sub3440()
PTM = 1
RPS = 130
Sub2890()
KPH = RPM * .1292706 * GR * GDGR
TDValue = KPH
TwoDecimals()
TextWindow.Write(TDDisplay)
TextWindow.WriteLine(" kph.")
TextWindow.WriteLine("")
TDL = 0
Sub1510()
'Road hazards
CR = 0
TextWindow.WriteLine("")
Sub1760()
'Mechanical breakdowns
If TYPE[DAY] = 3 AND GR > 2.7 Then
PP[1] = PP[1] + 10
PPT = PPT + 10
PPX = 1
EndIf
TextWindow.WriteLine("")
Sub2140()
'Physical problems
If PPX = 1 Then
PPX = 0
PP[1] = PP[1] - 10
PPT = PPT - 10
EndIf
TextWindow.WriteLine("")
TextWindow.Write("Time for a quick breather. You have about ")
TextWindow.WriteLine(Math.Floor(20 + 20 * Math.GetRandomNumber(999)/1000) +"
km to go.")
TextWindow.WriteLine("")
TextWindow.WriteLine("Press Enter when you're ready to go.")
JJJ = TextWindow.Read()
TextWindow.WriteLine("Okay, on the road again ... ")
'
'Sprint at end of stage
Sub3440()
```

```
TextWindow.Clear()
TextWindow.WriteLine("You're coming up on 10 km from the end.")
LN3441:
TextWindow.Write("How far out do you want to start your sprint? ")
DSP1 = TextWindow.ReadNumber()
If DSP1 < 0 OR DSP1 > 10 Then
TextWindow.CursorTop = 1
TextWindow.Write("Try again. ")
Goto LN3441
EndIf
TextWindow.WriteLine("Here's the countdown:")
Sub3440()
TextWindow.WriteLine("")
For DSP = 10 To 0 Step -.1
'Count down from 10km by 0.1 increments
TextWindow.CursorTop = 4
TextWindow.CursorLeft = 5
TDValue = DSP
TwoDecimals()
TextWindow.WriteLine("Distance Remaining: " + TDDisplay + " km    ")
Program.Delay(50)
'need logic to stop countdown - 'goto LN1070 when stopped
If DSP <= DSP1 Then
  Goto LN1070
EndIf
EndFor
Goto ln1070
KSR = 1
Goto LN1090
LN1070:
TextWindow.WriteLine("")
PTM = DSP / 2
RPS = 140
Sub2890()
KSR = RPM * .396
'Sprint speed
TDValue = KSR
TwoDecimals()
TextWindow.Write(TDDisplay)
TextWindow.WriteLine(" kph.")
TextWindow.WriteLine("")
LN1090:
TMSD = DSP / KSR
TMRD = (DIST[DAY] - DSP) / KPH
TTM[1] = TMSD + TMRD + TDL
If DSP > 3 Then
  TextWindow.WriteLine("Puff ... puff ... puff. That was a L-O-N-G sprint!")
EndIf
'
'Calculate top six riders
TextWindow.WriteLine("")
TextWindow.WriteLine("Race summary (total times in hours):")
TextWindow.WriteLine("Rider        1-You    2        3        4        5
6")
TTS = TTM[1]
```

```
WS = 1
TextWindow.Write("Stage time")
TDValue = TTM[1]
TwoDecimals()
TextWindow.CursorLeft = 13
TextWindow.Write(TDDisplay)
If TYPE[DAY] = 3 Then
GQ = .3
ELSE
GQ = .4
EndIf
For I = 2 To 6
RPM = 70 + 20 * Math.GetRandomNumber(999)/1000
TTM[I] = DIST[DAY] / (GQ * RPM) + 1.4 * Math.GetRandomNumber(999)/1000
TDValue = TTM[i]
TwoDecimals()
TextWindow.CursorLeft = 13 + (I - 1) * 9
TextWindow.Write(TDDisplay)
If TTM[I] < TTS Then
TTS = TTM[I]
WS = I
EndIf
EndFor
TTT = 1000
WT = 0
TextWindow.WriteLine("")
TextWindow.Write("Total time")
For I = 1 To 6
TTR[I] = TTR[I] + TTM[I]
TDValue = TTR[I]
TwoDecimals()
TextWindow.CursorLeft = 13 + (I - 1) * 9
TextWindow.Write(TDDisplay)
If TTR[I] < TTT Then
TTT = TTR[I]
WT = I
EndIf
EndFor
TextWindow.WriteLine("")
TextWindow.WriteLine("")
TextWindow.WriteLine(" Stage winner: Rider "+ WS+ "   Overall leader : Rider
"+ WT)
WSG[WS] = WSG[WS] + 1
If DAY < 22 Then
  Goto LN540
EndIf
'
'End-of-race summary
TextWindow.WriteLine("")
TextWindow.WriteLine("The Tour de France has ended!")
TextWindow.WriteLine("")
X = 0
FOR I = 1 TO 6
If WSG[I] > X Then
X = WSG[I]
```

```
WS = I
EndIf
EndFor
TextWindow.Write("Winner of the most stages ("+ X+ ") was Rider " +WS)
If WS = 1 Then
TextWindow.WriteLine(" That's YOU!")
ELSE
TextWindow.WriteLine("")
EndIf
TextWindow.Write("Overall winner by elapsed time was Rider "+ WT)
If WT = 1 Then
TextWindow.WriteLine(" That's YOU!")
ELSE
TextWindow.WriteLine("")
EndIf
TTT = 1000
WT = 0
For I = 1 To 6
If TTR[I] - 2 * WSG[I] < TTT Then
TTT = TTR[I] - 2 * WSG[I]
WT = I
EndIf
EndFor
TextWindow.Write("Overall points winner (time and stages) was Rider "+ WT)
If WT = 1 Then
TextWindow.WriteLine(" That's YOU!")
ELSE
TextWindow.WriteLine("")
EndIf
finished="true"
sub2700()
'
Sub Sub1430
'Subroutine to set event probabilities
PR[1] = 5
PR[2] = 10
PR[3] = 15
PR[4] = 20
PR[5] = 25
PR[6] = 30
PR[7] = 35
PR[8] = 40
PR[9] = 45
PR[10] = 50
PRT=50

PM[1] = 5
PM[2] = 10
PM[3] = 15
PM[4] = 20
PM[5] = 25
PM[6] = 30
PM[7] = 40
PM[8] = 45
PMT=45
```

```
PP[1] = 8
PP[2] = 13
PP[3] = 18
PP[4] = 23
PP[5] = 28
PP[6] = 33
PP[7] = 38
PP[8] = 43
PP[9] = 48
PP[10] = 56
PP[11] = 61
PP[12] = 66
PP[13] = 71
PP[14] = 74
PPT=74
EndSub
'
Sub Sub1510
'Subroutine to deal with road hazards
RN = Math.Floor(PRT * Math.GetRandomNumber(999)/1000)
For I = 1 To 10
If RN <= PR[I] Then
  Goto LN1511 'If event happened, exit loop
EndIf
EndFor
I = 10
LN1511:
If (I = 1) Then
  Goto LN1550
ElseIf (I = 2) Then
  Goto LN1570
ElseIf (I = 3) Then
  Goto LN1590
ElseIf (I = 4) Then
  Goto LN1610
ElseIf (I = 5) Then
  Goto LN1630
ElseIf (I = 6) Then
  Goto LN1650
ElseIf (I = 7) Then
  Goto LN1670
ElseIf (I = 8) Then
  Goto LN1690
ElseIf (I = 9) Then
  Goto LN1720
ElseIf (I = 10) Then
  Goto LN1740
EndIf
LN1550:
TextWindow.WriteLine("Mostly gravel roads this stage. You'll have to slow
down.")
TDL = TDL + .8
Goto LN1759
LN1570:
```

```
TextWindow.WriteLine("The roads in this area are very bumpy and will slow you
down.")
TDL = TDL + .5
Goto LN1759
LN1590:
TextWindow.WriteLine("Hot weather in this area has caused the roads to become
very")
TextWindow.WriteLine("slippery from oil seepage.")
TDL = TDL + .3
Goto LN1759
LN1610:
TextWindow.WriteLine("The wind is at your back making for a very fast ride!")
TDL = TDL + -.3
Goto LN1759
LN1630:
TextWindow.WriteLine("You're heading straight into the wind today. Tough
going.")
TDL = TDL + .5
Goto LN1759
LN1650:
TextWindow.WriteLine("There is a gusty sidewind today creating balance
problems.")
TDL = TDL + .3
Goto LN1759
LN1670:
TextWindow.WriteLine("Dreary day: drizzle, fog, and clammy chill in the
air.")
TDL = TDL + .2
Goto LN1759
LN1690:
TextWindow.WriteLine("Horrible weather! Icy rain that hits you like 1000
needles,")
TextWindow.WriteLine("stinging your face and arms. Your shoes are soaked. And
there")
TextWindow.WriteLine("are few spectators to cheer you on.")
TDL = TDL + .5
Goto LN1759
LN1720:
TextWindow.WriteLine("Mud and puddles on the road cause you to slide and skid
all over.")
TDL = TDL + .4
Goto LN1759
LN1740:
TextWindow.WriteLine("Today is a crisp, clear day in the French
countryside.")
LN1759:
EndSub
'
Sub Sub1760
'Subroutine to deal with mechanical breakdowns
RN = Math.Floor(PMT * Math.GetRandomNumber(999)/1000)
For I = 1 To 8
'Select event
If RN <= PM[I] Then
  Goto LN1761 'If event happened, exit loop
```

```
EndIf
EndFor
I = 8
LN1761:
If (I = 1) Then
  Goto LN1800
ElseIf (I = 2) Then
  Goto LN1830
ElseIf (I = 3) Then
  Goto LN1850
ElseIf (I = 4) Then
  Goto LN1890
ElseIf (I = 5) Then
  Goto LN1930
ElseIf (I = 6) Then
  Goto LN1970
ElseIf (I = 7) Then
  Goto LN1990
ElseIf (I = 8) Then
  Goto LN2120
EndIf
LN1800:
TextWindow.Write("You have a broken spoke. Want to fix it now? ")
AD = TextWindow.Read()
Sub3350()
If AD = "Y" Then
TDL = TDL + .1
ELSE
TDL = TDL + .15
EndIf
Goto LN2122
LN1830:
TextWindow.WriteLine("You got a flat tire. You'll have to change it now.")
TDL = TDL + .1
Goto LN2122
LN1850:
TextWindow.WriteLine("Your brakes tend to lock every time you apply them
hard. You can")
TextWindow.Write("nurse them along or fix them here. Want to fix them now? ")
AD = TextWindow.Read()
Sub3350()
If AD = "Y" Then
TDL = TDL + .2
ELSE
TDL = TDL + .4
EndIf
Goto LN2122
LN1890:
TextWindow.WriteLine("You seem to be missing shifts to your 19 cog. Perhaps
one or")
TextWindow.WriteLine("more teeth are worn. You can shift around it or fix it
here.")
TextWindow.Write("Want to fix it now? ")
AD=TextWindow.Read()
Sub3350()
```

```
If AD = "Y" Then
TDL = TDL + .2
Goto LN2122
EndIf
TDL = TDL + .4
Goto LN2122
LN1930:
TextWindow.WriteLine("On a tight corner, you narrowly missed a spill, but
your toe clip")
TextWindow.Write("got bent on a boulder near the road. Want to bend it out
now? ")
AD = TextWindow.Read()
If AD = "Y" Then
TDL = TDL + .1
ELSE
TDL = TDL + .2
EndIf
Goto LN2122
LN1970:
TextWindow.WriteLine("Uh oh! Chain broke. You've no choice but to fix it
now.")
TDL = TDL + .15
Goto LN2122
LN1990:
TextWindow.WriteLine("WHOOPS! Took a corner too fast, lost traction, slid,
and CRASHED!")
sub3440()
CR = 1
RN = Math.GetRandomNumber(999)/1000
If RN < .03 Then
Goto LN2080
ELSEIF RN < .5 THEN
goto LN2040
EndIf
TextWindow.WriteLine("You pick up yourself and your bicycle. You're both")
TextWindow.WriteLine("scratched and a bit beaten up but there seems to be
no")
TextWindow.WriteLine("serious damage so you get on your way.")
TDL = TDL + .3
Goto LN2122
LN2040:
TextWindow.WriteLine("You twisted your ankle and it is very painful. You know
it will")
TextWindow.WriteLine("slow you down. However, there is no way you would drop
out of the")
TextWindow.WriteLine("race, so you pick up your bicycle and get on your
way.")
TDL = TDL + .8
Goto LN2122
LN2080:
TextWindow.WriteLine("Blood is all over the place; ambulance is called and")
TextWindow.WriteLine("you are rushed to the local hospital.")
Sub3440()
TextWindow.WriteLine("Bad news! You dislocated your shoulder and you're out
of the race.")
```

```
finished = "false"
sub2700()
LN2120:
TextWindow.WriteLine("Bicycle ran like a charm today. No problems at all!")
LN2122:
EndSub
'
Sub Sub2140
'Subroutine to deal with physical problems
LN2150:
RN = Math.Floor(PPT * Math.GetRandomNumber(999)/1000)
For I = 1 To 14
If RN <= PP[I] Then
  goto LN2151 'If event happened, exit loop
EndIf
EndFor
I = 14
LN2151:
If I > 10 Then
  Goto LN2190
EndIf
If (I = 1) Then
  Goto LN2200
ElseIf (I = 2) Then
  Goto LN2320
ElseIf (I = 3) Then
  Goto LN2340
ElseIf (I = 4) Then
  Goto LN2370
ElseIf (I = 5) Then
  Goto LN2390
ElseIf (I = 6) Then
  Goto LN2420
ElseIf (I = 7) Then
  Goto LN2440
ElseIf (I = 8) Then
  Goto LN2470
ElseIf (I = 9) Then
  Goto LN2500
ElseIf (I = 10) Then
  Goto LN2530
EndIf
LN2190:
If (I - 10 = 1) Then
  Goto LN2560
ElseIf (I - 10 = 2) Then
  Goto LN2600
ElseIf (I - 10 = 3) Then
  Goto LN2640
ElseIf (I - 10 = 4) Then
  Goto LN2660
EndIf
LN2200:
X = Math.Floor(DIST[DAY] / 50)
If X < 2 Then
```

```
  X = 2
EndIf
TextWindow.WriteLine("You're pushing yourself to the absolute limit and after
"+ X +" hours")
TextWindow.WriteLine("you totally collapse. The medics give you oxygen and
bring you")
TextWindow.WriteLine("around, but warn you against resuming the race.")
If CL > 0 Then
  Goto LN2290
EndIf
CL = 1
If Math.GetRandomNumber(999)/1000 > .8 Then
  Goto LN2270
EndIf
Sub3440()
TextWindow.WriteLine("But nothing can defeat your competitive spirit and
you")
TextWindow.WriteLine("vow to press on regardless.")
TDL = TDL + 1
Goto LN2699
LN2270:
Sub3440()
TextWindow.WriteLine("You heard of another rider dying from overexertion
last")
TextWindow.WriteLine("year, so you follow the doctor's advice and withdraw.")
finished = "false"
sub2700()
LN2290:
Sub3440()
TextWindow.WriteLine("This is the second time you collapsed in this race,")
TextWindow.WriteLine("so you reluctantly concede that this just isn't your
year")
TextWindow.WriteLine("and you withdraw from the race.")
finished = "false"
sub2700()
LN2320:
TextWindow.WriteLine("You have a terrible abdominal pain ... something you
ate, perhaps?")
TextWindow.WriteLine("You'll have to slow down a bit.")
TDL = TDL + .4
Goto LN2699
LN2340:
TextWindow.WriteLine("You're having difficulty breathing and you're feeling
lightheaded.")
LN2350:
TextWindow.WriteLine("You recognize this as an early warning signal of total
collapse")
TextWindow.WriteLine("and wisely decide to slow your pace a bit.")
TDL = TDL + .3
Goto LN2699
LN2370:
TextWindow.WriteLine("You seem to be seeing through a haze ... and it's not
the weather.")
TextWindow.WriteLine("Occasionally, you can't seem to focus at all.")
Goto LN2350
```

```
LN2390:
TextWindow.WriteLine("Uh oh! A muscle in your calf seems to have turned to jelly. It's")
TextWindow.WriteLine("not particularly painful, but it seems to be completely out of")
TextWindow.WriteLine("control. You'll have to slow down a bit.")
TDL = TDL + .3
Goto LN2699
LN2420:
TextWindow.WriteLine("You have a sharp pain in your lower back. It doesn't seem to be")
TextWindow.WriteLine("injured ... perhaps you're just overly tense.")
TDL = TDL + .2
Goto LN2699
LN2440:
TextWindow.WriteLine("The gearing you've been using is really tough on your legs and")
TextWindow.WriteLine("you have developed shin splints. You'll have to back off your")
TextWindow.WriteLine("blistering pace a bit.")
TDL = TDL + .3
Goto LN2699
LN2470:
TextWindow.WriteLine("Terrible pain in the balls of your feet. Your toe clip seems to be")
TextWindow.WriteLine("adjusted correctly. Maybe it's these new cleats. In any event,")
TextWindow.WriteLine("you decide to back off a bit ... just for today.")
TDL = TDL + .3
Goto LN2699
LN2500:
TextWindow.WriteLine("A medic takes a look at you during lunch break and declares you")
TextWindow.WriteLine("have a salt/water imbalance. 'Drink more water along the way,'")
TextWindow.WriteLine("he recommends, 'and don't forget your salt pills.'")
Goto LN2699
LN2530:
If TYPE<>3 Then
  Goto LN2660
EndIf
TextWindow.WriteLine("The altitude is getting to you in the mountains. You're short of")
TextWindow.WriteLine("breath and you feel lightheaded.")
goto LN2699
LN2560:
TextWindow.WriteLine("Your saddle feels like it has appended itself to your body. A cyst")
TextWindow.WriteLine("seems to be starting, something you want to avoid at all costs.")
TextWindow.WriteLine("You put some extra padding on the saddle and back off on your")
TextWindow.WriteLine("pace just a tad.")
TDL = TDL + .15
Goto LN2699
```

```
LN2600:
TextWindow.WriteLine("The blistering pace you've been keeping has played
havoc with your")
TextWindow.WriteLine("knees. You've heard of football players with bad knees,
but a")
TextWindow.WriteLine("bicycle racer? Nevertheless, you'll have to slow down a
bit.")
TDL = TDL + .2
Goto LN2699
LN2640:
TextWindow.WriteLine("You developed a bad cramp in your legs. You'll have to
take it")
TextWindow.WriteLine("just a bit easier.")
TDL = TDL + .15
Goto LN2699
LN2660:
If CR = 1 Then
  Goto LN2150 'Can't feel too great after a crash
EndIf
TextWindow.WriteLine("You're feeling fit as a fiddle and have no physical
problems today.")
LN2699:
EndSub
'
Sub Sub2700
If finished then
Goto LN2730
endif
'It's all over
TextWindow.WriteLine("")
TextWindow.WriteLine("Too bad. That's it for this year, but there's always")
TextWindow.WriteLine("next year....")
LN2730:
TextWindow.WriteLine("")
TextWindow.Write("Press Enter To End")
AD = TextWindow.Read()
Program.End()
EndSub
'
Sub Sub2760
'Subroutine to assign keys to pedals

EndSub
'


'
Sub Sub2890
'Subroutine to pedal bicycle
RPM = Math.Floor((RPS + (30 + 40 * Math.GetRandomNumber(999)/1000)) * FIT)
TextWindow.WriteLine("Pedaling your bicycle-at a rate of "+ RPM+ " rpm. ")
Sub3440()
TextWindow.Write("Calculating speed....")
EndSub
'
Sub Sub3050
```

```
CLINE = 1
DataFile = Program.Directory +"\routes.txt"
FileLine = File.ReadLine(DataFile, CLINE)
For I = 1 To 22
  GetNextItem()
  N = NextItem
  GetNextItem()
  PLACED[I] = NextItem
  GetNextItem()
  TYPE[I] = NextItem
  GetNextItem()
  DIST[I] = NextItem
EndFor
EndSub

Sub GetNextItem
  'find comma in FileLine
  KK = Text.GetIndexOf(FileLine, ",")
  If KK <> 0 Then
    NextItem = Text.GetSubText(FileLine, 1, KK - 1)
    FileLine = Text.GetSubTextToEnd(FileLine, KK + 1)
  Else
    NextItem = FileLine
    CLINE = CLINE + 1
    FileLine = File.ReadLine(DataFile, CLINE)
  EndIf
  EndSub

Sub Sub3300
'Subroutine to read words
TYPED[1] = "Mostly flat with small hills."
TYPED[2] = "Hills, gorges, steep slopes."
TYPED[3] = "Mountains."
TYPED[4] = "Time trial against the clock."
TYPED[5] = "Rest."
EndSub
'
Sub Sub3350
'Subroutine to read yes/no answer
LN3360:
sub3390()
If AD = "Y" OR AD = "N" Then
  Goto LN3389
EndIf
TextWindow.Write("Don't understand your answer. Enter 'Y' or 'N' please? ")
AD = TextWindow.Read()
Goto LN3360
LN3389:
EndSub
'
Sub Sub3390
'Subroutine to read first letter of answer and convert to uppercase
If AD = "" Then
AD = "Y"
Goto LN3339
```

```
EndIf
AD = Text.GetSubText(AD,1, 1)
If text.GetCharacterCode(AD) >= text.GetCharacterCode("A") AND
text.GetCharacterCode(AD) <= text.GetCharacterCode("Z") Then
  Goto ln3339
EndIf
AD = text.GetCharacter(text.GetCharacterCode(AD) - 32)
LN3339:
EndSub
'
Sub Sub3440
'Subroutine to make a short pause
Program.Delay(500)
Endsub

Sub Sub3470
'Subroutine to print a centered line
TextWindow.CursorLeft = (70 - Text.GetLength(XD))/2
TextWindow.WriteLine(XD)
EndSub
'
Sub Sub3500
'Subroutine to display initial scenario
XD = "Tour de France Bicycle Race"
Sub3470()
TextWindow.WriteLine("")
TextWindow.WriteLine(" You are a bicycle racer entered in the 22-day Tour de
France")
TextWindow.WriteLine("bicycle race around France. Your objective is to win
the race by")
TextWindow.WriteLine("having the lowest overall elapsed time. In addition,
you must try")
TextWindow.WriteLine("to win as many individual 'stages' or daily races as
possible, as")
TextWindow.WriteLine("wins on these stages count toward the overall points
prize.")
TextWindow.WriteLine(" Each day the computer pedals your bicycle after you
select the")
TextWindow.WriteLine("gears. While racing, various hazards occur (weather,
mechanical")
TextWindow.WriteLine("breakdowns, road conditions, and physical problems)
that hamper")
TextWindow.WriteLine("your progress.")
TextWindow.WriteLine(" At the end of each stage (day), you may sprint to the
finish")
TextWindow.WriteLine("line. The computer will count down the distance
starting ten")
TextWindow.WriteLine("kilometers from the end of the race. During this
countdown, you")
TextWindow.WriteLine("must decide when to start your sprint. Remember, if you
start too")
TextWindow.WriteLine("soon, you may become too exhausted to maintain your
sprint to the")
TextWindow.WriteLine("end, but if you start too late, other riders may
overtake you.")
```

```
EndSub

Sub TwoDecimals

  whole = Math.Floor(tdvalue)
  decimal = Math.Floor((TDValue - whole)*100)
  TDDisplay = text.append(whole ,".")
  If decimal < 10 Then
    TDDisplay = Text.Append(TDDisplay,"0")
  EndIf
  TDDisplay = Text.Append(TDDisplay,decimal)
EndSub
```

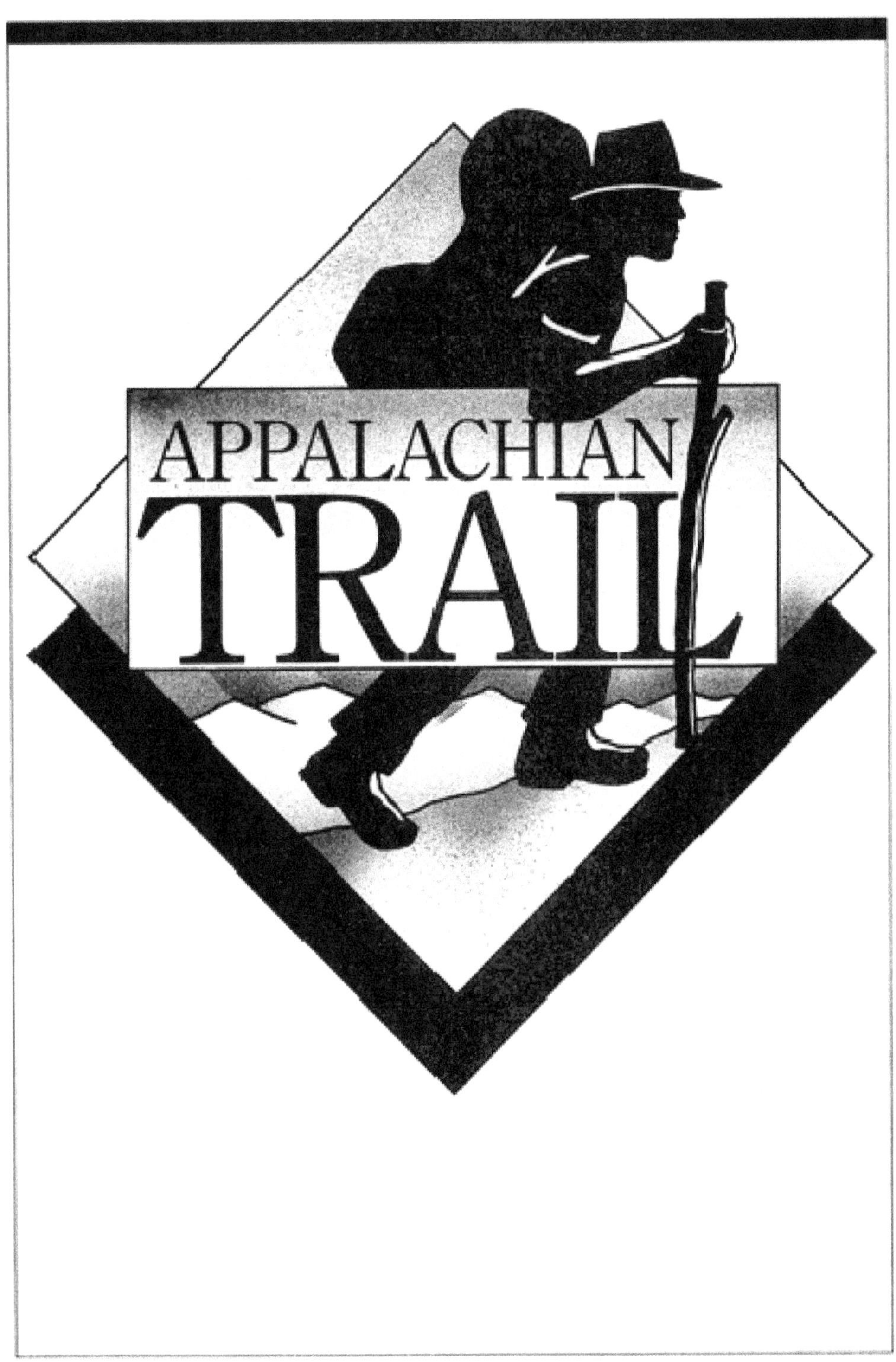
APPALACHIAN
TRAIL

Appalachian Trail

Appalachian Trail places you in the boots of a hiker whose goal is to walk the entire length of the 2000-mile Trail from Springer Mountain, Georgia, to Mt. Katahdin, Maine. Your journey begins in April as soon as the southern part of the Trail is clear of snow, and you must reach the northern terminus before the early snowfalls block the Presidential Mountain Range in New Hampshire.

Along the way, you encounter the same hazards reported in the diaries of hundreds of hikers. Some are natural hazards—prolonged heavy rain, late snowstorms, poison ivy; others are physical problems—hypothermia, excessive weight loss, blisters; and still other problems involve difficulties with equipment—torn raingear, worn-out boots, and broken zippers. It is not easy to complete the Appalachian Trail, but your chances of success will be better if you remember the following:

- Careful planning is important. When deciding what to pack, you must make many trade-offs—generally among comfort, weight, and food.
- Your method of food supply has a great effect on the success of your hike. You must choose one of the following methods:
    A. Bury caches of food along the trail. This has to be done prior to your hike and requires a great deal of planning.
    B. Purchase food as you go along. This is the cheapest method, but requires time-consuming off-trail excursions.
    C. Have a friend send food to post offices along the way. This is one compromise that works well for many hikers, but this method also requires a great deal of planning.
    D. The nutritional value of your food is important. You must decide how many calories you want to replenish each day and how to get them from each of the five food groups.

Prepare carefully and deal intelligently with the obstacles you encounter, and five million steps later you can join the elite group of fewer than 2000 hikers who have completed the Appalachian Trail. Happy hiking!

```
                          Appalachian Trail
     You are a hiker whose goal is to walk the entire 2007 miles of
the Appalachian Trail from Springer Mt., GA, to Mt. Katahdin, Maine.
You set out in April as soon as the Smokies are clear of snow, and
you must reach the northern terminus before it is blocked by snow.
     Your hike is divided into three-day segments.  Along the way,
you encounter natural hazards, difficulties with your equipment,
and physical problems.
     Careful planning for your hike is very important.  In deciding
what to pack, you have to make trade-offs--generally among comfort,
weight, and food.  Of course, everything must fit in your pack.
     You must decide how you will obtain food along the route, how
much to eat in each food group, and how many calories to replenish.
     You must decide at what pace you will walk, and how long to
hike each day.  Of course, a faster pace will cover mileage more
quickly than a slower one, but it is much harder on your body.
     You don't have many choices when dealing with mishap
assumed that you are a sensible hiker, make repairs
replace things that wear out, and see a doctor
Nevertheless, mishaps cost you time, of
spare as you take another of the
```

```
You must make some decisions about what to pack.

Tent:
  1 -- Sierra Designs Divine Light, 20 sq ft, max height 34 in.
         2 pounds 3 ounces, 214 cu in, price: $ 135
  2 -- Eureka! Crescent Bike, 22 sq ft, height 43 in.
         3 pounds, 353 cu in, price: $ 125
    -- Moss Starlet, 29 sq ft; with vestibule, 37; height 39 in.
         pounds 14 ounces, 334 cu in, price: $ 250
         Use trail shelters and sleep in open.
    ou want (number)? 1
```

```
June 1     You have walked 926 miles.
It has been raining steadily for the past week and you are
thoroughly soaked--your clothes, your sleeping bag, your food,
and, yes, your spirits.  What a bummer.
If it continues for another week, you're going to have fungus
growing on your skin.
```

```
August 19    You have walked 1954 miles.
The uppers on your boots are starting to separate from the soles.
You'll have to get them repaired by a shoemaker.
```

THE STORY

The Appalachian Trail is a continuous footpath that roughly follows the crest of the Appalachian mountain range through 14 states from Springer Mountain in northern Georgia to Mt. Katahdin in the central Maine wilderness.

In 1922, the first mile of the trail was cut and marked in Palisades Interstate Park in New York. Fifteen years later, in August 1937, the trail was proclaimed complete when the last two stretches—the south slope of Mt. Sugarloaf in Maine and a dense section near the Davenport Gap in Tennessee—were finally cut and marked. Over the years many sections have been relocated, particularly in the Great Smoky Mountains and Shenandoah National Park, but the total length of the trail remains a bit over 2000 miles.

The Appalachian Trail Conference, organized in 1925 when the project was barely under way, coordinated the effort to build what is today the longest marked footpath in the world. Today the Conference continues to coordinate the efforts of the organizations and individuals who maintain and preserve the Trail. Although the U.S. Department of the Interior is responsible for the administration of the Trail, volunteers still play the major role in clearing, maintaining, and "operating" the Trail.

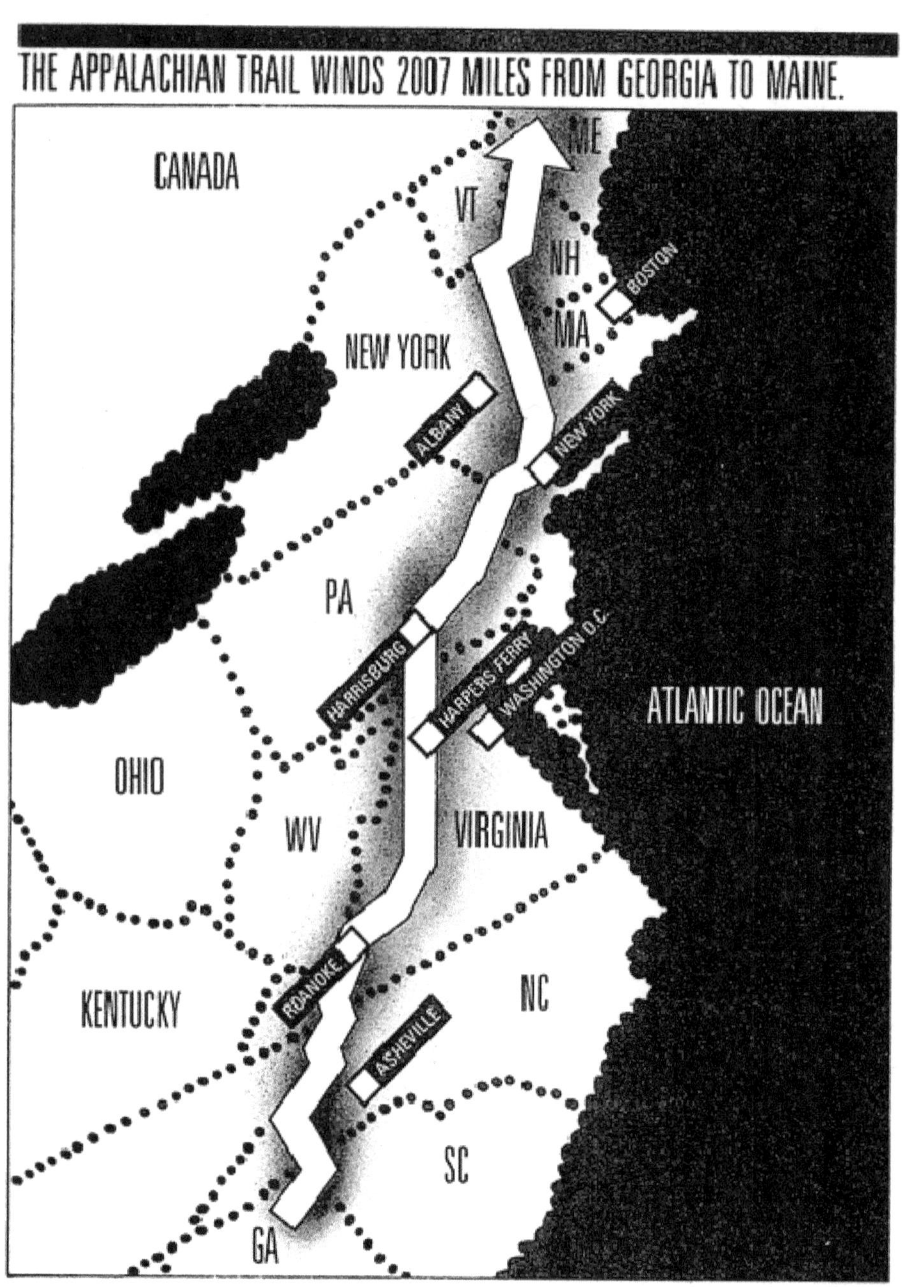

The Appalachian Mountain system is not an unbroken range, but consists of many mountain ranges often separated by deep valleys. Some of the more notable ranges include the Great

Smokies, the Blue Ridge Mountains, the Alleghenies, the Catskills, the Green Mountains, and the White Mountains.

The Trail passes through 14 eastern states. West Virginia has the least Trail mileage of any state—5.2 miles with another 20.0 miles along its border with Virginia—while Virginia boasts the longest section of trail—464.7 miles. The most mountainous stretches are in Vermont and New Hampshire. The roughest stretches are in Pennsylvania and New Jersey, and the worst weather is generally thought to occur in Maine.

Myron H. Avery was the first person to walk the entire length of the Appalachian Trail, starting in Maine in the 1920s when the Trail was still in its formative stage and finishing the last section 14 years later in the fall of 1936. Another early hiker who walked the entire trail, again in several sections, was George W. Outer-bridge, who started in 1932 and finished in 1939.

When in 1948 Earl Shaffer set out to walk the entire Trail in one continuous trip, most people thought the task quite impossible and him foolhardy to try it. Until that time, the Trail had been in existence for some 11 years and only six or seven people had walked the entire length, each doing so in a series of relatively short hikes over a period of years.

Shaffer had served 41/2 years in the Army in World War II, most of it in the Pacific theater, and had a yearning to spend some time alone in the wilderness. He prepared himself by doing jujitsu exercises and abstaining from smoking. He carried what was considered at the time a light load in a rucksack and set out from Mt. Oglethorpe in Georgia on April 4, 1948. He carried mostly dried foods augmented by food purchased along the route.

Shaffer had ordered a complete set of guidebooks and maps, but they did not arrive in time for his trip. Thus, he relied upon the trail markers, often quite poor, his compass, and instinct to find his way. The trail was in bad condition because maintenance had been curtailed during wartime; indeed, entire sections were obliterated by nettles, poison ivy, and briars, and logging had destroyed many blazed trees and markers.

Nevertheless, with a great deal of perseverance Shaffer managed to reach Mt. Katahdin in Maine on August 5, 1948, just 124 days after setting out. He averaged 16.5 miles per day, but because of detours and leaving the trail for food and supplies, his actual average daily mileage was probably closer to 18 or 19. This is a remarkable average, even for hikers today carrying lightweight equipment on a well-marked trail.

Seventeen years later, in 1965, when he was 45, Shaffer hiked the Trail again, this time from Mt. Katahdin to Springer Mountain. He thus became the first person both to hike the Trial continuously and to hike it continuously in both directions. On his second hike, he left on July 19, 1965 (after black-fly season in Maine) and reached Springer Mountain in freezing weather on October 25, exactly 99 days later. His average daily mileage was a spectacular 20.5, a rate few hikers have exceeded since.

Another early through hiker was Gene Espy, who, at age 24 in 1951, hiked from Mt. Oglethorpe, Georgia, to Mt. Katahdin in exactly four months. Unlike some other hikers, he prepared no food caches and made no arrangements to be met anywhere along the way. Like most early hikers, Espy carried a fairly heavy load—45 pounds—even though he had only minimal extra clothing and equipment.

Espy is one of the few hikers who report having seen more than one or two rattlesnakes. In his diary he records killing nearly 20, the largest nearly 4 feet long. He also notes seeing four copperheads within a 20-minute period along one section of the Trail in Pennsylvania. These snake encounters made Espy a staunch proponent of carrying a strong walking stick.

Another notable early through hiker was Mrs. Emma Gatewood, better known as Grandma Gatewood, who, in the summer of 1955 at age 67, walked the entire Trail, thus becoming the sixth person and the first woman to complete it. Seventeen months later, in April 1957, she was back on the Trail again, completing it in September. Her first journey took 146 days, and her second took 142 days. Her pack of less than 20 pounds was probably the lightest ever taken on the Trail, and she rarely cooked a meal. Unlike many other hikers who chose heavy military boots, Grandma Gatewood wore lightweight men's Keds, wearing out six pairs in the course of her journey. Neither did she carry a tent, sleeping bag, nor regular backpack; instead she carried a blanket and a rain cape in a homemade shoulder bag. Also, contrary to the rules of hiking, she carried no guidebook, map, or compass.

Over the next seven years, Grandma Gatewood continued to hike various sections of the Trail, some in a north-south direction and, in 1964, when she was age 77, these sections totaled a third completion of the Trail. Moreover, she took time out in 1959 to walk the entire Oregon Trail in honor of its 100th anniversary.

The only other person to have completed the trail three times was also a woman, Dorothy Laker. In contrast to Grandma Gatewood's style, Dorothy Laker did a thorough job of planning for her hikes and carried the best equipment she could afford. It paid off, and she completed her first trip in 1957 in 161 days. Her second trip, which started on June 14, 1962, had to be aborted on October 17 at Mt. Moriah, New Hampshire. On her third hike she got an earlier start, May 4, 1964, and successfully completed the Trail 151 days later on October 2.

Nine years later, in 1971, Laker attempted to complete the last section of her second hike, setting out from Mt. Moriah on August 23, 1971. Unfortunately, she twisted her ankle badly in a boggy area near Saddleback and shortly thereafter a stretch of particularly cold, wet weather set in. She pushed on, but she fell while fording the swollen Kennebec River, ending her attempt to finish the Trail that year. Finally, the next year, more determined than ever, she finished the last 152 miles in a grueling 12-day effort.

There are nearly as many approaches to hiking the Trail as there are people who attempt to do it. Let's consider the various pros and cons of different approaches.

Shelter: There are campsites along the Trail, in most cases no more than a day's hike apart. At many of these campsites there are roofed shelters, generally three-sided with an open front. Shelter facilities are, according to the Appalachian Trail Conference, "primarily provided for the long-distance hiker who may have no other means of shelter. Persons planning short hikes are asked to consider this and plan to carry tents." All very nice in theory, but scores of hikers note that all too often the shelters are packed with Boy Scouts, day campers, or fishermen who have made a shelter their base of operations.

The obvious alternative to using trail shelters is to carry a tent, although many hikers in the fifties and sixties reported great satisfaction in discarding a heavy tent along the way by cutting it up to use as a groundcloth. However, tent design has made great strides since then, and lightweight, modestly roomy tents are now widely available. Needless to say, the larger the tent, the more it weighs, although there is something to be said for a tent large enough to accommodate both you and your pack.

Sleeping: Grandma Gatewood and some other early hikers swore by blankets, but again, the latest lightweight sleeping bags weigh very little more than a single wool blanket yet are considerably more versatile. The key questions today usually boil down to bag shape (mummy—very confining and very warm; rectangular—roomy but heavy; and semi-rectangular—a cross between mummy and rectangular) and insulation material (goose down—warm, lightweight, and expensive—or a synthetic material—heavier than down but cheaper and much faster to dry when it gets wet).

Many of the shelters have bedframes with cut and broken springs. These are murder on sleeping bags, not to mention uncomfortable. Hikers are well advised to carry a heavy groundcloth to protect sleeping bags from these hazards, as well as for those nights when they must sleep outside on the ground. The floors of shelters are often made from rough logs that are equally uncomfortable; hence, an air mattress or foam pad is a practical necessity.

Cooking: For the most part, the campfire is an item of nostalgia due to the scarcity of dry wood and the danger of forest fires.

Indeed, open fires are not permitted anywhere along the Trail except in fireplaces provided at designated campsites. Therefore, most people carry a small stove. The technology of stoves has also improved greatly during the last decade, and extremely lightweight units which burn a variety of fuels (white gas, propane, and butane) are now available. Some of these fuels, especially white gas, can be purchased easily along the Trail, while others can be carried in compact cylinders or fuel bottles.

Of course, some hikers dispense with cooking altogether and eat cold food on the Trail, stopping for an occasional hot meal at a restaurant or store along the way.

Food supply: The three common methods of obtaining food are buried caches, packages sent ahead and held at post offices, and purchasing needed supplies at stores along the route. Each has its advantages and disadvantages. Food caches require no time-consuming off-trail excursions. Furthermore, canned goods can be buried along with the usual dried and concentrated foodstuffs, thereby giving the hiker a substantial dinner and breakfast when he digs up a cache. Depending upon how many caches are buried—some hikers bury as many as 50—the food load carried by the hiker can be potentially very light.

Purchasing food is the cheapest method of supply, because stores stock ordinary groceries rather than expensive trail mixes. On the other hand, this method requires many off-trail excursions, some of which can be quite long, and the food carried can be relatively heavy.

Food sent to and held at post offices along the way is a compromise; the hiker can send lightweight camp-supply meals and augment them with food purchased from stores, usually found near the post office.

No matter what the method of resupply, most hikers' diets are unbalanced and quite different from what they normally eat. Almost invariably the trail diet is deficient in fruits and fresh vegetables and abundant in grains and fibers. Because he is walking all day, the hiker burns up far more calories than he would in the course of a normal day at home. All these factors mean that he is calling upon his body to make some fairly radical adjustments in a short period of time. Some people's bodies adjust better than others', but nearly everyone experiences diet-related problems to some extent.

Water: It is advisable to carry a canteen or water bag to assure a supply of potable water. In many areas along the Trail the water is unsafe for drinking, and a considerable distance may pass before potable water can be found. All water obtained from unprotected or open sources should be purified by boiling or by chemical treatment before use.

Pack: Hikers constantly debate the relative merits of the external versus internal frame pack. The external frame pack rides farther away from the back and is cooler on hot days. Sleeping bag and mattress are usually carried on the outside and can be attached to the pack frame in a way that gives optimum weight distribution. Because these items are carried on the outside, an external frame pack generally holds more, but it also weighs more.

Everything normally is put inside of an internal frame pack, although some hikers still tie a sleeping pad to the outside. Proponents say that an internal frame pack keeps a hiker's things drier and is lighter and more compact than an external frame pack.

Footwear: Boots, say some hikers, make or break the trip.

Grandma Gatewood wouldn't agree, but in this she is clearly in the minority. Probably the major debate about footwear these days is leather versus synthetics. Many hikers still swear by a heavy handcrafted pair of one-piece leather boots, while others like a synthetic blend, alone or in some combination with leather, for its ability to breathe and dry quickly.

It is rare that a pair of boots, even the best custom-made pair, will last the entire trail without needing at least new soles. New soles usually last about 800 to 1000 miles; the rocky areas of Pennsylvania and New Jersey will do in a second pair; and the mountains of New England will finish off a third.

Raingear: When it rains on the Appalachian Trail it often comes down for days or weeks at a time. Thus, no matter what kind of raingear he carries, the hiker gets wet as the water seeps under his clothes, down his neck, and into his boots. Therefore, one approach is to not carry any raingear at all and to dry off when stopping at night but not otherwise. Most people still attempt to keep partially dry and carry a poncho or rain parka, and some hikers even carry rain pants.

Hazards: Most through hikers report that the first thing non-hikers ask about is snakes. In fact, snakes avoid human contact and many hikers have walked the entire Trail without seeing a single one. Nevertheless, it is probably better to err on the side of caution, and practically every hiker carries a 1 oz. snakebite kit.

For the most part, other animals also avoid humans, except if they have been fed by people (as have some of the bears in the Great Smoky Mountain National Park) or if they have been successful in the past finding food open in packs (raccoons, porcupines, and skunks usually do). Mice, which make their homes in many of the shelters, are always a problem.

But by far the most dangerous animals are the dogs found roaming about the small towns from Georgia to Pennsylvania. Not afraid of humans, they are perhaps the worst enemies hikers face on the trip. Against curs, as well as many other animals, the best defense is to avoid them and the second defense is a heavy hiking stick.

For many hikers, the worst hazard along the Trail is the poison ivy, oak, and sumac. In some stretches it is impossible to go around the thickets of poison ivy, and the hiker who has any susceptibility at all will probably come down with a case.

Probably the most common injury is a twisted ankle. The many rock scrambles, stream crossings, and boggy areas offer ample opportunity to put a foot down on an unstable surface.

A long hike is rough on equipment, and most hikers rip, tear, and wear out socks, pants, shirts, zippers, straps, stuff sacks, tents, groundcloths, and practically everything else at an amazing rate. It is vital to carry a small sewing kit and make repairs at the first sign of a rip. Worn socks should be replaced immediately to avoid blisters, whereas other items can be replaced later.

Trail markings: In theory, from each blaze on the Trail it is possible to see the next one. In practice, it isn't so. The Trail often has long sections where there are few opportunities for orientation or checking the route. The Trail guidebooks advise hikers never to proceed more than a quarter mile (roughly five minutes of hiking) without noticing some Trail indication. The cardinal mistake is an insistence on going forward when the route seems obscure or dubious.

Major stretches of the Trail are relocated almost every year because of commercial or residential development. Thus, even the latest maps and guidebooks are invariably out of date. The hiker must remain alert to the painted blazes and, if they deviate from the guidebook, should follow the blazes in preference to the printed data. In practice, this means that he will almost inevitably get lost—or at least stray from the Trail—more than once during the trip.

A decision to walk the Trail is not something to be undertaken lightly. A major physical and mental commitment is needed—a commitment to being alone and independent for three to seven months; a commitment to overcoming boredom, discomfort, weather, and hazards; a commitment to forcing the body to do more than it has ever done before; and a commitment to enjoying the challenge and adventure of a lifetime.

BIBLIOGRAPHY

Appalachian Trail Guides. *Appalachian Trail Conference.* Harpers Ferry, WV, 1984.

Fletcher, Colin. *The New Complete Walker.* New York: Knopf. 1982.

Hare, James R. (ed). *Hiking the Appalachian Trail* (2 vols). Emmaus, PA: Rodale Press, 1975.

Look, Dennis. *Joy of Backpacking.* Sacramento, CA: Jalmar Press, 1976.

Manning. Harvey. *Backpacking: One Step At a Time.* Seattle, WA: REI Press, 1972.

THE PROGRAM

The Appalachian Trail program is by far the largest in this book. There are two reasons for this: First, such a trip requires a tremendous amount of personal preparation—food, clothing, equipment, physical conditioning. Second, walking the Trail is a complex undertaking, requiring many decisions and trade-offs. For example, you may set a brisk hiking rate for yourself. However, this means you will burn more calories and have to eat (and carry) more food. In turn, this means that your load is heavier, which slows you down and causes you to burn even more calories.

Not all of the possible interactions have been included in the program and you may wish to modify it to include others. Some suggestions for doing this are included in the description of the program.

Because this program uses many of the same techniques and routines as other programs in this book, only those that are unique or suitable for modification are discussed.

You are asked to make decisions about seven major items of equipment: tent, pack, sleeping bag, foam pad, stove, boots, and raingear (starts at LN570). If you opt for an internal frame pack, everything you take must fit inside, whereas with an external frame pack, your sleeping bag and foam pad may be carried on the outside. I have assumed a volume of 3000 cu. in. for clothing, food, toilet supplies, eating utensils, guidebooks, etc. If you feel this is too little or too much, the volume can be changed. Also, the descriptions of the main items can be changed in the traildata.txt file. Each item requires four pieces of data: name, weight (ounces), price (dollars), and volume (cu. in.).

Actually, prices are not used, except to give you some idea of the cost of everything if purchased new. However, as many hikers seem to stay on rather limited budgets, it would be easy to add a routine to make sure that you stay within a certain total cost.

With respect to the food to be carried, you are asked to specify the percentage of each of five food groups that you want to eat (start at LN1050). Note that the screen is cleared at the beginning of this routine. This allows all five food groups to be listed on the screen and the cursor to be moved beside each group so you can enter its percentage in your diet.

It takes different weights of various types of food to produce one calorie of energy. For example, one gram of protein produces four calories, while a gram of fat produces nine calories. Thus, depending upon how many calories of energy you want to replenish each day, you must eat a certain weight of food. This calculation of food weight (FWT) is made near LN1330.

Because fat produces the most calories per gram, the lightest food load would consist of 100% fat. Obviously, no body could actually digest this, and it would be a disastrous choice. However, currently the program does not check for a balanced diet. Although you occasionally get indigestion (Sub2600) it is a random occurrence and happens whether or not you have specified a balanced diet.

The main program is extremely short, 13 lines, and simply calls a series of subroutines to deal with hiking pace and mishaps (LN1570). Currently the program checks on the hiker every three days. This could just as easily be done more or less often, or could be a function of distance. You might think that checking on a hiker every *x* miles might make more sense than every *x* days. However, after studying the accounts of scores of through hikers, it became apparent that far fewer things happened to faster hikers, while slower ones were plagued with problems. Thus, it seems that something happens every *x* days whether you are covering 8 or 28 miles a day.

Note that many mishaps are a function of date or distance or both. For example, you can't have snow in New England until you reach New England (distance > 1545 miles) and until September 13 (time in days > 166).

Sometimes in a program you want events to occur periodically as a function of a variable that is not increasing uniformly. For example, in this program, you have the opportunity to establish a new hiking pace and a new diet every 400 miles. But, depending upon initial hiking pace and mishaps, you may be walking a different distance every day. Thus, we put in a counter, STV, which is multiplied by 400 and compared with your cumulative mileage every three days.

```
If D > (STV + 1) * 400 Then
  Sub1820()   'Allow user to reset input variables
EndIf
```

The variable STV is incremented by 1 in the first line of the subroutine; thus, the second time around, this loop will look for 800 miles, and so on. Naturally, with this approach you will rarely hit a multiple of 400 miles on the button, but you will never go more than three days beyond the specified distance.

Many of the subroutines which deal with mishaps (Sub2070) have a counter that indicates how many times that mishap has occurred (HZArray). This is used to determine the maximum number of times that particular mishaps can occur. On the actual Trail, there is no limit to the number of times a snake can curl up in your boot or how often you can slip on rocks. Hence, if you wish, you can eliminate some or all of the tests for values of HZArray.

The remaining subroutines are more or less straightforward, although one particularly messy formula ought to be explained. It is found near LN1220 with a variation near LN3970, specifically:

```
CD = Math.Floor(WB * 11.5 + WB * DM * .3 + (WB + WP / 16) * DM * .21 + WB *
(15 - TW) * .22)
```

This formula calculates your daily usage of calories. The first element of calorie usage is daily body maintenance (basal metabolism) of 1150 calories per day per 100 pounds of body weight, i.e, WB (body weight in pounds) times 11.5. Actually, women have a basal metabolism of 1100 calories per 100 pounds, and men 1200; you can easily make this correction, since the program asks for your sex.

The second element is calories burned due to walking. This is proportional to the rate of walking times the time of walking (which, of course, is distance). According to studies done at Carnegie-Mellon University, the average person burns 90 calories per 100 pounds of body weight per hour at a walking speed of 3 mph. Thus, the second element in the formula equals 0.3 times body weight (in pounds) times rate (mph) times time (hours).

The third element is the calorie usage due to climbing. Assuming a body efficiency of about 30%, you use about 110 calories in raising every 100 pounds of total weight (body weight plus pack weight) each 1000 feet in elevation. Since, on average, the Trail involves a climb of 200 feet per mile, factoring these values together leads to the third element of the equation: 0.21 times (body weight + pack weight) times distance.

The fourth element of daily calorie usage is that from non-walking chores (cooking, dishwashing, eating, dressing, writing, etc.). If most of these activities are reasonably non-strenuous, calorie usage will be about 22 calories per 100 pounds of body weight per hour. Assuming nine hours of sleep (24 - 9 = 15), we subtract walking hours from 15 (your 15 waking hours) and multiply those hours by 0.22 times body weight.

There are many interesting modifications that can be made to this program to make it more realistic, but I leave it to you to discover these and incorporate them into the program.

PROGRAM VARIABLES

```
A Answer to input query, numeric value
AD Answer to input query, string
CADD Calories added due to carrying weight of food
CAL Calories to eat per day, user input
CALOFF Calories of weight lost per day
CD Calorie usage per day
COST[n] Cost of item in pack (n = 1 to 7)
CSTArray [n] Cost of item in pack, temporary (n = 1 to 4)
CT Total of food groups
D Distance into hike, cumulative
DB Distance when sole put on boot
DDAYS Distance walked in 3 days
DINPT Distance per day, calculated from player input
DLCArray[n] Distance from one location to the next (n = 1 to 21)
DM Distance per day, theoretical from player input
DMAX Distance per day, maximum due to physical condition
DY Days of food to be carried
FD[n] Diet percentage of each food group (n = 1 to 5)
FOOD Type of food resupply
FWT Food weight (oz.)
HZ[n] Hazard indicator (n = 1 to 25)
I Temporary iteration variable
ITEMD[n] Item to pack (n = 1 to 7)
ITMDArray[n] Item to pack, temporary (n = 1 to 4)
IVY Sensitivity to poison ivy, player input
J Temporary iteration variable
LCDArray[n] Location name (n = 1 to 21)
MD Day of month
MOD Month name
PC Physical condition, player input
R[n] Reduction in walking rate due to mishaps (n = 1 to 10)
RAIN Feelings about rain, player input
RM Rate of walking multiplier
RT Rate-of-walking multiplier, temporary
RW Rate-of-walking, player input (mph)
SNO Snow indicator (number of times of heavy snow)
SPDArray[n] Categories of stuff to pack (n = 1 to 7)
STK Walking stick (0 = no, 1 = yes)
STV Stop to get new input variable (400 - mile markers)
T Time into hike (days)
TD Time, temporary (days)
TM Time delay due to mishap (days)
TS Time since last weight-loss calculation
TSLOW[n] Time slowed down by mishap (n = 1 to 10)
TT Temporary indicator that date has been printed
TW Time of walking per day, player input (hours)
U Changes of underwear
VLArray[n] Volume of item in pack (cu. in.), temporary (n = 1 to 4)
VOL[n] Volume of item in pack (cu. in.) (n = 1 to 7)
```

VOL1 Volume of tent, stove, and raingear
VOL2 Volume of sleeping bag and mattress
WADD Weight added to pack for food
WB Weight, body (lbs.)
WHTArray[n] Weight of item in pack, temporary (oz.) (n = 1 to 4)
WP Weight of pack (oz. in input section, lbs. in hiking section)
WT[n] Weight of item in pack (oz.) (n = 1 to 7)
WTLOSS Weight loss since last weight-loss calculation
WTLOST Weight loss, total
WTOZ Weight in oz. (for printing only)
WTPND Weight in lbs. (for printing only)
XD Temporary string variable
X Temporary average miles per day

SMALL BASIC PROGRAM LISTING

```
TextWindow.CursorTop = 10
XD = "Appalachian Trail"
Sub5590()
TextWindow.CursorTop = 13
XD = "(c) by David H. Ahl, 1986"
Sub5590()
TextWindow.CursorTop = 23
XD = "Press Enter to Continue."
Sub5590()
JJJ = TextWindow.Read()
TextWindow.Clear()
Sub5620()
'read in data file
For I = 1 to 7
SPDArray[i]=File.ReadLine(Program.Directory +"\traildata.txt", (I-1)*5 + 1)
For J = 1 To 4
  FileLine = File.ReadLine(Program.Directory +"\traildata.txt", (I-1)*5 + J +
1)
  'get four numbers separated by commas
  KK = Text.GetIndexOf(FileLine, ",")
  ITMDArray[I][J] = Text.GetSubText(FileLine, 1, KK - 1)
  FileLine = Text.GetSubTextToEnd(FileLine, KK + 1)
  KK = Text.GetIndexOf(FileLine, ",")
  WHTArray[I][J] = Text.GetSubText(FileLine, 1, KK - 1)
  FileLine = Text.GetSubTextToEnd(FileLine, KK + 1)
  KK = Text.GetIndexOf(FileLine, ",")
  CSTArray[I][J] = Text.GetSubText(FileLine, 1, KK - 1)
  VLArray[I][J] = Text.GetSubTextToEnd(FileLine, KK + 1)
EndFor
EndFor
FOR I = 1 TO 21
  FileLine = File.ReadLine(Program.Directory + "\traildata.txt", 35 + I)
  'get two numbers separated by commas
  KK = Text.GetIndexOf(FileLine, ",")
  DLCArray[I] = Text.GetSubText(FileLine, 1, KK - 1)
  LCDArray[i] = Text.GetSubTextToEnd(FileLine, KK + 1)
Endfor
DB = 300
'New boot gives 300 extra mi
'
'Data Input Section
TextWindow.WriteLine("First we need some data about you.")
TextWindow.WriteLine("")
LN210:
TextWindow.Write("Your sex (M or F)? ")
AD = TextWindow.Read()
Sub5540()
If AD<>"M" AND AD<>"F" Then
TextWindow.WriteLine("Answer 'M' or 'F' please.")
GOTO LN210
EndIf
LN230:
TextWindow.Write("Your weight in pounds? ")
```

```
WB = TextWindow.ReadNumber()
If WB > 79 AND WB < 401 Then
  Goto LN260
EndIf
TextWindow.WriteLine("Surely you jest. Let's try that one again.")
Goto LN230
LN260:
TextWindow.Write("What is your physical condition (1 = excellent, 2 = good,
")
TextWindow.Write("3 = fair, 4 = poor)? ")
PC = TextWindow.ReadNumber()
If PC < 1 OR PC > 4 Then
TextWindow.WriteLine("Answer 1, 2, 3, or 4 please.")
GOTO LN260
EndIf
TextWindow.WriteLine("")
TextWindow.WriteLine("Walking pace: You may change your pace as the hike
progresses.")
TextWindow.WriteLine("Remember, a faster pace covers the distance more
quickly but")
TextWindow.WriteLine("burns more calories and has a higher risk of injury.")
TextWindow.WriteLine("Slow and deliberate......1.7 mph")
TextWindow.WriteLine("Moderate and vigorous......3 mph")
TextWindow.WriteLine("Fast and very difficult....4 mph")
LN350:
TextWindow.Write("At what rate in mph do you wish to walk (number & decimal
okay)? ")
RW = TextWindow.ReadNumber()
If RW < 1 OR RW > 4.2 Then
TextWindow.WriteLine("A rate of "+ RW+ " mph is silly.")
GOTO LN350
EndIf
TextWindow.WriteLine("")
TextWindow.WriteLine("Walking hours per day: You may change this as time goes
on.")
LN380:
TextWindow.Write("To start, how many hours do you wish to walk per day? ")
TW = TextWindow.ReadNumber()
If TW > 14 Then
TextWindow.WriteLine("That's just too ambitious.")
GOTO LN380
EndIf
If TW * RW < 7 Then
TextWindow.WriteLine("You won't even reach NJ by Christmas.")
GOTO LN380
EndIf
TextWindow.WriteLine("")
TextWindow.WriteLine("Your sensitivity to poison ivy:")
TextWindow.WriteLine(" (1) Highly sensitive")
TextWindow.WriteLine(" (2) Moderately sensitive")
TextWindow.WriteLine(" (3) Immune")
TextWindow.WriteLine(" (4) Had series of desensitization shots")
LN440:
TextWindow.Write("Which number describes you? ")
IVY = TextWindow.ReadNumber()
```

```
If IVY < 1 OR IVY > 4 Then
TextWindow.WriteLine("What's that? Let's try again.")
GOTO LN440
EndIf
TextWindow.WriteLine("")
TextWindow.Write("People who have hiked the Trail have different feelings ")
TextWindow.WriteLine("about rain:")
TextWindow.WriteLine(" (1) Let it pour, I love it.")
TextWindow.WriteLine(" (2) No problem as long as the sun comes out every few
days.")
TextWindow.WriteLine(" (3) Five solid days of rain really gets me down.")
TextWindow.WriteLine(" (4) If I foresee a long stretch of rain, I'll hole up
in a")
TextWindow.WriteLine(" shelter or motel and wait it out.")
LN520:
TextWindow.Write("Which number most closely describes your feeling? ")
RAIN = TextWindow.ReadNumber()
If RAIN < 1 OR RAIN > 4 Then
TextWindow.WriteLine("Not possible. Again please.")
GOTO LN520
EndIf
'
'Data on what to carry
TextWindow.WriteLine("")
TextWindow.WriteLine("You must make some decisions about what to pack.")
LN570:
For I = 1 To 7
  TextWindow.WriteLine("")
  TextWindow.WriteLine(SPDArray[I] +":")
  For J = 1 To 4
    TextWindow.WriteLine(J +" .. " +ITMDArray[I][J])
    WEIGHT = WHTArray[I][J]
    TextWindow.Write(" ")
    Sub5430()
    If VLArray[I][J] > 0 Then
      TextWindow.Write(", " +VLArray[I][J]+ " cu in")
    EndIf
    If CSTArray[I][J] > 0 Then
      TextWindow.WriteLine(", price: $" +CSTArray[I][J])
    EndIf
  EndFor
LN630:
TextWindow.Write("Which one do you want (number)? ")
A = TextWindow.ReadNumber()
If A < 1 OR A > 4 Then
TextWindow.WriteLine("Come on now; answer 1, 2, 3, or 4")
GOTO LN630
EndIf
ITEMD[I] = ITMDArray[I][A]
WT[I] = WHTArray[I][A]
COST[I] = CSTArray[I][A]
VOL[I] = VLArray[I][A]
EndFor
VOL1 = VOL[1] + VOL[5] + VOL[7]
VOL2 = VOL[3] + VOL[4]
```

```
TextWindow.WriteLine("")
If COST[2] > 135 Then
IF VOL[2] > 3000 + VOL1 THEN
Goto LN720
ELSE
goto LN690
EndIf
EndIf
If VOL[2] > 3000 + VOL1 + VOL2 Then
  Goto LN720  'Internal pack hold stuff?
EndIf
LN690:
TextWindow.WriteLine("Your pack is too small to hold all those things plus
clothes and")
TextWindow.WriteLine("food. You'll have to take a larger pack or some smaller
items.")
TextWindow.WriteLine("")
TextWindow.WriteLine("Let's try again ...")
Goto LN570
LN720:
TextWindow.Write("How many changes of underwear do you want to take? ")
U = TextWindow.ReadNumber()
If U > 6 Then
TextWindow.WriteLine("This is not a picnic. Take fewer.")
GOTO LN720
EndIf
TextWindow.Write("Do you want to take a walking stick (Y or N)? ")
AD = TextWindow.Read()
Sub5540()
If AD = "Y" Then
STK = 1
ELSE
STK = 0
EndIf
TextWindow.WriteLine("")
TextWindow.WriteLine("To summarize, here is what you have chosen:")
For I = 1 To 7
TextWindow.WriteLine(SPDArray[I] +": "+ ITEMD[I])
EndFor
TextWindow.WriteLine("Changes of underwear: " +U)
If STK = 1 Then
  TextWindow.WriteLine("Walking stick.")
EndIf
TextWindow.WriteLine("")
TextWindow.WriteLine(" In addition, you must carry (or wear) a hat, short-
sleeve shirt,")
TextWindow.WriteLine("chamois shirt, light jacket, long underwear, hiking
shorts, long")
TextWindow.WriteLine("pants, 3 pairs socks, eating gear, water bottle, soap,
toilet tissue,")
TextWindow.WriteLine("toilet supplies, towel, first-aid kit, snakebite kit,
flashlight,")
TextWindow.WriteLine("100' nylon cord, watch, compass, lighter, bandanna,
sewing kit, insect")
```

```
TextWindow.WriteLine("repellent, Swiss Army knife, water-purifier tablets,
notebook, maps,")
TextWindow.WriteLine("guidebook, stuff sacks, moleskin, camera, and money.")
TextWindow.WriteLine("")
For I = 1 To 7
WP = WP + WT[I]
CST = CST + COST[I]
EndFor
'Summarize weights
WP = WP + 190 + U * 4
If STK = 1 Then
  WP = WP + 24
EndIf
TextWindow.WriteLine("If you bought everything new, the total cost would be
$" +(225 + CST))
TextWindow.Write("The total weight of what you are wearing and carrying is ")
WEIGHT = WP
Sub5430()
TextWindow.WriteLine("")
TextWindow.WriteLine(".... not including food or water.")
'
'Data on food
Sub5390()
TextWindow.Clear()
TextWindow.WriteLine("")
TextWindow.WriteLine("Common systems of food supply include:")
TextWindow.WriteLine(" (1)Caches buried along the trail. Pros: no wasted time
leaving")
TextWindow.WriteLine(" the Trail for food, heavy items can be buried.")
TextWindow.WriteLine(" (2) Food sent to post offices along the way. Pros:
more flexible")
TextWindow.WriteLine(" than caches. Cons: P.O.s closed nights, Sat pm and
Sun.")
TextWindow.WriteLine(" (3) Grocery stores and restaurants. Pros: good
variety, cheap.")
TextWindow.WriteLine(" Cons: wasted time leaving Trail, limited opening
hours.")
LN1010:
TextWindow.Write("Which will be your major method of food supply? ")
FOOD = TextWindow.ReadNumber()
If FOOD < 1 OR FOOD > 3 Then
TextWindow.WriteLine("Sorry, try again.")
GOTO LN1010
EndIf
If FOOD = 1 Then
RT = 1
ELSE
RT = .95  'Off-trail excursions reduce walking rate
EndIf
RM = RT
Sub5510()
'Short pause before screen clears
LN1050:
TextWindow.Clear()
```

```
TextWindow.WriteLine("Obviously, you will carry your food in the most
efficient form:")
TextWindow.WriteLine("dried, dehydrated, concentrated, etc. However, you must
specify")
TextWindow.WriteLine("the percentage of your diet accounted for by each of
the following")
TextWindow.WriteLine("food groups (remember, all five must add up to 100).")
TextWindow.WriteLine(" (1) Dairy foods, cheese, yogurt")
TextWindow.WriteLine(" (2) Fruits and vegetables")
TextWindow.WriteLine(" (3) Meat, poultry, fish, eggs")
TextWindow.WriteLine(" (4) Bread, cereal, seeds, nuts,")
TextWindow.WriteLine(" (5) Margarine, lard, oils, fats")
CT = 0
For I = 1 To 5
TextWindow.CursorTop = I + 3
TextWindow.CursorLeft = 39
TextWindow.Write("? ")
FD[I] = TextWindow.ReadNumber()
CT = CT + FD[I]
EndFor
TextWindow.CursorTop = 10
TextWindow.CursorLeft = 39
TextWindow.WriteLine(CT+ "%")
TextWindow.WriteLine("")
If CT = 100 Then
TextWindow.WriteLine("Very good.")
GOTO LN1220
EndIf
TextWindow.WriteLine("Sorry, but your percentages add up to "+ CT+ " rather
than to 100%.")
TextWindow.WriteLine("")
TextWindow.WriteLine("Press Enter when you're ready to try again.")
JJJ = TextWindow.Read()
Goto LN1050
'
LN1220:
'Calculate calorie usage
DM = RW * TW
If DM > 30 Then
  DM = 30  'Desired distance = rate * time
EndIf
LN1250:
'Calories = metabolism + walking + climbing + camp activities
CD = Math.Floor(WB * 11.5 + WB * DM * .3 + (WB + WP / 16) * DM * .21 + WB *
(15 - TW) * .22)
TextWindow.WriteLine("")
TextWindow.WriteLine("Given your weight and that of your supplies, your
walking")
TextWindow.WriteLine("speed, and your walking time per day, you can expect")
TextWindow.WriteLine("to burn at least " +CD+ " calories per day.")
LN1290:
TextWindow.WriteLine("")
TextWindow.Write("How many calories worth of food do you want to eat? ")
CAL = TextWindow.ReadNumber()
If CAL > .6 * CD Then
```

```
  Goto LN1330
EndIf
TextWindow.WriteLine("Your body will rebel against burning that much body
fat.")
TextWindow.WriteLine("Better eat a bit more ...")
Goto LN1290
LN1330:
If CAL > 1.5 * CD Then
TextWindow.WriteLine("No blimps allowed on the trail.")
GOTO LN1290
EndIf
FWT = Math.Floor(CAL * 3.2/(4 * FD[1] + 3 * FD[2] + 4 * FD[3] + 4 * FD[4] + 9
* FD[5]))
WEIGHT = FWT
TextWindow.Write("That means eating an approx food weight per day of ")
Sub5430()
TextWindow.WriteLine("")
TextWindow.WriteLine("")
If FOOD = 3 Then
DY = 2
ELSE
DY = 3 'Avg days of food carried
EndIf
WADD = DY * FWT + 17
CADD = WADD * DM * .21
WP = WP + WADD
CD = CD + CADD
TextWindow.WriteLine("Food and water add " +WADD+ " oz. to your trail weight
bringing your")
TextWindow.Write("total weight (worn and carried) to ")
WEIGHT = WP
Sub5430()
TextWindow.WriteLine("")
TextWindow.Clear()
XD = "Preparations are finally complete!"
Sub5590()
Sub5510()
'
'Main Hiking Section
'Initial calculations, data, and messages
WP = WP / 16
Sub1930()
'Calculate true hiking pace
TextWindow.WriteLine("")
TextWindow.WriteLine("")


'Read locations
TextWindow.WriteLine(" It is April 1 and you briskly step out on the approach
trail")
TextWindow.WriteLine("at Amicalola Falls, Georgia. You hike the 6.9 miles to
the peak")
TextWindow.WriteLine("of Springer Mountain and sign the trail log, the first
of many")
```

```
TextWindow.WriteLine("that you intend to sign. Your hike will take you
through 14")
TextWindow.WriteLine("states as the Trail wanders 2007 miles along the
Appalachian")
TextWindow.WriteLine("Mountains to Baxter Peak on Mt. Katahdin in Maine. It
is a")
TextWindow.WriteLine("challenging trail with an average climb of 200 feet
each mile.")
TextWindow.WriteLine("Fewer than 2000 people have walked its entire length.
Good luck!")
TextWindow.WriteLine("")
Sub5390()
'
'Main loop starts here
LN1570:
T = T + 3
TD = Math.Floor(T + .5)
TextWindow.WriteLine("")
Sub5200()
'Check on the hiker every 3 days
DDAYS = 3 * RM * DINPT
D = D + DDAYS
If D > 1999 Then
  Goto LN4560
EndIf
TextWindow.Write("You have walked " +Math.Floor(D)+ " miles. ")
FOR I = 1 TO 21
If D > DLCArray[I] - 17 AND D < DLCArray[I] + 17 Then
  Goto LN1620  'Near anyplace?
EndIf
EndFor
TextWindow.WriteLine("")
Goto LN1630
LN1620:
TextWindow.WriteLine("You are near" +LCDArray[I])
LN1630:
If D > 1466 Then
R[10] = .85
TSLOW[10] = 2007  'Slow going in mountains
EndIf
Sub1710()
'Any mishaps recently?
If T > 12 Then
  Sub4030()  'Long stretch of rain?
EndIf
If D > 1545 AND T > 166 Then
  Sub4260()  'Snow in New England
EndIf
If D > 1845 AND KEN = 0 Then
  Sub4380() 'Kennebec River crossing
EndIf
If D > (STV + 1) * 400 Then
  Sub1820()  'Allow user to reset input variables
EndIf
Sub5390()
```

```
Goto LN1570
'Go back to start of hiking loop
'
Sub Sub1710
'Subroutine to determine which mishap, if any, occurs
TM = 0
RN = Math.Floor(1 + 40 * Math.GetRandomNumber(999)/1000)
If RN > 35 Then
  RN = 36  'Mishap occurs
EndIf
If RN > 12 Then
  Goto LN1760
EndIf
If (RN = 1) Then
  Sub2070()
ElseIf (RN = 2) Then
  Sub2110()
ElseIf (RN = 3) Then
  Sub2150()
ElseIf (RN = 4) Then
  Sub2220()
ElseIf (RN = 5) Then
  Sub2260()
ElseIf (RN = 6) Then
  Sub2300()
ElseIf (RN = 7) Then
  Sub2320()
ElseIf (RN = 8) Then
  Sub2340()
ElseIf (RN = 9) Then
  Sub2390()
ElseIf (RN = 10) Then
  Sub2410()
ElseIf (RN = 11) Then
  Sub2430()
ElseIf (RN = 12) Then
  Sub2460()
EndIf
Goto LN1800
LN1760:
If RN > 24 Then
  Goto LN1790
EndIf
If (RN - 12 = 1) Then
  Sub2530()
ElseIf (RN - 12 = 2) Then
  Sub2570()
ElseIf (RN - 12 = 3) Then
  Sub2600()
ElseIf (RN - 12 = 4) Then
  Sub2630()
ElseIf (RN - 12 = 5) Then
  Sub2670()
ElseIf (RN - 12 = 6) Then
  Sub2710()
```

```
ElseIf (RN - 12 = 7) Then
  Sub2750()
ElseIf (RN - 12 = 8) Then
  Sub2770()
ElseIf (RN - 12 = 9) Then
  Sub2790()
ElseIf (RN - 12 = 10) Then
  Sub2820()
ElseIf (RN - 12 = 11) Then
  Sub2870()
ElseIf (RN - 12 = 12) Then
  Sub2910()
EndIf
Goto LN1800
LN1790:
If (RN - 24 = 1) Then
  Sub2960()
ElseIf (RN - 24 = 2) Then
  Sub2990()
ElseIf (RN - 24 = 3) Then
  Sub3010()
ElseIf (RN - 24 = 4) Then
  Sub3040()
ElseIf (RN - 24 = 5) Then
  Sub3070()
ElseIf (RN - 24 = 6) Then
  Sub3100()
ElseIf (RN - 24 = 7) Then
  Sub3130()
ElseIf (RN - 24 = 8) Then
  Sub3170()
ElseIf (RN - 24 = 9) Then
  Sub3200()
ElseIf (RN - 24 = 10) Then
  Sub3220()
ElseIf (RN - 24 = 11) Then
  Sub3260()
ElseIf (RN - 24 = 12) Then
  Sub3340()
EndIf
LN1800:
T = T + TM 'Time delay resulting from mishap
Sub2020()
EndSub

Sub Sub1820
'Subroutine to let user reset input variables
STV = STV + 1
TextWindow.Write("Want to change walking pace or hours of walking? ")
AD = TextWindow.Read()
Sub5540()
If AD<>"Y" Then
  Goto LN1910
EndIf
LN1850:
```

```
TextWindow.Write("New walking pace (mph)? ")
RW = TextWindow.ReadNumber()
If RW < 1 OR RW > 4.5 Then
TextWindow.WriteLine("A rate of " +RW+ " mph is silly.")
GOTO LN1850
EndIf
LN1870:
TextWindow.Write("New hours per day on the trail? ")
TW = TextWindow.ReadNumber()
If TW > 14 Then
TextWindow.WriteLine("Come now; that's just too ambitious.")
GOTO LN1870
EndIf
If STK = 1 Then
Goto LN1910
ELSE
TextWindow.Write("Want to change your mind and carry a ")
EndIf
TextWindow.Write( "walking stick? ")
AD  = TextWindow.Read()
Sub5540()
If AD = "Y" Then
  STK = 1
EndIf
LN1910:
TextWindow.WriteLine("")
Sub1930()
EndSub
'
Sub Sub1930
'Subroutine to establish true hiking pace
DINPT = RW * TW
'Desired distance = walking rate * hours per day
If D > 600 Then
  PC = 1  'Under 600 miles physical condition limits mileage
EndIf
DMAX = 6 + 6 * (5 - PC)
If DINPT > DMAX Then
  DINPT = DMAX
EndIf
If WB / WP > 6 Then
  Goto LN1990  'Body weight to pack weight ratio under 6?
EndIf
DINPT = (.49 + .086 * WB / WP) * DINPT
'Heavy pack cuts down speed
LN1990:
If STV = 0 Then
  Goto LN2019  'No chance to change diet at the start
EndIf
Sub3820()
LN2019:
EndSub

'Chance to change diet as trip progresses
'
```

```
Sub Sub2020
'Subroutine to alter hiking rate due to mishaps
RM = RT
FOR I = 1 TO 10
If TSLOW[I] > T Then
  RM = RM * R[I]
EndIf
EndFor
EndSub
'
'Subroutines for 35 assorted mishaps follow
Sub Sub2070
If D > 360 OR HZArray[6] = 1 Then
Goto LN2017
ELSE
TM = .5
HZArray[6] = 1
EndIf
TextWindow.WriteLine("You run into Rangers on military exercises who advise
you to avoid")
TextWindow.WriteLine("the trail for the next few miles because of booby
traps.")
LN2017:
EndSub
'
Sub Sub2110
If D < 800 OR HZArray[12] = 1 Then
goto LN2111
ELSE
TM = 1
HZArray[12] = 1
EndIf
TextWindow.WriteLine("The back-support strap on your backpack has worn
through. You'll")
TextWindow.WriteLine("have to find a shoemaker to sew on a piece of heavy
leather.")
ln2111:
EndSub
'
Sub Sub2150
If D - DB < 500 Then
Goto LN2151
ELSEIF HZArray[15] = 1 THEN
goto ln2180
ELSE
TM = 1
HZArray[15] = 1
EndIf
TextWindow.WriteLine("The soles of your boots have worn through. You'll have
to get new")
TextWindow.WriteLine("soles at a shoemaker.")
Goto LN2151
LN2180:
If D - DB < 800 Then
Goto ln2151
```

```
ELSE
TM = 1.5
DB = D
HZArray[15] = 0
EndIf
TextWindow.WriteLine("Your repaired boot soles are going again. You'll have
to buy a new")
TextWindow.WriteLine("pair of boots along the way.")
LN2151:
EndSub
'
Sub Sub2220
If D - DB < 700 Then
Goto ln2221
ELSEIF HZArray[24] = 1 THEN
goto ln2221
ELSE
TM = 1
HZArray[24] = 1
EndIf
TextWindow.WriteLine("The uppers on your boots are starting to separate from
the soles.")
TextWindow.WriteLine("You'll have to get them repaired by shoemaker.")
LN2221:
EndSub
'
Sub Sub2260
If D < 1000 OR HZArray[23] = 1 Then
Goto LN2261
ELSE
TM = .4
HZArray[23] = 1
EndIf
TextWindow.WriteLine("The seat of your pants has worn through. You can take
off the")
TextWindow.WriteLine("pockets and sew them over the holes.")
LN2261:
EndSub
'
Sub Sub2300
TM = .3
TextWindow.WriteLine("Mice got into your food last night. Yuck.")
EndSub
'
Sub Sub2320
TM = .3
TextWindow.WriteLine("Some Boy Scouts kept you awake 'til 1 am last night.")
EndSub
'
Sub Sub2340
If D > 900 Then
Goto LN2341
ELSE
TM = .1
EndIf
```

```
TextWindow.WriteLine("Curs attack you as you are walking through a small
town.")
If STK = 1 Then
TextWindow.WriteLine("You drive them off with your walking stick." )
goto ln2341
EndIf
TextWindow.WriteLine("They nip at your heels. You should really carry a
stick.")
ln2341:
EndSub
'
Sub Sub2390
TM = .3
TextWindow.WriteLine("Trail is poorly marked and you get temporarily lost.")
EndSub
'
Sub Sub2410
TM = .2
TextWindow.WriteLine("Broken zipper on your pack. Lose time drying stuff.")
EndSub
'
Sub Sub2430
TM = .3
TextWindow.WriteLine("Route marked on map is out of date. You lose time
trying")
TextWindow.WriteLine("to get back on the trail.")
EndSub
'
Sub Sub2460
If HZArray[1] > 1 Then
Goto ln2461
ELSE
TM = 2
HZArray[1] = HZArray[1] + 1
DOC = 1
EndIf
TextWindow.WriteLine("You forget to shake out your boot and a snake has
curled up inside")
TextWindow.WriteLine("for the night. You're scared and he's mad.")
Sub5510()
If Math.GetRandomNumber(999)/1000 < .9 Then
TextWindow.WriteLine("He slithers away and all is okay. Whew!")
Goto ln2461
EndIf
TextWindow.WriteLine("It's a rattler and he bites you. You'll have to get a
doctor.")
Sub3360()
ln2461:
EndSub
'
Sub Sub2530
If D > 165 OR HZArray[7] = 1 Then
Goto LN2531
ELSE
HZArray[7] = 1
```

```
RN = Math.Floor(1 + 4 * Math.GetRandomNumber(999)/1000)
TM = RN
EndIf
TextWindow.WriteLine("Late snow in the Smokies. The trail is unpassable for
"+ RN+ " days.")
LN2531:
EndSub
'
Sub Sub2570
If HZArray[8] > 3 Then
Goto ln2571
ELSE
HZArray[8] = HZArray[8] + 1
R[1] = .9
TSLOW[1] = T + 14
EndIf
TextWindow.WriteLine("You have some nasty blisters that will slow your
pace.")
LN2571:
EndSub
'
Sub Sub2600
If HZArray[9] > 2 Then
Goto LN2601
ELSE
HZArray[9] = HZArray[9] + 1
R[2] = .7
TSLOW[2] = T + 3
EndIf
TextWindow.WriteLine("You have bad indigestion from an unbalanced diet.")
LN2601:
EndSub
'
Sub Sub2630
If D > 870 OR HZArray[10] = 1 Then
Goto LN2631
ELSE
HZArray[10] = 1
TM = .5
EndIf
TextWindow.WriteLine("A bear got into your food and ripped your pack last
night. It's")
TextWindow.WriteLine("a good thing he wasn't hungry for human burgers.")
LN2631:
EndSub
'
Sub Sub2670
If HZArray[11] > 1 Then
Goto LN2671
ELSE
HZArray[11] = HZArray[11] + 1
R[3] = .75
TSLOW[3] = T + 6
EndIf
```

```
TextWindow.WriteLine("You twisted your ankle crossing a stream. That will
slow your")
TextWindow.WriteLine("pace for a few days. Be more careful!")
LN2671:
EndSub
'
Sub Sub2710
If HZArray[2] = 1 Then
Goto ln2711
ELSE
HZArray[2] = 1
DOC = 2
EndIf
TextWindow.WriteLine("You slipped on some rocks on a ledge. It's incredibly
painful!")
TextWindow.WriteLine("Better see a doctor.")
Sub3360()
LN2711:
EndSub
'
Sub Sub2750
TM = .3
TextWindow.WriteLine("A branch snaps in your eye. Lose time to treat it.")
EndSub
'
Sub Sub2770
TM = .3
TextWindow.WriteLine("Bad case of constipation. Better change diet.")
EndSub
'
Sub Sub2790
TM = .5
TextWindow.WriteLine("You fell in a stream and everything got wet. Lose
time")
TextWindow.WriteLine("drying out your sleeping bag and clothes.")
EndSub
'
Sub Sub2820
If HZArray[13] = 1 Then
Goto LN2821
ELSE
HZArray[13] = 1
TM = 1.5
EndIf
TextWindow.WriteLine("Last night you saw an animal moving near you and
swatted at it.")
Sub5510()
TextWindow.WriteLine("Big mistake! It was a skunk. You'll have to wash")
TextWindow.WriteLine("what you can and replace the rest.")
LN2821:
EndSub
'
Sub Sub2870
If HZArray[14] = 1 Then
Goto LN2871
```

```
ELSE
HZArray[14] = 1
TM = 2
EndIf
TextWindow.WriteLine("Lowliest of the low! Someone stole your pack while you
were taking")
TextWindow.WriteLine("a shower. You'll have to replace everything.")
LN2871:
EndSub
'
Sub Sub2910
If HZArray[3] = 1 Then
Goto LN2911
ELSE
HZArray[3] = 1
TM = 3
DOC = 3
EndIf
TextWindow.WriteLine("After five solid days of rain, everything is soaked and
you just")
TextWindow.WriteLine("can't stop shivering. You feel so terrible that you'll
have to")
TextWindow.WriteLine("see a doctor.")
Sub3360()
LN2911:
EndSub
'
Sub Sub2960
If HZArray[16] = 1 Then
Goto LN2961
ELSE
HZArray[16] = 1
TM = .4
EndIf
TextWindow.WriteLine("You cut your hand badly with your knife. Be careful!")
LN2961:
EndSub
'
Sub Sub2990
TM = .3
TextWindow.WriteLine("Socks worn through. You'll have to buy new ones.")
EndSub
'
Sub Sub3010
If HZArray[17] = 1 Then
Goto LN3011
ELSE
HZArray[17] = 1
TM = 1
EndIf
TextWindow.WriteLine("Bad toothache. You'll have to find a dentist soon.")
LN3011:
EndSub
'
Sub Sub3040
```

```
If HZArray[18] = 2 OR WT[1] = 0 Then
Goto ln3041
ELSE
HZArray[18] = HZArray[18] + 1
TM = .5
EndIf
TextWindow.WriteLine("Tent ripped. You'll have to sew on a patch.")
LN3041:
EndSub
'
Sub Sub3070
If D < 1000 OR HZArray[19] = 1 Then
Goto LN3071
ELSE
HZArray[19] = 1
TM = .3
EndIf
TextWindow.WriteLine("Your groundcloth is in shreds. Must buy a new one.")
LN3071:
EndSub
'
Sub Sub3100
If D < 500 OR HZArray[20] = 1 OR WT[7] = 0 Then
Goto LN3101
ELSE
HZArray[20] = 1
TM = .4
EndIf
TextWindow.WriteLine("Bad rip in raingear. Must get a replacement.")
LN3101:
EndSub
'
Sub Sub3130
If D < 600 OR HZArray[21] = 1 OR STK = 0 Then
Goto LN3131
ELSE
HZArray[21] = 1
R[4] = .9
TM = .4
EndIf
TextWindow.WriteLine("Your walking stick breaks. You can get a new one in the
next")
TextWindow.WriteLine("town. Maybe they make 'em better up here.")
TSLOW[4] = T + 4
LN3131:
EndSub
'
Sub Sub3170
If HZArray[22] = 1 Then
Goto LN3171
ELSE
HZArray[22] = 1
TM = .4
EndIf
```

```
TextWindow.WriteLine("Your water bag springs a leak. Better get a new one
soon!")
LN3171:
EndSub
'
Sub Sub3200
TM = .2
TextWindow.WriteLine("You run out of toilet tissue. Yucko!")
EndSub
'
Sub Sub3220
TextWindow.WriteLine("You run out of water and the springs marked on the map
seem")
TextWindow.WriteLine("to have vanished or dried up. Better take it easy for a
bit.")
HZArray[5] = 1
R[5] = .9
TSLOW[5] = T + 3
EndSub
'
Sub Sub3260
If HZArray[4] = 3 Then
Goto LN3261
ELSE
HZArray[4] = HZArray[4] + 1
DOC = 4
EndIf
TextWindow.WriteLine("Oh oh, you stumble into a thicket of poison ivy.
Zowie!")
If IVY = 1 OR (IVY = 2 AND Math.GetRandomNumber(999)/1000 > .5) Then
Goto LN3290
ELSE
goto LN3300
EndIf
LN3290:
TextWindow.WriteLine("You got it really bad. You'll have to see a doctor.")
Sub3360()
LN3300:
TextWindow.WriteLine("Like it or not, you got a mild case. It itches like
crazy but the")
TextWindow.WriteLine("calamine seems to have it under control. It slows you
down tho'.")
R[6] = .9
TSLOW[6] = T + 7
TM = .4
LN3261:
EndSub
'
Sub Sub3340
TextWindow.WriteLine("Walking ... walking ... walking ... walking.")
EndSub
'
Sub Sub3360
'Subroutine to deal with serious injuries and illnesses
TextWindow.WriteLine("")
```

```
TextWindow.WriteLine("You're feeling horrible, but you found a nice country
doctor.")
If (DOC = 1) Then
  Goto LN3410
ElseIf (DOC = 2) Then
  Goto LN3480
ElseIf (DOC = 3) Then
  Goto LN3570
ElseIf (DOC = 4) Then
  Goto LN3640
ElseIf (DOC = 5) Then
  Goto LN3700
EndIf
'
'Rattlesnake bite
LN3410:
TextWindow.WriteLine("He examines your swollen leg and says,")
Sub5510()
TextWindow.WriteLine("'Good thing you got here so quickly. I'll give you a
shot of anti-")
TextWindow.WriteLine("venin but you're going to be out of commission for a
good 4 days?")
TextWindow.WriteLine("and even after that you'll have to take it easy for a
while.'")
TM = 4
R[7] = .7
TSLOW[7] = T + 15
Goto LN3801
'
'Broken or sprained leg
LN3480:
TextWindow.WriteLine("He examines your leg and says,")
Sub5510()
If Math.GetRandomNumber(999)/1000 > .7 Then
  Goto LN3520
EndIf
TextWindow.WriteLine("'That's a very nasty sprain. I'll tape it up, but
you'll have to")
TextWindow.WriteLine("take it easy for at least a month.'")
TM = 1.5
R[8] = .6
TSLOW[8] = T + 30
Goto ln3801

LN3520:
TextWindow.WriteLine("'Bad news, my young friend. Your leg is broken. I'm
surprised you")
TextWindow.WriteLine("got here under your own power. But this is the end of
your hike.")
TextWindow.WriteLine("Sorry, but maybe you can try again next year.'")
Sub4610()
'
'Hypothermia
LN3570:
TextWindow.WriteLine("He examines you and says,")
```

```
Sub5510()
TM = Math.Floor(5 + 6 * Math.GetRandomNumber(999)/1000)
TextWindow.WriteLine("'That prolonged rain and cold has put you in a
condition that we")
TextWindow.WriteLine("call hypothermia. You can stay in town here at a motel
and I'll")
TextWindow.WriteLine("keep an eye on you, but you can't go back on the Trail
for at")
TextWindow.WriteLine("least "+ TM +" days. Sorry, but that's the way it
is.'")
Goto ln3801
'
'Poison Ivy
LN3640:
TextWindow.WriteLine("He only needs a glance to see that you are suffering
from an")
TextWindow.WriteLine("extremely bad case of poison ivy. He puts you in a
clinic for")
TextWindow.WriteLine("a few days and tells you what you already knew?that
you'll just")
TextWindow.WriteLine("have to let it run its course.")
TM = 5
Goto ln3801
'
'Excessive weight loss
LN3700:
TextWindow.WriteLine("He examines you and says," )
Sub5510()
If WTLOST > .33 * WB Then
  Goto LN3770
EndIf
TextWindow.WriteLine("'You may want to lose some weight, but it's coming off
far too")
TextWindow.WriteLine("quickly. Your body just can't cope. I'm going to keep
you here")
TextWindow.WriteLine("for a week on a controlled diet?and then for the rest
of the trip")
TextWindow.WriteLine("you'll have to go at a slower pace. Also, I want you to
consume")
TextWindow.WriteLine("at least as many calories per day as your body is using
up.'")
WB = 1.18 * WB
TM = 7
R[9] = .8
TSLOW[9] = T + 30
Goto LN3801

LN3770:
TextWindow.WriteLine("'Believe it or not, you are in an advanced stage of
starvation.")
TextWindow.WriteLine("You're going to have to remain here for a few weeks on
a controlled")
TextWindow.WriteLine("diet to stabilize your body chemistry. And then you
will go home?")
TextWindow.WriteLine("yes, HOME, and not back to the Trail this year.'")
```

```
Sub4610()

LN3801:
EndSub
'
Sub Sub3820
'Subroutine to examine weight loss
CALOFF = CD - 1.03 * CAL
'Augment diet by 3% with ice cream, etc.
TS = T - TL
TL = T
'Time (in days) of this trip segment
WTLOSS = CALOFF * TS / 3500
WTLOST = WTLOST + WTLOSS
If WTLOSS < 1 Then
  Goto LN4010
EndIf
TextWindow.WriteLine("Since the start of the trip, you have lost "
+math.floor(WTLOST) +" pounds.")
If WTLOST > .07 * WB Then
  Goto LN3900  'Lost more than 7% of orig body weight?
EndIf
TextWindow.WriteLine("Right now you are feeling fit as a fiddle, but
remember, you")
TextWindow.WriteLine("still have a long way to go.")
Goto LN3970
LN3900:
If WTLOST>.15 * WB Then
  Goto LN3930  'Lost more than 15% of orig body weight?
EndIf
TextWindow.WriteLine("You occasionally feel a bit lightheaded and shaky. You
really")
TextWindow.WriteLine("should eat a bit more.")
Goto LN3970
LN3930:
TextWindow.WriteLine("That's far too much weight to lose in this short period
of time.")
If WTLOST > .24 * WB Then
HZArray[5] = 1
DOC = 5
Sub3360()
GOTO LN3970
EndIf
TextWindow.WriteLine("You frequently feel lightheaded, nauseated, and
sluggish. You'd")
TextWindow.WriteLine("better add to your diet?and soon!")
LN3970:
WB = WB+WTLOSS
CD = Math.Floor(WB * 11.5 + WB * DINPT * .3 + (WB + WP) * DINPT * .21 + WB *
(15 - TW) * .22)
TextWindow.WriteLine("At your current pace, you are burning " +CD+ " calories
per day.")
TextWindow.WriteLine("")
TextWindow.Write("How many calories worth of food do you want to eat? ")
CAL = TextWindow.ReadNumber()
```

```
If CD - CAL > 400 Then
  TextWindow.WriteLine("Okay, suit yourself.")
EndIf
LN4010:
EndSub
'
Sub Sub4030
'Subroutine to deal with a long period of rain
If Math.GetRandomNumber(999)/1000 < .94 Then
HZArray[5] = 0
Goto LN4250 '6% chance of heavy rain
EndIf
If HZArray[5] = 1 Then
HZArray[5] = 0
goto ln4250 'In a dry stretch?
EndIf
HZArray[25] = HZArray[25] + 1
TM = RAIN * 1.7
If HZArray[25] > 4 Then
  HZArray[25] = 4
EndIf
If (HZArray[25] = 1) Then
  Goto LN4080
ElseIf (HZArray[25] = 2) Then
  Goto LN4130
ElseIf (HZArray[25]= 3) Then
  Goto LN4150
ElseIf (HZArray[25] = 4) Then
  Goto LN4180
EndIf
LN4080:
TextWindow.WriteLine("It has been raining steadily for the past week and you
are")
TextWindow.WriteLine("thoroughly soaked ... your clothes, your sleeping bag,
your food,")
TextWindow.WriteLine("and, yes, your spirits. What a bummer.")
Sub5510()
TextWindow.WriteLine("If it continues for another week, you're going to have
fungus")
TextWindow.WriteLine("growing on your skin.")
Goto LN4250
LN4130:
TextWindow.WriteLine("Good grief! More rain ... torrential, blustery,
miserable rain.")
TextWindow.WriteLine("This is really beginning to get you down.")
Goto LN4250
LN4150:
TextWindow.WriteLine("Would you believe it? It is raining again. Not the
pitter-patter")
TextWindow.WriteLine("of the songwriters, but steady, heavy, cold rain.")
Sub5510()
TextWindow.WriteLine("... and more rain. Won't it ever stop?")
Goto LN4250
LN4180:
```

```
TextWindow.WriteLine("Unbelievable ... it is raining again?and has been for
the past week.")
If (RAIN = 2 OR RAIN = 3) AND D < 1900 Then
Goto LN4230
ELSE
Goto ln4250
EndIf
If RAIN = 4 Then
TextWindow.WriteLine("Okay, you resign yourself to wait it out.")
goto LN4250
EndIf
TextWindow.WriteLine("Even your cheerful attitude toward rain is taking a
beating, but")
TextWindow.WriteLine("you keep slogging along, hoping for a letup.")
Goto LN4250
LN4230:
Sub5510()
TextWindow.WriteLine("")
TextWindow.WriteLine("That's it. You can't take any more. Maybe")
TextWindow.WriteLine("you'll try again next year, but that's it for now.")
Sub4610()
LN4250:
EndSub
'
Sub Sub4260
'Subroutine to deal with snow in New England
If T > 200 AND Math.GetRandomNumber(999)/1000 > .5 Then
  Goto LN4290  '50% chance of snow after Oct 15
EndIf
If Math.GetRandomNumber(999)/1000 > .2 Then
  Goto LN4611 '20% chance of snow
EndIf
LN4290:
SNO = SNO + 1
TextWindow.WriteLine("Oh oh, New England is getting some snow ...")
If SNO = 1 Then
TextWindow.WriteLine("but you keep pushing on." )
Goto LN4611
EndIf
If SNO > 2 Then
  Goto LN4350  '3 heavy snowfalls and you're out
EndIf
TextWindow.WriteLine("You pushed through the last flurries but this looks")
TextWindow.WriteLine("more serious. You say to yourself, 'I've gone this")
TextWindow.WriteLine("far, I'm going to go all the way.' And on you go ...")
Goto LN4611
LN4350:
TextWindow.WriteLine("You made a gallant attempt to get through, but the
Park")
TextWindow.WriteLine("Rangers won't let you go on. Too bad.")
Sub4610()
LN4611:
EndSub
'
Sub Sub4380
```

```
'Subroutine to deal with the Kennebec River
KEN = 1
TextWindow.WriteLine("")
TextWindow.WriteLine("You have arrived at the Kennebec River.")
TextWindow.Write("Did you make prior arrangements to get across? ")
AD = TextWindow.Read()
Sub5540()
If AD<>"Y" Then
Goto LN4450
ELSE
RN = Math.GetRandomNumber(999)/1000
IF RN > .5 THEN
goto LN4440
EndIf
EndIf
TextWindow.WriteLine("Fortunately the person you called showed up to meet you
with")
TextWindow.WriteLine("a canoe. You get across in jig time.")
TM = .5
Goto LN4540
ln4440:
Sub5510()
TextWindow.WriteLine("Too bad; the guy you called didn't show up.")
Goto LN4460
LN4450:
TextWindow.WriteLine("That wasn't very sensible. What will you do now? ")
Sub5510()
LN4460:
If Math.GetRandomNumber(999)/1000 > .7 Then
  Goto LN4520  '30% chance you can ford the river
EndIf
TextWindow.WriteLine("The river is running very high and the logs from the
sawmill are")
TextWindow.WriteLine("very dangerous. You'll have to hang around until
another hiker")
TextWindow.WriteLine("(who, hopefully, has arranged for a canoe) shows up or
hope that")
TextWindow.WriteLine("someone comes along.")
Sub5510()
TM = Math.Floor(2 + 3 * Math.GetRandomNumber(999)/1000)
TextWindow.WriteLine("Finally ... you're across, but it cost you "+ TM +"
days.")
Goto LN4540
LN4520:
TextWindow.WriteLine("Fortunately the river isn't running too high and you
can probably")
TextWindow.WriteLine("wade across downstream at the ford. Boy, were you
lucky!")
TM = .6
LN4540:
T = T + TM
EndSub
'
LN4560:
'Reached end of trail!
```

```
TextWindow.WriteLine("You reached the end of the trail at Baxter Peak on Mt.
Katahdin!")
For J = 1 To 3
Sub5510()
EndFor
TextWindow.Clear()
For J = 1 To 10
Sound.PlayBellRing()
XD = "CONGRATULATIONS!"
TextWindow.CursorTop = 12
Sub5590()
Program.Delay(100)
TextWindow.clear()
Program.Delay(50)
EndFor
D = 2007
Sub4610()

Sub Sub4610
'game done
TD = Math.Floor(T + .5)
D = Math.Floor(D)
X = (Math.Floor(.5 + 10 * D / TD)) / 10
'End game statistics
TextWindow.WriteLine("")
TextWindow.Write("It is now ")
Sub5220()
TextWindow.WriteLine(" and you have been on the")
LN4630:
TextWindow.WriteLine("trail for " +TD+ " days. You have covered " +D +"
miles. Your average")
TextWindow.Write("speed, considering all the delays, was ")
TextWindow.Write(X)
TextWindow.WriteLine(" miles per day.")
WB = Math.Floor(WB + .5)
WL = Math.Floor(WTLOST + .5)
If WL > 0 Then
XD = "less"
GOTO LN4680
EndIf
XD = "more"
WL = -WL
LN4680:
TextWindow.WriteLine("You weighed "+ WB +" pounds at the end, " +WL+" "+ XD+
" than at the start.")
TextWindow.WriteLine("Nice going!")
TextWindow.WriteLine("")
TextWindow.Write("Press Enter to End")
AD = TextWindow.Read()
Program.End()
EndSub
'
'
Sub Sub5200
'Subroutine to print the date
```

```
If TT = TD Then
Goto ln5201 'Printed this date already?
EndIf
sub5220()
LN5201:
EndSub

Sub Sub5220
If TD < 31 Then
Goto LN5250
ELSEIF TD < 62 THEN
Goto LN5260
ELSEIF TD < 90 THEN
Goto LN5270
EndIf
If TD < 121 Then
Goto LN5280
ELSEIF TD < 152 THEN
goto LN5290
ELSEIF TD < 182 THEN
goto LN5300
EndIf
If TD < 213 Then
Goto LN5310
ELSEIF TD < 225 THEN
Goto LN5320
ELSE
GOTO LN5340
EndIf
LN5250:
MOD = "April"
MD = TD
Goto LN5330
LN5260:
MOD = "May"
MD = TD - 30
Goto LN5330
LN5270:
MOD = "June"
MD = TD - 61
Goto LN5330
LN5280:
MOD = "July"
MD = TD - 89
Goto LN5330
LN5290:
MOD = "August"
MD = TD - 120
Goto LN5330
LN5300:
MOD = "September"
MD = TD - 151
Goto LN5330
LN5310:
MOD = "October"
```

```
MD = TD - 181
Goto LN5330
LN5320:
MOD = "November"
MD = TD - 212
LN5330:
TextWindow.Write(MOD+" "+ MD+ " ")
TT = TD
Goto LN5389
LN5340:
TextWindow.WriteLine("")
TextWindow.WriteLine("It's November 12 and all the New England states are covered")
TextWindow.WriteLine("with snow. You have no chance of finishing the trail. Better")
TextWindow.WriteLine("luck next year. You have been out on the")
TD = Math.Floor(T + .5)
D = Math.Floor(D)
X = (Math.Floor(.5 + 10 * D / TD)) / 10
Goto LN4630
ln5389:
EndSub
'
Sub Sub5390
'Subroutine to temporarily break execution
TextWindow.WriteLine("")
XD = "Press Enter to continue"
Sub5590()
YYY = TextWindow.Read()
EndSub
'
Sub Sub5430
'Subroutine to print weights by pounds and ounces
WTPND = Math.Floor(WEIGHT / 16)
WTOZ = WEIGHT - 16 * WTPND
If WTPND > 1 Then
  TextWindow.Write(WTPND+ " pounds ")
  GOTO LN5470
EndIf
If WTPND = 1 Then
  TextWindow.Write("1 pound ")
  GOTO LN5470
EndIf
LN5470:
If WTOZ > 1 Then
  TextWindow.Write(WTOZ+" ounces")
  Goto LN5509
EndIf
If WTOZ = 1 Then
  TextWindow.Write("1 ounce")
EndIf
LN5509:
EndSub
'
Sub Sub5510
```

```
'Subroutine to make a short pause
Program.Delay(1000)
EndSub
'
Sub Sub5540
'Subroutine to extract the first letter of an input answer
If AD = "" Then
AD = "Y"
Goto LN5589
EndIf
AD = Text.GetSubText(AD,1, 1)
If text.GetCharacterCode(AD) >= text.GetCharacterCode("A") AND
text.GetCharacterCode(AD) <= text.GetCharacterCode("Z") Then
  Goto ln5589
EndIf
AD = Text.GetCharacter(Text.GetCharacterCode(AD) - 32)
LN5589:
EndSub
'
Sub Sub5590
'Subroutine to print centered lines
TextWindow.CursorLeft = (70 - Text.GetLength(XD))/2
TextWindow.Write(XD)
EndSub
'
Sub Sub5620
'Subroutine to print the instructions
XD = "Appalachian Trail"
Sub5590()
TextWindow.WriteLine("")
TextWindow.WriteLine("")
TextWindow.WriteLine(" You are a hiker whose goal is to walk the entire 2007
miles of")
TextWindow.WriteLine("the Appalachian Trail from Springer Mt., GA, to Mt.
Katahdin, Maine.")
TextWindow.WriteLine("You set out in April as soon as the Smokies are clear
of snow, and")
TextWindow.WriteLine("you must reach the northern terminus before it is
blocked by snow.")
TextWindow.WriteLine(" Your hike is divided into three-day segments. Along
the way,")
TextWindow.WriteLine("you encounter natural hazards, difficulties with your
equipment,")
TextWindow.WriteLine("and physical problems.")
TextWindow.WriteLine(" Careful planning for your hike is very important. In
deciding")
TextWindow.WriteLine("what to pack, you have to make trade-offs?generally
between weight")
TextWindow.WriteLine("and comfort. Of course, everything must fit in your
pack.")
TextWindow.WriteLine(" You must decide how you will obtain food along the
route, how")
TextWindow.WriteLine("much to eat in each food group, and how many calories
to replenish.")
```

```
TextWindow.WriteLine(" You must decide at what pace you will walk, and how
long to")
TextWindow.WriteLine("hike each day. Of course, a faster pace will cover
mileage more")
TextWindow.WriteLine("quickly than a slower one, but it is much harder on
your body.")
TextWindow.WriteLine(" You don't have many choices when dealing with mishaps.
It is")
TextWindow.WriteLine("assumed that you are a sensible hiker, make repairs
when necessary,")
TextWindow.WriteLine("replace things that wear out, and see a doctor if you
get sick.")
TextWindow.WriteLine("Nevertheless, mishaps cost you time, of which you have
little to")
TextWindow.WriteLine("spare as you take another of the five million steps
towards Maine.")
TextWindow.WriteLine("")
XD= "Press Enter when you're ready to go."
Sub5590()
JJJ = TextWindow.Read()
TextWindow.Clear()
EndSub
```

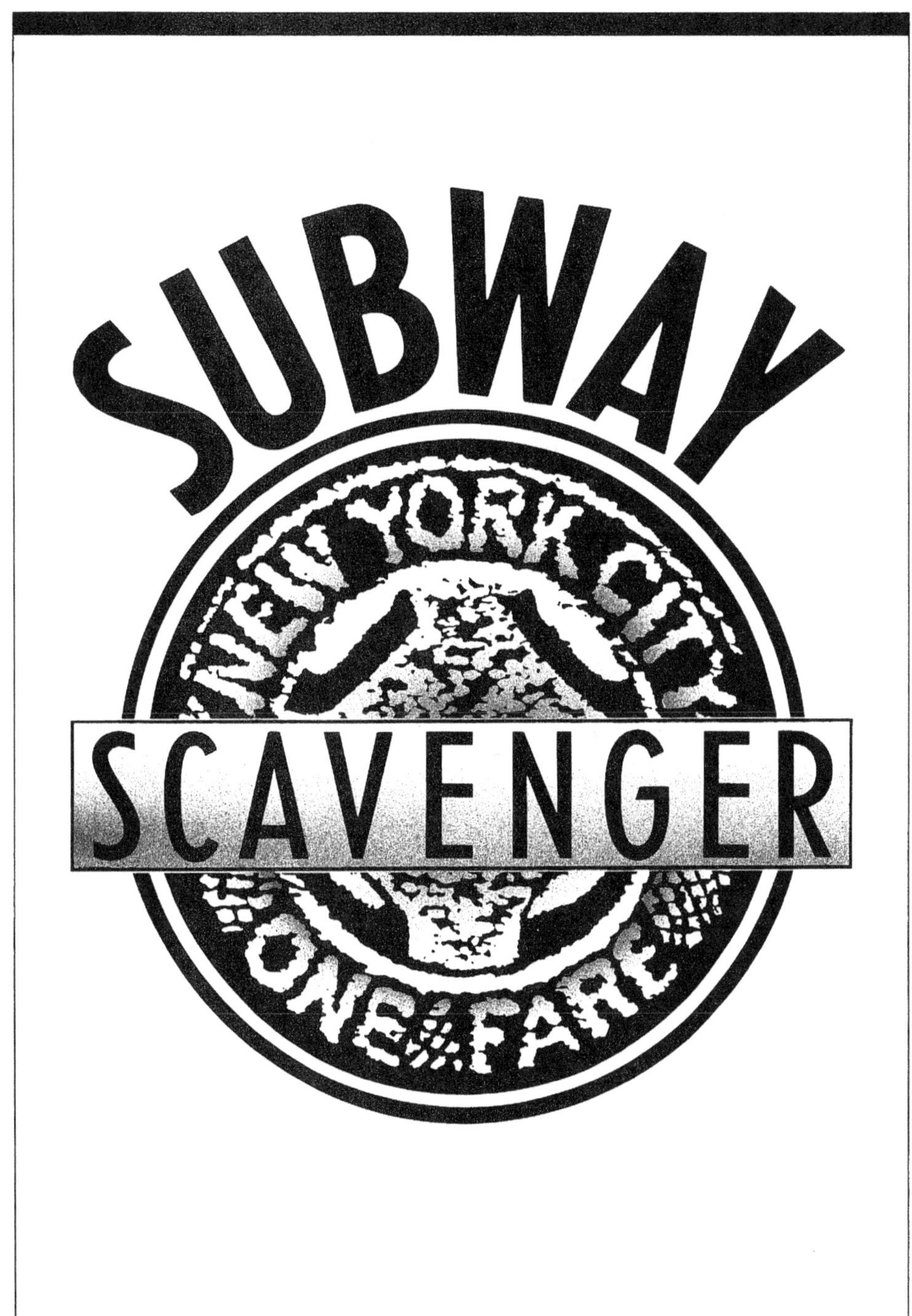
SUBWAY
NEW YORK CITY
SCAVENGER
ONE FARE

Subway Scavenger

In Subway Scavenger, you are a messenger hired to pick up and deliver packages all over New York City. Starting at 9:00 A.M., your log will show five deliveries and five pickups. You start from your office in the Port Authority Bus Terminal at 8th Avenue and 42nd Street and work until quitting time. During the course of your day, you face typical New York subway hazards—stuck doors, track fires, and unsavory characters—but the clock is your biggest enemy. The following rules govern your progress through your delivery schedule:

- When you arrive at a station on foot, you are told which trains stop at that station. You buy a token for $1 and board whichever train you wish.
- At each station, you can either get off or stay on. If you get off, you can then take another train (if the station is an interchange point) or make a delivery or pickup (if the station is within walking distance of your destination). Remember that express trains don't stop at all stations. The following clues should help non-New Yorkers:
    - » Brooklyn Academy of Music is abbreviated BAM.
    - » Rockaway Boulevard in Woodhaven (Queens) is on the A Train line.
    - » Harlem is serviced by the A, B, and D Lines.
    - » The World Trade Center is an easy walk from Chambers Street.
    - » The New York Stock Exchange is an easy walk from Wall Street.
    - » Grand Street and Canal Street run through Chinatown.
- The game is easier if you make a map as you go along.

By the time you complete a few games of Subway Scavenger, you will feel like a native New Yorker—and probably be qualified for a high-paying job as a subway courier. Write if you get work!

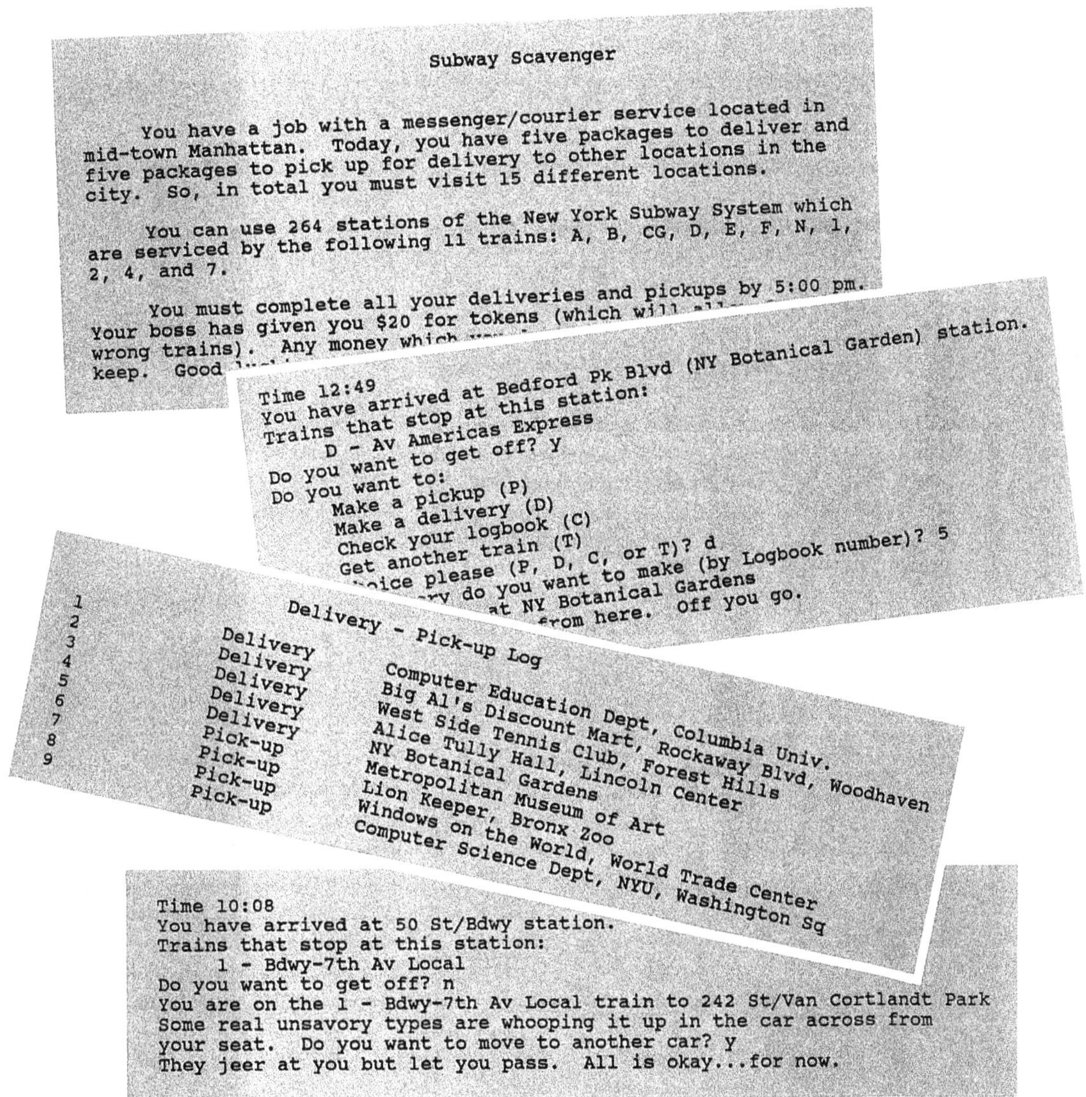

Subway Scavenger
You have a job with a messenger/courier service located in mid-town Manhattan. Today, you have five packages to deliver and five packages to pick up for delivery to other locations in the city. So, in total you must visit 15 different locations.
You can use 264 stations of the New York Subway System which are serviced by the following 11 trains: A, B, CG, D, E, F, N, 1, 2, 4, and 7.
You must complete all your deliveries and pickups by 5:00 pm.
Your boss has given you $20 for tokens (which
wrong trains). Any money
keep. Good
Time 12:49
You have arrived at Bedford Pk Blvd (NY Botanical Garden) station.
Trains that stop at this station:
D - Av Americas Express
Do you want to get off? y
Do you want to:
Make a pickup (P)
Make a delivery (D)
Check your logbook (C)
Get another train (T)
ice please (P, D, C, or T)? d
do you want to make (by Logbook number)? 5
at NY Botanical Gardens
from here. off you go.
Delivery - Pick-up Log
1 Delivery Computer Education Dept, Columbia Univ.
2 Delivery Big Al's Discount Mart, Rockaway Blvd, Woodhaven
3 Delivery West Side Tennis Club, Forest Hills
4 Delivery Alice Tully Hall, Lincoln Center
5 Delivery NY Botanical Gardens
6 Pick-up Metropolitan Museum of Art
7 Pick-up Lion Keeper, Bronx Zoo
8 Pick-up Windows on the World, World Trade Center
9 Pick-up Computer Science Dept, NYU, Washington Sq
Time 10:08
You have arrived at 50 St/Bdwy station.
Trains that stop at this station:
1 - Bdwy-7th Av Local
Do you want to get off? n
You are on the 1 - Bdwy-7th Av Local train to 242 St/Van Cortlandt Park
Some real unsavory types are whooping it up in the car across from your seat. Do you want to move to another car? y
They jeer at you but let you pass. All is okay...for now.

THE STORY

The first underground subway system in the world went into service in London, England in 1863. Other early subway systems include those of Glasgow (1886), Budapest (1896), Boston (the first in the United States, 1898), Paris (1900), Berlin (1902), New York (1904), Madrid (1919), Tokyo (1927), Moscow (1935) and Chicago (1943). Toronto's subway, completed in 1954, was the first in Canada.

Some subways consist of only a single line, but most, such as the Métropolitain in Paris, the New York Subway System, and the London Underground, are networks. By far the largest underground transportation system in the world is that of New York City, which includes 230 route miles of track and 465 stations. But development of the system did not occur quickly or easily.

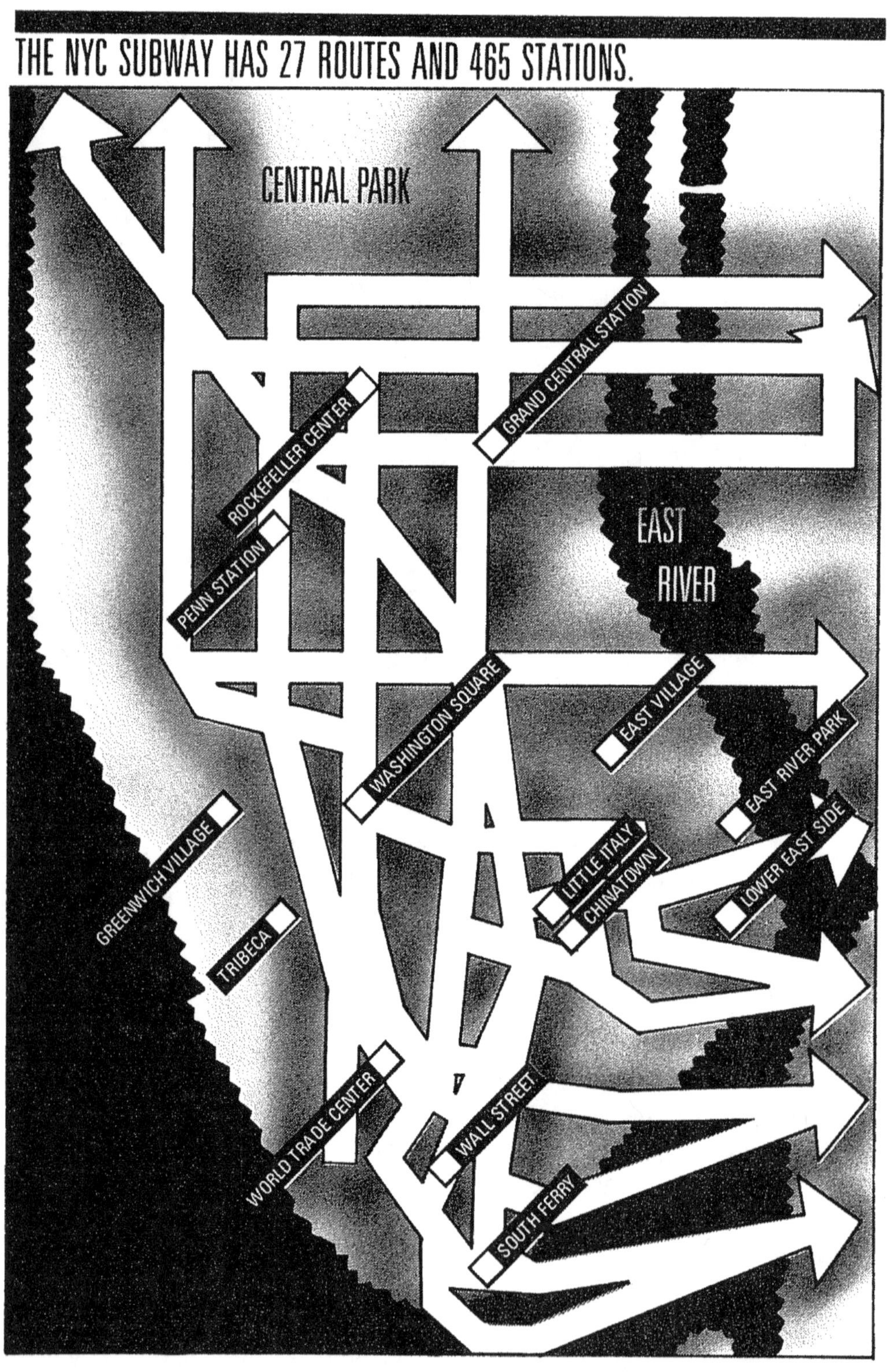
THE NYC SUBWAY HAS 27 ROUTES AND 465 STATIONS.
CENTRAL PARK
GRAND CENTRAL STATION
ROCKEFELLER CENTER
PENN STATION
EAST RIVER
WASHINGTON SQUARE
EAST VILLAGE
EAST RIVER PARK
GREENWICH VILLAGE
LITTLE ITALY
CHINATOWN
LOWER EAST SIDE
TRIBECA
WORLD TRADE CENTER
WALL STREET
SOUTH FERRY

As immigrants poured into New York in the early 1800s, the City grew so fast that street congestion soon became a major problem for pedestrians and drivers of horse-drawn wagons, omnibuses, and carriages. As a result, several mass-transit systems were proposed for New York City, with a subway suggested as early as 1864. However, it was an elevated railway that got the approval of both backers and politicians, and the first one, a cable-operated affair along Ninth Avenue, went into operation on February 14, 1870.

The cable frequently broke, disrupting service, so, on October 27, 1871, the line installed a steam locomotive to pull the cars. At the same time, a passing track was built in the center of the line, enabling trains to run in two directions. Running time over the entire route from Dey Street (near the Battery at the southern tip of Manhattan) to 29th Street was 28 minutes. The success of this line—more than 5000 fares daily—convinced a legion of skeptics that the "el" was the panacea for all of Manhattan's street-level traffic problems, and for the next 20 years the els spread like cucumber vines all over the City.

The disadvantages of the elevated railways were that they were noisy, smelly, dirty, and a detriment to the neighborhoods over which they rolled. An inventor, Frank J. Sprague, had a solution: electricity. Sprague had built an experimental electric car and won the attention of Jay Gould, the great New York railroad financier. Sprague persuaded Gould to take a ride in his experimental car. Anxious to show it off, Sprague enthusiastically yanked the controller to set the train in motion. But he pulled the controller too abruptly, and a fuse blew. The noise, which sounded like a bomb exploding, completely unnerved Gould, who instantly abandoned all interest in electric traction. Sprague was forced to look elsewhere for backing.

"Elsewhere" turned out to be Chicago, Illinois, Richmond, Indiana and St.Joseph, Missouri. Sprague's electrified, multiple-unit trains worked so well in these cities that in 1898 Brooklyn's steam-operated els began converting to electricity, and by 1903 all of New York's els were re-equipped with Sprague locomotives. More important, electric locomotives opened the possibility of building underground railways in Manhattan, an idea that had previously been dismissed because of the danger of smoke and steam in long underground runs.

Ground was broken in March 1900 for the first underground line in New York, a five-mile run from City Hall downtown up the East Side to Grand Central Terminal at 42nd Street. Rather than using the London and Glasgow method of boring an underground tunnel, New York's planners used the open-trench approach that had been employed successfully in Budapest. Using this approach, a huge, deep trench was cut; a roof was made of steel girders; and fill and paving were added above the roof. While this method was infinitely cheaper, easier, and faster than boring a tunnel, it was not popular with shopkeepers who wondered if the din and disruption would ever end. Eventually it did, and the first subway was put into service on October 27, 1904.

By this time, the promoters had vastly extended their plans, and the line, the Interborough Rapid Transit (IRT), extended from City Hall to 145th Street and Broadway in upper Manhattan. The length of the route was 13 1/2 miles, and the travel time was 26 minutes. Extensions and other lines were soon opened to meet increasing public demand for service. By 1912, a tunnel to Brooklyn was opened, and a few years later, one took trains under the Harlem River to the Bronx.

Meanwhile, the directors of the Brooklyn Rapid Transit (BRT) Company, a holding company that owned several els in Brooklyn, were enviously watching the success of the IRT. To grab a piece of the subway pie, they proposed to the city an ambitious plan to build a new subway from lower Manhattan up Broadway to the Queensboro Bridge, connecting it with tunnels to both Brooklyn and Staten Island. The directors of the IRT and newly-formed Hudson-Manhattan Tubes Company weren't happy about this, particularly when the City announced a splitting of the routes in what became known as "the Dual (IRT-BRT) Contracts." The BRT (later the BMT) benefited the most, getting 87.8 route miles all over Manhattan, Queens, and Brooklyn. The tunnel to Staten Island, incidentally, was never built.

The third big line to be built was the Independent Subway (IND), City-owned and operated right from the start. Although known for years as simply the Eighth Avenue Subway, that was a misnomer because the IND actually encompassed six basic routes: Washington Heights, Bronx-Grand Concourse, Coney Island, Queens-Manhattan, Sixth Avenue-Houston St., and Brooklyn-Queens crosstown. A seventh was added in 1939 to service the World's Fair at Flushing Meadow. Unlike the Victorian IRT with its mosaic-decorated stations or the BMT with its flamboyant rolling stock, the IND was a no-nonsense, modern line with bright, spacious stations, well-engineered cars, and speedy express runs.

In June 1940, New York City purchased the privately-owned Interborough Rapid Transit (IRT) and the Brooklyn Manhattan Transit (BMT) and combined them with the City-built Independent Subway System (IND) under the jurisdiction of the New York Transit Authority (TA). Today more than 6100 cars, connected in trains of from 3 to 12 units, operate day and night over 27 routes and make nearly 6400 trips on an average weekday. The lines use 12 bridges and 11 underwater tunnels and carry approximately one billion passengers per year.

In 1978, the New York City Transit Authority (TA) became a subsidiary of the Metropolitan Transportation Authority (MTA), the nation's largest transportation system. MTA vehicles carry nearly two billion riders per year, 6.3 million on an average weekday, or 57% of the population in its operating area. This exceeds the combined ridership of the systems of Chicago, Boston, and Philadelphia—the second, third, and fourth largest people movers in the country. With nearly 8000 rail cars, the MTA has a train fleet larger than all of America's other rapid-transit and commuter railroads combined.

The New York TA is charged with the operation of the subway system and surface bus fleet. The subway system alone employs nearly 28,000 workers and operates its own police department. Although accidents, track fires, delays, and crime regularly make the nightly news, the TA steadfastly maintains that the subway is actually one of the fastest and safest ways to travel around the city.

Just ask Rebecca Morris. Hailing from Youngstown, Ohio, with degrees in library science and English literature, Rebecca is not the sort of a person you would expect to find in the record books—particularly not for being the first woman to ride every inch of track from Brooklyn to the Bronx, from Queens to Manhattan, in one marathon odyssey. But, in the fall of 1973, she did—on 67 trains in 26 hours and 36 minutes.

Herman Rinke was the first person to tour the entire system for a single 5-cent fare. In 1940, just days before the three lines were unified under TA control, he rode for 25 hours. Since that day, more than 70 other people—recorded in an unofficial file at the TA Public Relations Department—have ridden the entire system. The 1961 subway map notes that a Flushing youth rode all the routes for a single token in 25 hours and 36 minutes. On April Fool's Day of 1966, the MIT Rapid Transit Club used a computer to route their attempt but failed to beat the best time to date, 24 hours and 56 minutes, set by Geoffrey Arnold in 1963. But on August 3, 1967, James Law and six high school buddies rode the entire system in 22 hours, 11 minutes, a time still cited in the *Guinness Book of World Records*.

People are fanatic about many facets of the subway. Bob Leon takes pictures of every transit nook and cranny. Howard and Suzanne Samuelson run an antique store devoted exclusively to transit material. Don Howard is a walking encyclopedia of transit lore, as are Hugh Dunne and Stan Fischler. Most of them look nostalgically back on earlier days—days of kerosene marker lanterns, days when people came to New York to ride the IRT, and days before graffiti.

In 1985, the TA set a goal of having 28% of the cars clean and graffiti-free. They succeeded, but just barely. Another goal for 1985 was to have working lights and loudspeakers, functioning climate control, accurate destination signs, and readable maps on 90% of the subway fleet. While these goals—particularly with respect to maps—were not quite realized, the TA made notable strides in meeting most of them. In 1985, for example, 78 of the TA's 465 subway stations were repainted.

Of the subway fleet of 6125 cars, 760 have been in service since the 1940s. Although in the past, the TA had purchased 200 to 400 new cars per year, these purchases were severely curtailed during the City's fiscal crisis in the mid-seventies. However, a contract was recently negotiated to purchase 1375 new cars from Japan, with the older cars being phased out as the new Japanese-built R-62 cars are delivered. The first 260 cars were delivered under this contract in 1984, and they will continue to be delivered at the rate of roughly 250 per year through 1988.

When the subway first opened in 1904, the fare was a nickel, which was a relatively large amount at the turn of the century. However, the fare did not change for over 50 years, and by 1956 the 5-cent fare was a real bargain. In contrast, over the next 30 years the fare was raised eight times until it reached its current level of $1.

As the fare has increased, so has the number of people who try to beat it by putting slugs in the turnstiles. Indeed, as of the end of 1985, the TA was collecting more than 13,000 slugs per day, resulting in a financial loss of almost $3 million per year. In an attempt to thwart cheaters, the TA has changed the design of the token to one with a stainless-steel center that looks like a "bull's-eye," an apt name as they are targeted at slug users. In mid-1986, all 2600 turnstiles at 749 entry locations were changed to accept only the new token.

The next time you're in New York, ride the subway. There is no better or faster way to get around—and after you master Subway Scavenger you'll really know how to do it.

BIBLIOGRAPHY

Annual Report (1984). Metropolitan Transportation Authority, 347 Madison Ave., New York, NY 10017.

Fischler, Stan. *Uptown, Downtown.* New York: Hawthorne Books, 1976.

New York City Subway Map (Spring 1985). New York City Transit Authority, 370 Jay St., Brooklyn, NY 11201. (Note: If you request a subway map from the TA, include a #10 business-size self-addressed, stamped envelope.)

THE PROGRAM

At first glance, the Subway Scavenger program may look quite complicated, because of both its length and the complexity of many program statements. In fact, the program is shorter than it seems and is relatively easy to understand—as well as being exceptionally versatile and powerful.

Its versatility and power stem from its general framework, which could be used to represent almost any kind of system with intersecting nodes. In this particular version, the framework is used to represent the New York City Subway System. However, it could just as easily accept data from any other subway (London, Tokyo, Moscow, San Francisco, etc.), train (Amtrak, BritRail, etc.), bus, or, for that matter, pedestrian system (Disneyland, a large building, manufacturing plant, etc.). It could even be used to model a mixed-mode system like a university with foot, auto, and bus transportation. Nor is the framework limited to transportation problems; it could also be used to simulate electronic-message traffic over a data network or a mixed system using voice, data, and manual transmission of messages.

The Subway Scavenger program is of modest length. Indeed, when the player instructions, prompts, and minor subroutines are stripped out, the main program is only about 80 lines long. Most of the information needed by the program is read from several data files.

Before discussing the program itself, it is important to be familiar with the three main types of data. First are the data about the nodes of the system, in this case the subway stations (data file stations.txt). To each node (or station) we must assign a number (STA), and we probably want to give it a name as well (STATIOND[STA]). We must also know how many lines of transportation (subway lines) intersect the node (STANU[STA]) and which ones they are (STATR[STA][n]).

Second, to each line of transportation (data file trains.txt), we must assign a number (TR) and possibly a name (TRAIND[TR]). In addition, we must know how many nodes it intersects (TRSTOP[TR]) and which ones they are (TRSTA[TR][n]). For convenience, we may also want to know the starting and ending point, so we can differentiate point-to-point routes from circular or continuous ones. In fact, the New York Subway System has only point-to-point routes, unlike the London Underground which has a mixture of circular and point-to-point routes.

Third, once the system is described, we must know what is to be transmitted (in this case, packages carried by a human being; data file deliveries.txt). To each package, we must assign a number (PKG) and, optionally, a name (PKGDESD[PKG]). We must also know where it is coming from and where it is going in terms of the nodes of the system (PKGSTA[PKG][n]). We don't really care which subway line it is carried on as long as it reaches its destination. In some cases, the building to which a package is to be delivered can be reached from more than one subway station. Naturally, it is usually preferable to use the closest station, because you spend less time walking. However, in some cases it is more efficient to walk a few extra blocks if you can reach a destination without having to ride out of your way to a station at which you can transfer to a closer line.

The main program consists of six major sections. The first one, "Arrive at station," (start at LN340) prints the name of the station at which you have arrived and the names of the trains that stop there. You can arrive on foot or by train. If you arrive on a train and that station is the end of the line, you must get off.

Otherwise, you can choose to get off or stay on the train.

If you get off the train, you must decide what to do next: make a pick-up, make a delivery, check your logbook, or catch another train. If you decide to catch another train, the program branches to the "Trains coming" section (start at LN530). LN550 picks a random train to arive at the station:

```
RN = Math.Floor(1 + STANU[STA] * Math.GetRandomNumber(999)/1000)
```

Recall that STANU[STA] is the number of trains that stop at a particular station; thus, RN will be an integer between 1 and STANU[STA]. RN is then used as the argument of STATR[STA][RN] to recover the actual number of the train:

```
TR = STATR[STA][RN]
```

The next two lines check to see if the current station (STA) is at one end of the line or the other for train TR. If so, that station is eliminated as a possible destination for train TR. Otherwise, train TR could have as its destination either end of the line. If you decide to board a particular train, the routine in above LN649 performs the important function of determining just where that train is along its route. This may sound unnecessary; after all, the program knows you are at station STA. However, station STA may be the fourth stop for train 1 and the twelfth stop for train 2, and so on; it is this index value that is determined by:

```
For I = 1 TO TRSTOP[TR]
'Find out where train is
If TRSTA[TR][I]=STA Then
  Goto LN649
EndIf
EndFor
LN649:
TRSTX = I
```

First, the For statement iterates through all the possible stops for train TR. In the data, these are station numbers. The If statement compares each station number (TRSTA[TR][I]) with the current station STA and, if a match is not found, goes on to the next one. When a match is found, LN649 assigns the index value I to the train station identification index, TRSTX.

Next, the "Train travel" routine (starts at LN690) adds or subtracts one from TRSTX depending upon which way you are traveling, and determines what the next station will be. This routine also calls the "Trip hazards" subroutine (Sub1210) which deals with sticky doors, muggers, track fires, and so on. After determining the next station, the program simply branches back to the "Arrive at station" section.

If you decide to make a pickup or delivery at a given station, the routine at LN750 determines whether or not that is a valid option (Has it been made already? Is your destination close enough to the station?) The subsequent routines simply update your logbook and check to see if all the pickups and deliveries have been made. If more deliveries remain, a list of nearby subway stations is displayed, and you must walk to one of them.

Throughout the program, two "costs" are assigned. First is the cost of tokens ($1 each), which is added each time you arrive at a station on foot to take a train (Sub1100). If you run out of money, the game ends.

The second "cost" is time. Activities and events that take time are travel (two to three minutes between stations, near LN690), waiting (one minute per train, LN600), walking and delivery (two minutes per block, six minutes per delivery, near LN870), delays due to malfunctioning doors (in Sub1100) and track fires (in Sub1100), and lunch (in Sub5140). If the total time exceeds eight hours (or nine hours in the easier version), your day has ended at 5:00 P.M. (or 6:00 P.M.), no more deliveries can be made, and the game ends.

The subroutine in Sub5560 shuffles the list of packages. Shuffling is discussed in detail in the description of the Orient Express program. However, you should note that in addition to shuffling a list of integers (PN[n]), this program shuffles four other variables that are associated with the list (package names, destinations, etc.). Thus, we see that shuffling can be a general function that is not limited to a list of integers.

PROGRAM VARIABLES

A Answer to input query (most often logbook no.)
AD Answer to input query, string
B Answer to query about station to walk to
DELTOT Total number of deliveries completed
DES Train destination (1 = north or west end of line, 2 = south or east end of line)
DORP([n] Delivery or pickup flag (n = package no.) (0 = open, 1 = delivery, 3 = pickup, 4 = done)
HD, HP, HR Hours, for printing
I Temporary iteration variable
J Temporary iteration variable
K Temporary shuffling variable
LGMAX Highest entry in logbook to date
LGPKG[n] Logbook number (n = package no.)
LUN Lunch indicator (0 = no lunch, 1 = had lunch)
MIN Minutes of elapsed time from start
MN Minutes, for printing
PERS Person indicator (0 = on foot, 1 = on train)
PKGDESD[n] Package destination name (n = package no.)
PKGSTA[n][s] Subway stations near package destination (n = package no., s = station no.)
PKSTDS[n][s] Distance from package destination to subway station (n = package no., s = station no.)
PKSTNU[n] Number of stations near package destination (n = package no.)
PN[n] Package number
PS Total packages
RN Random number
STA Station number
STANU[s] Number of trains that stop at station (s = station no.)
STATIOND[s] Station name (s = station no.)
STATR[s][t] Trains that stop at station (s = station no., t = train no.)
STNS Total stations
TK Token indicator (0 = company money, 1 = own money)
TKMAX Maximum amount of money available for tokens
TM Maximum minutes to play (480 hard, 540 easier)
TMD Maximum time to play (5:00 hard, 6:00 easier)
TOKEN Number of tokens used
TR Train number
TRDESD(t][2] Stations at each end of a line
TRAIND[t] Train name (t = train no.)
TRNS Total trains

TRSTA[t][p] Stations that train stops at (t = train no., p = stop no.)
TRSTOP[t] Number of stops made by train (t = train no.)
TRSTX Train station index
TRX Train heading (1 = south or east, -1 = north or west)

XD Temporary string variable

PROGRAM LISTINGS

```
TextWindow.CursorTop =10
XD = "Subway Scavenger"
Sub5530()
TextWindow.CursorTop =13
XD = "(c) by David H. Ahl, 1986"
Sub5530()
TextWindow.CursorTop =23
Sub5500()
Sub1650()
TextWindow.CursorTop =21
XD = "(Initializing data ... please be patient)"
Sub5530()
PS = 20
STNS = 264
TRNS = 11
MIN = 0
'For reading data: packages, stations, trains
Sub5660()
LGMAX = 10
TKMAX = 20
'Packages to start
Sub1780()
Sub2050()
Sub4760()
Sub5560()
'Starting station - had to do some initialization
STA = 21
DES = 1
TR = 1
TRSTX = 10
TRX = -1
TextWindow.CursorLeft = 60
TextWindow.WriteLine(" ")
Sub5500()
TextWindow.Clear()
TextWindow.WriteLine("")
TextWindow.Write("Do you want to be able to deliver after 5:00 pm (easier)?
")
AD = TextWindow.Read()
Sub5300()
If AD = "Y" Then
  TM = 540
  TMD = "6:00"
  GOTO LN270
EndIf
TM = 480
TMD = "5:00"
LN270:
For I = 1 To 5
'Information about deliveries
DORP[I] = 1
EndFor
For I = 6 To 10
```

```
'Information about pick-ups
DORP[I] = 2
EndFor
textwindow.Clear()
TextWindow.WriteLine("You may want to print or copy this screen for later
reference.")
TextWindow.WriteLine("")
Sub5390()
TextWindow.Clear()
'Print package log
'
LN340:
'Arrive at station routine
Sub5140()
'Print time
TextWindow.WriteLine("You have arrived at " +STATIOND[STA] +" station.")
TextWindow.WriteLine("Trains that stop at this station:")
For I = 1 To STANU[STA]
TextWindow.WriteLine("  "+TRAIND[STATR[STA][I]])
EndFor
If PERS = 0 Then
Sub1100()
GOTO LN530  'If on foot, buy token
EndIf
If STA<>TRSTA[TR][1] AND STA<>TRSTA[TR][TRSTOP[TR]] Then
  Goto LN430
EndIf
TextWindow.WriteLine("End of the line. You'll have to get off.")
Goto LN450
LN430:
TextWindow.Write("Do you want to get off? ")
AD = TextWindow.Read()
Sub5300()
If AD = "N" Then
  Goto LN690  'If you want to stay on train, branch to train travel
EndIf
LN450:
PERS = 0
TextWindow.WriteLine("Do you want to: ")
TextWindow.WriteLine(" Make a pickup (P)")
TextWindow.WriteLine(" Make a delivery (D)")
TextWindow.WriteLine(" Check your logbook (C)")
TextWindow.WriteLine(" Get another train (T)")
TextWindow.Write("Your choice please (P, D, C, or T)? ")
AD = TextWindow.Read()
LN490:
sub5350()
If AD = "P" OR AD = "D" Then
Goto LN750
ELSEIF AD = "T" THEN
Goto LN530
EndIf
If AD = "C" Then
Sub5390()
GOTO LN450
```

```
EndIf
TextWindow.Write("Not a valid choice. Enter P, D, C, or T please.? ")
AD = TextWindow.Read()
Goto LN490
'
LN530:
'Trains coming routine
Sub5140()
'Print time
LN550:
RN = Math.Floor(1 + STANU[STA] * Math.GetRandomNumber(999)/1000)
'Which train is coming?
TR = STATR[STA][RN]
If STA = TRSTA[TR][1] Then
DES = 2
GOTO LN600  'At one end of line?
EndIf
If STA = TRSTA[TR][TRSTOP[TR]] Then
DES = 1
GOTO LN600  'or the other?
EndIf
DES = Math.Floor(1 + 2 * Math.GetRandomNumber(999)/1000)
'Destination?
LN600:
TextWindow.WriteLine("Here comes the "+ TRAIND[TR] +" train to "
+TRDESD[TR][DES])
MIN = MIN + 1
TextWindow.Write("Do you want to get on? ")
AD = TextWindow.Read()
Sub5300()
If AD = "N" Then
  Goto LN550  'If don't get on train, wait for next one
EndIf
For I = 1 TO TRSTOP[TR]
'Find out where train is
If TRSTA[TR][I]=STA Then
  Goto LN649
EndIf
EndFor
LN649:
TRSTX = I
'Train station identification index
If DES = 1 Then
TRX = -1
ELSE
TRX = 1
EndIf
'
LN690:
'Train travel routine
PERS = 1
TextWindow.WriteLine("You are on the "+ TRAIND[TR] +" train to "
+TRDESD[TR][DES])
Sub1210()
'Possible trip hazards
```

```
TRSTX = TRSTX + TRX
STA = TRSTA[TR][TRSTX]
MIN = MIN + Math.Floor(2 + 1.3 * Math.GetRandomNumber(999)/1000)
Goto LN340
'Go to next station routine
'
LN750:
'Pickup and delivery routine
If AD = "P" Then
XD = "pickup"
ELSE
XD = "delivery"
EndIf
TextWindow.Write("Which "+ XD)
TextWindow.Write(" do you want to make (by Logbook number)? ")
A = TextWindow.ReadNumber()
If DORP[A]<>0 Then
  Goto LN820
EndIf
TextWindow.Write("That number seems to be in error. Want to check your
logbook? ")
AD = TextWindow.Read()
Sub5300()
If AD = "Y" Then
  Sub5390()
EndIf
Goto LN450
LN820:
TextWindow.WriteLine("That " +XD +" is at "+ PKGDESD[A])
For I = 1 To PKSTNU[A]
If PKGSTA[A][I] = STA Then
  Goto LN870
EndIf
EndFor
TextWindow.WriteLine("which is too far to walk from this station.")
TextWindow.WriteLine("Perhaps you should try something else.")
Goto LN450
LN870:
If PKSTDS[A][I] > 1 Then
XD = "s"
ELSE
XD = ""
EndIf
TextWindow.WriteLine("which is " +PKSTDS[A][I]+ " block"+ XD +" from here.
Off you go.")
'
'Successful pickup or delivery
MIN = MIN + 2 * PKSTDS[A][I] + 6
'Add to time (2 min per block, 6 at destination)
DELTOT = DELTOT + 1
If DORP[A] = 2 Then
  Goto LN950  'Is this a pick-up?
EndIf
TextWindow.WriteLine("")
TextWindow.WriteLine("You find someone to sign for the package.")
```

```
DORP[A] = 0
Goto LN990
'Mark delivery completed
LN950:
LGMAX = LGMAX + 1
TextWindow.WriteLine("You pick up a package and log it in as no. " +LGMAX)
TextWindow.WriteLine("The address on it is " +PKGDESD[LGMAX])
DORP[A] = 0
DORP[LGMAX] = 1
Goto LN1020
'
LN990:
'Check if all pickups and deliveries made
If DELTOT = 15 Then
  Goto LN1580  'Have all deliveries been made?
EndIf
If PKSTNU[A] = 1 Then
XD = ""
ELSE
XD = "S"
EndIf
LN1020:
TextWindow.WriteLine("From here you can walk to the following subway station"
+XD+ ":")
If PKSTNU[A] = 1 Then
TextWindow.WriteLine(" "+ STATIOND[PKGSTA[A][1]])
GOTO LN340
EndIf
For I = 1 To PKSTNU[A]
'Iterate through possible stations
TextWindow.WriteLine(" " +I+ " ... " +STATIOND[PKGSTA[A][I]])
EndFor
LN1060:
TextWindow.Write("Which station do you want to go to (by number)? ")
B = TextWindow.ReadNumber()
If B < 1 OR B > PKSTNU[A] Then
TextWindow.WriteLine("Not a valid response." )
GOTO LN1060
EndIf
STA = PKGSTA[A][B]
MIN = MIN + 3 + PKSTDS[A][B]
Goto LN340
'
Sub Sub1100
'Buy token subroutine
TOKEN = TOKEN + 1
If TOKEN <= TKMAX Then
  Goto LN1190
EndIf
TextWindow.WriteLine("")
TextWindow.WriteLine("You have spent the entire $20 your boss gave you on
tokens.")
If TK = 0 Then
  Goto LN1150  'Used own money yet?
EndIf
```

```
TextWindow.WriteLine("Moreover, you have used up your own money as well.")
Goto LN1520
LN1150:
TK = 1
TextWindow.Write("Do you want to buy tokens with your own money? ")
AD = TextWindow.Read()
Sub5300()
If AD = "N" Then
TextWindow.WriteLine("Okay, that's it then.")
GOTO LN1520
EndIf
RN = Math.Floor(300 + 600 * Math.GetRandomNumber(999)/1000) / 100
TextWindow.Write("You have exactly $"+ RN)
TextWindow.WriteLine("so you can buy "+Math.Floor(RN) +" more tokens.")
TKMAX = TKMAX + Math.Floor(RN)
LN1190:
EndSub
'
Sub Sub1210
'Trip hazards subroutine
'Door refuses to close
If Math.GetRandomNumber(999)/1000 > .05 Then
  Goto LN1290  '5% chance of a sticky door
EndIf
TextWindow.WriteLine("One of the car doors refuses to close and the train
can't move.")
RN = Math.Floor(1 + 2.5 * Math.GetRandomNumber(999)/1000)
MIN = MIN + RN
If RN > 1 Then
XD = "s"
ELSE
XD = ""
EndIf
TextWindow.WriteLine("You're stuck here for " +RN+ " minute"+ XD +".")
'
'Possible mugging
LN1290:
If Math.GetRandomNumber(999)/1000 > .35 Then
  Goto LN1430  '35 - 65% chance of mugging or fire on the tracks
EndIf
If Math.GetRandomNumber(999)/1000 > .05 Then
  Goto LN1649 '5% chance of tough characters
EndIf
TextWindow.WriteLine("Some real unsavory types are whooping it up in the car
across from")
TextWindow.Write("your seat. Do you want to move to another car? ")
AD = TextWindow.Read()
Sub5300()
If AD = "Y" Then
  IF Math.GetRandomNumber(999)/1000 > .05 THEN
    GOTO ln1350
  ELSE
    GOTO ln1370
    EndIf
    EndIf
```

```
If Math.GetRandomNumber(999)/1000 > .05 Then
Goto LN1360
ELSE
GOTO LN1380
EndIf
ln1350:
TextWindow.WriteLine("They jeer at you but let you pass. All is okay...for now.")
Goto LN1649
LN1360:
TextWindow.WriteLine("They look at you and try to bait you, but you avoid them.")
Goto LN1649
LN1370:
TextWindow.WriteLine("Uh oh. Two of them get up and block your way.")
LN1380:
TextWindow.WriteLine("Oh my, oh my. They're all moving to surround you.")
TextWindow.WriteLine("They pull knives and demand your money.")
Sub5470()
TextWindow.WriteLine("You, deciding that discretion is the better part of valor, give")
TextWindow.WriteLine("them all your money and call it quits for the day.")
Goto LN1520
'
LN1430:
'Fire on the track
If Math.GetRandomNumber(999)/1000 > .008 Then
  Goto ln1769 '0.8% chance of fire on the tracks
EndIf
TextWindow.WriteLine("Uh oh. The train is slowing down and seems to be stopping.")
Sub5470()
TextWindow.WriteLine("You're stuck here in the tunnel.")
Sub5470()
TextWindow.WriteLine("A trainman finally comes through and announces, 'It's just a")
RN = Math.Floor(10 + 35 * Math.GetRandomNumber(999)/1000)
MIN = MIN + RN
TextWindow.WriteLine("fire on the tracks folks. We'll be under way in a few minutes.'")
TextWindow.WriteLine("In fact, the delay is more like " +RN +" minutes!")
Goto ln1649
'
LN1520:
'End of game routine
If DELTOT = 15 Then
  Goto LN1580  'Were all deliveries made?
EndIf
TextWindow.WriteLine("")
TextWindow.WriteLine("You made it to " +DELTOT+ " locations, but")
TextWindow.WriteLine("your log still shows the following items:")
Sub5390()
Sub5250()
TextWindow.WriteLine("Perhaps you'll be able to do better tomorrow.")
Goto LN1610
```

```
LN1580:
Sub5250()
TextWindow.WriteLine("")
TextWindow.CursorLeft = 25
TextWindow.WriteLine("CONGRATULATIONS !")
TextWindow.WriteLine("")
TextWindow.WriteLine("You made all your deliveries and pick-ups successfully
in the")
TextWindow.WriteLine("Largest city in the world. Very good!")
LN1610:
TextWindow.WriteLine("You used $"+ TOKEN+ " for tokens.")
TextWindow.WriteLine("")
TextWindow.Write("Press Enter to End")
AD = TextWindow.Read()
Sub5300()
ln1649:
EndSub

Sub Sub1650
TextWindow.Clear()
XD = "Subway Scavenger"
Sub5530()
TextWindow.WriteLine("")
TextWindow.WriteLine("")
TextWindow.WriteLine(" You have a job with a messenger/courier service
located in")
TextWindow.WriteLine("mid-town Manhattan. Today, you have five packages to
deliver and")
TextWindow.WriteLine("five packages to pick up for delivery to other
locations in the")
TextWindow.WriteLine("city. So, in total you must visit 15 different
locations.")
TextWindow.WriteLine("")
TextWindow.WriteLine(" You can use 264 stations of the New York Subway System
which")
TextWindow.WriteLine("are serviced by the following 11 trains: A, B, CG, D,
E, F, N, 1,")
TextWindow.WriteLine("2, 4, and 7.")
TextWindow.WriteLine("")
TextWindow.WriteLine(" You must complete all your deliveries and pickups by
5:00 pm.")
TextWindow.WriteLine("Your boss has given you $20 for tokens (which will
allow for a few")
TextWindow.WriteLine("wrong trains). Any money that you don't use on tokens
is yours to")
TextWindow.WriteLine("keep. Good luck! (You'll need it.)")
ln1769:
EndSub
'
Sub Sub1780
'Subroutine to read data about package deliveries
  For I=1 To PS
    FileLine = File.ReadLine(Program.Directory +"\deliveries.txt", I)
    'get PN
    KK = Text.GetIndexOf(FileLine, ",")
```

```
    PN[I] = Text.GetSubText(FileLine, 1, KK - 1)
    FileLine = Text.GetSubTextToEnd(FileLine, KK + 1)
    'get PKGDESD - surrounded by quotes
    KK = Text.GetIndexOf(FileLine, Text.GetCharacter(34))
    FileLine = Text.GetSubTextToEnd(FileLine, KK + 1)
    KK = Text.GetIndexOf(FileLine, Text.GetCharacter(34))
    PKGDESD[I] = Text.GetSubText(FileLine, 1, KK -1)
    FileLine = Text.GetSubTextToEnd(FileLine, KK + 1)
    'still have a comma to deal with
    KK = Text.GetIndexOf(FileLine, ",")
    FileLine = Text.GetSubTextToEnd(FileLine, KK + 1)
     'get PKSTNU
    KK = Text.GetIndexOf(FileLine, ",")
    PKSTNU[I] = Text.GetSubText(FileLine, 1, KK - 1)
    FileLine = Text.GetSubTextToEnd(FileLine, KK + 1)
    'get PKSTNU pairs  of numbers separated by commas
    For J=1 To PKSTNU[I]
      'first is PKGSTA
      KK = Text.GetIndexOf(FileLine, ",")
      PKGSTA[I][J] = Text.GetSubText(FileLine, 1, KK - 1)
      FileLine = Text.GetSubTextToEnd(FileLine, KK + 1)
      'second is PKSTDS
      KK = Text.GetIndexOf(FileLine, ",")
      If KK<>0 Then
        PKSTDS[I][J] = Text.GetSubText(FileLine, 1, KK - 1)
        FileLine = Text.GetSubTextToEnd(FileLine, KK + 1)
      Else
        PKSTDS[I][J] = FileLine
      EndIf
    EndFor
  EndFor
EndSub
'
Sub Sub2050
  'Subroutine to read data about subway stations
  For I=1 To STNS
    FileLine = File.ReadLine(Program.Directory +"\stations.txt", I)
    'get STA
    KK = Text.GetIndexOf(FileLine, ",")
    STA = Text.GetSubText(FileLine, 1, KK - 1)
    FileLine = Text.GetSubTextToEnd(FileLine, KK + 1)
    'get STATIOND - surrounded by quotes
    KK = Text.GetIndexOf(FileLine, Text.GetCharacter(34))
    FileLine = Text.GetSubTextToEnd(FileLine, KK + 1)
    KK = Text.GetIndexOf(FileLine, Text.GetCharacter(34))
    STATIOND[I] = Text.GetSubText(FileLine, 1, KK -1)
    FileLine = Text.GetSubTextToEnd(FileLine, KK + 1)
    'still have a comma to deal with
    KK = Text.GetIndexOf(FileLine, ",")
    FileLine = Text.GetSubTextToEnd(FileLine, KK + 1)
     'get STANU
    KK = Text.GetIndexOf(FileLine, ",")
    STANU[I] = Text.GetSubText(FileLine, 1, KK - 1)
    FileLine = Text.GetSubTextToEnd(FileLine, KK + 1)
    'get STANU numbers separated by commas
```

```
    For J=1 To STANU[I]
      KK = Text.GetIndexOf(FileLine, ",")
      If KK<>0 Then
        STATR[I][J] = Text.GetSubText(FileLine, 1, KK - 1)
        FileLine = Text.GetSubTextToEnd(FileLine, KK + 1)
      Else
        STATR[I][J] = FileLine
      EndIf
    EndFor
  EndFor
EndSub
  '
Sub Sub4760
  'Subroutine to read data about subway trains
  CLINE = 1
  For I=1 To TRNS
    FileLine = File.ReadLine(Program.Directory +"\trains.txt", CLINE)
    'get TR
    KK = Text.GetIndexOf(FileLine, ",")
    TR = Text.GetSubText(FileLine, 1, KK - 1)
    FileLine = Text.GetSubTextToEnd(FileLine, KK + 1)
    'get TRAIND - surrounded by quotes
    KK = Text.GetIndexOf(FileLine, Text.GetCharacter(34))
    FileLine = Text.GetSubTextToEnd(FileLine, KK + 1)
    KK = Text.GetIndexOf(FileLine, Text.GetCharacter(34))
    TRAIND[I] = Text.GetSubText(FileLine, 1, KK -1)
    FileLine = Text.GetSubTextToEnd(FileLine, KK + 1)
    'still have a comma to deal with
    KK = Text.GetIndexOf(FileLine, ",")
    FileLine = Text.GetSubTextToEnd(FileLine, KK + 1)
     'get TRSTOP
    KK = Text.GetIndexOf(FileLine, ",")
    TRSTOP[I] = Text.GetSubText(FileLine, 1, KK - 1)
    FileLine = Text.GetSubTextToEnd(FileLine, KK + 1)
    'get TRSTOP numbers separated by commas
    For J=1 To TRSTOP[I]
      KK = Text.GetIndexOf(FileLine, ",")
      If KK<>0 Then
        TRSTA[I][J] = Text.GetSubText(FileLine, 1, KK - 1)
        FileLine = Text.GetSubTextToEnd(FileLine, KK + 1)
      Else
       TRSTA[I][J] = FileLine
        'read another line?
        If J<> TRSTOP[I] Then
          CLINE = CLINE + 1
          FileLine = File.ReadLine(Program.Directory +"\trains.txt", CLINE)
        EndIf
      EndIf
    EndFor
    TRDESD[tr][1] = STATIOND[TRSTA[tr][1]]
    TRDESD[tr][2] = STATIOND[TRSTA[tr][TRSTOP[tr]]]
    CLINE = CLINE +1
  EndFor
 EndSub
  '
```

```
Sub Sub5140
'Subroutine to check for lunch and end of workday
If MIN > TM Then
  Goto LN5220  'After 5 pm?
EndIf
Sub5250()
If LUN = 1 Then
  RETURN : 'Had lunch already?
EndIf
If MIN < 180 Then
  Goto LN1521 'Before 12 noon?
EndIf
If PERS = 1 Then
  Goto ln1521 'On a train?
EndIf
TextWindow.WriteLine("")
TextWindow.WriteLine("Time for a lunch break. Chili dog and cola. Burp!")
TextWindow.WriteLine("")
MIN = MIN + Math.Floor(24 + 20 * Math.GetRandomNumber(999)/1000)
LUN = 1
Goto ln1521
LN5220:
TextWindow.WriteLine("")
TextWindow.WriteLine("So sorry, it is after "+ TMD+ "pm and the places to
which")
TextWindow.WriteLine("you want to go will be closed.")
Goto LN1520
LN1521:
EndSub
'
Sub Sub5250
  'Subroutine to print the time
HR = Math.Floor(MIN / 60)
MN = MIN - 60 * HR
If HR < 4 Then
HP = 9 + HR
ELSE
HP = HR - 3
EndIf
HP = 100 * HP + MN + 10000
HD = HP
TextWindow.WriteLine("")
TextWindow.WriteLine("Time "+ Text.GetSubText(HD, 2, 2)+ ":" +
Text.GetSubTextToEnd(HD, 4))
EndSub
'
Sub Sub5300
'Subroutine to read yes/no answer
If AD = "" Then
AD = "Y"
Goto ln5319
EndIf
LN5320:
Sub5350()
If AD = "Y" OR AD = "N" Then
```

```
  Goto ln5319
EndIf
TextWindow.Write("Don't understand your answer. Enter 'Y' or 'N' please? ")
AD = TextWindow.Read()
Goto LN5320
LN5319:
EndSub
'
Sub Sub5350
'Subroutine to read first letter of answer
AD = Text.GetSubText(AD, 1,1)
If text.GetCharacterCode(AD) >= text.GetCharacterCode("A") AND
text.GetCharacterCode(AD) <= text.GetCharacterCode("Z") Then
  Goto ln5349
EndIf
AD = Text.GetCharacter(Text.GetCharacterCode(AD) - 32)
LN5349:
EndSub
'
Sub Sub5390
'Subroutine to print delivery/pick-up log
TextWindow.WriteLine("")
TextWindow.CursorLeft = 20
TextWindow.WriteLine("    Delivery - Pick-up Log")
TextWindow.WriteLine("")
For I = 1 To 15
If DORP[I] = 0 OR DORP[I] = 3 Then
  Goto LN5450
EndIf
If DORP[I] = 1 Then
XD = "Delivery"
ELSE
XD = "Pick-up"
EndIf
TextWindow.Write(I)
TextWindow.CursorLeft = 4
TextWindow.Write(XD)
TextWindow.CursorLeft = 15
TextWindow.WriteLine(PKGDESD[I])
LN5450:
EndFor
TextWindow.WriteLine("")
Sub5500()
EndSub
'
Sub Sub5470
'Subroutine to make a short pause
Program.Delay(1000)
EndSub
'
Sub Sub5500
XD = "Press Enter to continue."
Sub5530()
JJJ = TextWindow.Read()
TextWindow.WriteLine("")
```

```
EndSub
'
Sub Sub5530
'Subroutine to print centered lines
TextWindow.CursorLeft = (70 - Text.GetLength(Xd))/2
TextWindow.WriteLine(xd)
EndSub
'
Sub Sub5560
'Subroutine to shuffle the list of packages
For I = 1 To PS
DUM[I] = I
EndFor
For I = 1 To PS - 1
K = I + Math.Floor((PS + 1 - I) * Math.GetRandomNumber(999)/1000)
J = PN[I]
PN[I] = PN[K]
PN[K] = J
XD = PKGDESD[I]
PKGDESD[I] = PKGDESD[K]
PKGDESD[K] = XD
A = PKSTNU[I]
PKSTNU[I] = PKSTNU[K]
PKSTNU[K] = A
For J = 1 To 3
A = PKGSTA[I][J]
PKGSTA[I][J] = PKGSTA[K][J]
PKGSTA[K][J] = A
A = PKSTDS[I][J]
PKSTDS[I][J] = PKSTDS[K][J]
PKSTDS[K][J] = A
EndFor
EndFor
EndSub
```

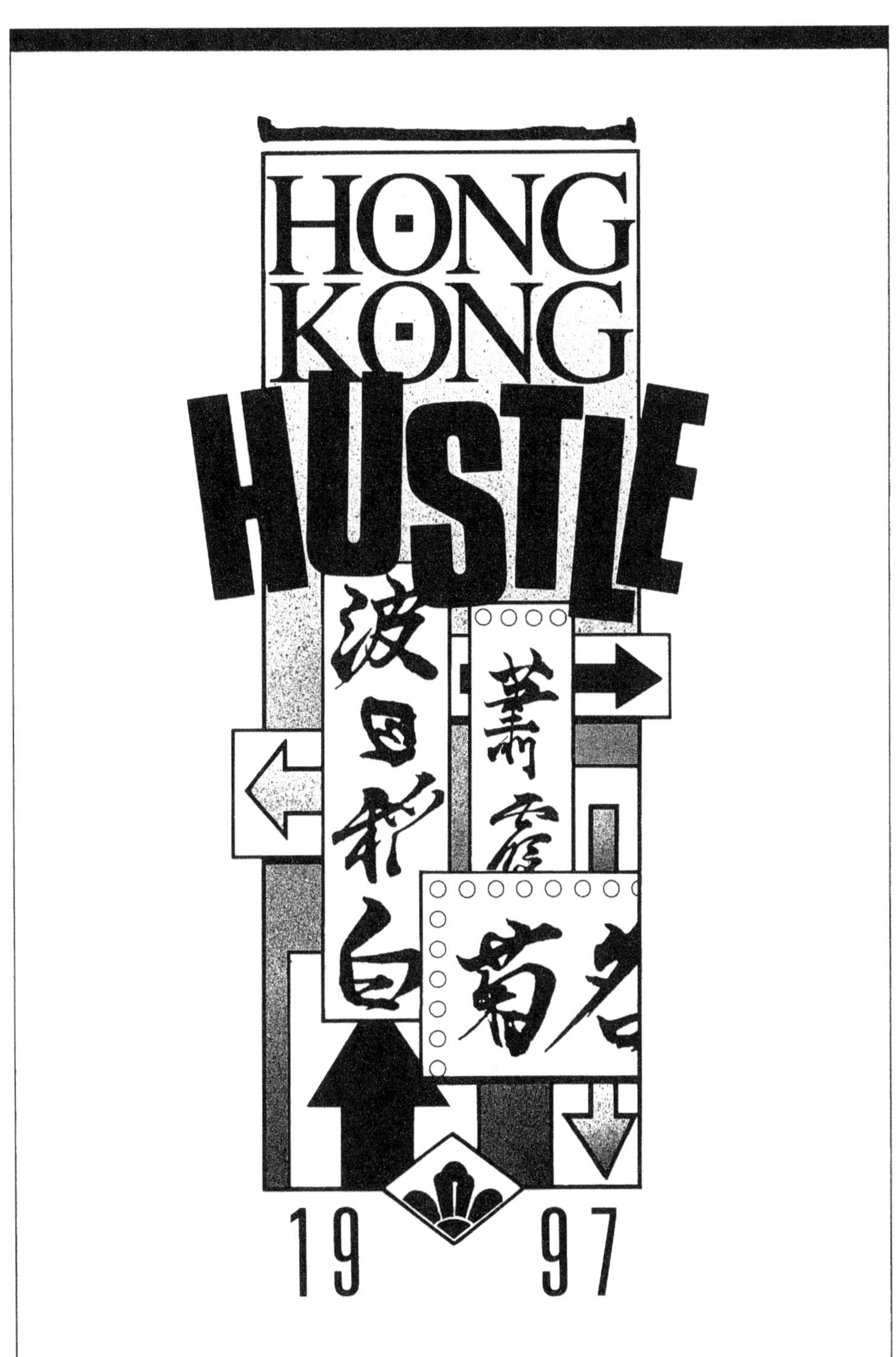
HONG
KONG
HUSTLE
19
97

Hong Kong Hustle

In Hong Kong Hustle, you are the Tai Pan of the largest international trading house in Hong Kong. It is June 30, 1997, and China is due to take over the Colony on July 1. You have just learned that the Chinese intend to confiscate much of the property of the major trading houses. Your objective is to collect 15 bags of gold and jewels, which you have stored around the city, get them to your boat before midnight, and escape.

You disguise yourself as a factory worker and set out from Repulse Bay, using only public transportation, to visit the locations in your notebook. Here are some hints to help you in your quest to remain the wealthiest trader in Southeast Asia:

- At the beginning of the game, your boat is docked near the Macau Jetfoil Pier. You can safely move it once to another pier near Tsuen Wan in the New Territories, but to move it more than once would be very dangerous.
- You may encounter members of the Green Triad, Hong Kong's organized-crime faction. For the most part, they are interested only in money, but it is best to avoid them.
- You will find the game extremely difficult until you develop a map of the transit routes of Hong Kong. If you have a map the colony, you can navigate more easily. If you don't, you can develop your own by riding the various buses, ferries, and trains from one end of the line to the other.
- You will find that most, but not all, of your destinations can be reached by more than one transit line. Generally, travel on the MTR (Mass Transit Railway) and the Canton/Kowloon Railway is faster than travel on buses and trams.
- You will probably want to complete all pickups on Hong Kong Island before moving your boat to Tsuen Wan, which is a better base of operations in the New Territories. Pickups in Kowloon can be made equally well from either pier.

Hong Kong Hustle is, perhaps, the most challenging game in this book. Completing the assignment, therefore, is especially rewarding. And as you ride the transit system you can be planning how to spend all that gold—if you succeed. Good joss!

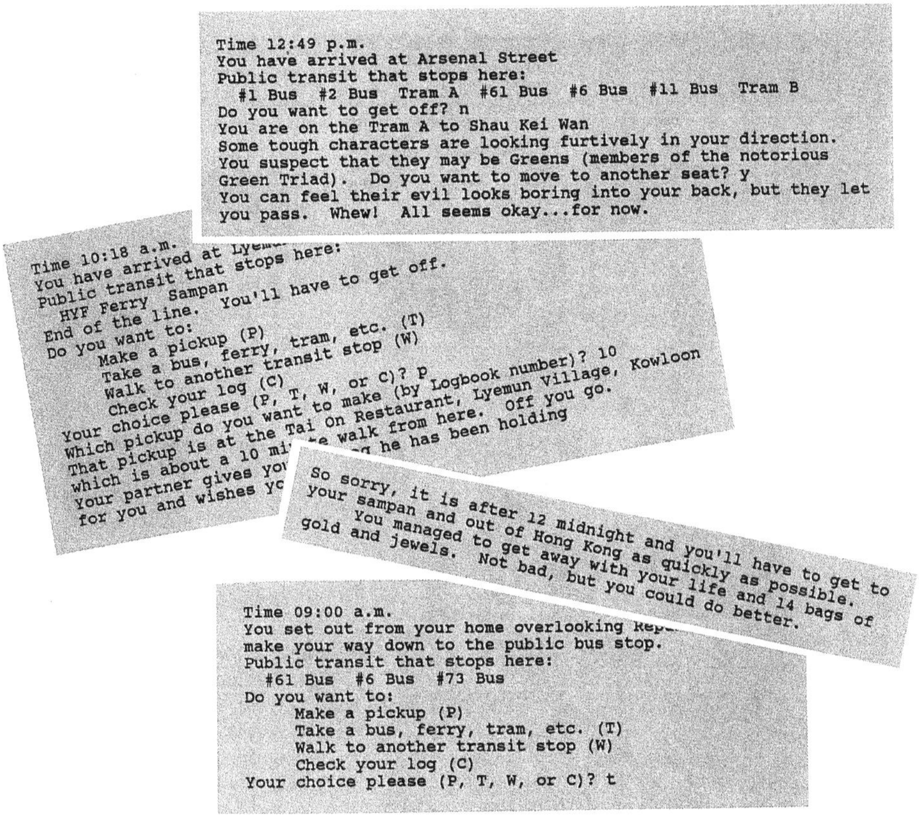

```
Time 12:49 p.m.
You have arrived at Arsenal Street
Public transit that stops here:
  #1 Bus  #2 Bus  Tram A  #61 Bus  #6 Bus  #11 Bus  Tram B
Do you want to get off? n
You are on the Tram A to Shau Kei Wan
Some tough characters are looking furtively in your direction.
You suspect that they may be Greens (members of the notorious
Green Triad).  Do you want to move to another seat? y
You can feel their evil looks boring into your back, but they let
you pass.  Whew!  All seems okay...for now.
```

```
Time 10:18 a.m.
You have arrived at Lyem
Public transit that stops here:
  HYF Ferry  Sampan
End of the line.  You'll have to get off.
Do you want to:
     Make a pickup (P)
     Take a bus, ferry, tram, etc. (T)
     Walk to another transit stop (W)
     Check your log (C)
Your choice please (P, T, W, or C)? p
Which pickup do you want to make (by Logbook number)? 10
That pickup is at the Tai On Restaurant, Lyemun Village, Kowloon
which is about a 10 mi      e walk from here.  Off you go.
Your partner gives yo        he has been holding
for you and wishes yo
```

```
So sorry, it is after 12 midnight and you'll have to get to
your sampan and out of Hong Kong as quickly as possible.
     You managed to get away with your life and 14 bags of
gold and jewels.  Not bad, but you could do better.
```

```
Time 09:00 a.m.
You set out from your home overlooking Rep
make your way down to the public bus stop.
Public transit that stops here:
  #61 Bus  #6 Bus  #73 Bus
Do you want to:
     Make a pickup (P)
     Take a bus, ferry, tram, etc. (T)
     Walk to another transit stop (W)
     Check your log (C)
Your choice please (P, T, W, or C)? t
```

THE STORY

Hong Kong Island was a small uninhabited rocky island at the mouth of the Pearl River until the 1830s when, during the days of the tea and opium trade, British sea captains discovered its magnificent protected harbor. Its name derives from two Chinese characters "Heung Kong" meaning fragrant harbor. Some historians suggest that the name might have been inspired by the scent of opium-laden ships in the harbor. Others think the name may have been a reference to the incense and joss stick industries on the south and west coasts of the island. The origin of the name, however, was unimportant to the British who settled on the island and made it an important port for all Far East trade.

HONG KONG, KOWLOON, AND THE NEW TERRITORIES ARE CONNECTED BY NEARLY 100 TRANSIT ROUTES.

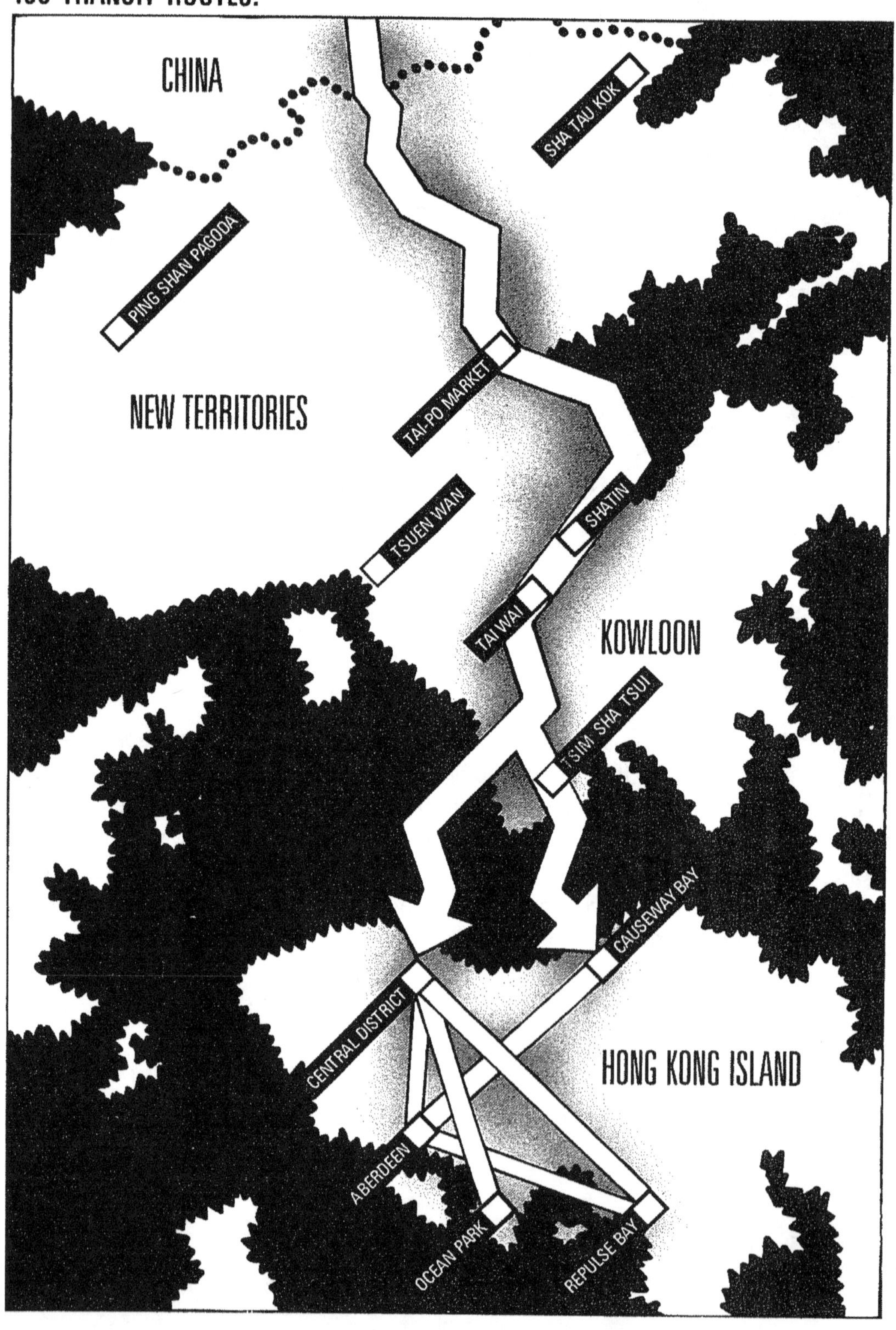

During the Nineteenth Century, Britain concluded three treaties with China relating to Hong Kong: the Treaty of Nanking, signed in 1842 and ratified in 1843 under which Hong Kong Island was ceded in perpetuity; the Convention of Peking in 1860 under which the southern part of the Kowloon Peninsula and Stonecutters Island were ceded in perpetuity; and the Convention of 1898, under which the New Territories and outlying islands (comprising 92% of the total land area of the colony) were leased to Britain for 99 years from July 1, 1898.

Hong Kong and the Kowloon Peninsula are relatively small—35 square miles—while the New Territories and outlying islands (235 of them) comprise a much larger land area—377 square miles. Although the British settled Hong Kong, today they represent just 2% of the population, with most of the remaining 5.3 million residents being Chinese.

It was the fact that the New Territories are subject to a lease that caused the current British Government to enter into negotiations on the future of Hong Kong with the People's Republic of China in the late 1970s. The Chinese Government has consistently taken the view that the whole of Hong Kong is Chinese territory. Its position for many years was that the question of Hong Kong fell into the category of unequal treaties of the past; that it should be settled peacefully when conditions were right; and that pending a settlement, the status quo should be maintained.

Of course, subtle hints were dropped from time to time. All of Hong Kong's water and a substantial amount of its food come from China and the New Territories, and it would be difficult for the residents of the island to exist without them. But, officially, the position was that the matter should be settled through diplomatic channels.

In the late 1970s, as the duration of the New Territories lease decreased, concern about the future of Hong Kong began to be expressed both in the colony itself and among foreign investors. In particular, there was increasing concern about individual land leases granted in the New Territories, all of which were set to expire three days before the expiration of the New Territories lease in 1997. It was clear that the short duration of these leases and the inability of the Hong Kong Government to grant new ones extending beyond 1997 would deter future investment and undermine confidence.

The British Government determined that the situation would become untenable by the mid-1980s if nothing was done. Thus, the Governor of Hong Kong visited Peking in March 1979 and attempted to solve the specific question of leases in the New Territories. He was not successful and not much happened for another two years. Then, finally, in 1982 Chinese officials indicated to a visiting British delegation that they were prepared to enter into negotiations over Hong Kong. Accordingly, Prime Minister Margaret Thatcher met with Chairman Deng Xiaoping on September 24, 1982, and jointly they "agreed to enter into talks through diplomatic channels with the common aim of maintaining the stability and prosperity of Hong Kong." During these negotiations, Hong Kong and British delegates explained in detail the legal and commercial systems which prevail in Hong Kong and the importance to these systems of the British role and link. Following extensive discussion, however, it became clear that the continuation of British administration in any form after 1997 would be unacceptable to the Chinese.

The British then agreed to explore the possibility of a bilateral arrangement coupled with a high degree of autonomy under Chinese sovereignty to ensure lasting stability and prosperity for Hong Kong. Discussions intensified after April 1984, resulting in a Joint Declaration issued on September 26, 1984.

The declaration formally states that China will resume the exercise of sovereignty over Hong Kong Island, Kowloon, and the New Territories as of July 1, 1997. Hong Kong will be established as a "Special Administrative Region" called Hong Kong, China, which will be under the direct authority of the Central People's Government of the People's Republic of China. The Hong Kong Special Administrative Region will be vested with executive, legislative, and independent judicial power, and laws currently in force in Hong Kong will remain basically unchanged.

The government of Hong Kong will consist of officials nominated by the Central People's Government. Local Hong Kong inhabitants, British, and other foreign nationals may be employed as advisors and even hold certain (unspecified) posts in various government departments.

Because free trade has made Hong Kong what it is today, it will retain its status as a free port and a separate customs territory. Nor will it be taxed by China. In the interim, the British will continue to govern Hong Kong with the important provision that land leases can be written through the year 2047.

Reaction to the pact is mixed. Most people in Hong Kong have no other place to go and, even if they did, would have difficulty getting a permanent visa. Hence, they tend to think that Hong Kong should accept the agreement and try to make the most of it. Some British managers and administrators in Hong Kong are quietly making contingency plans, but many intend to stay and give it a try. Hong Kong-born Chinese in Britain and other parts of the world have been quick to condemn Britain's negotiations as a "giveaway" and a "farce." As one said, "Hong Kong people are trying to convince themselves that the agreement will bind China, but it's just not true. China will do what she likes as she always has in the past." Another expressed concern that "there is nothing to prevent Hong Kong from being ruled by the mainland."

Chinese officials, of course, declare that the people of Hong Kong have nothing to fear. On October 3, 1984, Deng Xiaoping told a group of visiting Hong Kong delegates, "The Chinese Government will not change its policy, nor can anyone else change it." He went on, "We have kept our word in external affairs even during periods of chaos. It is the tradition of the Chinese nation to honor its commitments."

All of which sounds good, critics say, except that when July 2, 1997, rolls around, Hong Kong will no longer be considered an "external affair" by China. As for China honoring its commitments, skeptics urge the people of Hong Kong to ask scores of American wheat farmers what happened to their three-year contracts with that country when its harvests improved in 1985. Or to ask the managers of the Ameripex International Philatelic Exposition about China's withdrawal from the exposition on opening day to protest the participation of Taiwan.

Today, Hong Kong is still a thriving, cosmopolitan city of many contrasts—elegant shops and crowded street markets, first-class restaurants and outdoor food stalls, luxury hotels and teeming tenements, bustling factories and peaceful duck farms, noisy discos and ancient temples. After Tokyo, it i the main commercial hub of the Far East, and, as the Tourist Association brochure proclaims, it is "one of life's great adventures."

BIBLIOGRAPHY

China Daily (Sept. 27, 1984, Oct. 4, 1984), Beijing, China.

Hong Kong Discovery Guide. Hong Kong Tourist Association, Connaught Centre, Hong Kong. 1986.

Hong Kong Standard (Sept. 27, 28, 29, 1984), Kowloon, Hong Kong.

Places of Interest by Public Transport, Hong Kong Tourist Association. 1985.

THE PROGRAM

The Hong Kong Hustle program is built upon the same basic framework as Subway Scavenger. It has one important addition, namely, allowing for variable-length journey segments. In Subway Scavenger, each trip on a train was assumed to last only two or three minutes.

However, it was not feasible to use such a narrow time range for journeys in the Hong Kong simulation, because some trips could be as short as two minutes (tram, MTR), while others could be as long as 20 minutes (ferry, bus over the mountains).

Another less important change was incorporated in Hong Kong Hustle, specifically the option to allow the player to walk from one transit stop to another (assuming, of course, that the stops are within walking distance).

The length of time between transit stops is contained in the data file (transit.txt) for each transit line. Note that the first file line for each transit line is the same as the data for the trains in the subway program: the name of the transit line, the number of stations, and the identification number of each station. A second data line contains the frequency of service (which is not currently used in the program) followed by the time (in minutes) between stations on the line.

These data are used in the travel routine (starts at LN690). Note that if the vehicle is traveling in a "forward" direction (from the beginning of the line to the end), the time (TRT[t][s]) associated with the previous stop is used. However, if the vehicle is traveling "backwards" (from the end of the line to the beginning), then the time associated with the next stop is used.

The following example should make it easier to understand this concept:

Index	Bus Stop No.	Time to next stop
1	1	5
2	2	4
3	3	8
4	4	7
5	5	

If a bus is traveling from Stop 2 to Stop 4, for example, the elapsed time between Stop 2 to Stop 3 (four minutes) is stored as Time 2, and the time between Stop 3 to Stop 4 (eight minutes) is stored as Time 3.

Thus, the total time for the bus to go from Stop 2 to Stop 4 is Time 2 plus Time 3, or 12 minutes. On the other hand, if the bus is going from Stop 4 to Stop 2, it still takes 12 minutes, so we would not want to add Time 4 to Time 3 (15 minutes), but rather, Time 3 to Time 2.

The routine that allows walking from one transit stop to another (starts at LN1130) works like the one that lets you walk from a pickup location to two or more transit stops in Subway Scavenger. It, of course, also requires more data than that program requires. These data, STAWLK[s] and STAWK[s][k], are tagged onto the end of the data about each station, specifying station name and transit lines that stop at that station.

Hong Kong Hustle is a rather difficult game to complete successfully. There are several ways to make it easier. The easiest way is to lower the number of bags of gold and jewels to be collected.

This variable, BG, is currently set equal to 15 in the beginning of the program. Try setting BG equal to 11 or 12, and see how you make out. Of course, if you become very proficient at the game, you can raise BG to 17 or 18 for a real challenge.

Another way to make the game easier is to extend the time deadline past midnight, say to 4:00 A.M. or 5:00 A.M. For each hour you want to extend it, add 60 to the constant 899 in Sub4620:

```
If MIN > 899 Then
  Goto LN4650 '12 midnight yet?
EndIf
```

Unfortunately, times after 12 midnight will not be displayed correctly, but if you feel ambitious, you can modify the routine to print the time (Sub4680) to allow for times later than 12 midnight.

A third way to make the game easier is to deal with packages in only Hong Kong Island (locations 1 to 9) or only Kowloon and the New Territories (locations 10–23). This is not an easy modification to make (you must both decrease the number of bags to be collected and change the limits of the For loop in Sub4910 which shuffles the list of locations). In fact, it is probably easier to keep practicing with the current game than to try to modify it in this way, but the option is there for those who are especially ambitious and/or frustrated.

PROGRAM VARIABLES

```
A Answer to input query
AD Answer to input query, string
B Answer to query about station to walk to
BAG Total bags currently being carried
BG Total bags to be collected
BGMAX Maximum number of bags that can be collected
BGTOTAL Total bags aboard sampan
BGX Maximum number of bags that can be carried
DES Destination of arriving transit vehicle
FRD[9] Alternate words for "friend"
HD, HP, HR Hours for printing
I Temporary iteration variable
J Temporary iteration variable
K Temporary iteration variable
LGPKG[n] Logbook number (n = package no.)
MIN Total minutes of elapsed time
MN Minutes for printing
PERS Person indicator (0 = on foot, 1 = riding)
PICK[g] Pickup flag (g = logbook no.)
PKGDESD[n] Package destination name (n = package no.)
PKGSTA[n][s] Transit stops near package destination (n = parlfAge no., s =
stop c.)
PKSTOS[n][s] Time to walk from transit stop to package destination (n-package
no., s = stop no.)
PKSTNU[n] Number of stations near package destination (n = package no.)
PLACED[s] Place name (s = transit stop)
PN[n] Package number
PS Total packages
RN Random number
STA Transit stop number
STANU[s] Number of transport lines at transit stop (s = stop)
STATR[s]t] Transit lines that stop at transit stop (s = stop no., t = transit
lines)
STAWK[s][x] Identification of transit stops within walking distance (s = stop
no., x = index no.)
STAWLK[s] Transit stops within walking distance of another transit stop (s =
stop no.)
STNS Total transit stops
TR Transit line number
TRAIND[t] Name of transit line (t = transit line no.)
TRDESD[t][2] Transit stops at each end of line (t = line no.)
TRFREQ[t] Frequency of service on line (t = line no.)
TRNS Total transit lines
TRSTA[t][s] Transit stops on a transit line (t = transit line no., s = stop
```

```
no.)
TRSTOP[t] Number of stops on transit line (t = line no.)
TRSTX Transit stop identification indicator
TRT[t][s] Time between stops (t = line no., s = stop no.)
TRX Travel direction indicator
X Temporary numeric variable
XD Temporary string variable
```

Note: "Package" refers to bag of gold or jewels to be picked up.

PROGRAM LISTINGS

```
TextWindow.CursorTop = 10
XD = "Hong Kong Hustle, 1997"
Sub5030()
TextWindow.CursorTop = 13
XD = "(c) David H. Ahl, 1986"
Sub5030()
TextWindow.CursorTop = 23
Sub5000()
Sub1880()
'DIM PKGDESD[25), PKSTNU[25), PKGSTA[25, 5), PKSTDS[25, 5), LGPKG[25),
STAWLK[130)
'DIM PLACED[130), STANU[130), STATR[130, 11), TRAIND[35), PICK[20),
STAWK[130, 4)
'TRSTOP[35), TRSTA[35, 25), TRDESD[35, 2), TRFREQ[35), TRT[35, 25), PN[25)
PS = 23
STNS = 127
TRNS = 34
BG = 15
BGMAX = BG
Sub2100()
'Read words
Sub2150()
'Read about pickups
Sub2450()
'Read data about stations
Sub3820()
'Read about transit routes
Sub4900()
'Shuffle pickups
TextWindow.CursorLeft = 60
Sub5000()
TextWindow.Clear()
TextWindow.WriteLine("You may want to print or copy this screen for later
reference.")
TextWindow.WriteLine("")
TextWindow.WriteLine("Before setting out, you make a list of the various
places to stop.")
Sub4830()
'Print pickup log
Sub4620()
TextWindow.WriteLine("You set out from your home overlooking Repulse Bay
and")
TextWindow.WriteLine("make your way down to the public bus stop.")
'INITIALIZE THINGS
For I =1 TO 20
PICK[I] = 0
ENDFOR

PERS=0
STA = 23
BGX = 0
Goto LN360
'
```

```
LN330:
'Arrive at place routine
Sub4620()
'Display the time
TextWindow.WriteLine("You have arrived at " +PLACED[STA])
LN360:
TextWindow.WriteLine("Public transit that stops here:")
For I = 1 To STANU[STA]
TextWindow.Write(" " +TRAIND[STATR[STA][I]])
EndFor
TextWindow.WriteLine("")
If PERS = 0 Then
  Goto LN440  'If on foot, go to choice
EndIf
If STA<>TRSTA[TR][1] AND STA<>TRSTA[TR][TRSTOP[TR]] Then
  Goto LN420
EndIf
TextWindow.WriteLine("End of the line. You'll have to get off.")
Goto LN440
LN420:
TextWindow.Write("Do you want to get off? ")
AD = TextWindow.Read()
Sub4740()
If AD = "N" Then
  Goto LN690  'If want to stay on, go to transit travel
EndIf
LN440:
If STA = 5 OR STA = 50 Then
  SUB1430() 'Put gold in sampan?
EndIf
LN450:
PERS = 0
TextWindow.WriteLine("Do you want to:" )
TextWindow.WriteLine(" Make a pickup (P)")
TextWindow.WriteLine(" Take a bus, ferry, tram, etc. (T)")
TextWindow.WriteLine(" Walk to another transit stop (W)")
TextWindow.WriteLine(" Check your log (C)")
TextWindow.Write("Your choice please (P, T, W, or C)? ")
AD = TextWindow.Read()
LN500:
SUB4780()
If AD = "P" Then
Goto LN760
ELSEIF AD = "T" THEN
goto LN540
EndIf
If AD = "W" Then
Goto LN1130
ELSEIF AD = "C" THEN
SUB4830()
GOTO LN450
EndIf
TextWindow.Write("Not a valid choice, Enter P, T, W, or C please? ")
AD = TextWindow.Read()
Goto LN500
```

```
'
LN540:
'Transit arriving routine
Sub4620()
'Display the time (again)
LN560:
TR = STATR[STA][Math.Floor(1 + STANU[STA] * Math.GetRandomNumber(999)/1000)]
If STA = TRSTA[TR][1] Then
DES = 2
GOTO LN600 'At one end of line?
EndIf
If STA = TRSTA[TR][TRSTOP[TR]] Then
DES = 1
GOTO LN600 'or the other?
EndIf
DES = Math.Floor(1 + 2 * Math.GetRandomNumber(999)/1000 )
'Destination of next transit to arrive
LN600:
TextWindow.WriteLine("Here comes the " +TRAIND[TR] +" to "+ TRDESD[TR][DES])
MIN = MIN + 1
TextWindow.Write("Do you want to get on? ")
AD = TextWindow.Read()
Sub4740()
If AD = "N" Then
  Goto LN560 'If don't get on, wait for next transit
EndIf
For I = 1 to TRSTOP[TR] 'Find out where train is
  If TRSTA[TR][I]=STA Then
  Goto GotSTA
EndIf
EndFor
TextWindow.WriteLine("ERROR in station location")
GotSTA:
TRSTX = I
'Transit station identification index
If DES = 1 Then
TRX = -1
ELSE
TRX = 1 'Which way are we going?
EndIf
'
LN690:
'Travel routine
PERS = 1
TextWindow.WriteLine("You are on the " +TRAIND[TR]+ " to " +TRDESD[TR][DES])
Sub1240() 'Possible trip hazards
If TRX = 1 Then
MIN = MIN + TRT[TR][TRSTX]
ELSE
MIN = MIN + TRT[TR][TRSTX - 1]
EndIf
TRSTX = TRSTX + TRX
STA = TRSTA[TR][TRSTX]
Goto LN330
'Arrive at next location
```

```
'
LN760:
'Pickup routine
If BGX = 0 Then
  Goto LN790 'Maximum limit not set yet?
EndIf
If BAG >= BGX Then
TextWindow.WriteLine("You can't carry any more bags.")
GOTO LN880
EndIf
LN790:
TextWindow.Write("Which pickup do you want to make (by Logbook number)? ")
A = TextWindow.ReadNumber()
If PICK[A] = 0 Then
  Goto LN840
EndIf
TextWindow.Write("That number seems to be in error. Want to check your
logbook? ")
AD = TextWindow.Read()
sub4740()
If AD = "Y" Then
  SUb4830()
EndIf
Goto LN450
'Goto choice routine
LN840:
TextWindow.WriteLine("That pickup is at the " +PKGDESD[A])
For I = 1 To PKSTNU[A]
If PKGSTA[A][I] = STA Then
  Goto LN890
EndIf
EndFor
TextWindow.WriteLine(" ... which is too far to walk from here.")
LN880:
TextWindow.WriteLine("Perhaps you should try something else.")
Goto LN450
LN890:
TextWindow.WriteLine("which is about a " +PKSTDS[A][I]+ " minute walk from
here. Off you go.")
'
'Successful pickup
Sub5060()
MIN = MIN + PKSTDS[A][I] + Math.Floor(5 + 10 *
Math.GetRandomNumber(999)/1000)
BAG = BAG + 1
'Add to time
TextWindow.WriteLine("Your "+ FRDArray[Math.Floor(1 + 9 *
Math.GetRandomNumber(999)/1000)] +" gives you the bag he has been holding")
TextWindow.WriteLine("for you and wishes you good joss.")
PICK[A] = 1
'
'Check to see if you are overloaded
If BAG < 3 Then
  Goto LN1030 'If carrying fewer than 3 bags then no problem
EndIf
```

```
If BGX = 0 Then
  BGX = Math.Floor(3 + 3 * Math.GetRandomNumber(999)/1000) 'Set maximum bags
EndIf
If BAG < BGX Then
  Goto LN1030 'Haven't reached load limit yet?
EndIf
TextWindow.WriteLine("That last bag was a heavy one. You can't carry any
more. You'll")
TextWindow.WriteLine("have to return to your sampan and unload.")
'
LN1030:
'Walk from pickup back to transit stop
X = PKSTNU[A]
If X = 1 Then
XD = ""
ELSE
XD = "s"
EndIf
TextWindow.WriteLine("")
TextWindow.WriteLine("From here you can walk to the following transit stop"
+XD+ ":")
If X = 1 Then
MIN = MIN + PKSTDS[A][1]
TextWindow.WriteLine(" "+ PLACED[STA])
GOTO LN330
EndIf
For I = 1 To PKSTNU[A]
'Iterate through nearby transit stops
TextWindow.WriteLine(" " +I +".. " +PLACED[PKGSTA[A][I]])
EndFor
LN1090:
TextWindow.Write("Which place do you want to go to (by number)? ")
B = TextWindow.ReadNumber()
If B < 1 OR B > PKSTNU[A] Then
TextWindow.WriteLine("Not a valid response.")
GOTO LN1090
EndIf
STA = PKGSTA[A][B]
MIN = MIN + PKSTDS[A][B]
Goto LN330
'
LN1130:
'Walk to another location routine
X = STAWLK[STA]
If X > 1 Then
  Goto LN1160
EndIf
TextWindow.WriteLine("It would take too long to walk to another transit
stop.")
Goto LN450
LN1160:
TextWindow.WriteLine("")
TextWindow.WriteLine("From here you can walk to the following transit
stops:")
TextWindow.WriteLine(" 1  ...  " +PLACED[STA]+ " (where you are now)")
```

```
For I = 2 To STAWLK[STA]
TextWindow.WriteLine(" "+ I +" ... " +PLACED[STAWK[STA][I]])
EndFor
LN1200:
TextWindow.Write("Which place do you want to go to (by number)? ")
B = TextWindow.ReadNumber()
If B < 1 OR B > STAWLK[STA] Then
TextWindow.WriteLine("Not a valid response." )
GOTO LN1200
EndIf
STA = STAWK[STA][B]
MIN = MIN + Math.Floor(6 + 6 * Math.GetRandomNumber(999)/1000)
Goto LN330
'

Sub Sub1240
EndSub


Sub Sub1430
'Travel Hazards Subroutine
TextWindow.Write("Do you want to put the bags you are carrying aboard your
sampan? ")
AD = TextWindow.Read()
SUB4740()
If AD = "N" Then
TextWindow.WriteLine("Okay, it's up to you." )
GOTO LN1510
EndIf
TextWindow.WriteLine("Good. You stow them safely out of sight.")
MIN = MIN + 8
BGTOTAL = BGTOTAL + BAG
BAG = 0
BGX = 0
If BGTOTAL >= BGMAX Then
  Goto LN1600
EndIf
If STA = 50 Then
  Goto LN1869
EndIf
LN1510:
TextWindow.Write("Do you want to move the sampan to Tsuen Wan? ")
AD = TextWindow.Read()
Sub4740()
If AD = "N" Then
TextWindow.WriteLine("Okay; the captain is ready when you are." )
goto LN1869
EndIf
TextWindow.WriteLine("Okay. You shove off and make your silent way across the
harbor.")
MIN = MIN + Math.Floor(20 + 20 * Math.GetRandomNumber(999)/1000)
STA = 50
Sub4680()
TextWindow.WriteLine("You are at Tsuen Wan, New Territories.")
TextWindow.WriteLine("Public transit that stops here:")
```

```
For I = 1 To STANU[STA]
TextWindow.Write(" " +TRAIND[STATR[STA][I]])
EndFor
TextWindow.WriteLine("")
Goto LN1869
'
LN1600:
'All gold collected before midnight?
TextWindow.WriteLine(" You managed to pick up all "+ BG+ " bags of gold and
jewels")
TextWindow.WriteLine("before midnight.")
TextWindow.WriteLine("")
If BGTOTAL >= BG Then
  Goto LN1680
EndIf
TextWindow.WriteLine(" It's too bad that you lost " +(BG - BGTOTAL)+ " of
them along the way.")
LN1680:
TextWindow.WriteLine("")
TextWindow.WriteLine(" You sail away on your sampan and start your next")
TextWindow.WriteLine("great empire in Morristown, New Jersey.")
TextWindow.WriteLine("")
XD = "Good Joss !"
Sub5030()
Goto LN1840
'
LN1720:
'Time ran out
BGTOTAL = BGTOTAL + BAG
If BGTOTAL < BG Then
  Goto LN1770
EndIf
BGTOTAL = BGTOTAL - 1
TextWindow.WriteLine("")
TextWindow.WriteLine("Too bad, in your rush to escape you had to drop a bag
of gold.")
LN1770:
If BGTOTAL < .6 * BG Then
  Goto LN1800
EndIf
TextWindow.WriteLine(" You managed to get away with your life and " +BGTOTAL+
" bags of")
TextWindow.WriteLine("gold and jewels. Not bad, but you could do better.")
Goto LN1840
LN1800:
TextWindow.WriteLine(" You barely managed to escape with your life and only
"+ BGTOTAL)
TextWindow.WriteLine("bags of gold and jewels. You lost much face and you
will have")
TextWindow.WriteLine("difficulty becoming Tai Pan of a new venture.")
'
LN1840:
' end game
TextWindow.WriteLine("")
TextWindow.WriteLine("")
```

```
TextWindow.Write("Press Enter to End")
AD = TextWindow.Read()
Program.End()
LN1869:
EndSub
'
Sub Sub1880
XD = "Hong Kong Hustle"
Sub5030()
TextWindow.WriteLine("")
TextWindow.WriteLine("")
TextWindow.WriteLine(" It is June 30, 1997 and China will take over the British")
TextWindow.WriteLine("Colony of Hong Kong on July 1. While the transition was supposed")
TextWindow.WriteLine("to be smooth and amicable, you just Learned that the Chinese intend")
TextWindow.WriteLine("to confiscate much of the property of the great trading houses.")
TextWindow.WriteLine(" You, the Tai Pan, are being closely watched, so you disguise")
TextWindow.WriteLine("yourself as a common factory worker and set out, using only public")
TextWindow.WriteLine("transport, to recover as much of your liquid assets (gold & jewels)")
TextWindow.WriteLine("as possible before the day ends. You deposit them on an inconspic-")
TextWindow.WriteLine("uous sampan initially tied up near the Macau Jetfoil Pier.")
TextWindow.WriteLine(" You may move the sampan from the pier on Hong Kong Island to")
TextWindow.WriteLine("another pier near Tsuen Wan in the New Territories, but to move it")
TextWindow.WriteLine("more than once would be very dangerous.")
TextWindow.WriteLine(" You can use any of 34 different transit lines (bus, train,")
TextWindow.WriteLine("subway, ferry, tram, and public sampan) which service 125 stops")
TextWindow.WriteLine("throughout Hong Kong Island, Kowloon, and the New Territories. Of")
TextWindow.WriteLine("course, only 15 of these stops are of really keen interest to you.")
TextWindow.WriteLine(" Depending upon how much gold you pick up at various locations,")
TextWindow.WriteLine("you may have to return to your sampan more than once. Time, of")
TextWindow.WriteLine("course, is your biggest enemy, and you'll have to leave at midnight")
TextWindow.WriteLine("no matter what. Good luck!")
TextWindow.WriteLine("")
EndSub
'
Sub Sub2100
'Subroutine to read words
FRDArray[1] = "associate"
```

```
FRDArray[2] = "friend"
FRDArray[3] = "confidant"
FRDArray[4] = "ally"
FRDArray[5] = "comrade"
FRDArray[6] = "colleague"
FRDArray[7] = "mate"
FRDArray[8] = "partner"
FRDArray[9] = "compatriot"
EndSub
'
Sub Sub2150
'Subroutine to read data about gold pickups
CLINE = 1
DataFile = Program.Directory +"\pickups.txt"
FileLine = File.ReadLine(DataFile, CLINE)
For I = 1 To PS
  GetNextItem()
  PN[I] = NextItem
  GetNextItem()
  PKGDESD[I] = NextItem
  GetNextItem()
  PKSTNU[I] = NextItem
  For J = 1 To PKSTNU[I]
    GetNextItem()
    PKGSTA[I][J] = NextItem
    GetNextItem()
    PKSTDS[I][J] = NextItem
  EndFor
EndFor
EndSub

Sub GetNextItem
  'find comma in FileLine
  KK = Text.GetIndexOf(FileLine, ",")
  If KK <> 0 Then
    NextItem = Text.GetSubText(FileLine, 1, KK - 1)
    FileLine = Text.GetSubTextToEnd(FileLine, KK + 1)
  Else
    NextItem = FileLine
    CLINE = CLINE + 1
    FileLine = File.ReadLine(DataFile, CLINE)
  EndIf
EndSub

Sub Sub2450
'Subroutine to read data about transit stops
CLINE = 1
DataFile = Program.Directory +"\transit.txt"
FileLine = File.ReadLine(DataFile, CLINE)
For I = 1 To STNS 'STNS = number of stations
  GetNextItem()
  STA = NextItem
  GetNextItem()
  PLACED[I] = NextItem
  GetNextItem()
```

```
  STANU[I] = NextItem
  GetNextItem()
  STAWLK[I] = NextItem
  For J = 1 To STANU[I]
    GetNextItem()
    STATR[I][J] = NextItem 'Read trains, buses, etc. that stop here
  EndFor
  For J = 1 To STAWLK[I]
    GetNextItem()
    STAWK[I][J] = NextItem 'Read other stations within walking distance
  EndFor
EndFor
EndSub

Sub Sub3820
'Subroutine to read data about transit routes
CLINE = 1
DataFile = Program.Directory +"\hkroutes.txt"
FileLine = File.ReadLine(DataFile, CLINE)
For I = 1 To TRNS 'TRNS = number of trains, buses, etc.
  GetNextItem()
  TR = NextItem
  GetNextItem()
  TRAIND[I] = NextItem
  GetNextItem()
  TRSTOP[I] = NextItem
  For J = 1 TO TRSTOP[I]
    GetNextItem()
    TRSTA[I][J] = NextItem 'Read station numbers for transit vehicle
  EndFor
  GetNextItem()
  TRFREQ[I] = NextItem
  For J = 1 TO TRSTOP[I]-1
    'Read travel times
    GetNextItem()
    TRT[I][J] = NextItem
  EndFor
  TRDESD[TR][1] = PLACED[TRSTA[TR][1]] 'Place name at one end of line
  TRDESD[TR][2] = PLACED[TRSTA[TR][TRSTOP[TR]]] 'and at other end
EndFor
EndSub

'
Sub Sub4620
'Subroutine to check for out of time
If MIN > 899 Then
  Goto LN4650 '12 midnight yet?
EndIf
Sub4680()
Goto LN4669
LN4650:
TextWindow.WriteLine("")
TextWindow.WriteLine("So sorry, it is after 12 midnight and you'll have to
get to")
```

```
TextWindow.WriteLine("your sampan and out of Hong Kong as quickly as
possible.")
Goto LN1720
LN4669:
EndSub
'
Sub Sub4680
'Subroutine to print the time
HR = Math.Floor(MIN / 60)
MN = MIN - 60 * HR
If HR < 4 Then
HP = 9 + HR
ELSE
HP = HR - 3
EndIf
If MIN < 181 OR MIN > 900 Then
XD = "a.m."
ELSE
XD = "p.m."
EndIf
HP = 100 * HP + MN + 10000
HD = HP
TextWindow.WriteLine("")
TextWindow.WriteLine("Time: "+Text.GetSubText(HD, 2,
2)+":"+Text.GetSubText(HD, 4, 2))
EndSub
'
Sub Sub4740
'Subroutine to read yes/no answer
LN4750:
sub4780()
If AD = "Y" OR AD = "N" Then
  Goto LN4789
EndIf
TextWindow.Write("Don't understand your answer. Enter 'Y' or 'N' please? ")
AD = TextWindow.Read()
Goto LN4750
LN4789:
Endsub
'
Sub Sub4780
'Subroutine to read first letter of answer
If AD = "" Then
AD = "Y"
Goto LN4829
EndIf
AD = Text.GetSubText(AD, 1, 1)
If text.GetCharacterCode(AD) >= text.GetCharacterCode("A") AND
text.GetCharacterCode(AD) <= text.GetCharacterCode("Z") Then
  Goto LN4829
EndIf
AD = text.GetCharacter(text.GetCharacterCode(AD) - 32)
LN4829:
EndSub
'
```

```
Sub Sub4830
'Subroutine to print pickup log
TextWindow.WriteLine("")
TextWindow.WriteLine("Your pickup notebook shows:")
For I = 1 To BG
If PICK[I] = 1 Then
  Goto LN4880
EndIf
TextWindow.WriteLine(I+"    "+PKGDESD[I])
LN4880:
EndFor
TextWindow.WriteLine("")
Sub5000()
EndSub
'
Sub Sub4900
'Subroutine to shuffle the list of pickups
For I = 1 To PS - 1
K = I + Math.Floor((PS + 1 - I) * Math.GetRandomNumber(999)/1000)
J = PN[I]
PN[I] = PN[K]
PN[K] = J
XD = PKGDESD[I]
PKGDESD[I] = PKGDESD[K]
PKGDESD[K] = XD
A = PKSTNU[I]
PKSTNU[I] = PKSTNU[K]
PKSTNU[K] = A
For J = 1 To 4
A = PKGSTA[I][J]
PKGSTA[I][J] = PKGSTA[K][J]
PKGSTA[K][J] = A
A = PKSTDS[I][J]
PKSTDS[I][J] = PKSTDS[K][J]
PKSTDS[K][J] = A
EndFor
EndFor
EndSub
'
Sub Sub5000
XD = "Press Enter to continue."
Sub5030()
JJJ = TextWindow.Read()
EndSub
'
Sub Sub5030
'Subroutine to print centered lines
TextWindow.CursorLeft = (70 - Text.GetLength(XD))/2
TextWindow.WriteLine(XD)
EndSub
'
Sub Sub5060
'Short delay
Program.Delay(1000)
EndSub
```

VOYAGE★TO
NEPTUNE
2100

Voyage to Neptune

VOYAGE*TO NEPTUNE 2100

In Voyage to Neptune, you are in command of the first manned spaceship journeying from Earth to Neptune. The year is 2100, and manned space stations have been established at roughly 500-million-mile intervals along your route. These stations are at Jupiter (orbiting Callisto), Saturn (orbiting Titan), Uranus (on Ariel), and at several points midway between Saturn and Uranus, and Uranus and Neptune.

Navigation of your spacecraft is highly computerized, and you have a competent personnel officer on board to handle the inevitable people problems that will arise during a six-year journey. Your primary function as captain, therefore, is to maintain the delicate balance that will provide your ship with enough energy to reach its destination and return to Earth.

The following hints will help to speed you on your way:

- Your spaceship uses both solar energy and nuclear fuel. Because you cannot carry enough nuclear fuel for the entire trip, you also have on board a multi-celled breeder reactor, which takes the spent fuel from the propulsion engines along with a small amount of primary fuel and turns it—somewhat inefficiently—back into primary fuel for propulsion. You must decide how much fuel to use for propulsion and how many breeder reactor cells to operate on each leg of the trip.
- At each space station along the way, you may trade nuclear fuel for breeder-reactor cells and vice versa. You may not trade more fuel than you have; nor may you trade so many cells that your breeder reactor ceases to function.
- You may have problems with your engines along the way, but there is little you can do to lessen this possibility. Likewise, if you are unlucky, some of your fuel may decay.

If all goes well and you make judicious use of your resources, you can reach Neptune in just under six years with plenty of fuel left for your return voyage. Can you do it the first time or will you need a few trial runs?

```
Current conditions are as follows:
   Location: Earth
   Distance to Neptune: 2701 million miles.
Pounds of nuclear fuel ready for use: 3000
Operational bre[illegible] reactor cells: 120
```

```
How many cells would you like to trade? 5
At this distance from the sun, your solar collectors can fulfill
 40 % of the fuel requirements of the engines. How many pounds
of nuclear fuel do you want to use on this segment? 2300
How many breeder reactor cells do you want to operate? 115
You have only enough fuel to seed 91 breeder cells.
Please adjust your number accordingly.
How many breeder reactor cells do you want to operate? 91
```

```
                  ENGINE MALFUNCTION !

You will have to operate your engines at a 23 % reduction
in speed until you reach Titan.
```

```
                    Voyage to Neptune

     It is the Year 2100 and you are in command of the first manned
spaceship to Neptune.  Manned space stations have been established
which orbit Callisto, Titan, and Ariel, as well as at two inter-
mediate points between Saturn and Uranus, and Uranus and Neptune.
You must travel about 2700 million miles.  At an average speed of
over 50,000 miles per hour, the entire trip should take about
six years.
     Your spaceship is a marvel of 21st century engineering.  Since
you may have to stop at space stations along the way, you will not
be able to use the gravitational 'slingshot' effect of the planets.
However, your engines are highly efficient using both energy from
the sun captured by giant parabolic arrays and nuclear fuel carried
on board.  You will not be able to carry enough fuel for the whole
trip, so you also have a multi-celled nuclear breeder reactor
(which takes spent fuel from your engines along with a small amount
of primary fuel and turns it into a much greater amount of primary
fuel).
     The space stations along the way usually have a small stock of
engine repair parts, breeder reactor cells, and nuclear fuel which
are available to you on a barter basis.

                  Press any key to continue.
```

THE STORY

Although fictional accounts of space voyages date back to the 1500s, the first serious rocket motor for space flight was not devised until the twentieth century. In 1903, K.E. Tsiolkovsky, a Russian pioneer of astronautics, proposed using a liquid-propelled rocket motor for space flight. The first rocket to employ an engine of this type was fired by Robert H. Goddard in the United States in 1926.

In Germany during World War II, Werner von Braun developed the V2 weapon, the first long-range liquid-fuel rocket. After the war, von Braun and most of the other German rocket specialists went to the United States, where they were instrumental in the development of rockets for satellite launches and space exploration.

Russia was also working on rockets and space vehicles and, on October 4, 1957, launched Sputnik I, the event that marked the real beginning of the space age. Other Soviet satellites followed and in 1958 the United States launched its first satellite, Explorer I, which provided the first information about the Van Allen radiation belts that surround the Earth.

In January 1959, the Soviet satellite Luna I was the first successful lunar probe, bypassing the moon at 3728 miles. A year later another Soviet satellite was the first to circle the moon. On April 12, 1961, the USSR launched the first manned spacecraft, Vostok I, with Yuri Gagarin aboard. The flight made one complete circuit of the Earth at a height ranging from 112 to 187 miles, and lasted one hour and 29 minutes. Three weeks later on May 5, Alan Shepard became the first American space traveler, making a short 15-minute suborbital "hop" in a Mercury vehicle.

In the 1960s, the U.S. undertook a major program to put a man on the moon. Milestones in this project included docking maneuvers between Gemini spacecraft in December 1965; the first manned flight around the moon by Frank Borman, James Lovell, and William Anders in December 1968; and finally, the lunar landing by Neil Armstrong and Edwin Aldrin on July 20, 1969.

Space stations have had a somewhat controversial history since they were first proposed by Tsiolkovsky in the 1920s. Stations are felt by some to be the most efficient method of launching deep space probes, because the probe vehicle will not have to overcome the force of Earth's gravity. Others feel that the cost of space stations cannot be justified in view of the marginal benefits.

Skylab, the first and only American space station, was launched on May 14, 1973 and was manned by three successive crews for a period of 171 days. The Soviets have made a greater commitment to space stations and have launched several different types, which they have manned for periods exceeding one year.

The spectacular success of the Voyager 1 and 2 probes to Jupiter, Saturn, Uranus, and Neptune indicates that the technology required to send spacecraft to the outer planets is in place.

However, for manned planetary exploration, particularly beyond Mars, it seems that some system of manned or unmanned way stations will be necessary.

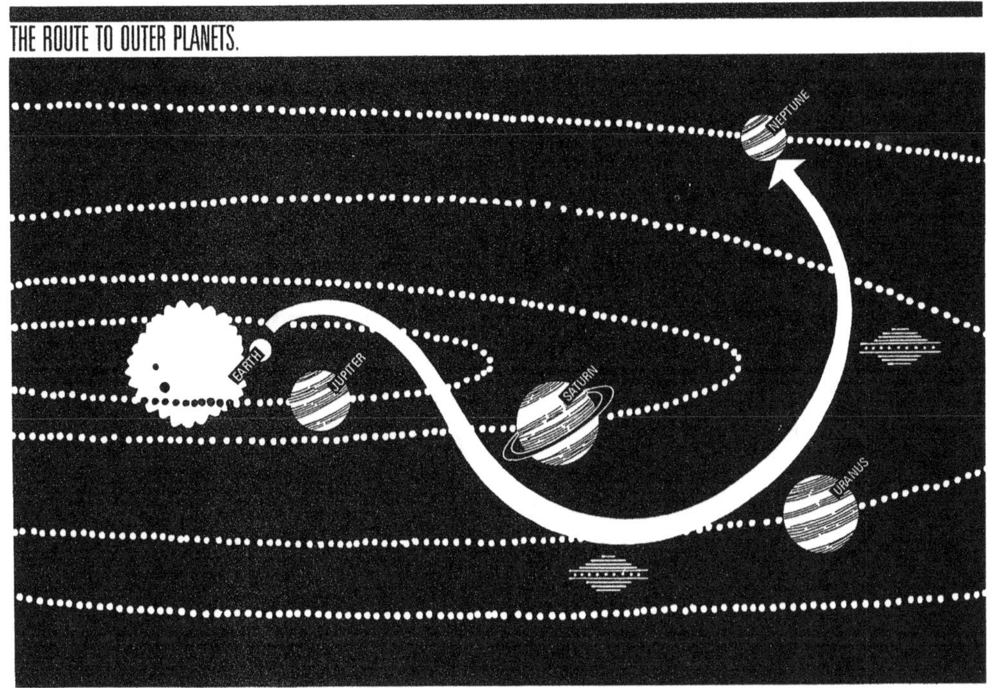

THE ROUTE TO OUTER PLANETS.

This computer program, Voyage to Neptune, leaps ahead to a time when a series of manned space stations have been established on the route to the outer planets. We are assuming stations at roughly equal intervals of 400 to 500 million miles. They are at Jupiter (orbiting Callisto, the largest Jovian moon), Saturn (orbiting Titan, a moon larger than Mercury), Alpha 1 (midway between Saturn and Uranus). Uranus (on Ariel, the innermost moon), and Theta 2 (507 million miles beyond Uranus).

The voyage itself is all fiction. Your spaceship has engines which can operate using both solar energy (captured by giant parabolic collecting arrays) and nuclear fuel. Because solar radiation diminishes as you get further from the sun and you will not be able to carry enough nuclear fuel for the entire trip, you also have a multi-celled nuclear breeder reactor which takes the spent fuel from the propulsion engines along with a small amount of primary fuel and turns it all back into primary fuel.

The space stations along the way usually have a small stock of engine-repair parts (you also carry spare parts), breeder-reactor cells, and nuclear fuel, which are available to you on a barter basis.

Your objective in the game is to make the 2700-million-mile trip to Neptune in six years or less. It is possible but far from easy. Bon voyage.

THE PROGRAM

The Voyage to Neptune program consists of five main program segments, initialization and summarization segments, and six short subroutines. It is a relatively short program; nevertheless, the game is challenging and entertaining.

In the initialization section, the title is displayed and variables are initialized. The trip-segment counter (variable SEG) loops through the trip segments until the seventh destination is reached, at which time program execution branches to the End Trip segment at LN940.

The current-conditions section (following the initialization) prints the current location, condition of the ship, fuel supply, and performance during the last trip segment.

The trading section (starts at LN350) allows you to trade nuclear fuel for breeder reactor cells and vice versa. Checks are made to make sure you are not trading more than you have or that you don't trade so many cells that your breeder reactor becomes inoperative.

The engine-power section (starts at LN570) calculates the amount of power you receive from your solar collectors. Initially solar power meets 48% of your requirements, but that power decreases by 8% during each leg of the trip. You enter the amount of nuclear fuel you want to burn, and the program checks to be sure it is not more than you have.

In the breeder-reactor usage section (starts at LN650), you enter the number of breeder-reactor cells you wish to operate. As the breeder cells need both primary nuclear fuel (5 pounds for each cell) and spent fuel from the engines (20 pounds for each cell), these conditions must be met.

The calculations section (starts at LN730) is the heart of the program. Efficiency (EFF) of the main engines is calculated; it is the sum of the energy from the solar collectors plus the nuclear fuel. Maximum engine output is 104%. There is a 10% chance of an engine malfunction; if it occurs, you are told about the problem, and the reduced efficiency of the engines is calculated (Sub860).

Rate of speed (RATE) in mph and total distance (DIST) in millions of miles are calculated, then speed and distance are used to calculate the time (TIME, in days) of this leg of the trip.

The amount of fuel (FUBR) produced by the breeder-reactor cells is calculated; not being highly efficient, they produce from 16 to 33 pounds of fuel per cell.

This new fuel is added to the total fuel. There is a 20% chance that some of the fuel in storage will decay to an unusable state; this amount, if any, is calculated after setting a value for FUTOT.

The end-of-trip segment (LN940) calculates the total time it took to reach Neptune, number of operational breeder-reactor cells, and remaining amount of fuel. Appropriate messages are printed about each factor, after which the game ends.

The subroutines to print the scenario (Sub1180); set location names and distances (Sub1420); calculate and print time in years, months, and days (Sub1460); temporarily break program execution (Sub1550); and print centered lines (Sub1680) do exactly what their names describe in a straightforward way.

The subroutine to extract the first letter of an input string (Sub1630) does just that using the familiar GetSubString function. However, if the letter extracted is not uppercase (between A and Z), it is converted to a numeric ASCII value, subtracts 32 (lowercase letters have ASCII values 32 higher than their corresponding uppercase letters), and converts the resulting value back to a string. While three distinct functions are performed, they can be accomplished with a single statement:

```
AD = Text.GetCharacter(Text.GetCharacterCode(AD) - 32)
```

There are several ways to make the game easier or more difficult. You can increase or decrease the propulsion efficiency of the nuclear fuel this line near LN730:

```
EFF = 56 - SEG * 8 + FUSEG / 40
```

Dividing FUSEG by a value smaller than 40 will increase efficiency, while dividing by a value larger than 40 will decrease efficiency. In the same line, you can allow for engine speeds over 104% of normal if you wish. You can also improve the efficiency of the reactor by increasing either of the constants (16 or 18) in the first equation in this line:

```
FUBR = Math.Floor(16 + 18 * Math.GetRandomNumber(999)/1000)
```

You can also change the barter price of fuel and breeder cells in this line:

```
TRADE = Math.Floor(150 + 80 * Math.GetRandomNumber(999)/1000)
```

although doing so is a two-edged sword because sometimes you want to buy and other times to sell; best to leave it alone.

PROGRAM VARIABLES

A	Answer to input query, value
AD	Answer to input query, string
BREED	Total breeder - reactor cells on ship
DIS[n]	Distance between segments (n = 1 to 7)
DIST	Cumulative distance traveled (million miles)
DY	Days
EF	Engine-efficiency malfunction value
EFF	Engine efficiency
FD	Fuel-decay indicator
FUBR	Fuel produced by each breeder cell
FUDCY	Fuel that decayed in storage
FUSEG	Fuel used on trip segment
FUTOT	Fuel, total available
MO	Months
RATE	Rate of speed (mph)
RN	Seed for random-number generator
PLAND[n]	Planet or satellite name (n = 1 to 7)
SEG	Trip-segment counter
TIME	Time of trip segment (days)
TM	Time, temporary
TOTIME	Cumulative total time of trip
UBREED	Breeder-reactor cells in use
XD	Temporary string
YR	Years

PROGRAM LISTINGS

```
TextWindow.CursorTop = 10
XD = "Voyage to Neptune, 2100"
Sub1680()
TextWindow.CursorTop = 13
XD = "(c) by David H. Ahl, 1986"
Sub1680()
TextWindow.CursorTop = 23
Sub1550()
TextWindow.Clear()
Sub1180()
'Display initial scenario
BREED = 120
FUTOT = 3000
Sub1420()
'Set initial values
'
'Loop through trip segments
LN190:
SEG = SEG + 1
'Trip segment counter
If SEG = 7 Then
  Goto LN940 'Reach Neptune?
EndIf
'
'Print current conditions
TextWindow.WriteLine("")
TextWindow.WriteLine("Current conditions are as follows:")
TextWindow.WriteLine(" Location: " +PLAND[SEG])
TextWindow.WriteLine(" Distance to Neptune: " +(2701-DIST)+ " million
miles.")
If SEG = 1 Then
  Goto LN350  'First trip segment?
EndIf
TextWindow.WriteLine(" Distance from Earth: "+ DIST+ " million miles.")
TextWindow.WriteLine("Over the last segment, your average speed was "+
Math.Floor(RATE) +" mph,")
TextWindow.WriteLine(" and you covered "+ DIS[SEG - 1] +" million miles in "
+TIME+ " days.")
TM = .81 * DIST
TextWindow.Write("Time est for this total distance")
Sub1460()
TM = TOTIME
TextWindow.WriteLine("")
TextWindow.Write("Your actual cumulative time was ")
Sub1460()
TextWindow.WriteLine("")
TextWindow.WriteLine("You used " +UBREED +" cells which produced " +FUBR +"
pounds of fuel each.")
If FUDCY = 0 Then
  Goto LN350
EndIf
TextWindow.WriteLine(FUDCY +" pounds of fuel in storage decayed into an
unusable state.")
```

```
LN350:
TextWindow.WriteLine(" Pounds of of nuclear fuel ready for use: " + FUTOT)
TextWindow.WriteLine(" Operational breeder-reactor cells: "+ BREED )
TextWindow.WriteLine("")
'
'Trade fuel for breeder-reactor cells
TRADE = Math.Floor(150 + 80 * Math.GetRandomNumber(999)/1000)
If SEG > 1 Then
  Goto LN420
EndIf
TextWindow.WriteLine("Before leaving, you can trade fuel for breeder-reactor
cells at")
Goto LN430
LN420:
TextWindow.WriteLine("Here at " +PLAND[SEG] +", breeder cells and nuclear-
fuel trade at")
LN430:
TextWindow.WriteLine("the rate of " +TRADE+ " pounds of fuel per cell.")
TextWindow.WriteLine("")
If FUTOT - TRADE < 1501 Then
TextWindow.WriteLine( "You have too little fuel to trade.")
GOTO LN500
EndIf
TextWindow.Write("Would you like to procure more breeder cells (Y or N)? ")
AD = TextWindow.Read()
Sub1590()
If AD<>"Y" Then
  Goto LN500
EndIf
LN470:
TextWindow.Write("How many cells do you want? ")
A = TextWindow.ReadNumber()
F = FUTOT - A * TRADE
If F > 1500 Then
FUTOT = F
BREED = BREED + A
GOTO LN570
EndIf
TextWindow.WriteLine("That doesn't leave enough fuel to run the engines.")
Goto LN470
LN500:
TextWindow.Write("Would you like to trade some breeder cells for fuel? ")
AD = TextWindow.Read()
Sub1590()
If AD<>"Y" Then
  Goto LN570
EndIf
LN520:
TextWindow.Write("How many cells would you like to trade? ")
A = TextWindow.ReadNumber()
F = BREED - A
If F > 49 Then
BREED = F
FUTOT = FUTOT + A * TRADE
GOTO LN570
```

```
EndIf
TextWindow.WriteLine("That would leave only " +F +" cells. The reactor requires a minimum")
TextWindow.WriteLine("of 50 cells to remain operational.")
Goto LN520
'
LN570:
'Engine power
TextWindow.WriteLine("At this distance from the sun, your solar collectors can fulfill")
TextWindow.WriteLine((56 - SEG * 8) +"% of the fuel requirements of the engines. How many pounds")
LN600:
TextWindow.Write("of nuclear fuel do you want to use on this segment? ")
FUSEG = TextWindow.ReadNumber()
If FUSEG <= FUTOT Then
FUTOT = FUTOT - FUSEG
GOTO LN650  'Enough fuel?
EndIf
TextWindow.WriteLine("That's more fuel than you have. Now then, how many pounds")
Goto LN600
'
'Breeder reactor usage
LN650:
TextWindow.Write("How many breeder-reactor cells do you want to operate? ")
UBREED = TextWindow.ReadNumber()
If UBREED > BREED Then
TextWindow.WriteLine( "You don't have that many cells." )
GOTO LN650
EndIf
If FUSEG / 20 >= UBREED Then
  Goto LN700  'Enough spent fuel from engines?
EndIf
TextWindow.WriteLine("The spent fuel from your engines is only enough to operate " +FUSEG / 20)
TextWindow.WriteLine(" breeder reactor cells. Again please... ")
Goto LN650
LN700:
If UBREED * 5 <= FUTOT Then
  Goto LN730  'Enough new seed fuel?
EndIf
TextWindow.WriteLine("You have only enough fuel to seed " +Math.floor(FUTOT / 5)+ " breeder cells.")
TextWindow.WriteLine("Please adjust your number accordingly.")
Goto LN650
LN730:
FUTOT = FUTOT - 5 * UBREED
'
'Calculate the results of input data
EFF = 56 - SEG * 8 + FUSEG / 40
If EFF > 104 Then
  EFF = 104  'Efficiency = 104% max
EndIf
EF = Math.GetRandomNumber(999)/1000
```

```
If EF < .1 Then
  Sub860()  '10% chance of engine problem
EndIf
RATE = EFF * 513.89
DIST = DIST + DIS[SEG]
'Rate in mph, dist in million miles
TIME = Math.Floor(DIS[SEG] * 41667 / RATE)
'Time in days
TOTIME = TOTIME + TIME
'Total trip time
FUBR = Math.Floor(16 + 18 * Math.GetRandomNumber(999)/1000)
FUTOT = FUTOT + FUBR * UBREED
'New fuel from breeder
FD = Math.GetRandomNumber(999)/1000
If FD < .2 Then
  FUDCY = Math.Floor(FD * FUTOT)  'How much fuel decayed?
Else
  FUDCY = 0
EndIf
FUTOT = FUTOT - FUDCY
'Decrease fuel by amount that decayed
Goto LN190
'
Sub Sub860
'Subroutine for engine problem
TextWindow.Clear()
For J = 1 To 7
TextWindow.WriteLine("")
XD = "ENGINE MALFUNCTION !"
TextWindow.CursorTop = 12
Sub1680()
TextWindow.Clear()
Sound.Stop(Program.Directory+"\ding.wav")
Sound.Play(Program.Directory+"\ding.wav")
EndFor
TextWindow.WriteLine("You will have to operate your engines at a "
+Math.Floor(300 * EF)+"% reduction")
TextWindow.WriteLine("in speed until you reach " +PLAND[SEG + 1]+ ".")
TextWindow.WriteLine("")
EFF = EFF * (1 - 3 * EF)
EndSub
'
LN940:
'End of trip segment
TextWindow.WriteLine("")
TextWindow.Write("You finally reached Neptune in ")
TM = TOTIME
Sub1460()
TextWindow.WriteLine("Had your engines run at 100% efficiency the entire way,
you would")
TextWindow.WriteLine("have averaged 51, 389 mph and completed the trip in
exactly 6 years.")
If TM > 2220 Then
  Goto LN1000
EndIf
```

```
TextWindow.WriteLine("")
XD = "Congratulations! Outstanding job!"
Sub1680()
TextWindow.WriteLine("")
Goto LN1070
LN1000:
TM = TOTIME - 2190
TextWindow.WriteLine("")
TextWindow.Write("Your trip took longer than this by ")
Sub1460()
TextWindow.Write( "Your performance was ")
YR = YR + 1
If YR > 4 Then
  YR = 4
EndIf
If (YR = 1) Then
  Goto LN1030
ElseIf (YR = 2) Then
  Goto LN1040
ElseIf (YR = 3) Then
  Goto LN1050
ElseIf (YR = 4) Then
  Goto LN1060
EndIf
LN1030:
TextWindow.WriteLine("excellent (room for slight improvement).")
Goto LN1070
LN1040:
TextWindow.WriteLine("quite good (but could be better).")
Goto LN1070
LN1050:
TextWindow.WriteLine("marginal (could do much better).")
Goto LN1070
LN1060:
TextWindow.WriteLine("abysmal (need lots more practice).")
LN1070:
textwindow.WriteLine("")
If BREED < 105 Then
  Goto LN1100
EndIf
TextWindow.WriteLine("Fortunately you have "+ BREED +" operational breeder-
reactor cells")
TextWindow.WriteLine("for your return trip. Very good.")
Goto LN1120
LN1100:
TextWindow.WriteLine("I guess you realize that the return trip will be
extremely")
TextWindow.WriteLine("chancy with only "+BREED+ " breeder-reactor cells
operational.")
LN1120:
TextWindow.WriteLine("With your remaining " +FUTOT +" pounds of fuel and "+
BREED+ " breeder")
TM = 42250 / (8 + FUTOT / 40)
If TM < 405 Then
  TM = 405
```

```
EndIf
TextWindow.Write("cells, to get back to Theta 2 will take ")
Sub1460()
TextWindow.WriteLine("")
TextWindow.Write("Would you like to try again (Y or N)? ")
AD = TextWindow.Read()
sub1590()
If AD = "Y" Then
  'RUN ELSE CLS : KEY ON : PRINT "Bye!" : END
EndIf
'
Sub Sub1180
'Subroutine to print the scenario
TextWindow.Clear()
XD = "Voyage to Neptune"
Sub1680()
TextWindow.WriteLine("")
TextWindow.WriteLine("")
TextWindow.WriteLine(" It is the Year 2100 and you are in command of the
first manned")
TextWindow.WriteLine("spaceship to Neptune. Manned space stations have been
established")
TextWindow.WriteLine("which orbit Callisto, Titan, and Ariel, as well as at
two inter-")
TextWindow.WriteLine("mediate points between Saturn and Uranus, and Uranus
and Neptune.")
TextWindow.WriteLine("You must travel about 2700 million miles. At an average
speed of")
TextWindow.WriteLine("over 50, 000 miles per hour, the entire trip should
take about")
TextWindow.WriteLine("six years.")
TextWindow.WriteLine(" Your spaceship is a marvel of 21st century
engineering. Since")
TextWindow.WriteLine("you may have to stop at space stations along the way,
you will not")
TextWindow.WriteLine("be able to use the gravitational 'slingshot' effect of
the planets.")
TextWindow.WriteLine("However, your engines are highly efficient using both
energy from")
TextWindow.WriteLine("the sun captured by giant parabolic arrays and nuclear
fuel carried")
TextWindow.WriteLine("on board. You will not be able to carry enough fuel for
the whole")
TextWindow.WriteLine("trip, so you also have a multi-celled nuclear breeder
reactor")
TextWindow.WriteLine("(which takes spent fuel from your engines along with a
small amount")
TextWindow.WriteLine("of primary fuel and turns it into a much greater amount
of primary")
TextWindow.WriteLine("fuel).")
TextWindow.WriteLine(" The space stations along the way usually have a small
stock of")
TextWindow.WriteLine("engine repair parts, breeder-reactor cells, and nuclear
fuel which")
TextWindow.WriteLine("are available to you on a barter basis.")
```

```
Sub1550()
TextWindow.Clear()
EndSub
'
'Subroutine to read location names and distances
Sub Sub1420
PLAND[1] = "Earth"
DIS[1] = 391
PLAND[2] = "Callisto"
DIS[2] = 403
PLAND[3] = "Titan"
DIS[3] = 446
PLAND[4] = "Alpha 1"
DIS[4] = 447
PLAND[5] = "Ariel"
DIS[5] = 507
PLAND[6] = "Theta 2"
DIS[6] = 507
PLAND[7] = "Neptune"
DIS[7] = 0
EndSub

Sub Sub1460
'Subroutine to calculate and print time in years
YR = Math.Floor(TM / 365)
If YR < 1 Then
  Goto LN1490
EndIf
If YR = 1 Then
TextWindow.Write( " 1 year")
ELSE
textwindow.Write(YR +" years")
EndIf
LN1490:
MO = Math.Floor((TM / 365 - YR) * 12)
If MO < 1 Then
  Goto LN1510
EndIf
If MO = 1 Then
TextWindow.Write( ", 1 month")
ELSE
TextWindow.Write(", "+ MO+ " months")
EndIf
LN1510:
DY = Math.Floor(TM - YR * 365 - MO * 30.5)
If DY < 1 Then
TextWindow.WriteLine( ".")
Goto LN1549
EndIf
If DY = 1 Then
TextWindow.Write( ", 1 day.")
ELSE
textwindow.Write(", "+ DY+ " days.")
EndIf
LN1549:
```

```
EndSub
'
Sub Sub1550
'Subroutine to temporarily break execution
TextWindow.WriteLine("")
XD = "Press Enter to continue."
Sub1680()
JJJ = TextWindow.Read()
RN = RN + 1
TextWindow.WriteLine("")
TextWindow.WriteLine("")
EndSub
'
Sub Sub1590
'Subroutine to read yes/no answer
LN1600:
sub1630()
If AD = "Y" OR AD = "N" Then
  Goto ln1601
EndIf
TextWindow.Write("Don't understand your answer. Enter 'Y' or 'N' please? ")
AD = TextWindow.Read()
Goto LN1600
LN1601:
EndSub
'
Sub Sub1630
'Subroutine to extract the first letter of an input answer (in upper case)
If AD = "" Then
AD = "Y"
Goto ln1631
EndIf
AD = text.getsubtext(AD,1, 1)
If AD >= "A" AND AD <= "Z" Then
  Goto ln1631
EndIf
AD = Text.GetCharacter(Text.GetCharacterCode(AD) - 32)
LN1631:
EndSub
'
Sub Sub1680
'Subroutine to print centered lines
TextWindow.CursorLeft = (40 - Text.GetLength(XD)/2)
TextWindow.WriteLine(XD)
EndSub
```

APPENDIX: Microsoft® Small Basic

Downloading and Installing Small Basic

To write and run programs using Small Basic, you need the **Small Basic** program. This is a free product that you can download from the Internet. This simply means we will copy a file onto our computer to allow installation of Small Basic.

Start up your web browser (Internet Explorer, Netscape or other). Small Basic is hosted at Microsoft's **Beginner Development Learning Center**:

http://www.smallbasic.com

On the Small Basic web page, you should see a button that allows downloading Small Basic:

Download

Click the download button. This window will appear:

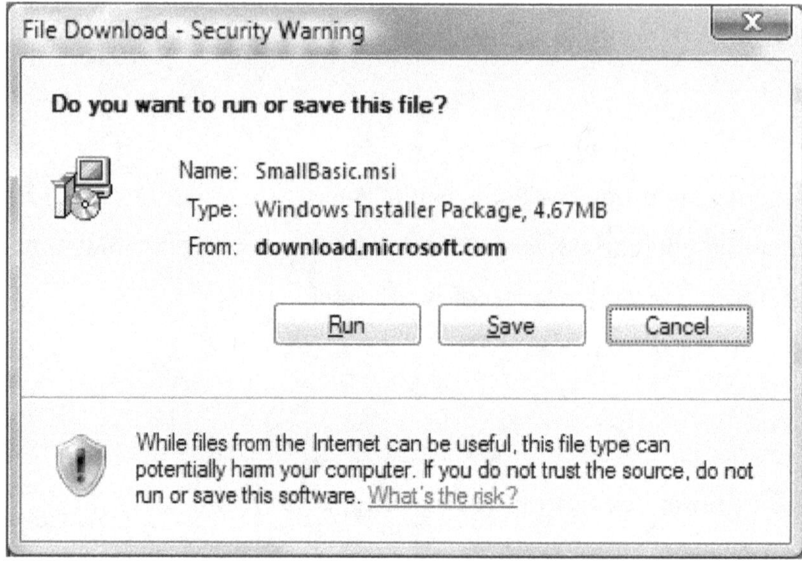

Click **Run** and the download of the installer begins:

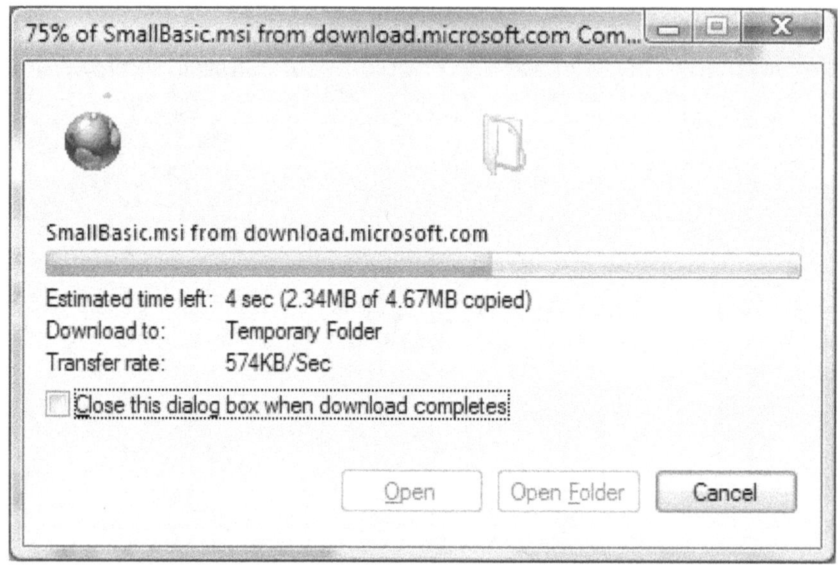

When complete, you should see:

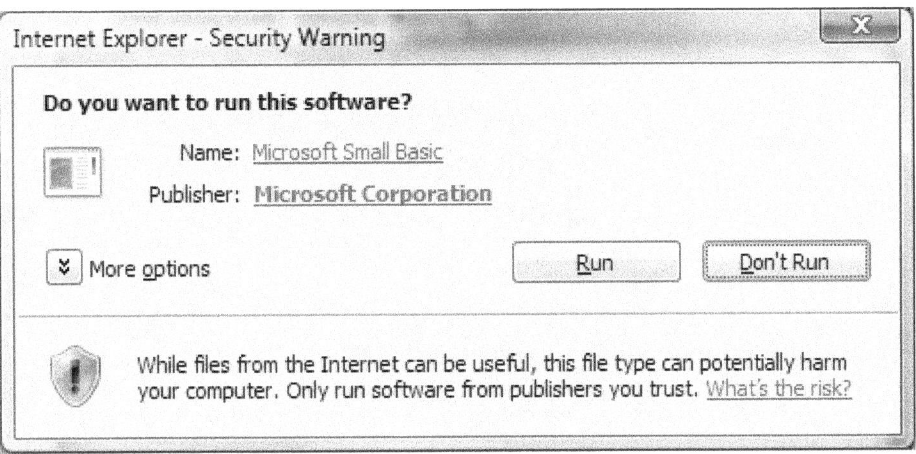

Again, click **Run** to see the Setup Wizard:

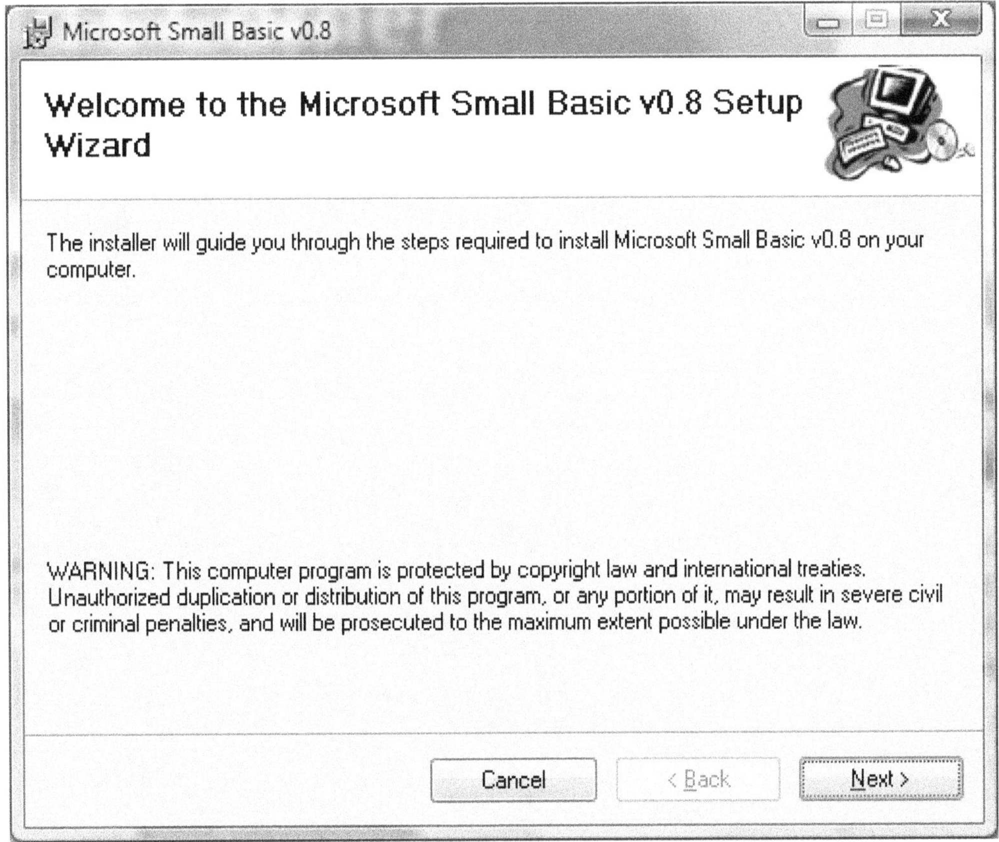

Click **Next** to start the installation process. Accept the licensing agreement. Then, for each screen afterwards, accept the default choice by clicking **Next**. When done you should see a screen announcing a successful installation.

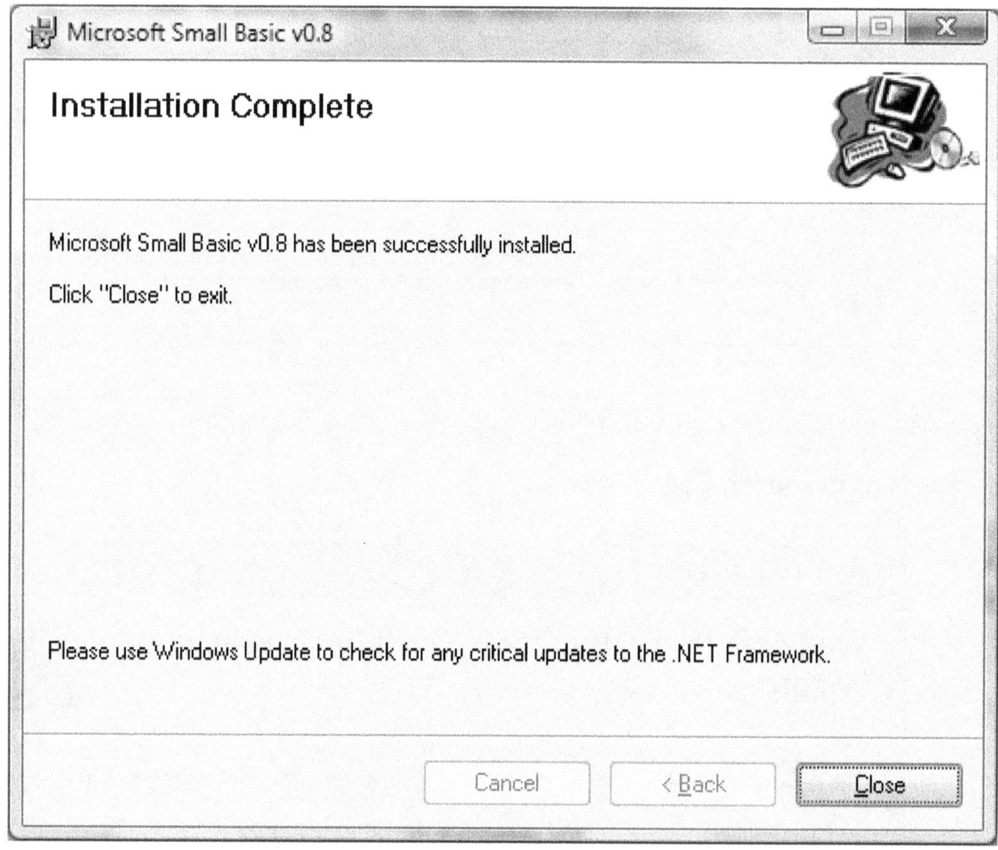

Starting Small Basic

We'll learn how to start **Small Basic**, how to load a Small Basic program, and how to run a program. This will give us some assurance we have everything installed correctly. This will let us begin our study of the Small Basic programming language.

Once installed, to start Small Basic:

1. Click on the **Start** button on the Windows task bar
2. Select **Programs**, then **Small Basic**
3. Click on **Microsoft Small Basic**

(Some of the headings given here may differ slightly on your computer, but you should have no trouble finding the correct ones.) The Small Basic program should start. Several windows will appear on the screen.

After installation and trying to start, you may see an error message that announces Small Basic cannot be started. If this occurs, try downloading and installing the latest version of the Microsoft .NET framework at:

http://msdn.microsoft.com/en-us/netframework/aa569263.aspx

This contains some files that Small Basic needs to operate and such files may not be on your computer.

Upon starting, my screen shows:

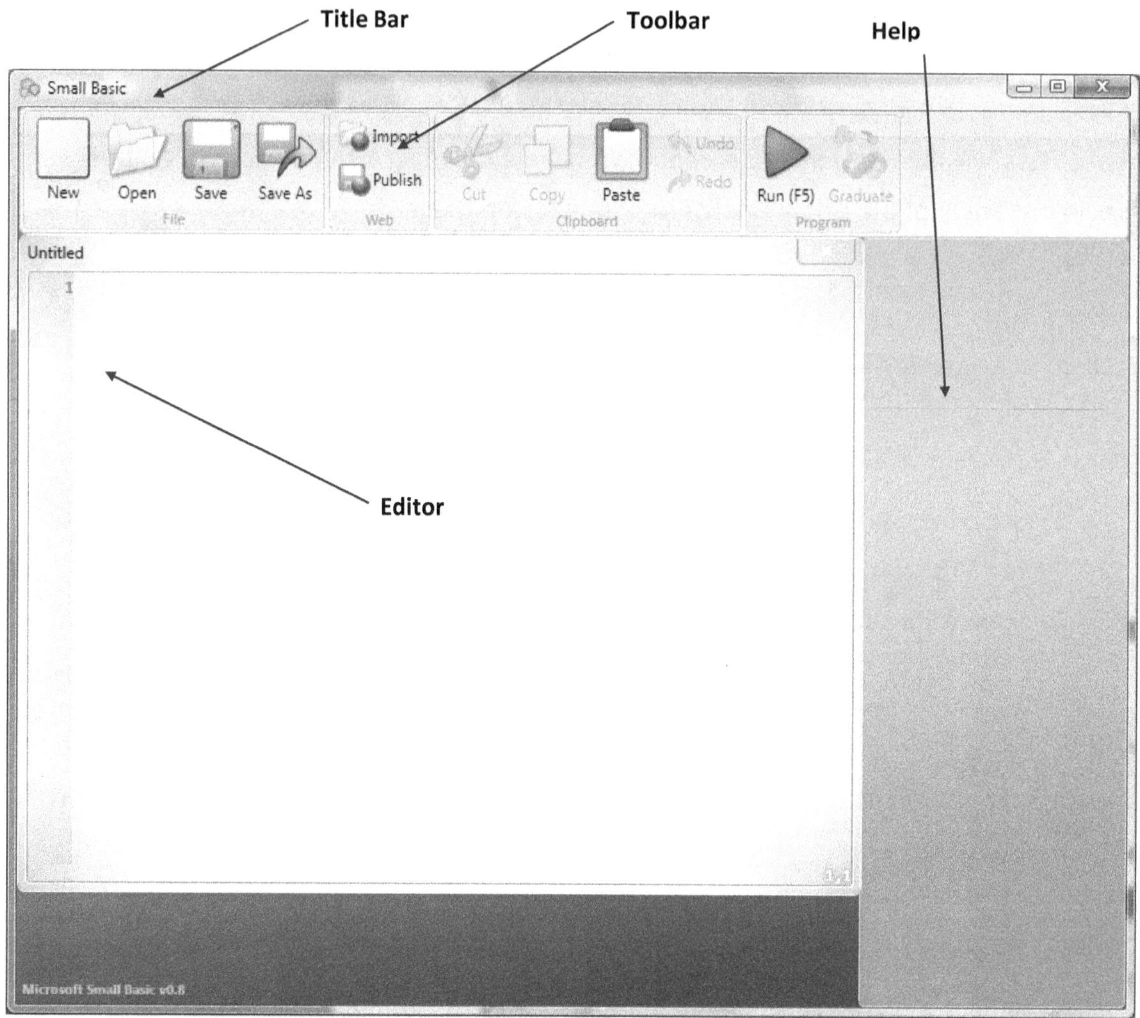

This window displays the **Small Basic Development Environment**. We will learn a lot more about this in Class 2. Right now, we're just going to use it to test our Small Basic installation and see if we can get a program up and running. There are many windows on the screen. At the top of the window is the **Title Bar**. The title bar gives us information about what program we're using and what Small Basic program we are working with. Below the title bar is a **Toolbar**. Here, little buttons with pictures allow us to control Small Basic. Almost all Windows applications (spreadsheets, word processors, games) have toolbars that help us do different tasks. This is the purpose of the Small Basic toolbar. It will help us do most of our tasks. In the middle of the screen is the **Editor**. This is where we will write our Small Basic programs. To the right is a **Help** area. Small Basic has great help features when writing programs. This area will display hints and tips while we write code.

Downloading the Small Basic Computer Adventures Source Code Files

If you purchased this book directly from our website you received an email with an individualized internet download link where you could download the compressed Program Solution Files. If you purchased this book through a 3rd Party Book Store like Amazon.com, the solutions files for this tutorial are included in a compressed ZIP file that is available for download directly from our website (after book registration) at:

http://www.kidwaresoftware.com/dasbca-registration.html

Complete the online web form at the webpage above with your name, shipping address, email address, the exact title of this book, date of purchase, online or physical store name, and your order confirmation number from that store. After we receive all this information we will email you a download link for the Source Code Solution Files associated with this book.

Warning: If you purchased this book "used" or "second hand" you are not licensed or entitled to download the Program Source Code Solution Files. However, you can purchase the Digital Download Version of this book at a highly discounted price which allows you access to the digital source code solutions files required for completing this tutorial.

Opening a Small Basic Program

What we want to do right now is **open a program**. Included with these notes are many Small Basic programs you can open and use. Let's open one now. Make sure **Small Basic** is running. We will open a program using the toolbar. Follow these steps:

Click the **Open Program** button:

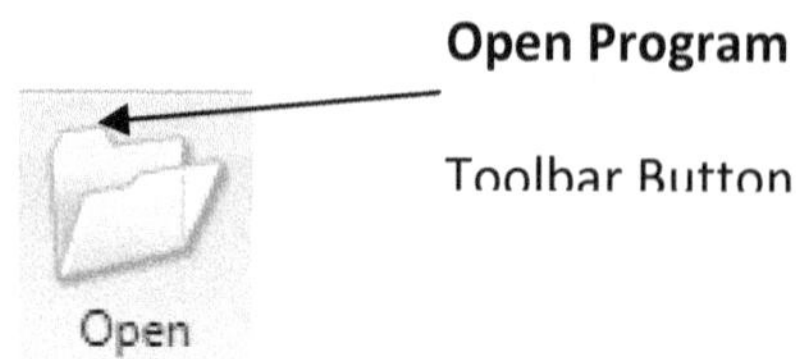

An **Open Program** window will appear:

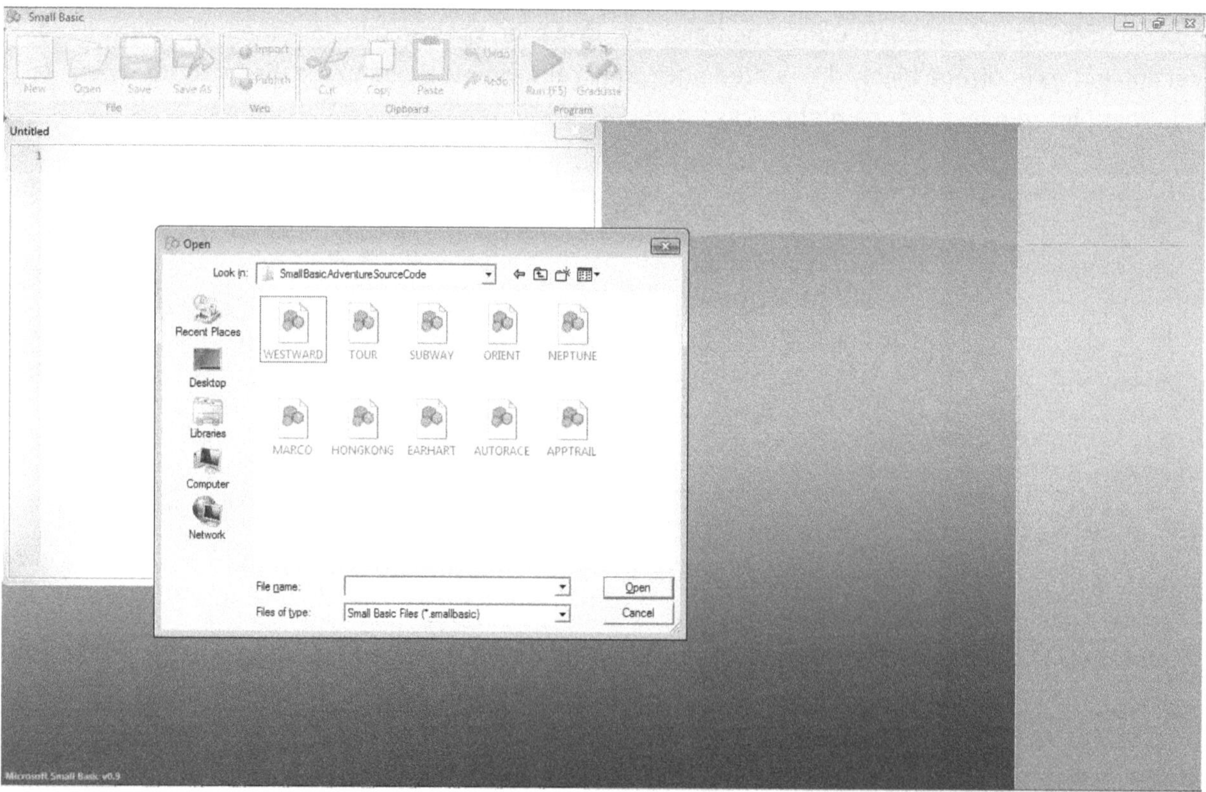

Find the folder named **SmallBasicAdventureSourceCode.** This is the folder that holds the Small Basic programs for this book. Open that folder then open any of the Small Basic Adventure Games.

Running a Small Basic Program

Look for a button that looks like the **Play** button on a VCR, CD player, or cassette tape player:

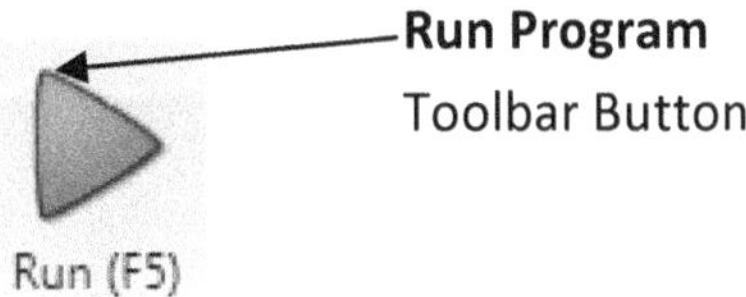

Click this button to run the **Small Basic Computer Game** that you opened previously. The Small Basic Computer Game will now run in a separate window.

You can also run a program by pressing the **<F5>** function key.

If you've gotten this far, everything has been installed correctly. If you don't see the game running, something has not been installed correctly. You should probably go back and review all the steps involved with installing Small Basic and Small Basic and make sure all steps were followed properly.

To stop this program, press any key or click the boxed **X** in the upper right corner of the window.

Stopping Small Basic

When you are done working with a Small Basic program, you want to leave the Small Basic environment. To stop Small Basic, click on the close button in the upper right hand corner of the main window. It's the button that looks like an **X**. Stop Small Basic now. Small Basic will close all open windows and you will be returned to the Windows desktop.

We publish several Self-Study or Instructor-Led Computer Programming Tutorials for Microsoft® Small Basic:

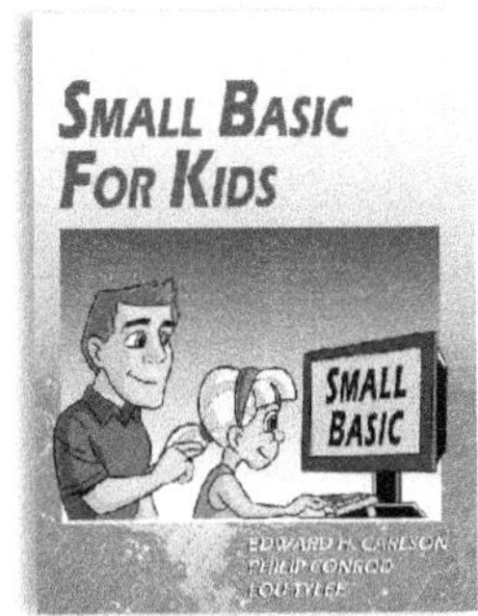

Small Basic For Kids is an illustrated introduction to computer programming that provides an interactive, self-paced tutorial to the new Small Basic programming environment. The book consists of 30 short lessons that explain how to create and run a Small Basic program. Elementary students learn about program design and many elements of the Small Basic language. Numerous examples are used to demonstrate every step in the building process. The tutorial also includes two complete games (Hangman and Pizza Zapper) for students to build and try. Designed for kids ages 8 and up.

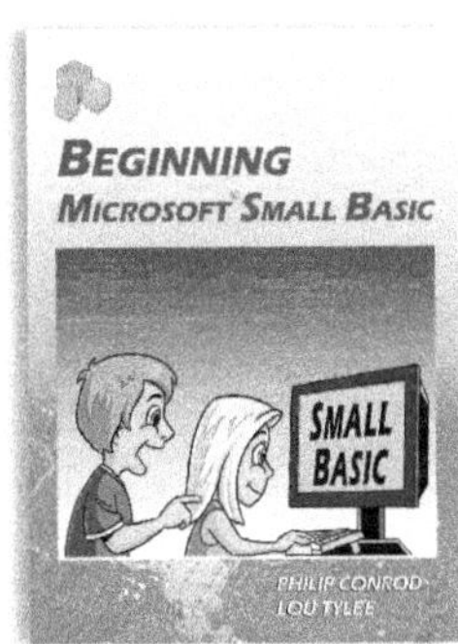

The Beginning Microsoft Small Basic Programming Tutorial is a self-study first semester "beginner" programming tutorial consisting of 11 chapters explaining (in simple, easy-to-follow terms) how to write Microsoft Small Basic programs. Numerous examples are used to demonstrate every step in the building process. The last chapter of this tutorial shows you how four different Small Basic games could port to Visual Basic, Visual C# and Java. This beginning level self-paced tutorial can be used at home or at school. The tutorial is simple enough for kids ages 10 and above yet engaging enough for beginning adults.

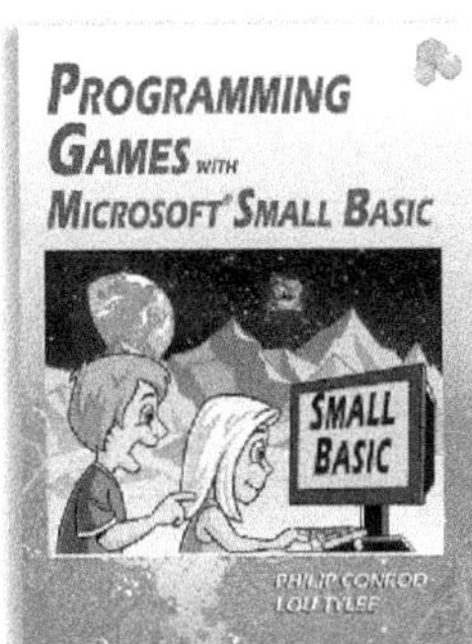

Programming Games with Microsoft Small Basic is a self-paced second semester "intermediate" level programming tutorial consisting of 10 chapters explaining (in simple, easy-to-follow terms) how to write video games in Microsoft Small Basic. The games built are non-violent, family-friendly, and teach logical thinking skills. Students will learn how to program the following Small Basic video games: Safecracker, Tic Tac Toe, Match Game, Pizza Delivery, Moon Landing, and Leap Frog. This intermediate level self-paced tutorial can be used at home or school. The tutorial is simple enough for kids yet engaging enough for beginning adults.

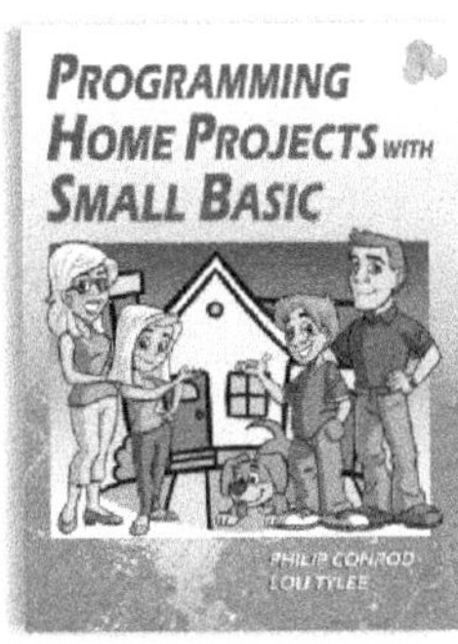

Programming Home Projects with Microsoft Small Basic is a self-paced programming tutorial explains (in simple, easy-to-follow terms) how to build Small Basic Windows applications. Students learn about program design, Small Basic objects, many elements of the Small Basic language, and how to debug and distribute finished programs. Sequential file input and output is also introduced.. The projects built include a Dual-Mode Stopwatch, Flash Card Math Quiz, Multiple Choice Exam, Blackjack Card Game, Weight Monitor, Home Inventory Manager and a Snowball Toss Game.

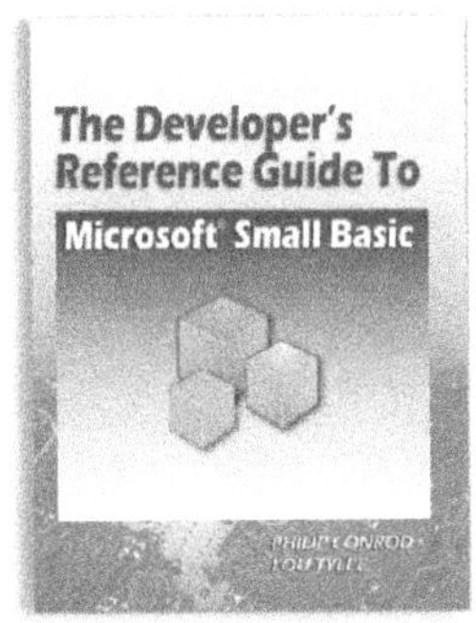

The Developer's Reference Guide to Microsoft Small Basic
While developing all the different Microsoft Small Basic tutorials we found it necessary to write The Developer's Reference Guide to Microsoft Small Basic . The Developer's Reference Guide to Microsoft Small Basic is over 500 pages long and includes over 100 Small Basic programming examples for you to learn from and include in your own Microsoft Small Basic programs. It is a detailed reference guide for new developers.

David Ahl's Small Basic Computer Adventures is a Microsoft Small Basic re-make of the classic *Basic Computer Games* programming *book* originally written by David H. Ahl. This new book includes the following classic adventure simulations; Marco Polo, Westward Ho!, The Longest Automobile Race, The Orient Express, Amelia Earhart: Around the World Flight, Tour de France, Subway Scavenger, Hong Kong Hustle, and Voyage to Neptune. Learn how to program these classic computer simulations in Microsoft Small Basic. This "intermediate" level self-paced tutorial can be used at home or school.

Basic Computer Games - Small Basic Edition is a re-make of the classic BASIC COMPUTER GAMES book originally edited by David H. Ahl. It contains 100 of the original text based BASIC games that inspired a whole generation of programmers. Now these classic BASIC games have been re-written in Microsoft Small Basic for a new generation to enjoy! The new Small Basic games look and act like the original text based games. The book includes all the original spaghetti code GOTO commands and it will make you appreciate the structured programming techniques found in our other tutorials.

We also publish several Self-Study or Instructor-Led Computer Programming Tutorials for Microsoft® Visual Basic® Express and Visual C#® Express:

Visual Basic® Express For Kids is a beginning programming tutorial consisting of 10 chapters explaining (in simple, easy-to-follow terms) how to build a Visual Basic Express Windows application. Students learn about project design, the Visual Basic Express toolbox, and many elements of the BASIC language. The tutorial also includes several detailed computer projects for students to build and try. These projects include a number guessing game, a card game, an allowance calculator, a drawing program, a state capitals game, Tic-Tac-Toe and even a simple video game. Designed for kids ages 12 and up.

Beginning Visual Basic® Express is a semester long self-paced "beginner" programming tutorial consisting of 10 chapters explaining (in simple, easy-to-follow terms) how to build a Visual Basic Express Windows application. The tutorial includes several detailed computer projects for students to build and try. These projects include a number guessing game, card game, allowance calculator, drawing program, state capitals game, and a couple of video games like Pong. We also include several college prep bonus projects including a loan calculator, portfolio manager, and checkbook balancer. Designed for students age 15 and up.

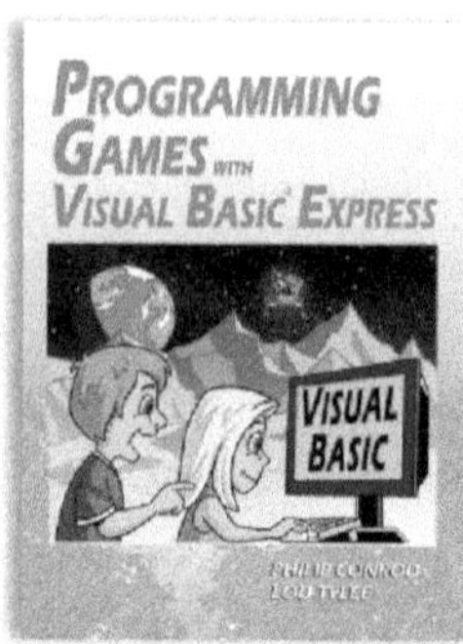

Programming Games with Visual Basic® Express is a semester long "intermediate" programming tutorial consisting of 10 chapters explaining (in simple, easy-to-follow terms) how to build Visual Basic Video Games. The games built are non-violent, family-friendly, and teach logical thinking skills. Students will learn how to program the following Visual Basic video games: Safecracker, Tic Tac Toe, Match Game, Pizza Delivery, Moon Landing, and Leap Frog. This intermediate level self-paced tutorial can be used at home or school. The tutorial is simple enough for kids yet engaging enough for beginning adults.

Programming Home Projects with Visual Basic® Express is a semester long self-paced programming tutorial explains (in simple, easy-to-follow terms) how to build a Visual Basic Express Windows project. Students learn about project design, the Visual Basic Express toolbox, many elements of the Visual Basic language, and how to debug and distribute finished projects. The projects built include a Dual-Mode Stopwatch, Flash Card Math Quiz, Multiple Choice Exam, Blackjack Card Game, Weight Monitor, Home Inventory Manager and a Snowball Toss Game.

Visual C#® Express For Kids is a beginning programming tutorial consisting of 10 chapters explaining (in simple, easy-to-follow terms) how to build a Visual C# Express Windows application. Students learn about project design, the Visual C# Express toolbox, and many elements of the C# language. Numerous examples are used to demonstrate every step in the building process. The projects include a number guessing game, a card game, an allowance calculator, a drawing program, a state capitals game, Tic-Tac-Toe and even a simple video game. Designed for kids ages 12 and up.

Beginning Visual C#® Express is a semester long "beginning" programming tutorial consisting of 10 chapters explaining (in simple, easy-to-follow terms) how to build a C# Express Windows application. The tutorial includes several detailed computer projects for students to build and try. These projects include a number guessing game, card game, allowance calculator, drawing program, state capitals game, and a couple of video games like Pong. We also include several college prep bonus projects including a loan calculator, portfolio manager, and checkbook balancer. Designed for students age 15 and up.

Programming Games with Visual C#® Express is a semester long "intermediate" programming tutorial consisting of 10 chapters explaining (in simple, easy-to-follow terms) how to build a Visual C# Video Games. The games built are non-violent, family-friendly and teach logical thinking skills. Students will learn how to program the following Visual C# video games: Safecracker, Tic Tac Toe, Match Game, Pizza Delivery, Moon Landing, and Leap Frog. This intermediate level self-paced tutorial can be used at home or school. The tutorial is simple enough for kids yet engaging enough for beginning adults.

Programming Home Projects with Visual C#® Express is a semester long self-paced programming tutorial explains (in simple, easy-to-follow terms) how to build a Visual C# Express Windows project. Students learn about project design, the Visual C# Express toolbox, many elements of the Visual C# language, and how to debug and distribute finished projects. The projects built include a Dual-Mode Stopwatch, Flash Card Math Quiz, Multiple Choice Exam, Blackjack Card Game, Weight Monitor, Home Inventory Manager and a Snowball Toss Game.

We also publish several Self-Study or Instructor-Led Computer Programming Tutorials for Oracle® Java®:

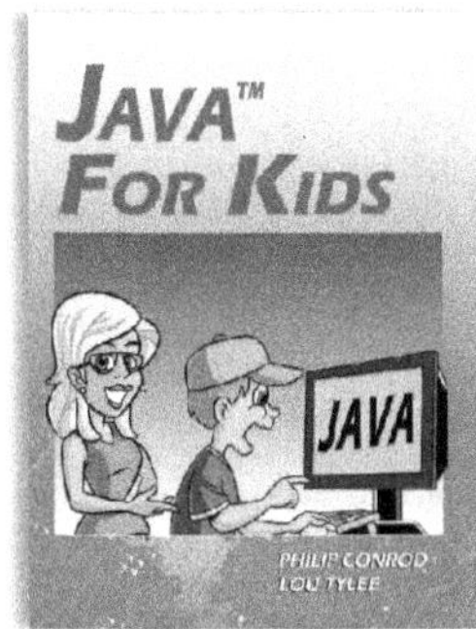

Java™ For Kids is a beginning programming tutorial consisting of 10 chapters explaining (in simple, easy-to-follow terms) how to build a Java application. Students learn about project design, object-oriented programming, console applications, graphics applications and many elements of the Java language. Numerous examples are used to demonstrate every step in the building process. The projects include a number guessing game, a card game, an allowance calculator, a state capitals game, Tic-Tac-Toe, a simple drawing program, and even a basic video game. Designed for kids ages 12 and up.

Beginning Java™ is a semester long "beginning" programming tutorial consisting of 10 chapters explaining (in simple, easy-to-follow terms) how to build a Java application. The tutorial includes several detailed computer projects for students to build and try. These projects include a number guessing game, card game, allowance calculator, drawing program, state capitals game, and a couple of video games like Pong. We also include several college prep bonus projects including a loan calculator, portfolio manager, and checkbook balancer. Designed for students age 15 and up.

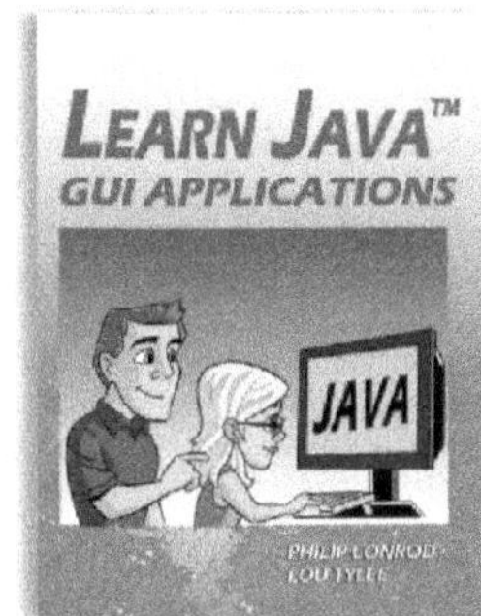

Learn Java™ GUI Applications is a 9 lesson Tutorial covering object-oriented programming concepts, using a integrated development environment to create and test Java projects, building and distributing GUI applications, understanding and using the Swing control library, exception handling, sequential file access, graphics, multimedia, advanced topics such as printing, and help system authoring. **Our Beginning Java tutorial is a pre-requisite for this tutorial.**

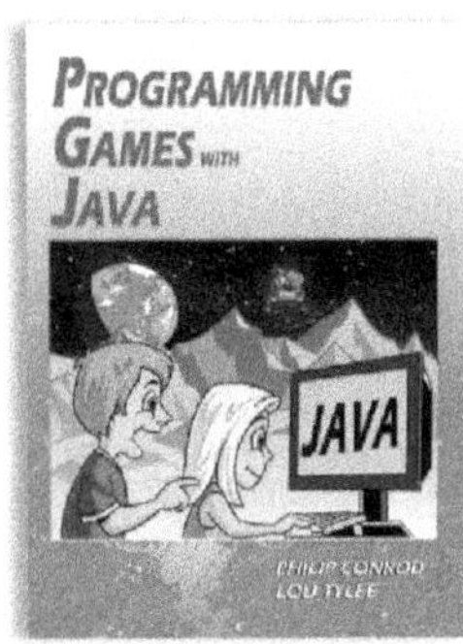

Programming Games with Java™ is a semester long "intermediate" programming tutorial consisting of 10 chapters explaining (in simple, easy-to-follow terms) how to build a Visual C# Video Games. The games built are non-violent, family-friendly and teach logical thinking skills. Students will learn how to program the following Visual C# video games: Safecracker, Tic Tac Toe, Match Game, Pizza Delivery, Moon Landing, and Leap Frog. This intermediate level self-paced tutorial can be used at home or school. The tutorial is simple enough for kids yet engaging enough for beginning adults. **Our Beginning Java and Learn Java GUI Applications tutorials are required pre-requisites for this tutorial.**

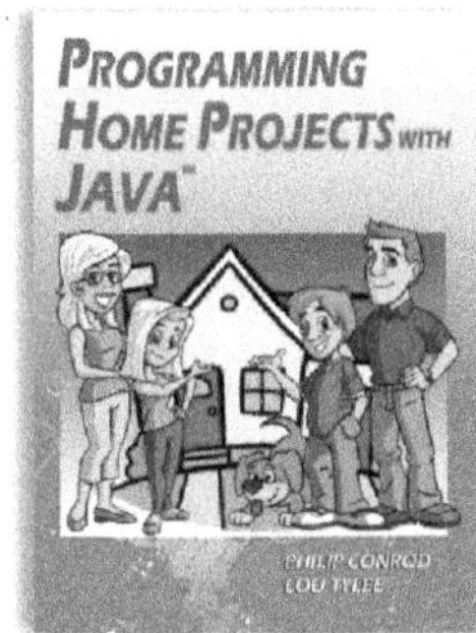

Programming Home Projects with Java™ is a Java GUI Swing tutorial covering object-oriented programming concepts. It explains (in simple, easy-to-follow terms) how to build Java GUI project to use around the home. Students learn about project design, the Java Swing controls, many elements of the Java language, and how to distribute finished projects. The projects built include a Dual-Mode Stopwatch, Flash Card Math Quiz, Multiple Choice Exam, Blackjack Card Game, Weight Monitor, Home Inventory Manager and a Snowball Toss Game. **Our Beginning Java and Learn Java GUI Applications tutorials are pre-requisites for this tutorial.**

We also publish several advanced Honors Level Self-Study or Instructor-Led "College-Prep" Computer Programming Tutorials for Microsoft® Visual Basic® Professional Edition and Visual C#® Professional Edition:

LEARN VISUAL BASIC PROFESSIONAL EDITION is a comprehensive college prep programming tutorial covering object-oriented programming, the Visual Basic integrated development environment, building and distributing Windows applications using the Windows Installer, exception handling, sequential file access, graphics, multimedia, advanced topics such as web access, printing, and HTML help system authoring. The tutorial also introduces database applications (using ADO .NET) and web applications (using ASP.NET).

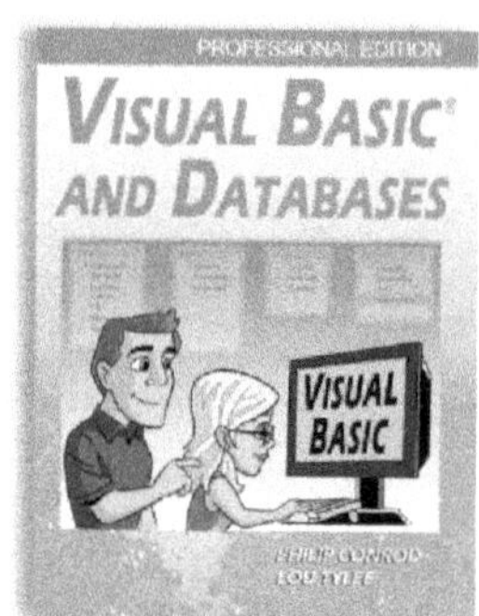

VISUAL BASIC AND DATABASES PROFESSIONAL EDITION is a tutorial that provides a detailed introduction to using Visual Basic for accessing and maintaining databases for desktop applications. Topics covered include: database structure, database design, Visual Basic project building, ADO .NET data objects (connection, data adapter, command, data table), data bound controls, proper interface design, structured query language (SQL), creating databases using Access, SQL Server and ADOX, and database reports. Actual projects developed include a books tracking system, a sales invoicing program, a home inventory system and a daily weather monitor.

LEARN VISUAL C# PROFESSIONAL EDITION is a comprehensive college prep computer programming tutorial covering object-oriented programming, the Visual C# integrated development environment and toolbox, building and distributing Windows applications (using the Windows Installer), exception handling, sequential file input and output, graphics, multimedia effects (animation and sounds), advanced topics such as web access, printing, and HTML help system authoring. The tutorial also introduces database applications (using ADO .NET) and web applications (using ASP.NET).

VISUAL C# AND DATABASES PROFESSIONAL EDITION is a tutorial that provides a detailed introduction to using Visual C# for accessing and maintaining databases for desktop applications. Topics covered include: database structure, database design, Visual C# project building, ADO .NET data objects (connection, data adapter, command, data table), data bound controls, proper interface design, structured query language (SQL), creating databases using Access, SQL Server and ADOX, and database reports. Actual projects developed include a books tracking system, a sales invoicing program, a home inventory system and a daily weather monitor.

www.ingramcontent.com/pod-product-compliance
Lightning Source LLC
LaVergne TN
LVHW060135070326
832902LV00018B/2812
* 9 7 8 1 9 3 7 1 6 1 1 7 0 *